NICHOLAS B

Sub specie aeternitatis

Articles Philosophic, Social and Literary

(1900-1906)

(Klepinina № 3)

Translated by Fr. S. Janos

frsj Publications

Sub specie aeternitatis

Articles Social, Philosophic and Literary (1900-1906)

ISBN: 978-0-9991979-2-9 *Hardcover*
ISBN: 978-0-9991979-3-6 *Paperback*

Library of Congress Control Number: 2019901801

Printed in the United States of America

Printed on acid-free paper.

For information address:

frsj Publications
Fr. Stephen J. Janos
P.O. Box 210
Mohrsville, PA 19541

Contents

Translator Comments

In the interest of clarity, mention of some bibliographic details seems appropriate. Berdyaev penned a prolific number of books and articles, bewildering even for a specialist to keep track of. And Berdyaev's titles in English at times quite vary from their Russian originals. Added to which, from, early on Berdyaev often re-used and re-cycled various of his journal articles into chapters in his books, at time interspersed with chapters uniquely written for the book. Some foreign language editions further compound this problem. A bewildering array of Berdyaev titles, spanning nearly half a century, addressing numerous areas, along with dim glimmerings of obscure figures and ideas from the past, all so charming and yet at times so confusing.

Our present book -- "*Sub specie aeternitatis: Articles Philosophic, Social and Literary,* (*1900-1906*)"[1] -- was published by Berdyaev in 1907 (S-Peterburg, M. V. Pirozhkov publisher, 437 p.). The current Russian reprint, from which our translation was made, is that of the year 2002 "Kanon" publisher, Moscow. Our present text was assigned as "№ 3" by Tamara Klépinine in her exceedingly invaluable 1978 Paris YMKA-Press "*Berdiaev Bibliographie*", in the initial "Books & Booklets" section.

Berdyaev actually published two books in 1907, both by the same publisher. The other book was "*The New Religious Consciousness and the Societal Aspect*", to which T. Klépinine assigned the "№ 2". This was seemingly prior to and independent of our present volume, and yet not so in both regards. Berdyaev penned a "dedication" in both of these 1907 books to his wife (of October 1904), Lidia Berdyaeva. A curious fact emerges: the Preface to the ("№ 3") "*Sub specie aeternitatis*" is dated as 25 February 1906; that of ("№ 2") "*New Religious Consciousness*" is dated later, 15 April 1907. Apparently, the M. V. Pirozhkov publisher, having two manuscripts in hand, published the shorter one first, contrary to the order intended by Berdyaev.

---

[1] in Russian: "*Sub specie æternitatis: опыты философские, социальные и литературные* (*1900-1906*)". С-ПЕТЕРБУРГЪ, Издание М. В. Пирожкова, 1907.

A further detail. "*Sub specie aeternitatis*", other than its opening and close, consists entirely of a sbornik-collection of *previously published* journal articles. And quite untypically, these articles are arranged chronologically; Berdyaev's methodology in such things is usually a shotgun approach, at times which is perceptible but to Berdyaev himself and the Holy Spirit. In Berdyaev's seemingly written later *"New Religious Consciousness"* tome, the chapters were are and uniquely written for the book. This latter work remains yet untranslated in English. By a quirk of fate, we seem to have followed out the sequence initially intended by Berdyaev.

Berdyaev's literary activity may be roughly divided into two phases, although somewhat an over-simplification. The first period comprises his work while still in Russia, prior to his 192w banishment. This was a formational period of dynamic intensity and wide ranging examination of European cultural figures and motifs, -- a fluidly transitional period during which his embryonic core motifs fully emerge. Berdyaev's post-1922 phase in the West may be regarded as Berdyaev's "mature period" -- when his core motifs and thought attain a crystaline clarity and assuredness, amidst the increasing attention of a Western audience and interaction with contemporary Western intellectual figures. Berdyaev's books written during this period were nearly all, during his lifetime, translated into English amidst many another language. This translation activity continued for a few short years after Berdyaev's death in 1948, and then ceased, leaving significant a portion of the total corpus of his writing untranslated. Hence, after respectfully waiting for others more qualified to do so, half a century later in our own twilight years, we have set about translating the "unfinished half" of Berdyaev's writings, -- both his many major Journal Put' and other articles written in the West, and also his "early period" books written while still in Russia (which includes the present volume).

Tamara Klépinine's 1978 "*Berdiaev Bibliographie*" is a masterfully arranged and truly invaluable resource, a precious and authoritative aid scientifically academic in the best sense of the word. But it is long out of print and rare if not virtually impossible to find. It lists a total of 483 writings by Berdyaev, not including those listed as "*sans signature*". Berdyaev's writings are categorised into sections: the first numbered section comprises "Books & Booklets" (with sub-listing of foreign language editions). Other sections variously comprise "anthology" contributions, prefaces, journal articles, etc. Separate lists of both Russian and Foreign Language journals are provided with "x-ref" to Berdyaev works included. All in all, supremely helpful. And in our own Berdyaev translations, whether in books or Online, we provide both a year of initial publication and the clarifying Klepinina №. To provide the current generation of readers some better sense of the sequential order of Berdyaev's "early period" books (apart from booklet-pamphlets), the following Kl. № /Year /Title listing may be helpful:

№ 1 - 1901 Subjectivism and Individualism in Societal Philosophy
№ 2 - 1907 The New Religious Consciousness and the Societal Aspect
№ 3 - 1907 Sub specie aeternitatis: Articles Philosophic, Social and Literary (1900-1906)
№ 4 - 1910 The Spiritual Crisis of the Intelligentsia
№ 5 - 1911 The Philosophy of Freedom
№ 6 - 1912 Aleksei Stepanovich Khomyakov
№ 8 - 1916 The Meaning of Creativity. On Justification of Man.[1]
№ 14 - 1918 The Crisis of Art
№ 15 - 1918 The Fate of Russia

* * *

Our present text, "*Sub specie aeternitatis*", represents thus one of Berdyaev's earliest books, and as such it contains core thoughts and motifs that will mature at depth over the course of years, decades even. Some of the themes are quite timely, others timeless. Indeed, our Latin title might be loosely translated as "Under the Guise/Aspect of Eternity" or alternately, "With an Eye to Eternity", or simply, "As regards Eternity". This is the cohesive intuitive theme and symbol threading its way through the book.

The obviating need for something eternal in life, the undying and ineradicable hunger for it, is clearly suggested in the quote opening the initial article, from Ibsen's "Solness the Master Builder": the need to build not merely habitations for mankind, but also lofty and upwards inspiring towers. "Daily bread" is of course a basic necessity to hold body and soul together. But "man lives not by bread alone" (Mt. 4: 4) -- said in answer to

---

[1] English title: "The Meaning of the Creative Act" (1955).

the facile and pragmatic materialist's temptation for "turning stones into bread". There mustneeds be something more -- to staunch the drift of modernity's desiccated souls into a "latent death-wish" epidemic of alcoholism, drugs and the life. The everyday gruel in life fails to satisfy, evokes an hunger for something more substantial and filling. This smugly bland positivist rationalism underlying the various contemporary trends leads then instead, among a portion of the Russian intelligentsia, onto the paths of philosophic idealism, and thence towards a return to Christianity. In this, Berdyaev was merely one voice, among others, in the searching out of new paths.

In historical a setting, the articles comprising our text span the dawning of s new -- the XX Century. Symbolically, the death of both Fr. Nietzsche and Vl. Solov'ev in the year 1900 mark marks a close to the old century, whilst prophetically having sown seeds for the next. The dawning of a new century is a time of expectant optimism, and an obliviousness to the cataclysmic horrors lying in wait. In Russia, there is also the added instability of turbulent years: the humiliating defeat from the 1904-1905 Russo-Japanese war, the shocking event of "Bloody Sunday" (22 January 1905), the subsequent failed "1905 Revolution" which in its excess evoked the subsequent "Reaction".

The primary source for philosophic thought, its centre, was Germany. Russians studied abroad in Germany and then uniquely russified the Germanic philosophic thought. This was already so back in the time of A. S. Khomyakov and the "Old Slavophils", on the one hand, and the "Westernisers" more superficially so, on the other -- as regards Hegel and his successors. Another dominant philosophic current contemporary with our text was Neo-Kantianism. Against its rationalistic gnosseological quests into the structures of knowledge, Berdyaev issues a demand for a realist ontologism, both as regards the knower and the known. Kant in his brilliance had posited the noumenal as unknowable, relegating knowledge in effect as but studies in phenomenology, the structure of cognition of appearances. Unless the knower as a noumenal subject ontologically exists, Neo-Kantianism remains a philosophic system "hanging suspended up in the air", without grounding, without a solid foundation. And yet, regarding ethics, Kant provides a continuing basis for Berdyaev's personalism.

Some several of our articles deal with Marxism, which for Russia from the 1890's among a portion of the radical intelligentsia came to supplant the variant trends of the older Russian Narodnik/Populism, of which N. K. Mikhailovsky had been significant a spokesman. Marxism, with its intellectual nexus in Germany, was seen as more "scientific" a socialist approach and totalitarian scope of view. As such, it assumes the form of a surrogate for religion in its "faithful", an indeed pseudo-religion. Marxist heretics like K. Bernstein in Germany are castigated, and the Marxist drift in Russia towards philosophic idealism by Berdyaev and others, merits an anathema towards such reprobates. Preserving the purity of the orthodox Marxist faith among its "true believers" -- the historical dynamics of splittings and deviations, such as with that of Mensheviks and Bolsheviks, bears parallels to the Reformation religious wars in the West, or the Sunni-Shia rivalry within Islam. In "religious" a template, the writings of Marx becomes an "inspired scripture", Vl. Lenin during this period is in the process of becoming its "St. Paul" (L. Trotsky its eventually erased-from-memory Barnabas?), and J. Stalin in time becomes its "pope" -- having purged the "faith" from any corruptions... Socialism absent a true respect for freedom leads instead to a coercive and oppressive collectivism; liberalism absent a responsible freedom likewise leads to contorted chaos.

Berdyaev's thought represents a critique of various trends, intellectual, societal and cultural. In this, freedom and the dignity of the concrete human person remain guiding constants. Among Berdyaev's great merits are a re-discovery and re-examination of significant forgotten figures from the past, including conservative voices considered "irrelevant" even among the contemporary pseudo-conservative chattering class. Who can soon forget the opening epigramme to Berdyaev's K. Leont'ev article, that Russian of a sort Nietzsche. And then too A. S. Khomyakov, about whom Berdyaev will write an entire book in 1912.

And it is not only Russian cultural figures that Berdyaev rescues from obscurity. Throughout his works are scattered a precious few intensive studies, -- such as on Léon Bloy (cf. our "The Crisis of Art" edition), and J. K. Huysmans (cf. the epilogue to Berdyaev's 1911 book, "Philosophy of Freedom").

The 2nd chapter of our present text similarly contains Berdyaev's 1902 article on dramatic plays by Maurice Maeterlinck (1862-1949) -- whom few if indeed any of our readers will ever have heard of; although "Pelléas and Mélisande" in music may evoke a faint echo. Berdyaev's article is itself an absolute artistic gem, introducing initially the Russian reader and now us -- to the creative genius of Maeterlinck. It invokes catharsis in the apprehension of an ensuing tragedy. In radical contrast to our modern crude and vulgar culture, we become re-acquainted on a profound level with a brittle fragility of soul undetected in those around us. All which transpires upon a more authentic and rarified plane of being. In Maeterlinck's "*The Blind*" -- the image of the priest vexingly resonates all too strongly with the priest-translator now penning these words, perceiving that his efforts all too resemble those of that priest...

In both the Maeterlinck article and the L. Shestov article on "Tragedy and the Everyday Ordinary", -- there is attention to a sense of "tragedy". How timelessly untimely a subject. In our modern culture, in our increasingly atomised society, people flee in terror before the face of the tragic, seek to blot out and efface its immediacy. Our vulgar common culture tries shallowly to treat everything as a "joke", amidst a numbing "laugh effect". The reaction to tragedy is something intensely personal. It involves not only sympathy, but also empathy, -- just as when we share in the inevitability of the long withering terminal illness of a dear close friend, a parent or a spouse. In all this there is a vast interplay of emotions and motifs. But in the face of the tragic inevitability, there is the ability to be able to care, of empathy, and ultimately a transcendent catharsis validating the eternal, "*sub specie aeternitatis*", over the temporal within the human soul and consciousness. In acceptance of the tragic, the acceptance becomes transcendent within the catharsis.

"*Sub specie aeternitatis*" -- under the guise of eternity -- even in the rare instance of abundant surfeit, "daily bread" fails to quell an innate hunger lodged deep within the heart and soul of man. It is almost a physiological problem of sorts, the need for a "balanced diet". And thus, our present tome opens forth in vital search for it...

8 February 2019
Fr. S. Janos

Sub specie aeternitatis

Articles Social, Philosophic and Literary

(1900-1906)

In Dedication to Li

Concerning Realism

(In Place of an Introduction)

I have decided to publish these articles of the past six years, although I intimately sense their imperfective and fragmentive quality, and seeming lack of inner connection. I am printing the articles in almost an unclear form and in chronological sequence. I know, that I shall be accused of contradictions, inconsistency and variance... But as regards this I want to say some several words about these apparent contradictions and about the active inner unity and consistency of the *searchings*, that connect my articles. And foremost of all I have in mind an unity psychological, a consistency subjective, i.e. a connection verymost real.

It seems to me, that in these fragmentive and insufficiently conclusive articles, from first to last, there threads singular a desire -- to figure out *the meaning* of life, of life personal and worldwide, a singular insight -- concerning modern culture and the modern societal aspect. The dichotomy and crisis of soul, reflected in this book, is perchance not of interest for me alone. A real egress from this dichotomy and crisis has always appeared for me only as one that is religious, and all the problems of being in the final extent boil down to a problem religious, although to examine them I have attempted to do so in philosophic a manner. Even when one is not yet endowed of wisdom, one might still nevertheless love wisdom, i.e. be a philosopher. However, the ultimate wisdom and real power obtain only within religious a gnosis. I ask pardon of the academics, in that philosophy for me is not "an abstract principle", in that it is connected for real with a living relationship of person to culture and the societal aspect; I ask pardon also of the societally-involved, of all the *social true-believers*, in that the societal aspect, the socialness likewise is not for me an "abstract principle", under which would be subordinated the creative aims of the person and the meaning of the world. The point of contention with "abstract" philosophies and "abstract" publicists, with the rationalists, severed off from life, from the real fullness of being, is determined not in the "abstract" departments of science, of politics, etc etc, but rather in the unknown by them higher instances, in the revealings of the Logos.

But in these essays there is also an objective, a logical progression of an inward movement of ideas. I tend to think, that in them I am not stumbling about on various sides, but rather instead move along towards a definite mental, considered sphere of purpose. In this book I see a gradual liberation from the mighty intellectual currents of our era: from Marxism, Kantianism and Nietzscheanism. A good portion is allotted to my critique of Marxism and Kantianism, with which in the initial articles I was still connected. Later on through an individualistic reorientation and decadent split I transitioned to a completely different grounding of problems, than initially posited. This framework of ideas, towards which I then gravitated, in all its components, is best of all to be characterised by the words -- *mystical realism.* The "Idealism", which in my first article I considered a battle shout and which was part of a larger trend, connected with "Problems of Idealism", was however a transitional condition. "Idealism" was fine for an initial criticism of Marxism and positivism, but within it there is nothing creative, and to remain upon it was impossible, as regards the real or religious. Amidst this a portion of the "idealists" then advances further towards mysticism, and combines with a current, possessing other sources, and hence transitions from idealist abstractions to mystical realities. Once there is manifest an awareness and consciousness of mystical realities, there then ceases the realm of illusionism, be it positivist, idealist or romantic, and there instead ensues new an era. I have to admit, that from what comprises the world, from its whatever real things, is what determines one's relationship to them, and sets the accounting od realities. I cannot be still a nihilist, cannot substitute mystifications for the mystic. And therefore necessary for me is metaphysical and religious knowledge. Therefore also my politics and my ideal of the societal aspect has to be constructed upon the real-mystic, i.e. religious groundings.

The loss of a feel for realities, a disconnection from the depths of being -- this is the essence of our era, and in this is the crisis of the contemporary consciousness. This loss is to be felt with both in philosophy, and in politics, and in art, and throughout the whole of modern life, suffused in a spectral realm of phenomena. The positivism all still prevailing among us at its root denies reality, declares being a metaphysical phantasm, admits of only phenomenology, processes, a condition of consciousness, it leads to endless an illusionism. Idealism in all its uncritical forms likewise does not lead us out from the realm of illusionism, and even consolidates it further, admitting only of a norm, an idea, a condition of consciousness, but not actual being.

The positivist Social-Democracy projects a pretend type state of being, the illusion of a phenomenal world and already at its evident limit it leads to non-being, already there is to be sensed within it the religion of a jolly neo-Buddhism. Everything -- is splintered, disoriented, "abstracted", everything becomes phantasmic and trite. Real only is the yearning for all-unity, for being that is concrete, individual and absolute. We have undergone a romantic sort of languishing.

But "realism" begins with oneself acknowledging the mystical reality, with a real self-awareness and self-consciousness. A solipcism sort of individualism cannot even admit the reality of the I. But once there is the I -- a mystical-metaphysical reality, then already from this there hence becomes inevitable a passing over to the reality of others that also are an I, the reality of God, the reality of the devil; the world is alive, the blood flows in its veins, and all again exists for real.

We are transitioning from the positivist, the idealist and other sorts of non-being, to being that is metaphysical and mystical. I therefore also get a grasp of knowledge that is for real, i.e. as my co-uniting, and not a dis-uniting from the world, from being. But metaphysical knowledge unites us for real with being not in an abstract, not in its rationalistic form, but the rather as part of the full religious gnosis. Our mysticism gravitates towards religion, i.e. towards a defining correlation with the mystical realities of the world, a mysticism which seeks to be perceptive, to grasp the meaning of the world. All the threads conjoin in the central idea of the Logos. Our politics ought to catch sight of the mystical realities behind the historical phenomena, ought to connect their aims with the religious meaning of the world. With the self-awareness and self-consciousness of *the person*, as a mystical reality, there begins a real knowledge, a real religious revelation and activity, a real creativity. On this victory of *realism*, on the surmounting of the imaginary and illusory reality of the positivist world, it would seem, depends a cultural and religious rebirth and true liberation. Mystical realism leads not to a static dogmatism, but rather to a dogmatism that is dynamic, always pulsing, creatively unbounded, insightful and transfigurative. A vital and real mysticism ought always to reveal something, to affirm something, ought to be an attempt to be productive and relate concerning the assayed and discerned, and it is "dogmatised" in the name of dynamic motion, in order that the motion be actual, in order that in the dynamic motion something real should happen. The sort of a non-dogmatism, not allowing us to stir, to reveal or affirm, rising up against every discerning of the meaning of things, against every creative "yes", -- is always dogmatised, always stagnant. In the modishly fashionable "adogmatic" mysticism there is no movement forward, no realism, it seeks as though to consolidate the blindness and illusory aspect to what is experienced, and in this it is terribly alike to its antipode -- the old dogmatism. They fail to understand, that religious a revelation, -- is an opening forth, it should involve continuation, and religious a creativity remains boundless only then, if in the past something was revealed, if in the future something is revealed. But to create from nothing -- is impossible. Religion however is of a discerning and real mysticism.

A real and discerning mysticism cannot remain something purely individual, hidden away from the experienced world, it ought to engage the world, affect the world. Religion ought to be concrete an aspect, something felt, connected with living history, beholden to the politics of life, or else religion never was nor will be a reality. Unneedful to me is a religion, which possesses no sort of any relationship to all the fullness of life, nor to the historical process, to the future of the human societal aspect. And indeed to no one is such a religion needful, since religion is no some separate corner of individual experiences, with which each would seek to comfort oneself, but rather the real deed of the salvation of humankind and the world, of the victory over death and non-being, the affirmation of the person within absolute being, the affirmation of life eternal and enriched. We have come towards a denial only of the human, the rationalistic, the abstractly-political and abstractly-moral paths of salvation amidst the affirmation of a path humanly religious. The acute setting of the problem of socialism and anarchism renders vivid the religious meaning of world history, helps us spurn the allure of the Grand Inquisitor -- the compulsory ordering of an earthly realm, in which felicitude and tranquility obtain at the sacrificing away of freedom and eternity.

My first and final thought -- is the invariable thought concerning *the person*, concerning liberation. The path I go is towards its universal affirmation, towards an uniting with the world Logos. I make an approach in these articles towards God-manhood, towards an embodiment of the Spirit into the societal aspect, towards a mystical unity of love and of freedom. And having moved away from the Marxist pseudo-sobornost', away from the decadent-romantic sort individualism, I instead go a path towards the Sobornost' of a mystical neo-Christianity.

S.-Peterburg, 25 February, 1906

The Struggle for Idealism

(1901 - 105)[1]

Hilda. First of all I shall look about all, that you have built here.
Solness. It will have you running about much.
H. Yes, you indeed have built quite much.
S. Very much. Especially the last few years.
H. And very many bell-towers also? So terribly high?
S. No. I no longer still build bell-towers. And likewise no churches.
H. What then do you build *now*?
S. Dwellings for people...
H. And could you not...also construct such towers over these dwellings?
S. What are you hinting at by this?
H. I think...that something such...might as it were point...forwards, towards freedom.
S. How strange you should say this. This is most of all what I would want.
H. Why indeed do you not?
S. Akh, people do not want this!
H. You say... they don't want this!
S. But now I am building for myself a new home. Just opposite.
H. For yourself?
S. Yes. It is almost ready. And on it will be a tower.
H. An high tower?
S. Yes.
H. Very high?
S. The public will say, actually, that it is too high, i.e. for a typical house.
H. I shall come to see this tower early tomorrow morning.

Hendrik Ibsen. "Solness the Builder" ["The Master Builder"].

It is no secret, that Marxism, that selfsame Marxism, which still not long ago represented such an organised, organic entity and satisfactory worldview, is now undergoing serious a crisis. If several years back the intellectual-societal life of the progressive portion of Russian society tended to revolve around the disputes between the Marxists and the Populists, now the centre of gravity has shifted and foremost appear the

---

[1] BOR'BA ZA IDEALIZM. Article originally published in the monthly journal "Mir Bozhii", S. Peterburg, jun. 1901, p. 1-26.

frownings of the critical ortodoks current within Marxism itself. Now for it the motifs of theoretical work are not as a critique of the Populist trend, but rather as self-criticism and the need for furthermost a developing of worldview. In Western Europe this crisis was occasioned generally by a noted book by Bernstein [Eduard, 1850-1932], but in my opinion, perhaps, it becomes clear, that a new critical trend is not primarily Bernsteinism in the particular sense of this word and, in any case, cannot simply remain Bernsteinism.

I want to take a look at the modern tumult within Marxism under a not at all typical point of view, I want to connect it with the crisis throughout all the worldview of the XIX Century. For any intensive look into the complex soul of the modern intelligent man, into his profound moral issues, into the modern trends within the spheres of philosophy and art, it ought to be clear, that we live in an epoch of spiritual tumult. Denying this would only be the man, hypnotised by some whatever dogma. The conventional progressive worldview of the recent past century has hit a dead end and upon the former path it is impossible to go any further. Needful is a review of the accepted formulas and the seeking out of new paths. I take upon myself the impudence to categorically assert, that the droll singsong of positivism, naturalism and hedonism throughout all its lines renders apparent *a struggle for idealism*, a struggle for a more joyful and bright world perception, in which the higher and eternal questions of the human spirit receive satisfaction.

Within philosophy they are beginning to understand the unsatisfactory aspect of positivism as a worldview, while instead the Platonic traditions are revived and the eternal truths of metaphysical creativity are acknowledged; in art is to be noted a reaction against a vulgarised naturalism, killing off any beauty, and in modern symbolism is reborn a romanticism of the finest artistic creations of the past; the eudaemonism, hedonism and utilitarianism prove themself bankrupt in the deciding of the moral problem, and there is noted a striving to establish an absolute value of the good, to revive the idealistic idea of "natural law", which is long already thread-bare, despite its tremendous historical merits. Very characteristic is this strong interest od modern man and especially of "forefront" man in questions of philosophy, art and morals. Every deep soul senses himself unsatisfied in his best inquiries and bears within him the burden of the duality of a transitional epoch. One can, certainly, meet with a great multitude of sated "positivists", who suffer no spiritual hunger, who understand not the strivings of Faust, but such people are not in the front ranks of any historical epoch. The bourgeois, the philistine spirit lives still within the progressive masses and faces a great task of spiritual revival. It will therefore be clear, that I have little in common with the declarations of Brunetière [Ferdinand, 1849-1906] and suchlike concerning the bankruptcy of science. A positive realistic science, on principle shunning any romanticism, this -- is the chief attainment of the XIX Century, this is an eternal contribution of the bourgeois epoch into the treasury of the human spirit and nothing derogatory against it is possible.

In order to posit a social-political diagnosis on this by the spiritual strivings, to which I point, it is needful first of all to dispel a certain historical misunderstanding. This historical misunderstanding states: theoretical idealism is connected with reactionary social impulses, as regards a practical materialism; a practical idealism and progressive strivings can only be connected with a theoretical realism or materialism; the inclination towards metaphysics almost always leads to thought about societal disorder, since metaphysics is as it were -- a worldview of the ruling classes. This misunderstanding holds an enormous grip over the average progressive man; this coarse prejudice very much indeed greatly inspires a superstitious terror in facing those inquiries, which everyone ought to reckon as most sacred, and without which life is rendered empty, grey and mindless. The modern progressive is terribly afraid of certain words, he wracks his soul over some unthreatening triteness, and he does not dare admit, that at times he thirsts to glance at life from the point of view of eternity. To future ages it will seem monstrous, that there was a time, when spiritual shabbiness was almost a matter of pride, and spiritual richness they reckoned best to hide away from their souls in daylight. We are attempting to show the historical roots of this misunderstanding, which in its own time was useful a lie, but now is only perhaps harmful, since it retards the formation of *the new man* for modern society.

In the life of various peoples there occur eras, which are termed "eras of enlightenment". Here the reasoning ability of man comes into its own right, having thrown off from itself the fetters of authority, beginning a relentless critique of the dogmatic worldview of the past, the time-worn religious and societal ideas, superstitions and prejudices, standing in the way against the ultimate developing of human society. These "eras of enlightenment" often purport their theoretical slogan of "materialism", a revolutionary materialism, which is rendered into a weapon of the struggle against darkness in the name of light, and to be a materialist in such eras often means to be an idealist. The reactionary forces of society get veiled with idealistic words and against these words contend the progressive forces, which themself out of a natural psychological reaction tend to veil over as materialistic, words that are actually idealistic in their content. Thus, for example, the medieval Scholastico-theological worldview and the societal forces, concealed behind this worldview, strongly exploited the terminology of an absolute idealism and the philosophers of the enlightenment era had to direct their critical arrows against all theoretical absolutes, in order to undermine the medieval Scholasticism and the mode of life resting upon it. The greatest of the eras of enlightenment was that experienced by France in the XVIII Century, and no other era can reckon in its ranks such an array of immense thinkers, nor such brilliant a literature. The task facing it was great: to demolish medieval society and the medieval worldview. I think, that the philosophy of the French Enlightenment figures of the XVIII Century, with its materialism directed against the medieval absolutism, is also indicative to its strong effect up til now upon the progressive man of our times. An analogous enlightenment era was experienced by Germany, as a land more backward, only so til the decade of the 40's of the XIX Century, finding therein its expression within L. Feuerbach and the Left Hegelians. Criticism in theology became a basic impelling motif of the then "materialism", and humanistic strivings set to it idealistic an imprint. In Russia in the decade of the 1860's there was an "era of enlightenment". Chernyshevsky and Pisarev -- were our "enlighteners", under the banner of materialism they contended against the darkness of pre-Reform society in the name of freedom of thought and human dignity. But we now have to esteem in Chernyshevsky and Pisarev not the "materialism", in which there was nothing original and for our time nothing of value, we esteem rather their "enlightened idealism". Our publicists of the decade of the 1860's fought against metaphysics, since that it was defended by the conservative elements, they fought against the cult of beauty, since behind it clung the landed gentry with its publicists, literateurs, poets and poetisers. They were historically correct. Their materialistic lie, amidst all its philosophic inconsistency, included within it an enormous practical truth.

That was then, but now?

During the XIX Century the correlation of societal forces changed, the revolutionary fervour of the "third estate" cooled down, it ceased to be "of the people" and became "bourgeois", having shown its exploitative claws. The creative powers of the bourgeoise, in the past century having accomplished great critical work, has begun to wear down and the character of its ideology has brusquely changed. Towards positive spiritual work it has seemed little capable. The bourgeois era of history denotes a lowering of the psychological type of the human person, a narrowing of its spiritual horizons. The bourgeois aspect, converting life into a retail shop, tends to murder all idealism, kills it within life, within philosophy, in art, in morality, in politics and holds tight only to positive science, as needful for its practical interests. It belittles every vivid individuality, is corrosive towards beauty and the striving to grasp the mystery of existence. The revolutionary materialism of the past century with its idealistic baggage tends to get replaced by positivism with its philosophic restraint and wont for accurateness. Positivism, as a demand for applying the scientific method to all the spheres of knowledge, is something perpetual; science can only be positive, and religious or metaphysical determinations on scientific questions inadmissible. Positivism however, as a worldview, represents a devaluing: it spiritually is coercive of man, and recommends an ignoring in response to the most profound inquiries of the human spirit.[1] Metaphysical idealism gets banished by the bourgeoise from the intellectual life of mankind as lacking in practical utility. In art, the bourgeois asserts realism and creates its most extreme manifestation -- naturalism. Naturalism faithfully reflects society in the XIX Century in all its ugliness. Beauty is banished from the art of the ruling classes, since it does not show forth in their life and art becomes relegated into a protocol, wherein the theoretics of naturalism propose transforming artistic creativity into a branch of experimental science. Idealism gets banished from human experiences and art impotent to render it. In the XVIII Century hedonism struggled against the authoritarian criteria of good and evil, and in this was its right to existence. In the XIX Century this idealistic current vanishes from the theories and practices of the ruling class and there stirs instead an utilitarian view on life, an outlook of the shop-keeper, knowing no morally lofty a beacon, than the income-account book. The moral life of bourgeois society, which revolves around making a profit, provides little nourishment for idealistic constructs, and ethical idealism finds itself no place within

---

[1] It is characteristic, that the father of positivism, Au. Comte, has termed all the revolutionaries as metaphysicians.

the bosom of this society. The XVIII Century advanced the profound idealistic idea of "natural rights" and relied on it in the political struggle; this idea was dethroned by the evolutionists of our era, and liberal opportunism was rendered the trend in the prevailing politics. Literally, alongside the bourgeois social aspect we ought also to acknowledge the deep spiritual and cultural bourgeoisness of society in the XIX Century, a bourgeoisness, distortive of life and lessening its value. I should want, that someone might venture to show, -- in what positive connection is there to be found the psychic mindset of the governing classes of bourgeois society with any sort of idealistic a philosophy, how and where in fact the capitalists, the industrialists or bankers have been affected by metaphysics? The life of the prevailing masses is abasedly empty and devoid of content, and a protest against it is an expression not only of *social-material*, but also *spiritual-ideal* an hunger. The spiritual summits of the aristocratic intelligentsia of the past itself contain psychological features moreso lofty, and in certain regards is closer to the future, than is the bourgeois-democratic intelligentsia of the capitalist era with its spiritual poverty and anti-idealist spirit.[1] Plato, Goethe or Fichte are people moreso of the future, than are Bentham, Zola or Spenser. In Russian progressive literature the enlightened materialism of the "idealists of the soil" has been transformed into a stultifying positivo-realist stereotype, from which long already has expired any practico-idealist content. The "positivism", which is defended by our traditional-progressive journalists against metaphysical incursions, is verymost bland a liberalism in its philosophy with all the signs of a liberal half-fastedness. And only something by way of a new word can satisfy the spiritual thirst of the finest people of our time.

This selfsame XIX Century created in its bosom an opposition to the bourgeois society. And herein the opposition became infected by the bourgeoisness, I say this for real, though my words sound as heresy and a paradox. The oppressed and down-trodden position of the opposition societal group, the tense character of the social struggle, directed at the attaining of a minimum for human existence, all this tended to narrow the horizons of the person, immersed in the struggle with the bourgeois

---

[1] I have intended to point out only in the most general of features the prevailing psychological aspect of the XIX Century, but I am assuredly mindful, that the historical actuality is extraordinarily complex and full of various hues and individual shadings.

society, and it set a peculiar imprint upon the ideology. In suchlike an era there could not be *the man himself of value*, there was only the crumbs of a man, a man, rendered into but a means. Marxism arose amidst suchlike an historical setting, whereof it could not develope within itself an idealistic anti-bourgeois content, which ought to be inherent to it, which in rudimentary form is in it to greater a degree, than in other currents. The ideology of Marxism is set upon very low a level of developement, and its philosophic world-understanding is not original. The ideologies of the oppressed producers of the mid-XIX Century were lacking, and to their lot befell the task of not having to extend their gaze into the spiritual distance, they were faced with more urgent work, which fatally slanted from them the ideal goals of mankind. I would formulate the greatest and enduring service of Marxism to be in the following manner: Marxism established first off, that only a material societal organisation can be the basis for ideal a developement of human life, that the human ends are to be realised only amidst the material conditions of economic mastery over nature; in practise namely it means to construct "dwellings for people". And here amidst the conditions of the historical moment all the theoretical and practical work has gone towards the working out of the material means, the social-economic premises; amidst psychological a conceptual illusion the means were confused of as ends, and the ends themself of human life were conceived of too materially. Marxism proved to be impoverished in its spiritual-cultural content, the ideal tasks of philosophy, morality, art were not sufficiently conceived of within its struggle with the social bourgeois era nor could it prevail over its own spiritual bourgeoisness. Marxism, as a philosophic worldview, is adjoined to the materialism of the enlightenment era, in part to the German enlightenment philosophy, from the bosom of which Marx and Engels emerged. They bespoke a new word and a great word only in the sphere of the social-economic, yet outside this sphere they added almost nothing to the critical work of the bourgeoise in the period of its revolutionary struggle against the medieval society and its theological worldview. The dialectical character of their materialism, borrowed from Hegelian idealism, does not alter the essential point of the matter, and in regard to their view on the world and life they were materialists and hedonists, with their spiritual scope circumscribed. Idealists as regards their social task -- they struggled against every idealism and were situated under the grip of that historical misunderstanding, upon which I attempted to cast a certain light. Historical Marxism stood in hostile a relationship towards philosophic idealism and metaphysics, towards also artistic idealism and romanticism, towards absolute a morality, towards all religion, which gets jumbled together with the old theology and churchliness. The "students" were faced with enormous a practical task, and yet moreover they popularised and defended from enemies the social-economic teaching of their teacher, but since then they have added to it nothing spiritually of value. And 50 years have passed, and during this time much water has flowed, and we live amidst different societal-historical conditions, wherein life and thought have gone forward and set new tasks.

In the social-political revolutionary movement of the XIX Century there is a certain feature, which imparts upon its fighters quite sharply an anti-bourgeois imprint, -- that of a social-political romanticism, which is accompanied by bravery. The whole effort of human idealism gets channeled into this side and creates beautiful heroic images. The human person gets mangled, its formula of life constricted, but it is idealism nonetheless, though also one-sided. We deeply esteem this idealism, but suchlike a bravery has no future, is rendered obsolete by the modern social situation; and the path, along which the idealism was channeled, little by little is closing, and the quite vivid manifestation of the anti-bourgeois spirit is dissipating. The producers are become the citizens of the world, there are being created certain elementary conditions for the furtherance of human life, their struggle assumes less sharp a character and their formula of life has expanded, wherein the human person is rendered not only into a means, but also an end in itself. On whatever side might expand the formula of life of the self-worthy human person, what is it that replaces the former form of idealism, how will man be a new citizen of the world, how will he differ from the former citizen, the bourgeois philistine? On this question, it seems, one might answer, that if the people of the future do not create a new idealism, if this idealism does not penetrate into the consciousness of the societal group, preparing for the new society, then the social movement will ultimately take on a bourgeois character and the new philistine will not be much more attractive a psychological type, than the old philistine, against whom the struggle is waged. The victory of the oppressed will weaken the acute character of the struggle, this is evident and nowise of regret, but it cannot and ought not to lead to such sort of improvements, that are everywhere seen with five-kopek cures. An all-encompassing sobriety tends to kill the poetics of the past and necessitates compensation for those spiritual losses, such as would accompany material a victory.

There has appeared the book by Bernstein. The spread of "Bernsteinism" -- is an important symptom. Amidst all his theoretical weakness and a certain practical dose of philistinism, Bernstein says much that is true, he is correct also in his appeal for self-criticism, and in the overthrowing of the theory of the necessity of the social catastrophe (Zusammenbruchstheorie and Verelendungstheorie), and in pointing out the one-sided character of the German social movement. But the moderate and accurate "Bernsteinism", belittling the spirit of the movement and denying the value of its ideal aim, the "Bernsteinism", in abolishing the romanticism and idealism of the past and presupposing no sort of a new romanticism and idealism -- is bourgeois, within it there is nothing still of a new society nor of a new man. I pointed above to the bourgeois aspect of the orthodox sort Marxism, whereas Bernsteinism however, naked and bare, if you please, is still moreso bourgeois and it impels especially towards an idealistic summoning forth, it witnesses to the necessity of introducing a new idealistic current into the social movement. When Bernstein presupposes to concentrate upon the means of struggle and pronounces the impudent phrase "the end-goal for me means nothing", he partially, in very narrow a sphere, is correct, but from a general, philosophic point of view, he is profoundly incorrect.[1] We admit of the material means, great and small, only in the name of the ideal ends, always great; we ought to be pervaded by these ends, pervaded to such a degree, that our life becomes not filled merely by the means of struggle, we ought more complexly to understand the means of struggle per se and in such manner to ennoble its soul. It seems to me, that there ensues a moment, when the historical misunderstanding has to dissipate and a practical idealism ought to enter into an uniting with a theoretical idealism, so as with combined forces to struggle against the social and cultural bourgeoisness and thereby prepare the soul of man for the future society. After this historical orientation, I shall move on to a consideration of the question concerning the struggle for an idealistic worldview per se.

---

[1] In the book of Bernstein it is possible to point out separate places, where he conceives of the necessity of empowering idealism alongside the realism, but these are only unclear allusions.

A theoretical struggle for idealism has to begin with a critique of hedonism or, in more elevated a terminology, eudaemonism, which is accepted on faith by a majority of the progressive and intelligentsia sport people of our time. The contemporary social movement builds "dwellings for people", it "no longer still yet builds bell-towers and churches". In the struggle of societal forces, which comprises the very essence experienced by our era, the social ideal inspires us. Social developement and the social struggle, amidst which it will be realised, will lead to a new form of the societal aspect, and amidst our sociological perspective, the new form of the societal aspect will be first of all a new form of production. Everyone, actually, tends to agree, that the new form of production itself per se is not the ideal, such being still remote. I say moreover, that not only every form of production, but every form of the societal aspect can only be a means and cannot be an end-goal, to speak about such as an end can only be conditional, only as a slogan in the social-political struggle. If you should actually demand an accounting of the end-goals of the struggle for a new society, if you put point blank the question concerning the ideal, which everyone tends to sanction and itself already has no need of an higher sanction, then the verymost, that you get, is the following: the end-purpose of every struggle, of every social organisation of life -- is *the happiness of people*. Marxism, from the lips of its founder, pronounced rightful a judgement upon Bentham, as upon an arch-philistine, having adopted the English shop-keeper as the type for the normal man, but Marxism itself proceeds no further than the typical hedonism or eudaemonism, and this is the most, that obligingly can be said of the average Marxist. Here however, actually will be introduced a modification and very essential a modification, and they will tell us, that the end-purpose of every vital struggle -- is *the happiness of the harmonically developing person*. And what such is the harmonically developing person, in this final instance? A person that is developing in the mental, the moral and aesthetic regards. And this means, that not every manner of happiness (about satisfaction I speak no further) is an ideal end-purpose of the social struggle of progressive mankind, but rather only some sort of *higher* happiness, presupposing the higher functions of the human spirit. And once there be admitted an happiness uplifting and an happiness demeaning, once within the human soul there exist *qualities* defying analysis into whatever the quantitative, then the hedonism falls into an inescapable circle, it would have to admit some whatever higher criterion of good and evil, even pronouncing judgement upon happiness itself. The utilitarian J. S. Mill said, that it is better to be a discontented Socrates, than to be a contented pig. Why better? On the basis of utilitarianism and hedonism it is impossible to extol the discontented Socrates against a contented pig, since for this it would be necessary to admit of something more lofty, more sacred, then every sort of contentedness in this world. Carlyle had every basis to term utilitarianism a swinish philosophy.

Psychology (the scientific, and not the metaphysical) long ago already has shattered this illusion, which suggests that man should only strive towards satisfaction, or more complexly stated, towards happiness, wherein this be the sole purpose of life. This could be safely asserted in the XVIII Century by Helvétius, but in our time to assert similar a position with aplomb can only be through boorish ignorance. Happiness is a consequence of the moral life of man, but never its end-purpose; a certain degree of contentment is a condition for the developing of life, but all the same not an end-purpose. Morality -- is independent a quality, -- a quality indissoluble, and this is first of all a psychological fact, which it is possible to deny only by way of sophistry, by way of violation against the very essence of human nature. I will recourse again to that ultimate instance of progressive hedonism -- of developement in all regards of the human person. In order for this principle not to be totally lacking in content, we should have to postulate, as its content, a mental, moral and aesthetic developement. But mental developement benotes an affinity towards *truth*, moral -- towards *good*, the aesthetic -- towards *beauty*. A fulfilling life of the human person is of an higher content, we inevitably find it grounded upon ideas of truth, the good and beauty, which prove higher than any sort of happiness and contentment, since only do they make for us an uplifting happiness, worthy of man, rather than of swine. And herein hedonism in vivid a manner comes nigh well to suicide. Let us consider, however, yet further an argument of the hedonists, utilitarianists and evolutionists in ethics. Truth, the good and beauty, they tell us, represent only social *matters of utility* in the human struggle for life. Marxism especially will insist, that all the so-called "ideology" is only a social matter of usefulness. *Illusionism* -- is the point of view of Marxism on spiritual aspects of the good. Herein ensues all that selfsame inescapable circle, and I would ask the reader to turn his particular attention to this. They tell us, that philosophy, morality, art, the word "ideology", exist for life, that they are of value, only as matters of usefulness in the social life of people, and in the given era -- only as matters of usefulness in the resolution of the "social question" of our days. The deciding of the "social question" ought to provide order for the life of people. And for what is this life itself, this selfsame life, for which everyone is for? Life is for living life, answers the highest wisdom of our era. This answer is too true and therefore it still says nothing; life is only a combination of all the vital processes. But indeed this life, for which all are for and which itself is for itself, is not merely a digesting of food, indeed not for this do we build "dwellings for people". And I say: everyone is for living life, but it is for a life uplifting, for a life in truth, the good and beauty, and by this I recognise the existence of the higher end-purposes of life and of its higher *meaning*. The question about the meaning and ends of life is an eternal one, not to be purged from the human soul by any sort of positivist-evolutionary phrases, and it is impossible to highly enough regard such writers, as Tolstoy and Ibsen, who with an extraordinary intensity posit this old and yet eternally new question. From all the above-adduced arguments is naturally to be garnered this extraordinarily important deduction, *that progress and striving for perfection are higher than happiness and contentment*. More than once already the reactionary nature of utilitarianism and hedonism has been pointed out, as deeply contrary to the very idea of progress and this point is completely correct. Progress presupposes an higher and all-obligatory purpose to the social life of mankind.

In another place I have attempted to show, deriving from Kant, that the basic principle of morality and the formal condition of every moral good is this -- the *self-integrity* of the human person and the *equal-integrity* of all human persons.[1] There are certain that might tend to think, that there is proffered here the old eudaemonistic principle, appealing to the happiness of the harmonically developed person. This would be a crude mistake, witnessing to an incapacity of orientation regarding the higher most succinct inquiries of the human spirit. First of all we admit of *the absolute value* of man, as an end-in-itself, and to this idea it is impossible to insert an empirical system.[2] Therefore, in admitting the sanctity of man,

---

[1] Vide my book, "*Subjectivism and Individualism in Societal Philosophy*". P. Struve likewise developes this thought in the preface to my book.

[2] In the above-named book I attempted to show, that in the conceivings of truth as an end-purpose of knowledge and of good as an

as an end-in-itself, and his equality in value with all other humans as an end-in-itself, we have in view not mere usefulness and happiness nor do we regard as our ultimate ethical idea as merely historical by choosing the usefulness of conditions overall for the selfsame happiness of people. Man -- is a sacred end-in-itself, is not some being merely digesting food and receiving from this an agreeable satisfaction, no, this is a spiritual being, a bearer of truth, the good and beauty, the realisation of an higher truth; for this end-in-itself the striving towards perfection and progress stands higher than contentment and happiness. For a consistent hedonist the word *man*, insofar as it have ethical a meaning, is empty a sound, a pretty phrase, whereas for us this word is full of utmost meaning and significance. The developement of the historical person to the extent of *man* is the triumph of spiritual values, values eternal and absolute, without which the life of people is not yet still human a life, without which it would be so vilely empty and aimless, so *bourgeois* in a most coarse and true meaning of this word.

There exists a myth, that metaphysical idealism -- is sundered off from life by abstraction, and that positivist-evolutionary science is much closer to life. This is first of all a verymost great a psychological lie. "Metaphysics, -- in the expression of Struve, -- is far richer an effort and far nigh closer to reality, i.e. to the fullness of human experiences". Only the perspective of a metaphysical idealism comes fully nigh close to the purposive experiences of the human soul, only herein does the human soul find a full and all-sided satisfaction. I further venture to express a thought, which directly might seem paradoxical: every actually living man, a man, in searching out truth, creating justice and the good or contemplating beauty -- is a metaphysician-idealist. You search for truth and this search fills your life with uplifting content and meaning, which you directly sense and experience, but indeed by precisely this point of departure you already presuppose, that truth is not an empty sound, rather instead that truth is a value, an absolute value, which you still do not know, but which you ought to recognise. The evolutionist at present would begin by showing you, how cognitive knowledge developed from a zoological condition right up to you, and would conclude with this, that while he admits of the idea of

---

end-purpose of moral life there is logically included an acknowledgement of their absoluteness and that this absolute value nowise contradicts the relativity of the theories and all the historical moralities.

truth, absolutely a value for you, as a living and seeking being, it is but useful an illusion, he produces chimerical an analysis and from the valuable experience, comprising the intimate nature of your spirit, there remains nothing. In suchlike a manner, it is possible to acquire a scientific position, but to receive it is irrelevant, since about it at a given moment you will not enquire, nor at some other time be interested by it. The evolutionist with his constant call to turn to the mollusks for an explanation of everything in the world, including also your search for truth, is correct in his partialised area, but to him belongs not the final word in the unraveling of world-knowledge. Philosophic idealism by its very essence always summons *forwards*, to the eternal values, which ought to be realised in life, and it fully come nigh to you, to your soul, thirsting for truth, it arouses the voice of your consciousness, loudly declaring to the value of your searching, of a value, upon which no sort of any evolutionism can infringe. As a living man, conscious of the great importance of the moral problem, you tend to say: this is good, and this is evil, good is a value, I sense myself as something unconditionally of value, and I want to serve the good and struggle against evil. At that moment, when you establish the qualitatively self-sufficing aspect of good in your soul, you acknowledge its absolute value and serve it, you make the greatest act of your life, a veritable divine-service, a service to the God of truth. But here comes along the evolutionist, he calls you back to an investigation of mollusks and importunes you promptly to demonstrate, that everything, what you perceive as sacred, is only useful an illusion in the struggle for existence, that the moral awareness decomposes down to whatever the particles, having nothing in common with morality, and that all this is irrefutably demonstrated by the level of the moral ideals of fish... Every societal fighter for justice tends to be a proponent of "natural law", he appeals for truth in human regards, for an assertion of the eternal rights of man, he is an idealist and agreeable to a martyr's crown for the idea of true-justice, which is experienced by him as absolute a value. The evolutionist endeavours rather to cool down his idealistic call for justice, he endeavours by evolutionary a path instead to demonstrate, that the "natural rights" of man as conceived by the idealist-struggler, which he so passionately wishes to embody in life, is but purest an illusion and from the mollusks it has emerged in suchlike a manner. Only philosophic idealism affirms and provides a basis to this thirst for truth and justice, which has filled the lives of the practical idealists, it acknowledges the absolute value of the moral good and the natural rights of man. The developing human soul contemplates beauty and is enraptured by it, it senses, that "beauty is a great power" -- and experiences the sense of beauty as something unconditionally of value. Man strives towards the beautiful in his feelings, in works of artistic creativity, within outward nature, and this striving uplifts him over the trivial in life. Evolutionary science does not know beauty as a value exhilarating for us, it decomposes it down to molecules and presents a demonstration of the developement of the sensation of beauty originating from the animal world up through the aesthetically refined man of our times. The critical method in philosophy, proclaimed by Kant, looks into the developing human consciousness and analyses it, soundly suggesting, that in it more readily can be found the keys to the mysteries of cognition and morality, than in the awareness of some whatever jellyfish.

But this nowise means to infringe upon the legitimacy and necessity of the *genetic* method of investigation. Everything stated above is directed not against evolutionary science, which we esteem no less than whatever any evolutionist, rather only as a protest against the full-blown positivist-evolutionary perspective and as a defense of the rights of philosophic idealism, which is closer to the experiences of the human soul, -- of living life moreso in the very broad sense of this world, than with evolutionary science, which deals only with one special function of life. At the present time it is impossible not to be an evolutionist, but amidst this, in order that the theory of developement should assume a philosophic meaning and significance, it is in need of revision. The scientifico-philosophic theory of developement ought first of all to admit something that many evolutionists fail to understand: Demokritos already knew, that *nihil ex nihilo*, that life cannot develope from an absence of life, the psychical from an absence of the psychical, morality from an absence of morality, cognition from an absence of cognition, nor beauty from an absence of beauty. There has to be that something, that developes. It is time already to be done dealing with the mechanical materialistic worldview, decomposing everything qualitative into a certain quantity of particles, from which in miraculous a manner everything emerges into the light. It is necessary to admit of the qualitative self-sufficing aspect of the elements of the universe; the world in its developing unfolds to only that content, which in an undeveloped condition was praeternally a given.

Moreover, in order to transform the theory of developement into a theory of *progress*, there needs to be brought in a teleological principle. Progress is the movement of a *being* along a direction towards a *need*, and is a triumph or rendering the needed into being. Another meaning of progress cannot be had and in a philosophy of progress we ought to return to the great idealists of the past, especially to Fichte, nowise altering the traditions of realistic science in general, or realistic sociology in the details. The whole meaning of social developement, the rendering of this developement as progress, consists only in this, that it is the sole means of the discerning of the *needed* within the life of humankind, i.e. of such *spiritual values*, as truth within human cognition, good within the human will, beauty within human feelings. Idealistic a metaphysics has to posit this as a social and world progress, as movement towards an upmost end-purpose of being, that singular truth, in the name of which *the needs* are rendered the whole deed of the world. Everything true, just and beautiful within the life of mankind -- is immortal, as immortal as that eternal and absolute truth, to which we become conjoined in our serving the good and our struggle against evil. And the evil, that evil, which so tangibly is felt within the empirical actuality, from higher a point of view is merely a "not-finding the path to good" and therein is consigned to a shameful ruination, to an inglorious death, still more degrading, than whatever punishment. Peer Gynt, in the remarkable play by Ibsen, prefers accepting hell's torments, rather than to go into the melting furnace, and he cites an appeal to his great sins, but in vain: even in evil he has accomplished nothing great and in his abasement he has proven himself worthy of only one fate: to go into the melting furnace, from which they prepare spoons. Evil as thoroughly negative and in denial, that stature within evil, which history knows, is but an optical illusion, within it is a great force of good, and not evil, a good, of obscure an historical setting, amongst which it will happen to become apparent. Suchlike is all the demonism with its strong will and strong protest. In the amoralist that is Fr. Nietzsche, the majestic impression proceeds from the good within him, and not evil. And nakedly triumphant evil never impresses, its impotent nature is evident to every moral gaze. The profoundly tragic aspect of human life lies in not so much the conflict of good and evil, as rather the multiplicity and complexity of the good itself. Thus, for example, the truly tragic conflict of the striving for embodying justice within human relationships in contrast with the striving freely to create truth and beauty within one's own life. The tragic writers illustrate the clash of human passions with moral duty, but great passions themself per se are not evil. The teaching of Fichte about the actualising I and about the world, as a material of duty, garbed in sensory a form, has, it would seem, a continuing significance and appears to be one of the greatest metaphysical conceptions, embodying within itself the idealistic spirit of progress. Evil is only an insufficient realisation of the oughtful due within the sensory world, an insufficient coming nigh of being towards the ideal end-purpose and therefore the nature of evil is totally negative. Philosophic idealism, situated nigh to the traditions of the immortal Plato, has to admit of a world of *ideal values*, extra-temporal and extra-spatial, which can be absent within the empirical actuality, and which within it never finds its legitimate expression, but which becomes realised within progress, by this singular empirically detectable sign of metaphysical uniting of the existent and the ought, and appears thus as a spiritual beacon of human life. They might ask us: where however is the absolute truth, the absolute good, the absolute beauty, point out to us the content of these ideas, that are constantly alluded to. In suchlike a setting of the question lurks a misunderstanding. No one man, nor any one historical era can pretend to a possession of absolute truth, absolute good and beauty, which are gotten only over the expanse of the whole of progress, as its final end-point. Every other manner of perspective would contradict the idea of an eternal developement, and progress would be transformed into aa moment of an absolute becoming. But everything in the life of mankind possesses an end-purpose only to the degree of proximity to those ideas as regards absolute a significance. The content of the whole of spiritual culture is relative, but receives meaning only as a striving towards the absolute.

P. V. Struve recently issued an appeal to return back to Lassalle [Ferdinand, 1825-1864] and I whole-heartedly join in with this appeal. In his philosophic and idealistic spirit Lassalle stands higher than Marx, and to him namely belongs the idealistic expounding on the "idea of the fourth estate", and he namely with extraordinary an ability posited the human-general character of this idea and imbued it with valuable moral content. And it is in his struggle for idealism namely that we ought to find a footing, for his historical image shows sufficiently, the extent of the progressive nature of philosophic idealism. It faces a great task: the preserving of a sober realism and an understanding of the necessity of material means, and to introduce into the social movement an idealistic spirit. Lassalle understood the necessity, understood it more widely and more profoundly than Marx. At the present moment there is particular need to insist upon this. The ideologies of a new society ought not to allow, that into this society should enter bourgeois souls, they ought to inculcate into man a valuable vital content. The progressive intelligentsia of our time face work over the *spiritual* regeneration of those elements of society, which ought to set into place the cornerstones of the future, and this spiritual regeneration ought to be closely interwoven with the social struggle, preparing "dwellings for the people". And upon the "dwellings" there can and ought to be built high "towers". If into these dwellings be settled a philistine contentment and bourgeois satiety, then to build them, certainly, is possible, but suchlike work would hardly be able to particularly inspire, and the awareness of the builder hardly to be particularly uplifted. We tend to think, that this will not be so, and that in the "dwellings of the future" will be settled the new man, spiritually regenerated, a man with broad a formula of life, a bearer of ideal values, imprinting upon life the seal of utmost a meaning.

Alongside the social democratisation of society ought to enter its spiritual aristocratisation. We cannot await a miracle, cannot expect, that on the next day of the birth of a new society suddenly there would appear a new man with broad spiritual horizons, if still on the eve he was filled with a spiritual bourgeoisness and the formula of his life was extraordinarily narrow, if beyond the material means of struggle he fails to perceive the ideal ends. The contemporary social struggle builds "dwellings for people", it ought also to build up the souls of people, for whom the dwelling is only a means, and it is impossible to postpone this in the hope, that everything somehow will happen by itself; this needs doing, needs doing today. Otherwise we risk entering into a new society, ultimately disoriented as regards the paths of its idealism, with diminished souls, all bourgeois the same, but happily digesting food and its benefits. What a frightful, truly tragic contradiction: we were ready to accept a martyr's crown for our ideal and manifest greatness of soul, but the ideal itself proves to be prosaically stale and insignificant, with no place in it for greatness of soul. It would not be surprising, if under such conditions the man of the future "would yearn for the fate of the fighter and prophet of cherished ideals". In this contradiction, part of the fault lies with a dialectical understanding of social developement with its theory of the necessity of a social cataclysm (Zusammenbruchstheorie) and in general of that mechanical and automatic expounding of the historical process, into which the orthodox sort Marxism frequently falls.

Marxism has made an attempt to provide an evolutionary-scientific basis of idealism via the dialectical method, and many of the "orthodox" up to the present see great a spirit in confessing the theory of the Zusammenbruch regarding capitalist society. But herein namely it is that Marxism stumbles, as the modern actuality and modern philosophic thought tends to demonstrate. This attempt seems a sort of evolutionary-historical utopianism, scientifically impermissible, and thus within it there is not and cannot be idealism. Idealism -- is in the depth and breadth of an ideal, idealism -- is in the active struggle, directed towards the realisation of the ideal, wherein betraying it is an iniquity, idealism -- is there in the greatness of spirit, pervading the social movement, of a spirit, which struggles for what is struggled for. The roots of idealism are metaphysical and the evolutionary historical process creates merely the conditions for its appearance. The dialectical theory of the necessity of social catastrophe however is not only unscientific, logically absurd and in contradiction with the facts of life, but also deeply anti-idealistic. A new society gets created in the dialectical moment of the negation of the old society, evil passes over into its contrary -- into good, rendered insurmountably atop its inner contradictions. Where is the genuine place for idealism, is it on this or on that side of the dialectical divide? I tend to think, that for idealism there will prove to be no place, if this point of view be taken to its logical conclusion.

On the one side of the divide is the idealism of former times, which the "orthodox" also assert; the social evil is so great and overwhelming, that the life of people has to be preoccupied with the material means of the struggle; the psychology of the producers [trans. i.e. "workers"] from the Zusammenbruch-theory perspective hence cannot be expanded upon nor deepened. And on the other side of the divide? Along that side the idealism, perchance, also arises by some sort of ungraspable miracle, but this idealism is situated outside the range of our contemporary view. If there is no penetration by the idealistic worldview, about which I am speaking in my article, then we will have to admit, that on that side of the divide of the old society the idealism will seem out-dated, no longer needed, since the bourgeois sense of contentment will spread to all the people and their souls become covered in too thick a layer of grease, unable to idealistically protest against the merciless triviality of life. That jolly and content man, who takes it upon himself boldly to declare, that the swan song of idealism within the history of mankind has already finished its singing, such a fellow will be of very repulsive a type, and if he proves correct, it will be then a death sentence signature for mankind and its higher spiritual experience.

We perceive somewhat rather different a divide regarding the old and the new society, and in this we stand closer to Lassalle. The sun-rise of a new society is not a dialectically wrought cataclysm, but rather consists in the appearance of a new world-historical era, with bears with it a new great idea, embodying within it an all-mankind sort of progress. Lassalle pointed to the "idea" of the modern era and to its bearers within a defining societal class. The moment of an ultimate realisation of a new societal form within the empirical actuality has no principal significance, it can be more or less remote and in any case it cannot be a social Zusammenbruch, since never in the past history of mankind has there occurred similar a manner of the realisation of a great world historical idea in a new form of the societal aspect.[1] Great is that idealistic spirit, which lives within the social movement and uplifts man above the trite daily struggle, and great is the rising sun, providing light and warmth to the life of strugglers for a new society. We herein on principle separate and hold ourself aloof from all the social reformers, who are incapable of seeing anything great beyond their own small doings, who cannot strongly desire and protest, nor deeply understand and foresee. Nothing is more trivial and banal, than to posit an idealism in expectation of a speedy or sudden realisation of the ideal: in this would be expressed a lack of understanding as to the nature of an ideal. Idealism on principle is preserved moreso amidst a total non-realisation of the ideal, since also then is possible an idealistic victory, amidst which would cease its sway and moderate its sense of duty, in preserving the faith and certitude of its ideal.

---

[1] This question mustneeds on principle be separated from the question on political revolutions in the traditional historical sense of this word. These latter are simply facts, which often are encountered within history and derive from these or some other concrete causes. An admitting of the possibility or impossibility of similar revolutions is nowise the same matter as speaking about the scientific understanding of the process of social developement.

The difficulties to be faced are far greater, than is presupposed by orthodox Marxism with its faith in the mechanical inevitability of the collapse of old forms and the birth of the new. But the presence of these difficulties ought not to dishearten the spirit, which is called to surmount them. We veer off from the area of that which of necessity will occur, and concentrate instead upon the area of that which ought to be created, and this reflects also a strengthening of human idealism, in which categories of the proper and the just prevail over the categories of the existing and the necessary. The new society will be the child of the human spirit, and the evolutionary historical process will create only the basis for its idealistic work. Such a point of view includes within it a partial rehabilitation of the utopianists. Their mistakes are already not terrible, and their correctness tends to be too forgotten.

I already hear the voice of an all-sneering sort, which maliciously says: you walk hand in hand with Bernstein, for it is Bernstein namely that sharply protests against a faith in the inevitability of a social catastrophe and by this exposes his bourgeois nature. First of all, I am not doing this, and whatever the combination of views Bernstein seemingly might represent, a partial coinciding of my views with his views nowise has me beholden to him. And on this I am very insistent. Bernstein -- is a legitimate offspring of orthodox Marxism, he inherited from it realistic elements, which he attempts to strengthen, and he is correct, insofar as he speaks as a voice for the modern social actuality, distinct the from actuality, which existed 50 years back. But in Bernstein there is a lack of the theoretical power of thought and of a practical power of spirit. Within orthodox Marxism Bernstein has not reached the idealism, and he himself has proven incapable of independent a creativity, he is not among those, who blaze new paths; he has tallied up a summation of the facts of life, loudly saying, that the social movement has fecklessly lost the romanticism, which upon a time had tinted it in vivid an idealistic hue, and... has become bereft of idealism. Bereft of idealism is not Bernstein alone, his particular tendency of disparaging the social movement for us is not especially important, the important thing is this, that the social movement itself of our day has become bereft of idealism. To resurrect the past, to resurrect that outlook, which was evoked by a different social-historical setting, is now impossible, since in the struggle for idealism it is necessary to go a new path, it is necessary to create, it is necessary to infuse a new idealistic content into those forms, which are fashioning the contemporary social developement. This will not be a repudiation of sober realism either in practise or in theory, which certainly ought to be preserved, but rather only as a reminder, as to the name of which this realism exists.

I have already pointed out, that orthodox Marxism often tends to fall into a mechanical understanding of the ideological developement of mankind. The question about the relationship between "ideology" and "economics" from the point of view of historical materialism has been little worked out and on account of this there tend to circulate very ridiculous presentations. A certain expression about "basis" and "superstructure" proves upon closest an analysis to be bereft of any whatever definite meaning, and this is a figure, supporting quite varied an interpretation. Frequently one chances to hear, that every ideology (science, philosophy, religion, morals, art) is created by "economics", by "the condition of the producer forces", by "the social medium" etc. These approaches within Marxist literature as expressions from a philosophic point of view can nowise sustain critique. How can this economic developement create an ideological developement? What does this mean, when they tell us, that the production relationships of whatever the era create its philosophy? What sort of an inner causal connection is there possible between economics, the forms of production and exchange, -- be this the discovery of a scientific law, the construct of a metaphysical system, the experience of moral ideals, or artistic creativity? Historical materialism, in consequence of its philosophic disarray and methodological naiveté, tends to further strengthen the typical fallacy of evolutionism, which believes in a miracle of creating something from nothing, a morality from whatever the elements absolutely foreign to it, a scientific knowledge from something, having nothing in common with knowledge etc. In general, it is time to quit this evolutionary superstition, and it need not be held on to by the doctrine of historical materialism, which undoubtedly has a future, as a very valuable sociological trend. An ideology does not automatically create economic developement, it is created by the spiritual work of people and ideological developement is only a disclosing of spiritual values, having eternal a significance, nowise dependent upon whatever evolution. But the ideology actually is *conditioned* by the composite of the productive forces, and economic developement actually creates the basis for the ideological developement of mankind, literally, and only amidst the ready at hand *material means* is there to be reached the *ideal ends* of life. In such manner we acknowledge the spiritual independence of every ideology and its aspect of social condition as affected by material productive forces, its dependence upon economic developement. All this has important a significance for an examination of a new task, which we are attempting to posit for the ideologies of a new society. Social-economic developement itself per se cannot automatically create that idealism, which ought to fill the life of people, it instead creates the conditions for the manifesting of *man* in the true sense of the word, but it does not create man himself. Into our consciousness should enter the great idea of constructing dwellings with lofty towers stretching upwards and we ought to make an approach to constructing this sort of tower, since it will never grow on its own. In what however consists this tower?

This -- is a manifold embodiment of the idealistic spirit within human life, the idealism within philosophy, in art, in morality, in the social-political struggle, in love. This idealistic spirit is called to uplift the earth to the heavens and bring the heavens to the earth; it should imprint upon all human affairs the seal of an higher meaning and therein explain our struggle, both temporal and ultimate, as a struggle towards *the eternal and the infinite*. It is only under this condition that the life of human person, this end-in-itself, will find tremendous a value and meaning. This will involve a revival of that romanticism, which comprises an eternal need for the human soul, at times swallowed up by the historical setting, but expressed an especial intensity in deep and complex natures. We live in a transitional era and the finest, the most refined and dissatisfied souls bear within them at times a fateful dividedness. Only a conscious effort of co-uniting theoretically a viably grounded idealism together with the progressive social strivings can surmount this dividedness.

I would define romanticism as the yearning of the human soul for that which is eternally of value. In love, this special area of romanticism, it is manifest as a desire for a love eternal, a love, realising an affinity of souls and having an unconditional value and significance. But a love absolute in its value never finds a full realisation in the empirically actual and upon this basis arises the profoundly tragic aspect of love, against which the philistine ideals of felicitude and contentment are to no avail. Social developement and the social struggle tend to remove only the obstacles for a manifestation of true love, to abolish the negative aspects as regards family and those oppressive social constraints, which hinder the cultivating of the psychological interacting of human souls. But this question still does not deal with love itself, the genuine question lies beyond that side of a social resolution of the problem. The ideals concerning love among the people of the progressive portion of society is not particularly as yet lofty nor profound. The ideal of an equal-rights partners union of a man and woman, presupposing the economic self-sufficiency of each and freedom from compulsory social constraints, does point to an elementary needful pre-condition, but it is nowise still a guarantee nor salvation from the prosaic tedium of life. This partnership union likewise often becomes a poetical graveyard of love, as in a compulsory marriage, since in it does not appear that invaluable content, which bears, regretably, so banal a term, -- a novel it is not. It serves as a fine illustration of a thought developed by me, that social forms are always -- means, never ends. Only contemporary modern art begins closely to make an approach to the question concerning love and demands a rebirth of romanticism in love in contrast to that swamp, in which naturalism has wallowed. The most recent art is beginning to understand the idealistic nature of love, and indeed only a poetry of love, only an ideal-romantic love has value, uplifts man over the prosaic aspect of life, from which is no true exit in the philistine ideal of felicity, such as is confessed by the greater multitude of the so-called "progressive" people. For example, Hendrik Ibsen in almost all his works provides more elevating, moreso poetic a relationship between a man and woman and passionately protests not only against modern social forms, but also against that bourgeois spirit, which inhabits them, and he -- is a revolutionary of spirit. And the preaching of "free love" -- the latest word of the progressive point of view on love -- once again seems only conditional a love, only a removing of social hindrances, while about love itself nothing here still is said. "Free love" is a means, and not an end. In declaring a struggle for idealism in this important area of human life, I think, that only an admitting of the metaphysical meaning of love can enable an heightening of the value of the human life, filling its soul with uplifting a content. The so-called "women's question", which also in like degree regards men, will be resolved, as part of the general "social question", and thereupon the problem of love will stand forth in all its clarity. Ideal love with its eternal romanticism, its beauty and poetry is one of the end-purposes of human life and the task of its fulfillment in life ought to be set onto the standards of the spiritual struggle for a new man, for which the social struggle readies a new edifice.

Metaphysical creativity within philosophy is likewise, if you please, romanticism and a romanticism eternal in its correlation of profoundest concerns of the human spirit. And first of all we would wish within life an embodiment of the philosophic spirit, the spirit of the great thinkers of the Athens aristocracy, the spirit of Plato and of Bruno, of Spinoza and Fichte, the spirit of all the great idealists, about whom the struggle for progress is only vaguely familiar with. For us, philosophic idealism is not some specialty, severed off from the life of theory, preached from philosophic cathedra-chairs, this rather -- is a star, lighting our life's path, a fully active struggle for the embodiment of truth. It would seem to be somewhat awkward to introduce for discussion the question about the tasks and contents of metaphysics and about those paths, which can lead to it. Yet only I would want to particularly stress the following important deduction: the process of the cognition of truth, finding its higher purpose in a metaphysical comprehension of the world, possesses independent a value, and this is not only useful in the struggle for the existence of means, this -- is an end, one of the ideal ends of life, elevating us to the level of *man*. And I think, that in the critique of bourgeois society, in its oppressing and compelling of man, a critique purported on the part of progressive societal science and likewise on the part of the direct feelings of the progressive strata of society, metaphysical idealism can add its own say. From the perspective of the eternal values bourgeois society and the servants of darkness will be brought to judgement and -- condemnation. The challenge, hurled by metaphysical idealism to modern life, filled with its ugliness, will be profound and greater than any other challenge, as the voice of eternal truth within mankind rendered nigh to it.

Idealism within ethics acknowledges the absolute value of good and evil, qualitatively and independently so. First of all and foremost of all idealists ought to insist on this, that moral perfection is an end-purpose of human life, and that the aspect of perfecting stands higher than mere contentment. It is time likewise to come to terms with that folly, which sees an higher manifestation of morals in the sacrificing of one's own soul in the name of the benefit of others. One's own life perhaps, sometimes one ought to devote it, but one's own soul it is impossible to surrender for anything in the world. Only a spiritually developing and perfecting soul can be an authentic fighter for progress, can bring into the life of mankind the light of truth, the good and beauty. Each human person, not broken nor ultimately crushed, ought to be aware of his own natural right to a spiritual perfecting, a right freely to create in one's own life absolute truth and beauty. The vulgarisation of spirit is the greatest moral crime. When it is done unconsciously, then behind it stands responsible the historical setting, but no one has the moral right consciously to debase his spiritual level. Societal utilitarianism, insofar as it impinges upon Faustian strivings and abases the soul of man, represents a reactionary current in human thought, irregardless whatever the democratic forms that veil it. When man bears sacrifice to the altar of *his own truth*, then his spirit is uplifted and we meet with the morally great. But there is nothing great in the idea of the sacrifice of one's own soul in the name of the philistine felicitude of X or Y. The fighters for idealism ought first of all to recognise the inherent value of the moral content of life and to perceive the democratisation of society as the aristocratisation of it. Hence results the great task of our time: to infuse an ideal moral content into those social forms, which reflect the progressive forces in society. This means to raise up the fourth estate to the "idea" of the fourth estate. This means likewise the creating of the *morally perfective aspect* of man, the spirit of which will be foreign to every sort of bourgeoisness and to open up all the possibilities and powers lodged within it, -- the figure of one more astute, more capable an inspiration towards the struggle, than the figure of simply a contented man. Material satisfaction is a means, an elementary necessary condition, but an ideal of perfective completion -- is the end-goal.

There is beginning in art a rebirth of idealism and romanticism, as a reaction against realism, which has gotten to be very trite, a very stale naturalism. Art is striving towards a new sense of beauty and a new setting of eternal questions, expressing more refined and complex a psyche, and extraordinarily subtle details. I see an healthy core aspect of "decadentism" in the reflections of delicate individual hues of the human soul and in protest against the bourgeois coarseness and complete absence of beauty within life. Symbolism finds itself a justification within theoretical aesthetics, which in any case cannot reckon art as merely a reflection of actuality. An idealistic worldview has to admit of the independent significance of beauty and of artistic creativity within the life of mankind. Beauty is an ideal end-purpose of life, uplifting and ennobling man. We recognise the idea of an independent significance for beauty, understanding by this that beauty is a value in itself, and in such manner we only but come nigh to the plenitude of human experiences. In bourgeois society and its art there is too little beauty and the opposition to this sort of society ought to enter into the life of mankind as a possibility for greater beauty, as a beauty within human feelings, within art, in all the segments of life. To the former views of protest thus is added an aesthetic protest against bourgeois society. Thus, for example, was the activism of the English aesthete Morris [William, 1834-1896]. On our side ought to be not only truth and justice, but likewise also beauty. Modern art with its "decadent" tendencies -- is the art of a transitional era and reflects in itself a nervous wreck amidst an unhealthy societal atmosphere, but in principle it makes progressive efforts to bespeak something new and to prepare for a new man with more beautiful a soul, full of individual mods and tints, infinitely of value for the intimate life of the human person. In such manner, art enables resolution to a great problem of our time: the forming of a fine human individuality. The ideal of beauty ought to be sketched into our sense of knowledge, since beauty is an integral aspect of singular a truth, to be realised within human progress. The man of the future ought to be fine a man, and only such a man stands to construct "dwellings". From this perspective we might say, that the ethical and aesthetic critique of Fr. Nietzsche possesses great significance, despite his social naiveté. And into the new culture there will be the need to introduce the element of "tragic beauty".

There is beginning in recent times to be revived the unjustly forgotten theory of "natural rights", and the idea of "natural rights" is also a genuine basis for idealism within politics. This idealism is not and cannot be consistent with the shallow idea of societal utilitarianism, nor in the logically absurd theory of the necessity of a social catastrophe. From the point of view of societal welfare it is possible to justify anything, howsoever improper. Societal utilitarianism cannot condemn the idyllic picturing of feudal rights, in which the landowner lives ideally and the peasantry lives well. For an adherent of the idealistic idea of "natural rights" an unlawful happiness is the greatest shame, and progress, which though also it destroy a given system of well-being, but still lead to the triumphing of human rights, is greatest a benefit. The most beautiful blossoms of a practical social idealism grow forth from the idea of the "natural rights" of man and the citizen. Idealism sees in the rights of man, in the equality of free individuals -- a value in itself, and not merely a means useful for prosperity. The "natural rights" of the human person is sacred a matter, upon which nothing and no one can infringe, it possesses metaphysical roots, but humankind comes nigh to it only by way of social developement. There is no such happiness and no such benefit, in the name of which should be snatched away from man his "natural rights". In the face of "natural rights" morally powerless is even a majority of voices, and the welfare of the people etc. There is need to struggle for a new society under the banner of "natural rights", raised above all the "petty matters". And this thought ought to have an especial significance for us, in our own land...

But there is a certain idea, upon which rests an idealistic view on the world and life, the idea of *a moral world-order*. If science transitions over into philosophy, then the philosophy transitions over into a religion. Without a religious faith in a moral world-order, in the vital connection of the individual with the general and incessant significance of every moral force -- it becomes impossible to live, since life is rendered meaningless and according to the remarkable French saying, "*rien ne vaut la peine de rien*" ["nothing is worth nothing"]. Many tend to live having a superstitious fear regarding religion, since they measure it all entirely by its historical forms. But it is time to recognise, that religion, despite the flow of its content, is an eternal, transcendental function of consciousness and that all the integral understanding and relationship to the world ought to be religious. The majestic surge of spirit and idealistic enthusiasm becomes possible only in such an instance, if I sense with all my being, that in serving human progress in its modern historical form, I therein serve an eternal truth, that my exertions and my efforts by their results become immortal and enter into the world-order. And I think, that the new man, having shaken off from himself the old world with its superstitions, will become pervaded anew by religion.

The tasks in the struggle for idealism befalls the lot of that societal group, which is manifest in the modern epoch as bearers of the idea of progress common to all humanity. The task cannot be fulfilled entirely by a social-political party, which pursues more specific aims. The "idea" of the future is to be realised not only by the struggle of some social-political party, the manner of its realisation is rather more complex and manifold... And hence all the time I have in view, that the struggle for idealism is not a struggle against realism. Idealistic philosophy cannot infringe upon positive science, nor can social idealism -- upon social realism. The position of a sober social realism is firmly established, it has the advantage over the old romanticism and the idealists of the latest form have to join in with its traditions. We well remember, that first of all there has to be a satisfying of the material demands of the human masses, as that which is most urgent, and that only power can serve as mid-wife to the birth of the new idea. I generally think, that there has to be intensified an effort, just as for our idealism, so also for our realism, but now especially it is necessary to insist upon idealistic a moment, since up to the present it has remains quite in the shadows. Ibsen's builder Solness accomplishes realistic work, and this is a symbol for scientific realism in theory and a sober social realism in practise. The fine image of Hilda itself symbolises philosophic idealism in theory and the idealistic spirit of practical life. Henceforth then Solness and Hilda will together build and indeed build the greatest and most wonderful in the world -- "airy castles upon strong foundations". Solness -- hearkens to Hilda, he is her builder and, heeding her call, he has to reach for the very top of the "tower". When Solness begins to build the lofty "tower" and Hilda receives finally her "crowning" -- the golden dreams of man are realised. We need to have occupying our spirit such outlooks, in order to rise above the ugly triteness of grey a life, in order to be pervaded by that enthusiasm, without which nothing great within history would have happened. The struggle for idealism -- is itself a legacy of the XIX Century for our XX Century. The onset of the XX Century belongs to the idealists, who not only seek to realise the social ideas of the second half of the XIX Century, but also will pour into new forms the uplifting spiritual content.

Towards a Philosophy of Tragedy

Maurice Maeterlinck

(1902 - 49)[1]

"Il y a un tragique quotidien qui est bien plus rèel, bien plus profond et bien plus conforme à notre être véritable que le tragique des grandes aventures. Il est facile de le sentir mais il n'est pas aisé de le montrer par ce que le tragique le tragique essentiel n'est pas simplement materièl ou psychologique. Il ne s'agit plus ici de la lutte déterminee d'un être contre un être, de la lutte desir contre un autre desir ou de l'eternel combat de la passion et du devoir. Il s'agirait plutôt de faire voir ce qu'il y a d'etonnant dans le fait seul de vivre. Il s'agirait plutôt de faire voir l'existence d'une ame en elle -- même, au milien d'une immensité qui n'est jamais inactive. Il s'agirait plutôt de faite entendre par dessus les dialogues ordinaires de la raison et des santiments, le dialogue plus solennelet ininterrompu de l'être et de sa destinée. Il s'agirait plutôt de nous faire suivre les pas hésitants et douloureux d'un être qui s'approche ou s'eloigne de sa vérité, de sa beauté ou de son Dieu".

Maeterlinck. "Le Trésor des Humbles". (*Vide endnote [a] p. 59*).

At the end of the 1860's in Germany appeared a book of charming beauty, which was a bold summoning to the spirit of the times. I speak about the book by Fr. Nietzsche, entitled "*The Birth of Tragedy from the Spirit of Music*". Nietzsche provides here a new philosophic interpretation of Greek culture: in the bright, vivacious spirit of the Hellenes, which many tend to perceive so crudely in hedonistic a manner, Nietzsche instead discerns a *tragic beauty*. This Dionysian principle finds its classical embodiment in the tragedies of Aeschylos and Sophokles, and the perishing of the spirit of tragedy was together with this a ruination of the whole of Greek culture. That rational attitude towards life, which Sokrates brought with him, and which is reflected already in the tragedies of

---

[1] K FILOSOFII TRAGEDII. MORIS METERLINK. First published in the sbornik anthology "Literaturnoe delo", S. Peterburg, 1902, p. 162-184.

Euripides -- was hostile to the god Dionysos, and to the spirit of tragic beauty.

The book by Nietzsche -- is the product of a passionate protest against the contemporary bourgeois culture, in which the great :immoralist" perceived the death of the tragic spirit and beauty. His religious soul recoiled at the prevalence of shallow reasoning and material interests. He believed, that the "Dionysian principle" will rise forth and that "the cloud covered Apollo" would be indulgent towards us and "the nigh coming generation will behold his auspicious doings in the aspect of beauty".[1] Nietzsche in his ultimate searchings went astray and more than once engaged in very striking contradictions with those of the ideal essence of his spirit, but this is already beyond the theme of our article. The important thing for us to note is the profound perspicacity, which Nietzsche displayed in "*The Birth of Tragedy*".

Several decades back the spiritual life of the European peoples had slackened to the extent, that within it, it seemed that the spirit of tragedy had ultimately perished. The hedonistic ideal of earthly contentment for people had won out over the awareness of an eternally tragic aspect of human life, the tragic aspect, with which is connected both all that is most tormentive, so also all that is most beautiful in life, uplifting above the everyday drollness and triteness. In the life of the progressive portion of society there has predominated a practical rational outlook. The material worries have evoked an intense awareness of the necessity of the material ordering of human life. This aspect has found itself a gifted expression in the teachings of Marx. Still not so long ago it was believed, that all the evil, all the contradictions in life would be removed by material and social developement, and positive science and the political struggle were admitted as the sole worthwhile and expedient weapons for societal progress, which would bring about the satisfaction and happiness of people. This was a triumph of the *outer* man over the *inner*, temporary, based on a psychological illusion, a triumph of the *means* of life over its *end-purpose*. Positivism, having triumphed in theory and practice, failed to understand the tragic aspect in life, closely bound up with its inner meaning, it saw only various forms of maladaption, which in the knowing are removed by science, in the practical life of social developement. And yet this or some other attitude towards tragedy, the tragic principle in life possesses

---

[1] *Nietzsche Werke*. Band I, p. 172.

enormous a significance, a touchstone as it were regarding worldview; herein lies one of the fundamental points of dissonance between two sharply differing types of attitude towards the world and life -- the idealistic and the realistic.

A primary tragic aspect in life involves the tragic aspect of death. Death is empirically unavoidable, and this inescapableness clashes with being alive in an human soul thirsting for life, thirsting for deathlessness, thirsting for infinite a perfection and infinite an ability. Science and the developements in societal regards can prolong life, can put man into better conditions of existence and lessen the extent of death from sickness and need, but they are still powerless against the tragic aspect involved in death. In facing the tragedy of death, the "positivist" is brought to an halt and senses his own impotence and helplessness. Sometimes he tries to scream and comfort himself with various phrases, which ordinarily would appear an infringement upon the very essence of the spiritual nature of man. "Positivists" always sense themself awkward in the face of death and the more sensitive among them prefer to remain silent. When a man has someone very close tragically perish, the man might bend under the weight of the grief crushing him, might continue standing, if he is a strong man, but his vulgar optimism has to perish, he has to be deeply shaken by the empirical meaninglessness of life, he has to begin feeling, that in the most fortunate, in the happiest minutes of the life man there lurks the tragic, and that from this tragic aspect there is no saving escape whether in good societal arrangement, nor in science, through which they might hide from in finely wrought edifices, nor in warm clothing, nor can knowledge of the laws of nature prove any solace.

Everyone well knows, what an enormous role in the life of people is played by love; I speak about the love between a man and a woman, to which is devoted such an endless multitude of dramas, comedies and tragedies. There is no need to resort to any sort of exceptional instances, to admit of the profoundly tragic aspect of love. At each step is encountered an unrequited love and bears with it a burning passion. To abolish this, this sometimes intense and mighty a thing, but often vapid and to the point of everyday triteness, this tragedy of unrequited love -- cannot be abolished by social progress, nor by progress in knowledge, and in general by none of the means, found in the empirically actual. But the tragic exists not only in unrequited love, the tragic exists in every love by its very essence, since it does not know contentment and respite, since it is of that ideal dreaminess, which the human soul fosters within itself, unable to realise it in life. There are many contented people that one can encounter, men content with their wife, wives content with their husband, but this is a philistine sort of satisfaction on the other side of love in the true meaning of this word. Love too often gets poisoned by jealousy and too often sullied by the poison of disenchantment and over-indulgence, the thirst for new impressions. According to a beautiful myth, recounted in the "Symposium" of Plato, the two halves of the human being can never get conjoined into an higher individuality and are consigned to an eternal yearning. The soul seeks a kindred soul and experiences a tragic conflict of the "monistic" ideal of love and its empirical "pluralism". Positivism proves just as impotent facing the tragedy of love, as it also does in facing the tragedy of death. Social developement can only remove the external hindrances of love and create moreso free the conditions for its manifestation. But this only intensifies an awareness of the inwardly tragic aspect of love, which earlier on has been debilitated by evil, by the minute sufferings of life.

In the everyday life of people the thirst for knowledge does not play such a role, as does love or death, but it is something each one has, in meriting the name of man. In the finest people this thirst for knowledge assumes tormentive dimensions, and this -- is a tragedy for those select ones. Our striving for absolute truth is profoundly tragic, and empirically irresolvable. The so-called refined science, based upon experience, does not provide a true and ultimate knowledge, it provides only this conditional and relative knowledge, which serves as a weapon in the struggle for existence. Positivism herein senses itself the expert and recommends refraining from questions, which can cause unwonted sufferings and paralyse the satisfaction in life. The empirically irresolvable thirst for absolute knowledge can find itself satisfaction only upon the groundings of an idealistic metaphysics and religion. The tragic aspect of life in general, and the tragic aspect of life in particular -- serve as an important argument to wit, in that the essence of the tragic aspect rests upon the profound non-correspondence between the spiritual nature of man and the empirical actuality. The imperative illusion of the material empirical world -- herein is the ultimate source of all the tragic aspect, a perception for philosophic spiritualism, and together with this a finding within it a way out, that egress, which does not obtain for positivism and empiricism.

Tragic the same is our striving for freedom, from which derives the whole social-political ideology. Social-political progress creates only a favourable setting for the triumph of inner freedom, from the autonomous self-determination of the person. But the ultimate quenching of that limitless thirst for freedom, which should brighten and uplift human life, gets connected with the attainment of an higher completeness, a supreme well-being. Therefore the empirically inescapable tragic aspect of human striving for freedom and perfection leads to a postulating of immortality.

The theme of Goethe's "Faust" -- is the tragic aspect of the mighty aspirations of man, becoming infinitely lost.

For me it has been important to point out, that the rational-practical European culture with its optimistic faith in the removal of everything bad, of all the contradictions, and instead the affirmation of the hedonistic ideal by way of scientific positivism and the social-political struggle, with its weak understanding of the ideal end-goals in life, -- this culture stands in contradiction to the tragic spirit. Beauty however is closely connected with the tragic aspect in life, and the death of tragedy would be the death of beauty. The age of positivism and hedonism had thought to bury and be done with tragedy in the life of people, and this was expressed, amidst other things, by a decline of dramatic form within literature, of a form undoubtedly higher, and given the exceptional predominance of the realistic novel, so accurately reflecting all the petty triteness of bourgeois society.

But in recent decades there is to be noted a rebirth of drama in European literature, and this is much significant a symptom. The progenitor of modern drama is manifest in the genius if the writer, Hendrik Ibsen. His influence upon all the successive drama in literature and the most recent trends in art are impossible to fully appreciate. Through the strength of his talent, through his extraordinary originality, through the extent of his influence upon the whole of modern literature, alongside Ibsen, there can be put only the remarkable Belgian dramatist, Maurice Maeterlinck.[1] Here is purest a presenter of tragedy not only in modern literature, but perhaps, also in the literature of all time. In Aeschylos and

[1] Regarding Maeterlinck very little has been written in Russian literature. One might mention a decent article by Z. Vengerova [Zinaida Afanas'evna, 1867-1941], entitled "*Морис Метерлинк*" (Nachalo, 1899, January/February). Already after my article there appeared a number of articles concerning Maeterlinck. But in the recent period of the creativity of Maeterlinck has met with disillusion, and decline.

Sophocles tragedy was the result of a clashing of man with fate, in Shakespeare -- the result of the clashing of human passions with the moral law. We see the same with Schiller and many others. Tragedy is always depicted as an intertwining of external events, which inevitably lead to catastrophes. In Ibsen we find not so much the tragedy, as rather the drama. The eternally tragic in human life is depicted by him not in pure a form, it gets refracted instead within the complex empirical actuality and is muted. The sphere of creativity in Ibsen is quite broad and only sometimes does he attain the heights of the purely tragic, as for example in "*Brandt*". Maeterlinck makes an enormous step forward in the history of tragedy, renders it deeper. He has an understanding of the inner very essence of human life, as tragedy. For the depiction of the tragic aspect of human life there is not needed a purely external intersecting of events, and unneeded are the plots, the catastrophes, the tumult and blood. The eternal inward tragedy transpires prior to this, it happens in quiet, it can hit the head of a man at any second, when he least of all expects it, since within the very essence of life lies concealed irresolvable tragic contradictions. There is no writer in the whole of the world literature, who with such depth and beauty has depicted the eternal, cleansed of all external touches, nor has depicted the tragic principle in life, as has Maeterlinck. In "*The Secrets of the Soul*" and "*The Intrusion of Death*" is depicted the inescapable tragic aspect of death eternally stalking us. This is a favourite theme of Materlinck. In "*Aglavaine and Selysette*" and "*Pelleas and Mélisande*" -- is the inescapable tragic aspect in love; in "*The Blind*" is the inescapable tragic aspect of the lack of knowledge. We shall limit ourself to an exposition and analysis of these five dramas of Maeterlinck, the finest and sufficiently characteristic to all his specifics.

The content in the dramas of Maeterlinck is very simple and yet amidst this, sublime. First of all we shall take a look at the smallish one-act drama "*Secrets of the Soul*" (*L'Interieur*). Herein immediately appears all the originality of tragedy in Maeterlinck. The scene presents the following setting. "An old garden, overgrown by willows. Deep amidst it the house, with three lighted windows on the lower floor. The view is of a clearly enough visible interiour of a room, a family spending the evening round a single lamp. The father sits next the chimney-corner. The mother pensively gazes directly in front of herself; one hand she has with elbow upon the table, the other holding the head of a child asleep beside her. Two young daughters sit at their embroidery, day-dreaming, and under the influence of the surrounding quiet, now and then they smile. When any of them get up, they walk or move stiffly, and their movement then seems grave, hesitant, perturbed, and the light, penetrating through the dim windows, bestows them a character somewhat auspicious". An old man and a passerby are on the point of entering, to say, that the daughter of these people, who are calmly sitting in the room not knowing, that she had just only died, had drowned. The old man and the passerby take a look towards the interiour of the room: where all are awaiting the return of the daughter.

The old man. "Let me first take a glance, whether they are all in the hall. Yes, yes... Here I see the father: he is sitting at the chimney-nook, hand set on the knee... as though waiting. The mother with elbow on the table"... *Passerby.* "She is looking at us"... *Old man.* "No; her gaze is far ranging, but it is as if she hardly knows, what she is looking at. And then too she could barely make us out in the shadow of these trees. But all the same don't you approach... The sisters of the deceased are likewise in the room, they leisurely embroider; and the child there is asleep. On the clock, standing there in the corner, it is now directly nine... They are all sitting silent and have no sort of premonition"...

They begin to discuss what course best to take on breaking the news about the misfortune that occurred. The old man says concerning the deceased:

"It is impossible to know anything here... Perhaps, she was one of those, who keep everything secret in the depths of their soul, and who of us does not have a moment, when death seems a wish? A strange soul -- murky; yet no trace of it evident, in that room... they are all on good terms... They chatter about certain trifles, and no one suspects anything... One can live whole months side by side with those, who almost no longer belong to this world, and whose soul is over-wrought; and one replies to them, not overly concerned over one's words: and suddenly it happens, what you did not expect. They appear like -- walking dolls, and how much do they happen to think and to feel... why perchance should she not live, like all the others? Why should she not say prior to her death: "a storm is coming", or: "today we will have thirteen at table"... With a smile they talk about fading flowers and cry on the quiet. Even an angel, perhaps, would not see it all, and a man would have his eyes opened only then, too late to undo the deed. Yesterday evening she sat here together with her sisters, and had this misfortune not happened, you would not be observing them and perceiving them, as it is... It seems to me, that I saw her here thus the first time... Yes -- in order to understand daily life a bit, something needs to be brought into it... Constantly you see them beside you, and you understand them only at the moment, when they forever forsake us... And what a strange sort of heart she must have had nonetheless in her bosom; woesome, naive, an unriddled sort of heart!... O, if she had done all, that was needful to do, if she had said all, that it was needful to say"...

And here further on the words of the old man, full indeed of profound symbolic meaning:

"They are nowise apprehensive for themself: the doors are locked, the windows fastened with iron rods; the walls of the old house they have reinforced, and in the oaken doors they have set bolts... They have overlooked nothing, that can be foreseen".

And thus continues the discussion of the old man and the passerby without deciding how to tell the frightful truth to those, who are situated within, behind the walls and the locked doors. The old man's granddaughter, Mary, arrives saying, "that peasants are carrying the deceased, and that they are already nearby and will soon be here". The old man, the passerby and Mary continue to observe the inhabitants of the house within, alert for the slightest indication of their distress. The old man says regarding those, bearing the deceased:

"The crowd with each step is getting closer and closer, and the misfortune here already after two hours is all growing... And they are in no condition to handle this. And those, who are bearing forth this grief, are altogether unable to halt it. It has itself overtaken them, and they are powerless to oppose it. It courses its own purpose and its own path... It is ceaseless, as though it had only one single thought: all have to yield to it under its power... and here, they thus wither and go... filled with pity, but, still forward they have to go".

There follows still the words of the old man, which provides a key to an understanding of all the whole play:

"I am already well beyond eighty years of age, and never before has the seeing of life struck me so, as now... why is it that all, what they are doing here, seems to me mysterious and important... They are simply gathered together round their lamp, as we also might do; but still nonetheless it seems to me, that I am looking at them from another world apart from here. And why? Because, that I know a small truth, which they do not yet know. Isn't that so, children? Say, why are you also so pale? Or is this something else, which it is impossible to express, and which compels us to weep. I did not know, that life at times would become so sorrowful and can lead to such terror among those, who look into it... This tranquilness of theirs already of itself breaks my heart... They too much believe in the world... they think, that nothing will happen, that the door is locked, and yet should some enemy be near, there is only these paltry windows to protect them from him... they fail to consider, that many an event happens inside of us, and that the world does not stop at our threshhold... Nor would the thought enter their mind, that many know more of their smallish life, than do they themself, nor that in a mere two steps from their door, that I, a decrepit old man, hold in his weak hands all their small happiness, exactly like some sick bird".

Then enters Martha, another granddaughter of the old man, and tells about what has already happened. Part of the crowd is filling the garden. The old man goes to the house, in order to relate the terrible news, and the rest peer through the window, at what is transpiring within. There inside plays out a frightening mute scene. The old man enters the room, and the father, the mother and sisters begin to suspect. A voice from the crowd exclaims: "He has told them, told them!" The old man stands without turning, pointing a finger towards the door, which is behind him. The mother, father and both sisters rush towards the door, and the father momentarily cannot open it. The old man tries to console the mother in the room. In the garden is a crush of people. All push towards another side of the house and disappear, except for the passerby, who remains at the window. In the room the door, finally, is thrown wide open; all rush out at once. The glimmering rays of the moon are seen in the fountain, and in the midst of the empty room the little child continues to sleep peacefully within its crib.

This simple but nonetheless profoundly symbolic tragedy produces devastating an effect. Here is depicted the inner tragedy of death, which the human soul experiences outside the external chain of events. Very characteristic with Maeterlinck and very profound is this separation into two worlds, setting opposite the inner inhabitants of the house, from those who observe it from the sides, regarding everything happening there. The inside of the house, -- is a symbol of the whole of human life. People tend to life from day to day, they handle their little affairs, they await the onset of a typical order of events and fail to know, how tragic their life is, how at any moment there can crash down upon their head some unexpected grief, they only sense some sort of an indefinite melancholy. But how tragic human life is, if viewed from the side, from the side always is seen the little sorts of truth, which can break a man. These walls, behind which people think to hide from the tragic, these doors, which they strongly reinforce, so that the bitter truth should not burst in upon them, cannot save people in the least. The entirety of the material culture of mankind, which is symbolised by these walls, doors and windows, is powerless to withstand the tragic in life, it does not offer protection from the empirically inescapable tragic aspect of death, of the same sort of protection as against the rain and weather.

The "*Intrusion of Death*" (*L'Intruse*) depicts a gloomy hall in an old castle. In it sits a blind grandfather, the father, an uncle and three daughters. In an adjoining room is a very ill mother of the family. All the members of the family speak in clipped phrases. All have a sense of something terribly disquieting, the presence of something foreign and strange. The slightest noise assumes particular a form. This mood builds and with extraordinary a force is transmitted to the reader. All are wholly seized by a sensation of the intrusion of death into the life of people, this sensation takes form in the quiet, amidst the very daily setting and becomes inexpressibly tormenting. Particular distress is felt by the blind grandfather, he lacks sight in the external world and therefore he is still more sensitive regarding that, what transpires in the depth of the soul. Only the uncle appears a sceptic, representative of healthy an outlook. Finally, the tenseness at the presence of something strange, the feeling that here something has to break, reaches extremest proportions. From the adjoining room a door opens and upon the threshhold appears a sister of mercy, in her black garb, and leaning forward, crosses herself signifying the death of the woman. All understand and silently go into the room of the deceased. The blind grandfather is left by himself alone.

Maeterlinck is endowed with an extraordinary gift of evoking very powerful, tense moods, and in this regard he has no rivals. This is particularly true regarding the "*Intrusion of Death*", an impressionistic play par excellence. It is close to the spirit of each man: much truly much has happened in his life to experience similar moments, -- moments of terrible stress, when a man anticipates, that now there is going to happen something tragic, something frightful is about to explode into daily life. Let those, who so readily sneer at the "symbolist" and "decadent" Maeterlinck, let them be mindful of his mood in the face of the intrusion of death into their own house, and they perhaps will understand, how profound, a life-gripping truth there is in this small tragedy, bereft of anything fabulous.

"*The Blind*" has quite broad a theme, this -- is an entire philosophy of history. Herein is depicted the inescapable tragic aspect of the aspiration of mankind towards the light and knowledge. "*The Blind*" is the same sort of one-act play, as the "*Secrets of the Soul*" and the "*Intrusion of Death*". The setting is as follows:

"Under the sky, studded with stars, spreads an old northern forest, seemingly endless. Amidst it in the deep gloom sits, wrapped in his broad black mantle, an aged priest. His body and his head, motionless, like death, the old man is slightly resting back against the empty trunk of a massive oak tree. His face, terribly pale, his half-opened lips gone blue. His blank and lifeless eyes glance no longer at nature and give the impression of frequent and from long ago sufferings and tears. White as the moon his sparse hair is fallen in straight strands down his face, alight and more wearied, than all that surrounded him in the silence of the gloomy forest. His frail stiff hands are clasped at his knees. On the right of him sit six blind old men, one on a stone, another on a stump, the others on dry leaves. On the left, opposite there sit, separated only by some clumps of rock and an uprooted tree, the same number of blind women. Three of them are praying, in subdued lament of voice. A fourth is very old. The fifth, in a condition of mute madness, holds on her knees a sleeping child. The sixth, still remarkably young, has her hair all twisted and falling down to the ground. The women, the same as the men, are garbed in dark same-hued broad garments. Most of them, resting elbows on their knees with their hands supporting their heads, sit in expectation of something; and it seems, that they all have gotten out of the habit of useless movements and moreover no longer are attentive to the subtle and soft sounds of the island. The large, sad trees: the yew, weeping willows and cypress cover them in shadow. Not far from the priest flower in the gloom of night a clump of spindly, sickly gold-flower asphodelus. The darkness reigns intensely, despite the moon shining, which off and on somewhat, attempts to dispel the gloom of the leaves".

The content of the tragedy is thus. Under the guidance of the old priest, the blind had come out into the forest from the poor-house, which had been their constant dwelling-place. In their clipped phrases they speak among themselves, and in their words sounds all the inescapable apprehension of the blind. They have lost their aged guide, they think, that he has gone off somewhere, and they begin to get alarmed. They themself are in no condition to leave the forest and return to the poor-house. The blind do not even know, where they are, the only one able to tell them this is the old priest, who alone has use of sight. Everything, that happens around them, in this endless forest, every noise, the slightest sound evokes in the blind a terrible alarm, even fear. The splash of the waves, breaking upon the craggy shore, the sound of the night bird flitting about and the falling of leaves to the ground, the sound of the wind -- all this is felt by the hapless blind, as something incomprehensible, strange and terrible. It is frightening for them in the forest, they seek their own nook, they want to return to the poor-house, but without success. They begin to complain.

First blind-born. "He has gotten very old. For a certain while, evidently, he has had weak eyesight, and he does not want to admit this, fearing, that some one else might occupy his place among us; but I suspect, that he is almost unable to see. We need a different leader: he no longer listens to us, and indeed gathered together we are too many. In the entire house there are only four with eyesight -- the three nuns and him, and they are all older than us! -- I am convinced, that we have strayed, and he is looking for the way, where has he gone to? He ought not to have forsaken us here!..."

The blind would have preferred to remain at the poor-house, they talk about the light, about the sun, about how they came to this island being already blind and had only seen the sun somewhere long, long ago, in another land.

Sixth blindman. "Was there any of us who were born on this island?" *Blind elder*. "You indeed know, that we all came". *Blind eldress*. "We came from afar". *First blind-born*. "I nearly died at the time of travelling across the sea". *Second blind-born*. "I likewise; -- we arrived together". *Third blind-born*. "We all three are from the same village". *First blind-born*. "They say, that on a clear day visible from here is our church; it is without a belfry". *Blind eldress*. "And I am from somewhere else". *Second blind-born*. "From whence are you?" *Blind eldress*. "Now I no longer still try and think about this, since every time, when I want to tell about something, I can remember almost nothing... It was so long ago"... *Blind girl*. "They brought me from somewhere far away". *First blind-born*. "From whence are you?" *Blind girl*. "I do not know how to express it. How would you describe it? -- It was very remote from here -- beyond the sea. I lived in a spacious land... I could point out many of its signs for you, but indeed we now can see nothing. I long wandered about... I saw the sun, and water, and fire, the mountains, faces and strange flowers... On this island there are no such flowers, here it is too dark and cold. At the time, when I lost my sight, I happened not moreover to pay attention, but I did see father, and mother and sister... back then I was too young, in order to know, where I was... I playing still at the shore of the sea... But how well I remember being able to see!... One time I looked at the snow atop a mountain... I began already to recognise these things, fated to become unhappy".

Finally on the dry leaves grows the sound of rapid, but still distant steps. The blind have their hope aroused, that it is the priest who has returned. A large dog rushes in from the forest and runs round among the blind.

First blind-born. "Who is it? -- Who are you? Have pity on us, we have been waiting for so long. (The dog stops and puts its front paws on the knees of the blind man). Akh! Akh, what is this you have put upon my knees?... Is this some animal? -- Is this, it seems a dog?... Yes! Yes! This is the dog from the poor-house... Come here! Come here! It has come to save us!"

The first blind-born gets up, enthused by the dog, which leads him to the priest and there stops. Here we approach the very heights of the inescapable tragedy, as the dog indicates, that among the blind there is some one dead and that the dead one -- is the old priest, their only guide. He had never forsaken them, he was all the time among them, but he was dead. The blind are then seized by a boundless fear.

The blind elder. "We never knew anything... never did see him... How could we know, what happens right in front of our poor blind eyes?... He never complained of anything... now it is already too late... I have had three near me die... But not such a death!... Now it is our turn"...

Occasionally they would have a ray of hope break forth, that a nun from the poor-house might come out or that they might be seen from the light-house, but then there again ensues a condition of hopelessness. It begins to snow. The child of the blind mad-woman begins to cry.

The blind girl. "He can see! He can see! He is crying, as though he sees something". The blind girl lifts the child over the heads of the blind. This child is their last straw, for them to snatch at.

The blind eldress. "Have pity on us!"

The symbolic meaning of this remarkable tragedy is clear. The tragic fate of the blind itself symbolises the tragic fate of all mankind. Man has arrived on earth from somewhere afar off, he dimly remembers, that he once saw a glimpse both of light, and the sun, he thirsts now to be able to see, he thirsts to know truth and what is right, but he wanders about in the dark. Man has not directly noticed, that religion has gone dead, and that he has been left in the dark forest of worldly life without any guide. In recognising, that religion has gone dead, man has tended to sense the inescapable tragedy of his position; for him there is no way out from the endless dark forest. Herein is totally expressed the pessimistic non-belief of Maeterlinck in human reason and progress. Salvation can be sought only in art and beauty, which perchance, is symbolised by the child, begotten of the blind mad-woman.

Now we turn to "*Aglavaine and Selysette*" and "*Pelleas and Mélisande*", very poetic works by Maeterlinck, exceptionally original and beautiful as regards form and devoted to the tragedy of love, which the first three plays did not deal with. "*Aglavaine and Selysette*" and "*Pelleas and Mélisande*" tend moreso to resemble former dramas, in that the are comprised of five acts and in them there is an individual sketching of character, which is not there in "*Secrets of the Soul*", nor in the "*Intrusion of Death*", nor in "*The Blind*". These instead are psychological dramas. Herein are portrayed the unique types of Maeterlinck's women, delicate, beautiful, angel-like. In all of world literature there are no works, in which the drama transpires in an atmosphere of suchlike an emotional beauty, as in these two plays by Maeterlinck.

"*Aglavaine and Selysette*" -- is a profound psychological tragedy, without complex a tale and without noisy outward events. The story line is old, but never yet has it been worked out so uniquely, nor has the inwardly tragic aspect of love been portrayed in such eternal a guise, so independent from everything external, from everything, that in people is spiteful and lacking in love, and from all the mud of life. And as always, with Maeterlinck the action occurs outside of time and expanse, within the depths of the human soul. In a castle quietly live two loving beings, Meleander and Selysette. Meleander is reading a letter from Aglavaine, the widow of Selysette's brother, a letter informing of her journey hither. She writes: "I have seen you only once, Meleander, at the time of the fuss and confusion of my wedding; my poor wedding, alas! For we failed to take note of the guest, whom they never invite and which always gets seated at the place of expected happiness. I have seen you only once, already more than three years back; and amidst this I come to you with the same peace of mind, as though we slept as babes in the same cradle... I am convinced of this, that I shall have found a brother!... We have said almost nothing to each other, but the some few words spoken by you have sounded for me different, than any, that I heard prior to this... And how anxious I am to greet Selysette with a kiss!... She has to be so good, she has to be so beautiful, since she loves you and you love her! I shall love her even moreso, than you love her, since I have all the more reason to love; I have been unhappy... and now I am fortunate, that is why I suffered, and I will share with you, what there is to be found in the sadness. Sometimes it seems to me, that the tribute, which I paid, suffices for the three of us; that fate will demand nothing moreover and that we can anticipate wonderful a life. We shall have no other care, except a care for happiness. Both for you, and for me, and for Selysette, by the little you have told me about her, the happiness will consist only in all the best, that is in our soul. We shall have only one concern, to make it as much possible all the more beautiful under the influence of the intensified love of all us three; and we shall be rendered the better from this love. We shall create so much beauty within us ourself and around us, that there will not moreso remain a place for misfortune and sorrow; and if misfortune and sorrow nonetheless should want to enter, they themself will have to be rendered beautiful, firstly, before they dare knock at our door"...

Selysette asks Meleander -- is Aglavaine beautiful? *Meleander.* "Yes, beautiful". *Selysette.* "Whom does she resemble?" *Meleander.* "She does not resemble other women... This is a different sort of beauty, altogether... A beauty moreso strange and moreso spiritual"... *Selysette.* "I know, that I am not a beauty"... *Meleander.* "Thou will not say this moreso, when she will be here. In her presence it is impossible to say, what one does not think or what is useless".

Here already is entangled the tragedy of love. Meleander tells Selysette, that after the arrival of Aglavaine they will love each other more, and otherwise, profoundly. To this Selysette answers: "Love her, if thou will love her. I shall leave".

She has sensed in her delicate and sensitive soul, that into their quiet life intrudes a being more powerful, who will be closer and more necessary for Meleander. Aglavaine then enters the scene. Aglavaine, Meleander and Selysette have so much needful to say to one another, but as always happens in these instances, they converse about trifles. The old grandmother of Selysette says, gazing intently at Aglavaine: "I did not know, that there could be such beauty".

In the following scene Aglavaine and Meleander meet in a garden. They talk about how they tend to fulfill each the other, how close their souls... This conversation is ineffably beautiful, in it there is not one banal word, and love is expressed in completely new uncommon forms.

Meleander. "When thou do speak to me, I first hear the voice of my own soul... *Aglavaine*. -- "I likewise, Meleander, when thou do speak to me, I hear my own soul; and when I am silent, I do hear thy soul... I should never yet have found my soul, except to have met thine. I cannot the more seek thy soul, save therein to find mine"... *Meleander*. "We comprise in ourself one and the same world... God did err, when He rendered two souls from our soul"... *Aglavaine*. "Where indeed wast thou, Meleander, over the course of these past two years, when such loneliness awaited me!" *Meleander*. "I likewise awaited loneliness and had ceased to hope".

And suddenly at the height of bliss they remember still about one other being, about Selysette. *Aglavaine*. "Why should she not be lifted together with us to a love, which knows not all merely the trite aspects of love? She is more beautiful, than thou dost think, Meleander,; let us extend an inviting hand to her: she is able to follow along with us; and aside us she will not have cause to cry"... *Meleander*. "Thou art not a sister to me, Aglavaine, I cannot love thee, as a sister"... *Aglavaine*. This is true, that thou be not a brother to me, Meleander; for which reason we shall have to suffer"... Over the course of this conversation Aglavaine pronounces words, very in character for Meleander, for his cult of delicacy and beauty: "I think, that often they err, when they attempt to assume that suffering is moreso proper to the weak, and thereby admit it in oneself". *Meleander*. "Thou art beautiful, Aglavaine". *Aglavaine*. "I love thee, Meleander"... *Meleander*. "This thou wilt lament, Aglavaine". *Aglavaine*. "No, for it is thou, Meleander". *Meleander*. "This we shall worry over"... *Aglavaine*. "Yes"... They kiss. From the trees a cry of pain is heard. It becomes evident, as Selysette flees to the castle.

In the next scene Aglavaine is asleep on a bench at the shore of a lake. Selysette enters and admonishes Aglavaine that she could fall off into the water. Aglavaine uses this opportunity, to have a soul to soul talk with Selysette. "I have seen into thy soul, Selysette, since thou hast loved me here in spite of thine intent", -- says she. Between these two rivals there does not exist the typical trite jealousy, for in them is too much an emotional beauty, softness and delicacy; they instead love each other.

Aglavaine. "He will love in thee that, what he loves in me, since this is the same... In the world there is not a man, who would be so attractive to me, as Meleander. How could he not love thee, and how could I love him, if he did not love thee?"... *Selysette.* "Ah, I do begin to love thee, Aglavaine!"... *Aglavaine.* "I long already do love thee, Selysette". After this scene between Aglavaine and Selysette there begins a struggle, but this is a struggle of two souls, from which each thirsts for the greatest beauty, and in this tragic struggle there is not lurking in the shadows the typical rivalry, petty malice nor spitefulness.

The emotional condition of Meleander is expressed in the following, profoundly sincere words, which he relates to Selysette: "When I am beside thee, I think of her; and when I am beside her, I think of thee".

In the play of Maeterlinck there is no falsehood, no lie. Meleander loves both Aglavaine and Selysette. This is a very bold and original setting of the question, in it there is a deep truth, which people, perhaps, do not quickly understand nor perceive.

Meleander says to Selysette: "Think thou, that the happiness, which would be based upon the sufferings of some sprig of a being, so pure, so delicate, as thou, would thus be a continuing and worthy happiness for us?... Think thou then, that if I were to kiss Aglavaine and she should love me, would one of us admit this as happiness? We love each other somewhere higher than us ourself, Selysette, we love each other there, where we are beautiful and pure, and therein we meet also thee".

Aglavaine says to Selysette: "We all three are bearing sacrifice to something, that does not even have a name and that nonetheless is quite more powerful than us... but is this not strange, Selysette? I love thee, I love Meleander, Meleander loves me, he likewise loves thee, and thou in turn love us both, and yet we cannot live happily, *because there has not yet ever ensued a time, when human beings can be united in such a manner* (italics. N. B.)".

It is on this immortal point, a genuine ethical and aesthetic revelation, for which some whenever be erected a memorial to Maeterlinck. In these words lies concealed all the whole meaning of the play. This is a beauty for some perchance future time, connected with some higher sort of mankind. "I want to kiss thee humanly, -- Aglavaine says to Selysette, -- as only one human being can kiss another". Aglavaine indeed wants to leave, since away from Meleander she can better preserve that which is beautiful in soul, and for which he loves her. But Selysette has also decided to leave, her frail being has its own plan. "Little Selysette likewise can be beautiful,... thou will see, thou will see,...Ah! You both will strongly love me moreso". She takes her little sister Yssaline and goes up to the summit of an old tower. There she leans over the shambles of a wall overlooking the sea. Part of the wall collapses, amidst the noise of its falling is heard a faint cry of fright. In the final scene, Aglavaine wants to learn from the dying Selysette the truth.

Aglavaine. "My poor little Selysette, I bow to thee, since thou art so beautiful... Thou hast rendered simple the most beautiful from all, that love can do, when it is mistaken... But now I ask thee to do further something more beautiful, in the name of different a love, which is not mistaken... Thou do hold at this moment upon thy small lips the profound composture to all our life". But Selysette has died, without answer, as to why she fell from the tower.

"*Aglavaine and Selysette*" is among the best of the works of Maeterlinck, works of genius, and perchance even prophetic. I stress in particular the profound ethical significance of this drama. In it are revealed those profound and spiritual groundings of love, which point to an egress from the tragic aspect, to its utmost surmounting. Only in the future can this be rendered more clear, than with Maeterlinck, but in any case the tragic love of Aglavaine, Selysette and Meleander is such a matter of beauty, uplifting above all the trite and transitory, and there is sensed some sort of resignation to the inescapable.

"*Pelléas and Mélisande*" is a play not so profound in content, as was "*Aglavaine and Selysette*", but it is very beautiful in form and the most poetic piece by Maeterlinck. This is a genuine music within the poetry. The plot is very simple. Golaud finds the frail, beautiful, mysterious being Mélisande in the forest, at the shore of a lake. He brings her to his castle and makes her his wife. Between Mélisande and the younger brother of Golaud, Pelléas, somewhere in the depth of soul, love quietly is born. An instinct of beauty holds sway over these "children", as Golaud calls them, and their love bears some sort of unearthly a character. Mélisande has found herself a kindred soul in Pelléas, he has lifted her grieving over heaven, which Golaud has failed to understand, while himself good and loving, he is still too old and coarse. The seal of a profound grief lays upon the love of Pelléas and Mélisande, it is manifest as an embodiment of tragic beauty. The scene, which occurs between Pelléas, ascending the winding staircase and Mélisande, leaning from a window, when her wondrous hair falls upon Pelléas, belongs among the pearls of world poetry. Golaud is in no condition to rise to an understanding of the beauty and the sanctity of the love of these "children", and they perish. But Mélisande has died not from the wound, inflicted upon her by Golaud, but in the words of the doctor, thus could die even a little bird, she was unable to live, she was born for death. "This was a fragile being, -- says Arkël, the grandfather of Golaud and Pelléas, -- so shy and quiet... This was a frail being, mysterious, as is also everything in the world".

Here again we stand face to face with the inwardly tragic aspect of love. The immense merit of Maeterlinck consists in this, that he has depicted this tragic aspect, as eternal a principle, cleansed from the transitory trivialities of empirical existence. The content of the tragic in Maeterlinck tends to digress from social bonds and historical sensibilities.

In his works, "*Le Trésor des Humbles*" ["The Treasure of the Humble"] and "*La sagesse et la destinée*" ["Wisdom and Destiny"], Maeterlinck provides the key to a philosophic understanding of his tragedies. The first article from the anthology "*Le Trésor des Humbles*" is entitles "*Le silence*" (molchanie, silence). Here with an extraordinary eloquence he developes his favourite thought, that everything important and great in human life transpires in quiet and silence, and that ordinary words fail to express that, what occurs in the depths of the human soul. This is very characteristic to the dramas of Maeterlinck. Everything, that is in the human soul, is soft, fragile and beautiful, and finds itself a reflection in Maeterlinck; everything, that in it is evil, coarse and cruel -- is incomprehensible and foreign to him. In him is not that power and protest, which we find with Nietzsche or Ibsen, in him there is too little of the Promethean. This is the passive Christian of our day, in him is moreso goodness and pity towards human suffering, than otherwise of modern writers. "In essence, -- says he, -- if each had the courage to hearken only to the most simple, most intimate, most genuine voice of one's own conscience, the sole indisputable duty would be to alleviate around oneself, in as possibly broader a circle, as much as possible a greater quantity of sufferings".[1] The originality of Maeterlinck consists in this, that he organically combines goodness and beauty. And I think, that the

[1] "*La sagesse et la destinée*", p. 2.

"Maeterlinck aspect" within the human soul is just as eternal, as is the "Nietzschean", since always within it will be a combining of the "angelic" and the "demonic".

The refined human soul, repelled by the coarseness of life round about, senses itself detached from it: it stands wounded by the moral problem, protests against its vulgarisation by hedonism and utilitarianism and together with this tends towards immoralism; it thirsts for religion and does not find it; it is indignant over quite many a thing, the evil at each step chokes it: and together with this it often idealises everything, fatalistically asserting, that everything that is, is for the best. In modern life there exists an entire trend, -- a trend very interesting, pointing to some sort of spiritual upheaval, to the search for new paths and new ideals. It is composed of people, all in soul protesting against the staleness of life, against the philistinism, against the quenching of spirit and the bourgeois absorption with external material interests. These new sort of people protest against the rational culture in the name of a culture of tragic beauty; but they too often stand at the sidelines of the great liberation movement of mankind and remain detached from the historical tragedies of human reason.

From philosophic a point of view, tragedy is empirically irresolvable. Tragedy shows, that life, as an empirical intersecting of phenomena, is bereft of meaning, but it is the tragic aspect namely that compels with especial a force the positing of questions concerning the meaning and ends of life. Spiritualistic a metaphysics overcomes the empirically-inescapable tragic aspect of life and leads to that higher, finalative optimism, which has nothing in common with trite contentment and even presupposes indignation, melancholy and sorrow. The world has to be justified not only as an aesthetic phenomenon, but just the same, as a phenomenon moral and reasonable.

I above indicated, that the tragedy of life, in the final end, is rooted in illusions of the empirical actuality. Within it there is no escape from the tragic, it remains impossible to find the meaning of life, it remains impossible to ultimately abolish evil, to have truth ultimately triumph and cease the sorrowing of the human spirit in its ideal dreaming. But philosophic idealism finds a way out. Demolishing naive realism within the theory of cognition, it leads to an acknowledging of the spiritual nature of man and the world and to a restoration of the truths of human reason, which ought to be in conjunction with the senses and judgement. In such manner, gnosseology thus overcomes one of the basic sources of pessimism -- agnosticism. Agnosticism -- this is a sickness of the nineteenth century, which the positivists attempted to elevate into a philosophic principle. This sickness was especially tormentive for many of the idealistically minded souls, infected by positivism. Maeterlinck and people of his spiritual type are likewise agnostics, they do not believe in the mightiness of thought, they are incapable of surmounting that positivism, which chokes them, which contends against them. They seek for a way out in a mysticism, which would compensate them for all the losses, instigated as the result of positivism and materialism within their idealistic soul. Mysticism always becomes a symptom for the need of a new worldview.

It is my deep and fundamental conviction regarding the tragedy of cognition that there is only one way out of such as is worthy of a man: a return to that fiery faith in human reason, such as lived within the greatest thinkers of mankind, in Plato and Aristotle, in Spinoza and Leibniz, Fichte and Hegel, -- a faith, which was strong in the Königsberg seer [i.e. Kant], addressing one side of his spirit towards agnosticism. The positivist-agnostics in vain do claim their descent from Kant. The philosophy of Kant was a critical upheaval within the history of metaphysics, in it was much of an healthy scepticism, but Kant never quenched a faith in human reason, and as the bearer of higher ideas, he wrote a critique of reason, and his critique was first of all his memorial, erected to the moral-rational nature of man. That Faustian thirst for knowledge, the thirst for absolute truth, which is full of the profoundly tragic and which leads weak and sickly souls to an irresolvable pessimism and blind mysticism, from the point of view of philosophic idealism opens to the human spirit the perspectives of eternity and infinitude, the perspectives of limitless developement towards an higher perfection, which each soul silently invokes as the Divinity. Set aright, human reason can create a new metaphysics, which will be merely the furthest step in the gradual discerning of the sole eternal metaphysics, based upon Plato.

That sort of human soul, which is reflected in his works by Maeterlinck and also by the whole of "decadent" literature, has lost faith not only in the power of thought, but also in the progress of mankind, that endless progress, which was the religion of the people of the XIX Century. But mankind is returning to the transformative idea of progress, understood in the spirit of the tragedy of Prometheus, and not in the spirit of trite hedonism. Only then will the tragedy of an ailing human will find itself valiant an exist, and forsake that pessimism, which leads to flabbiness. This is an appeal to a faith in life, in its growing value. I speak about progress, an idea ethical and religious, and not about evolution, not about a process, bereft of meaning and purpose. The fundamentals of this revolutionary-idealistic idea can sooner be found in the philosophy of Fichte, than in the philosophy of Spenser. The continuous perfecting of mankind presupposes a moral world-order and a supra-empirical world of ideal norms, by which everything is evaluated within the empirically actual. The progress of mankind opens before us an infinitude, and herein all human aspirations find an outlet. To create beauty and the good, to create that which is of a value, yearned of by man, can only be through the creating of higher forms of life and culture, and therefore the insofar as able participation of the liberation struggle of mankind, in the abolishing of oppression and injustice, is obligatory for every truly aware man. The expectations of a better future can be connected only with a synthesis of that realism, inherent to the modern social movement and finding its best expressions in Marxism, a synthesis with that idealism, which a spiritual aristocratism ought to introduce into the movement.

In summation. I would formulate thus the philosophic essence of the tragic aspect: the tragic beauty evidenced in sufferings and the eternally discontentedness is the sole path worthy of man on the way towards the bliss of the righteous. The tremendous, not only literary, but also in general cultural merit of Maeterlinck consists in this, that he introduces into the triteness filling the daily awareness of people, rather instead a spirit of tragic beauty, of extraordinary fragility and humanness, and in such manner he ennobles man, bestows him spiritually aristocratic an aspect, and therein points to some sort of higher destiny. The negative sides to Maeterlinck and of all the "decadentism" is in a non-belief in human reason, in an absence of activity. Modern art and "modern people", he soul of which is tormented by higher spiritual questings, ought to join in on the struggle for freedom and justice on earth, and then, perhaps, will vanish the flabbiness of some and the coarseness of others. And both sides ought first of all to be pervaded by an unconditional respect for reasoning and for the peole of theoretical thought, who search for the light and truth. It is time already to place foremost in mind for all our world-concept and our ethical considerations towards life -- the idea of the *person*, which includes within it the greatest spiritual content.

But only upon the basis of religion is possible an ultimate conjoining of truth, of the good and beauty and the acknowledging of their singular truth, manifold only within the empirically visual. Suchlike a religion is needful to man, since without it he cannot handle the tragic problems, posited by the enigma of existence. A new task ahead for mankind will be the building of a bridge between "the kingdom of God on earth", a kingdom of freedom and justice, and that "heavenly kingdom", towards which always will yearn the tragic spirit of man.

Endnote [a]:

"There is a tragic element in the life of the every day that is far more real, far more penetrating, far more akin to the true self that is in us than the tragedy that lies in a great adventure. But, readily as we all may feel this, to prove itis by no means easy, inasmuch as this essential tragic element comprises more than that which is merely material or merely psychological. It goes beyond the determined struggle of man against man, and desire against desire: it goes beyond the eternal conflict of duty and passion. Its province is rather to reveal to us how truly wonderful is the mere act of living, and to throw light upon the existence of the soul, self-contained in the midst of ever-restless immensities; to hush the discourse of reason and sentiment, so that above the tumult may be heard the solemn, uninterrupted whisperings of man and his destiny. It is its province to point out to us the uncertain, dolorous footsteps of the being, as he approaches, or wanders from, his truth, his beauty, or his God".

As quoted from Alfred Sutro's 1897 English translation of Materlinck's "The Treasure of the Humble", chapter entitled "The Tragical in Daily Life", p. 113-114.

The Ethical Problem in Light of Philosophic Idealism

(1902 - 50)[1]

Zwei Dinge erfüllen das Gemüth mit immer neuer und zunehmender Bewunderung und Ehrfurcht, je öfter und anhaltender sichdas Nachdenken damit beschäftigt: *Der bestirnte Himmel über mir, und das moralische Gesetz in mir...*
Kant. "Kritik der praktischen Vernunft".

Der Mensch und überhaupt jedes vernünftige Wesen, existirt als Zweck an sich selbst nicht bloss als Mittel zum beliebigen Gebrauche für diesen oder jenen Willen, sondern muss in allen seinen, sowohl auf sich selbst, als auch andere vernünftige wesen gerichteten Handlungen jederzeit als Zweck betrachtet werden.
Kant. "Grundlegung zur Metaphysik der Sitten".

Ich gehe durch dies Volk und halte die Augen offen: sie sind kleiner geworden und werden immer kleiner: -- das aber macht ihre Lehre von Glück und Tugend.
Zu viel schonend, zu viel nachgebend: so ist euer Erdreich! Aber dass ein Baum *gross* werde, dazu will er um harte Felsen harte Wurzein schlagen!...
Ach, dass ihr mein Wort verstündet: thut immerhin, was ihr wollt, -- aber seid erst solche, die wollen können!
Nietzsche. "Also sprach Zarathustra".

Ich lehre den Übermenschen. Der Mensch ist etwas, das überwunden werden soll. Was habt ihr gethan, ihn zu überwinden?
Nietzsche. "Also sprach Zarathustra". [Vide Endnote, "a": p. 103].

I.

The purpose of my article -- is to make an attempt at positing the ethical problem upon the basis of philosophic idealism. I shall want to accomplish this, albeit however in general aspects, but also through the possibility of delimited features. Our theme has something innate for each

---

[1] ETICHESKAYA PROBLEMA V SVETE FILOSOFSKOGO IDEALIZMA. Article was initially published in sbornik-anthology "Problemy idealizma", Moskva, publisher "Mosk. psikhologicheskogo obschestva", 1902, p. 91-136.

consciously aware man, especially now, when moral questions again arise with tormentive an intensity and when the idealistic wave gushing upon us demands a shedding of light upon all the timely social problems, from rather instead the perspective of the eternal ethical problem. The construct of philosophic an ethics, as higher an arbiter of all human strivings and doings is, perhaps, a most important task for modern thought and each mind in philosophising over the problems of life has to here carry its own weight. I speak not about the trifling practical morals, which barely it is philosophically possible to deduce and which imposes a fateful stamp of triteness upon the work of philosophy, I am speaking instead about the philosophic positing of the basic problems of moral life.[1] Ethics is not a sociological and psychological science, investigating the laws of existence, this rather is a philosophic discipline, establishing the norms of the imperative. "In practical philosophy, -- says Kant, -- something happens not on the grounds of this, that it happens, but rather in accord with the laws whereof, that it has to happen, irregardless whether it actually happen".[2]

Ethics begins with an opposition between the existent and the imperative comprising the ought, and only in consequence of this opposition does it become possible. A negation of the imperative ought, as independent a category, independent from the empirically existent and not

---

[1] In the philosophic literature I cannot point to a single practical ethics, which has not diminished the dignity of both philosophy and the philosopher. When one makes the transition, for example, from the theoretical portion of the "Ethik" of Wundt [Wilhelm, 1832-1920] to its practical morals, one then experiences an unpleasant sensation. The same can be said also about the ethics of Spenser [Herbert, 1820-1903], Paulsen [Friedrich, 1846-1908], Hoffding [Harald, 1843-1931] and many others. Onto the higher philosophic principles gets artificially hitched very ordinary philistine morals.

[2] Vide *Kant*. "Grundlegung zur Metaphysik der Sitten". Vide also the book of *Windelband* [Wilhelm, 1848-1915], "Präludien", chiefly the chapters entitled "Normen und Naturgesetze", "Kritische oder genetische Methode" and "Vom Prinzip der Moral". Vide likewise" *Simmel* [Georg, 1858-1918], "Einleitung in die Moralwissenschaft".

This indeed nowise, certainly, excludes the psychological and sociological investigation of the developing of morality.

derivative from it, would lead to the abolition not only of ethics, but also of the moral problem itself. Ethics in the sole worthy meaning of this word is not a scientific investigation of an existing morality, of moral druthers and moral concepts: the moral problem, which it involves, lies on different a side beyond the everyday, the conditional worldly morals and the empirical good and evil.

First of all, it is necessary to take a look at the ethical problem from its gnosseological side, and here we have to admit of a *formal* intrepidness of the category of the imperative ought (while not as yet addressing the content of this category). The attempts of the positivists and the immoralists to fashion an idea of the imperative ought and uphold exclusively what exists, is very naive, and sometimes even comical. The denier of the imperative ought at each step tends to betray himself and enters upon a very monstrous contradiction regarding his anti-ethical assertions. From the tongue of the "immoralist" quite often springs forth a protest against this or some other manifestation of the existent and, consequently, a depreciation of this existent, and quite often from his lips is heard an appeal to something that is not actual, an appeal to something better and higher from his point of view. A man ought to make a transvaluation of all moral values, a man ought to defend his "I" against everything which might infringe upon it, a man ought to lift himself above the shameful sense of pity, a man ought to be strong and powerful, a man ought to be a "superman". Thus speaks the Nietzschean and has the naiveté to consider himself an "immoralist", and it therein seems to him, that he stands "beyond this side of good and evil" and has ultimately buried the idea of the imperative ought, associated for him with an antipathy towards slave-like a morality. In actuality however, our "immoralist" stands only on this side of historical good and evil, on this side of the historical morals of this or some other era, and into the eternal idea of the imperative ought he attempts to insert some new moral content. Everything in Nietzsche is a passionate, tormentive protest against actuality, against what exists and a protest in the name of an idea, in the name of an imperative ought. I shall be speaking further about Nietzsche and we shall see, that the preaching of a "superman" is the preaching of an absolute imperative ought.[1]

---

[1] Vide the original and very sincerely written booklet by L. Shestov, "The Idea of the Good in the teachings of Graf Tolstoy and Fr. Nietzsche". Shestov speaks with repugnance about duty, about the

Quite often within history the given actuality with its moral tastes and demands tends to be regarded as an imperative ought, and the revolt against it gets seen as a transgression of the imperative ought. For the masses this rouses psychological illusions, which become embedded within false theoretical ideas. And nowise can they comprehend, that the pure idea of the imperative ought is an idea revolutionary, that it is the symbol of a revolt against the actual in the name of an ideal, against existing morals in the name of those higher, against evil in the name of good. I am now considering the category of the imperative ought in its formal gnosseological pure form, and further on I shall look at it from other sides. Kant did all the most for a finalative affirmation of the independence of the categorical imperative, as a principle which is given *a priori* within our consciousness, and in such manner he rendered ethics independent from scientific cognition.[1] This was his immortal contribution and the philosophic ethics of the imperative relates to Kant. The moral appraisal of the existing from the point of view of the imperative ought is present for every consciousness: all the disputes about good and evil, all the shiftings of various systems of morals occurs within the bounds of this eternal ethical function and it is impossible here to be "on the other side beyond". And thus, in following Kant, from gnosseological a perspective, we first of all already recognise the independence of the ethical categorical imperative, the necessity of an ethical point of view upon life and the world, sharply distinct from a perspective that is scientifically conceived: the moral problem, the problem of the imperative ought, cannot be deduced from the existent, from empirical being, and ethics, i.e. the philosophic teaching concerning the imperative ought, is a matter autonomous, it does not depend upon science, upon a cognition of what exists.[2]

---

moral philosophy of Kant, about every sort of moral preaching, but all this is overall a misperception. Mr. Shestov in essence thirsts for "the good" and not in vain he ends his book with the words: "It is needful to search for God".

[1] Vide the excellent study of the moral philosophy of Kant in the book by P. Novgorodtsev [Pavel, 1886-1924], "Kant and Hegel in their Teachings about Truth and the State".

[2] In order to avoid misunderstanding I should specify, that I am contrasting ethics only in regard to positive science. In what relates

Before passing on from the gnosseological premises into a further investigation of the ethical problem, I want to make several clarifications in regard to the ethical portion of my book, "*Subjectivism and Individualism in Societal Philosophy*", since it seems that I have caused some certain misunderstandings. Along with this I want more precisely to define its relationship to the point of view of P. B. Struve, as was developed in the preface to my book. From my explanation it will be clear, that with Struve I have quite notable gnosseological differences of opinion, but as to ethical differences of opinion there are almost none.

"For the theory of cognition, -- says Struve, -- there is no opposition moreso acute, than that of being and what ought to be, of what is true and what is imperative". In these words an indisputable truth gets interlaced with misunderstanding. And for us from the point of view of the theory of cognition no opposition is more acute, than the opposition between being and what ought to be, but this is not an objection against teleological criticism. A teleological criticism transcendentally (not empirically) unites truth and the good into a common conception of the normal, i.e. of the imperative ought, but it also does not purport to unite being with what ought to be, which can be aligned towards unity only upon the basis of metaphysics, towards which such theological criticists as, for example Windelband, do not incline.[1] I am totally unable to comprehend, why Struve regards it possible to align the opposition of "being and what ought to be" together with the opposition between "the true and the imperative ought". The concept of being cannot be considered identical with the concept of the true, since this would be based upon a confusing of

---

however to metaphysics, there is an uniting of ethics and science into an higher supra-empirical cognition.

[1] Vide: Windelband. "Präludien", "Normen und Naturgesetze". Windelband gives a classical and very refined exposition of Kantianism in a spirit of teleological criticism. Vide likewise the fine article of B. Kistyakovsky [Bogdan, 1868-1920], "The Category of Necessity and Justice" ("Zhizn", May, 1900). In this article is explored the parallelism of logical and ethical universal validity.

consciousness with knowing.[1] The true from the perspective of the theory of cognition is an imperative ought, and not an existent, although cognitively the imperative ought is by no means identical with the morally imperative, but only parallel to it. I concur with Struve, that the theory of cognition is first of all an analytic-descriptive discipline, but he indeed himself also admits, that at the furthest stage there arises a teleological problem. When we introduce into the theory of cognition the concept of truth, as the end-purpose of cognition, we posit the teleological problem. Truth is a value, which ought to be realised within our cognition, but is unable to be realised. The basic, the inner sign of truth is manifest by its *Geltung* [valid significance], and in this sign is encountered the good. The transcendental unification of truth and the good within the concept of an universally-binding norm (imperative) occupies a middle ground between a total empirical differentiation betwixt truth and the good, and their total metaphysical identity. Once again I stress, that amidst this is preserved the chasm, impassible within the bounds of empirical actuality and science, between being and the imperative ought. The dualism between ethics and science has been firmly established by Kant and I share this dualistic point of view no less than Struve. Alongside other teleological criticists I tend to posit an ideal universally-binding moral good not from the natural compelling aspect of experience, but from rather the ideal universally-binding aspect of truth.

All the arguments of the positivists-evolutionists against a non-dependence upon experience, against an absolute idea of an imperative ought, tend usually to miss the mark, since they render the moral law, which is present for the subject, as rather an object of scientific knowledge, i.e. they situate it within the experiential world, where all is relative. We first of all have an opposition of the absolute moral law, as an imperative ought, in contrast to all the empirical world, the existent, since it is very easy to show, that in the existent, which is manifest for us as the object of experiential knowledge, there is no absolute imperative necessity, but only by crude a misunderstanding can this be regarded as an argument against Kant and against those, who follow him in moral philosophy. From a perspective of scientific cognition, operative via experience, the positivist-

[1] Within Russian literature vide the book of S. Askol'dov [Sergei, 1871-1945], "Fundamental Problems in the Theory of Knowledge and Ontology", Chapter I, "Consciousness and Cognition".

evolutionist can show only, that the imperative ought (the moral law) does not exist, i.e. the imperative is not what exists, but it would be needless to demonstrate this, for we ourself well know and understand this, as the point of departure to our ethical constructs. The positivists do not want to comprehend, that the human consciousness possesses two distinct, parallel sides: the cognitive-theoretical, oriented towards the natural legitimacy of experience, i.e. the existent, and the moral-practical, oriented towards the normative legitimacy of the good, i.e. to the imperative ought.[1] Positivism (-empiricism) utilises the scientific-conceptual function of consciousness and then, when this goes astray, there goes with it the too naively believing in experience, in its singularity and finality, whilst forgetting, that this experience is but the product of our consciousness and moreover only one side of it. In this is expressed the limitedness of positivism, expressed a sort of blind spot, connected with a dogmatic self-smugness. Besides this existent, which within experience is conceptualised by science, there is an entire infinitude and in this infinitude there is quite possible much to make sense of from the angle namely of scientific cognition; yet in order not to remain blind, there is need here to make a transition over to a different side of consciousness, and in a certain sense very important. The greatest and indeed immortal merit of Kant consists in this, that he ultimately demolished the restrictive dogmatism, which believes only in the sensory world and takes upon itself the audacity to prove the emptiness and illusion behind the ideas of God, freedom and immortality. To demand scientific-logical proofs for ethical positions signifies however a failure to understand the essence of the ethical problem, since these positions possess their own specific ethical proof, they derive their value not from the perceptual activity of consciousness, but rather from a purely moral activity. In this infinitude, which is revealed on different a side from that of positive experiential perception, rests on firm foundations the moral law, the imperative. This -- is the object of ethics. And in such manner the gnosseology of critical idealism opens wide the doors to the free moral creativity of the human spirit.

---

[1] Metaphysics unites the existent and the imperative within absolute being.

II.

Before passing over from the gnosseological premises of ethics to a further look at the moral problem, I want to make several critical remarks concerning hedonism.[1] The perspective regarding hedonism in ethics is completely unsustainable and already sufficiently refuted by the whole of modern philosophy and science, but yet through a distortion, it gets expounded only by a low sort of philosophy, and generally a low sort of spiritual culture, although it all still continues to be the most widespread point of view: this is the typical view on the morality of the average man.[2] A final elimination of all the sophistries of hedonism has not only a philosophic-ethical, but also a social-cultural significance.

Man always strives towards satisfaction -- herein is the psychology of hedonism; man always ought to strive towards the greatest satisfaction -- herein is the ethical imperative of hedonism. Hedonism does not first of all hold up under even a slight bit of psychological criticism. Psychology definitely teaches, that man strives not towards satisfaction, -- this would be a striving completely lacking in content, but rather towards this or some other objects with a certain content. If I go to a concert to listen to music, then the object of my intent is not satisfaction, but rather the music, whereas the satisfaction -- is only a consequence. If I work at some scientific investigation, then the object of my desire is knowledge, and not satisfaction. The life of man is comprised of desires and strivings, directed towards an entire series of objects; the realisation of these desires and strivings involves the discharge of energies present within the human soul; there exists an organic connection between what a man desires, and that of how he is by his nature, since man tends to realise within his life not satisfaction and happiness, and by his nature he manifests his energy, though it be attained by way of suffering. Sufferings often presuppose

---

[1] I employ the very broad term hedonism, but I have in view also all its branches, i.e. eudaemonism, utilitarianism, etc.

[2] For a critique of hedonism, vide Simmel: "Einleitung in die Moralwissenschaft", Erster Band, p. 293-467. Wundt: "Ethik", p. 432-449. Guyau [Jean-Marie, 1854-1888]: "La morale anglaise contemporaine". Also an excellent critique of hedonism can be found with Mackenzie [John Stewart, 1860-1935]. Vide his "Ethics", p. 78-103.

satisfactions, they are interlaced within the very essence of the human individuality. When a man works at the resolution of some whatever complex problem of knowledge or struggles for the realisation of social justice, his emotional life tends to get concentrated upon these objects, and they become purposive ends. If a man during this while thinks instead about satisfaction as his conscious goal, then he will never resolve the problem of knowledge and will never realise justice. And by this we become ultimately convinced, that hedonism is a psychological *non sens* and contradicts the basic facts of emotional life. Even J. S. Mills says, that in order to be happy, is not a consequence of especial concern over being happy.[1] I say quite moreso: happiness -- is a wondrous thing and man constantly dreams about it, but psychologically it is impossible to make happiness the purposive end of life, the object of his desires and to consciously direct his activity at its realisation. Man finds his higher happiness in the realisation of something of value from the point of view of his conscious nature, i.e. the realisation of the good in his will, truth in his cognition, beauty in his feelings; these values are also purposive ends, from their realisation is comprised spiritual life. The whole content of the emotional life vanishes, when in the field of consciousness there obtains only satisfaction and happiness, as purposive ends. The quality of happiness is wholly determined by the quality of the objects of desire, i.e. by the spiritual nature of man. Here we meet up against insurmountable difficulties for the hedonistic theory of morality.

Quantitatively, the types of satisfaction defy making a sum total of them, and we can nowise say, in what is the greatest happiness. The satisfaction from fine roast-beef or champagne is impossible to compare with the satisfaction from a philosophic book or artistic work, it is impossible even to ask, what bestows a greater quantity of satisfactions. Literally, we have to admit, that satisfaction, -- is the result of an accomplished desire, -- qualitatively varied, and this qualitative aspect is dependent upon the objects desired, on the quality demanded. Happiness is less definable a concept, than is satisfaction, and the question about the quality of happiness cannot be adduced to its quantity. If happiness were to

[1] This sincere and honest thinker has often uncovered inner contradictions by his point of view, nor was he satisfied with the narrow positivist-utilitarian view on life. Vide the interesting and instructive "Autobiography" of Mills.

lose all its content for the human consciousness, were to lose that which bestows its qualitative hue, then there would result a completely empty concept, from which nothing could be inferred. But hedonistic ethics does not admit of any sort of qualitative criteria, it evaluates everything based on the quantity of satisfactions. We stand afront an evident absurdity. Hedonism should admit of its own psychological incompetence, since satisfaction -- is not the purposive end for life, and should also admit its ethical incompetence, since in recoursing to satisfaction, it is impossible to derive any sort of moral imperatives, and satisfaction tends to be evaluated not as regards its quantity -- quantitatively it is neither of any common measure nor comparable -- but rather it is evaluated as regards quality, which is operative upon altogether differing, actively ethical criteria.

We well know, that satisfaction is a plus, and suffering -- a minus, we know likewise, that happiness -- is something dreamt of by man, but all this has very little a relationship to ethics. Satisfaction can be ugly and immoral, happiness can be shameful, whereas suffering can be morally of value and valiant. The purposive end, which ethics seeks -- is not the empirical happiness of people, but rather their ideal moral perfection. And therefore, in opposition to the hedonists of every shade, I offer the following necessary psychological premise for ethics: morality -- is an autonomous quality of the human soul, and it is impossible to deduce it from any such non-ethical concepts, as satisfaction or happiness; happiness itself is subject to moral a judgement, and this judgement determines the quality of the happiness, acknowledging it as worthy or unworthy to the moral nature of man.

I have some several words more to say about those varieties of hedonism, which can be termed as a societal, altruistic utilitarianism. This is regarded as the most progressive trend in ethics, though hardly as an higher form of moral consciousness. The dogmas of societal utilitarianism have been converted into deadening formats and hinder any sort of profound penetration into the very core of the moral problem. The moral problem in essence here gets altogether displaced, since the question concerning usefulness is substituted in place of the question concerning value.

The general welfare, the greatest happiness of the greatest quantity of people -- herein is the ethical criterion, proposed by the societal altruistic utilitarianism. This current tends totally to be subject to the same critique as hedonism in general, but it has further its own deficiencies. If it be impossible to construct an ethics based upon the happiness of the individual, then universal happiness becomes moreover a completely fictitious concept. In what way is it possible to pass over from the individual happiness of a man to the universal happiness of mankind, in the name of what man is it possible to subsume the general welfare and regard him as the average? Why should an altruistic utilitarianism posit the happiness of some other man as higher than my own happiness, if the ultimate criterion be happiness all the same, and why should my doings be qualified as moral, only when I serve the happiness of someone else? To these questions there is no answer, and herein ensues a vicious circle. One can demonstrate, in what manner historical man contrives to the benefit of the common good, and consequently, to infer a genetic sort of justification of societal utilitarianism, but I am not asking about this, I am asking about an ethical justification. For ethics it is important to show, why suchlike a principle -- is an imperative ought, rather than why it should seem necessary. There is no sort of an ethical justification for transitioning over from the happiness of one man to that of the happiness of some other and to the happiness of all. When I look to my own satisfaction and happiness, then this would possess no sort of a moral value, but to look to the satisfaction and happiness of Peter and Ivan and even the Peters and Ivans in the world -- this likewise would not possess any sort of moral value, because that my satisfaction and happiness and the satisfaction and happiness of Ivan are completely differing valuations and they are completely alike outside the sphere of ethics, since they have nothing in common with the moral ends in life. The added up sum total from such ethical zeros, as the satisfaction and happiness of X or Y, makes it still impossible to result in anything. An egoistic hedonism includes within it less inner contradictions, than does the altruistic, and to extreme measure and bluntly enough it ignores the moral problem and lays bare the immoral nature of every hedonism. It is quite the same indeed, if it is shameful for a man to devote his life to his own greatest satisfaction, then also it is no less shameful to turn himself into an implement for foreign sort a greatest satisfaction.

Further along it will become evident, the extent to which hedonism and utilitarianism, whether the individual sort, and so also the societal, both acutely contradict the fundamental idea of ethics, -- the idea of the person and its growth towards a perfecting. These hedonistic teachings in essence are profoundly reactionary and it is only through misunderstanding and lack of thought that people of progressive strivings cling to them. That satisfaction and well-being, which hedonism and utilitarianism see as the sole end-purpose to life and morality, fail to include within them any sort of higher a developement, since where this developement would be needful to posit an higher satisfaction and happiness, would be contradictory to the basic principle of hedonism. That which hedonism regards as its final purposive-end -- is in only a temporary moment of equilibrium, i.e. a given personal or historical system of adaption, which constantly is assaulted by the furthermost growth towards all higher and higher forms of life. Progress, i.e. the movement towards uppermost a goal, happens by way of great dissatisfaction and great sufferings; those sufferings and this dissatisfaction comprise enormous a moral price, which contentment and well-being tend to lack.[1]

The evolutionary current in ethics attempts to introduce certain correctives to hedonism and utilitarianism, it introduces into ethics the idea of the developing of life.[2] But, regretably, evolutionism by-passes the moral problem, it does not provide any sort of answer to the question morally concerning *value*, concerning *the imperative ought*, and in the final end it rises no higher than does hedonism. The difference is only in this, that evolutionism speaks not about utility and the greatest satisfaction, but rather about the greatest adaptability, i.e. all the same again about something completely non-ethical. Particularly inherent to evolutionism is

---

[1] I cannot fail to mention the article of P. L. Lavrov [1823-1900] on morality, in which he very precisely revealed for his times an understanding of all the vulgarity and reactionary aspects of the hedonistic and utilitarian theories. [Berdyaev likely has in mind the 1870 P. Lavrov article, "Modern Teachings on Morality and its History"; also articles "Social-Revolutionary and Bourgeois Morality" and "Social Revolution and the Tasks of Morality"]. But his idealistic theory of the person could not be grounded and developed upon the basis of positivism. Within Russian literature vide likewise the critical comments contained in the [1898] book of P. Nezhdanov, "Morality". Nezhdanov accurately understood, that morality is suchlike a quality, as uplifts man.

[2] Vide H. Spenser. "The Principles of Ethics", tom I, p. 56-58. The universal ethical evolutionism of Wundt and Paulsen, in our view, is faulty from a gnosseological point of view.

the special and grievous sin -- bowing in worship to the God of necessity in place of the God of freedom. Evolutionary theory often successfully explains the historical developement of morals, moral concepts and tastes,[1] but morality itself eludes it, and the moral law is situated outside its narrow cognitive perview. I have already spoken about this from the point of view of gnosseology. Evolutionism can only point out, how morality, i.e. an eternal value of some sort, an absolute what ought to be, gets revealed within the process of societal developement, but it possesses no sort of right to infer the moral apart from the non-moral, and in its absence, it has to presuppose morality, as something obtaining prior to any evolution and within it only as unwinding, not creatively forming. Evolutionism has as little the same place within philosophic ethics, as it does within the theory of cognition, it is appropriate only to psychological and sociological investigations, and all the evolutionary arguments against an absolute morality are striking by their non-critical aspect. Marxism, as a philosophic worldview, shares in all the sins of evolutionism and particularly witnesses to the need for an ethical idealism.[2]

Now is not a time for breaking lances for a demonstrating of the idea, that everything that exists is developing, but from this indisputable truth it is impossible to derive even a single argument against an absolute moral law, which is conceived of by us, as a category of the imperative ought, rather than of the existent. From evolutionism it is possible to make only one accurate inference: the absolute moral law, the ethical norms ought only gradually to be realised within the life of mankind, i.e. by way of social developement to become established as part of the existent, of the empirical actuality. The ethical norms per se are as little able to evolve, as are the laws of logic; morality is inalterable, and becomes altered only to the degree of proximity to it. The absolute and eternal aspects of the moral law we see not to be in this, that it always and everywhere is present in the empirical existent, i.e. not in the inalterability of an already existing

[1] In this regard quite much can be provided by the Marxist understanding of history, which mustneeds be admitted as an higher form of sociological evolutionism.

[2] The modern critical current is elucidating the healthy and vital elements of Marxism and combines them with a philosophic and ethical idealism.

morality, but rather in its inalterable value, as an imperative ought, and in this, that the value is not dependent upon the empirical actuality, and that the moral law -- is the autonomous legislator of our consciousness and compulsory an effort has no power over the inherent value of the moral good.

No sort of a stagnantly frozen empirical content can make pretense to the name of an absolute morality; the absolute moral norm always is only a summoning forward, ever forward and forward, -- this is a beacon, which shines to us from infinitude. The moral law -- is an unmediated revealing of the absolute, -- this is the voice of God within man, given for "this world", but it is "not of this world". If evolutionism with its limitedness possesses no sort of significance for ethics, then nonetheless it possesses a great significance in the teleological idea of progress. We admit of the principle of a maximum of life, of its highest developement, but with us this principle possesses not the biological meaning that it does for the evolutionists, but rather ethical a meaning.

III.

Kant gave not only a formal, gnosseological basis to ethics, he provided quite more. The whole content of ethics can be constructed only by relying upon Kant. Kant recognised the absolute value underlying man: whence man -- is an end-in-itself, while from a moral point of view it is impossible to look at him as merely a means, and together with this all people are morally equivalent, of equal a value.[1] This eternal, absolute moral law, the basic condition to every realising of the moral good and all the derivative content of morality, can be deduced only from it and only be justified by it.[2] My whole further exposition will be an attempt to reveal

---

[1] Vide Kant. "Grundlegung zur Metaphysik der Sitten", p. 52-54, and "Kritik der praktischen Vernunft", p. 158.

[2] "Dieses Prinzip der Menschheit und jeder vernüftigen Natur überhaupt, als Zwecks *an sich selbst* (welche die oberste einschränkende Bedingung der Freiheit der Handlungen eines jeden Menschen ist), ist nicht aus der Erfahrung entlehnt, erstlich, wegen seiner Allgemeinheit, da es auf alle vernünftige Wesen überhaupt geht, worüber etwas zu bestimmen keine

and establish a grounding for the ethical principles of the human person, as an end-in-itself and of absolute value.

The basic idea of ethics is the idea of the person, as the sole bearer of the moral law. From the point of view of ethics -- what such is the person, in what regard stands the ethical idea of person to the empirical person with all its manifold, concrete content, in which appears a motley jumble of beauty together with ugliness, of the sublime with the vile? Here, it seems to me, is involved the close connection of ethics with metaphysics, and in the final end also with religion. Within the bounds of experience, with which positive science tends to deal, the ethical idea of person eludes notice, such that behind the empirical person we cannot recognise an absolute value, and in the empirical actuality man too often becomes not man, not that man, which we consider an end-in-itself and which ought to be therein sacred. This painful contradiction between the person empirical and the person ideal renders the moral problem into a tragic problem. There is a great, a truly tragic, moral turmoil in the impossibility for us, within the limits of our empirical attitudes, to remember in Judas the Betrayer also a man, i.e. of absolute value, to see in him a brother, i.e. in spirit equal to us as an end-in-itself. This leads us to the very depth of the moral problem. *The moral problem is first of all a problem of the relationship between the empirical "I" and the ideal,*

Erfahrung zureicht; zweitens, weil darin die Menschheit nicht als Zweck des Menschen (subjectiv), d. i. als Gegenstand, den man sich von selbst wirklich zum Zwecke macht, sondern als objectiver Zweck, der, wir mögen Zwecke haben, welche wir wollen als Gesetz die oberste einschränkende Bedingung aller subjectiven Zwecke ausmachen soll, vorgestellt wird, mithin aus reiner Vernunft entspringen muss. Es liegt nämlich der Grund aller praktischen Gesetzgebung objectiv in der Regel und der Form der Allgemeinheit, die sie in gesetz (allenfalls Naturgesetz) zu sein fähig macht (nach dem ersten Prinzip), subjectiv aber im Zwecke; das Subject aller Zwecke aber ist jedes vernüftige Wesen als Zweck an sich selbst (nach dem zweiten Prinzip); hieraus folgt nun das dritte praktische Prinzip des Willens, als oberste Bedingung der Zusammenstimmung desselben mit der allgemeinen praktischen Vernunft: die Idee *des Willens jedes vernünftigen Wesens als eies allgemein gesetzgebenden Willens*". Kant. "Grundlegung zur Metaphysik der Sitten", p. 55-56. ["Zweiter Abschnitt"].
[Endnote "b": p. 104].

spiritual, (normative-normal) "I".[1] Kant proceeds from the dualism of the "sensory" and the "moral-reasoning" nature of man and in this dualism he sees all the *raison d'être* of the moral problem. He admitted of moral value only to that, which issues forth from a respect towards the moral law, and not from sensory inclinations and instincts, which themself per se are neither moral nor non-moral. Kant thereby made certain false rigoristic deductions, directed against the life of the senses and the instinctive inclinations of human nature, but his thought was accurate and profound in this regard, that morality -- is a specific quality in man, independent of sensory life, and that this is the legislative capacity of the will (the practical reason).[2]

And thus, we come to this conclusion, that *morality is first of all an inner relationship of man to his own self, of the search for and the realisation of his own spiritual "I", the creation of a "normative" consciousness within the consciousness "empirical".* In ordinary language this is also called the developing of the person within man. Morality, as a relating of man to man, is the unconditional recognition in each man of his spiritual "I" and the unconditional respect for his rights. This is also what in ordinary language is termed humanness: to be human -- means to recognise and to respect each man as a brother in spirit, to regard his spiritual nature likewise as an end-in-itself, as is one's own, and to enable its developement on the grounds of universally an human spiritual culture.

From suchlike a positing of the question it is evident, that the moral problem is first of all a problem individual and becomes rendered a problem social only in its furthermost inferences. But an ethical individualism will remain hanging up in the air, lacking any support, if it remains upon the groundings of experience. The empirical person, as such, cannot lead to an ethical individualism, it shoves us rather into the embraces of hedonism and immoralism. Literally, the idea of the person and the moral problem, the subject of which is manifest as the person, is conceivable only upon the groundings of spiritualism. Kant was completely

---

[1] I employ the word "normal" here in the sense of corresponding with a "norm'. The entire empirical actuality (the realm of nature) in the strict philosophic sense of the word is *not normal*, normalist comprises only the ideal world of the imperative ought.

[2] Vide Kant, "Grundlegung zur Metaphysik der Sitten", p. 7.

consistent and he postulated spiritualism.[1] Man has absolute a value, since he is eternal a spirit, and people are equivalently of equal value, since they are of one and the same spiritual nature. The spiritual individuality possesses absolute inalienable rights, which it is impossible to appraise, and higher than it is nothing except its highermost developement. *The moral value in man is determined neither by the approval nor by the censure of other people, nor by usefulness for society, nor in general by anything outside it in the world, but rather in concurrence with its own inner moral nature, in relation to the verymost God.* Only in such manner is there removed that degrading and vile view on morality, which sees in it something on the outside issuing measures against man, something constricting him from the outside, something almost hostile to him. Usually they fail to understand, that it is namely Kant, that selfsame Kant, who set at the core of his moral philosophy the idea of the imperative ought, he identified morality with an inner freedom, and what is hostile to the person and its freedom is not the ethics of Kant, but rather moreso the utilitarian and evolutionary ethics, which recourses to purely external criteria, thereby evaluating the sacred rights of the person from a perspective of societal usefulness and adaptability and sees its moral idea in the disciplined herd of animals. The moral law is an autonomous legislative capacity of the moral-reasoning nature of man, and he is not bound to it from the outside, for it comprises the very essence of his spiritual individuality. In fulfilling the moral law, this does not mean the restricting of his own "I" in the name of the "not-I", this means rather the affirmation of his true "I"; the moral conscience is a responsibility facing him himself, facing his spiritual "I".

---

[1] The defect of Kant was in this, that he regarded the position of spiritualism as too shabby from the point of view of philosophic cognition and he constructed a metaphysics exclusively by way of the method of moral postulates. I disdain the Kantian agnosticism and both many Kantians and I myself believe in the possibility to construct a metaphysics along different lines.

IV.

And thus, the basic, the governing idea of ethics is the idea of the "I", and from it there has to be inferred the whole of morality. Here we come up against the question concerning the relationship between the "I" and the "thou" and we therein have to untangle s whole series of sophisms, connected with this central question in ethics. A large portion of moral systems admit of an ethical primacy of the "thou" over the "I", the primacy of the "other" over "oneself"; in the moral philosophy of the XIX Century this was termed "altruism", which they wanted to substitute as the true spiritual essence of human life. And one of the most significant merits of Fr. Nietzsche mustneeds be admitted in his protest against the degradation of the "I", which is wrought by ostensible moral conventions.[1] But only an affirmation of the primacy of the "I" over the "thou", from our point of view, would not comprise an "immoralism", on the contrary rather it would constitute the greatest triumph of a genuine morality.

The concepts of "I" and "thou" are relative, relational, and can be transposed optionally thus: if A is an "I", then B in relation to it will be a "thou", will be an "other", but indeed B is likewise an "I" and for it A is the "thou". Ethics from the sidelines looks at A and at B, since for ethics there does not exist the relative distinction between "I" and "thou". For ethics both A and B are alike an "I", i.e. human a person, and both of these "I" are equivalent, are of equal value. The "thou" is quite negative a concept, in the "other" can be found something positive, only if it be looked upon, as an "I". The current altruism in its utilitarian version always acknowledges the moral predominance of the "thou" and the sum of the "thou's", unified into a concept of the "not-I" over the "I", and by this it abolishes the "I", i.e. it does away with the sole bearer of the moral principle, and comes well nigh to absurdity. This implies the destroying of morality due to a moral zealousness, shoving together a whole series of restricted and negated "I's", wrought in the name of "others", and from the sum total of this it is impossible to receive an affirmation and developement of all the "I's".

---

[1] "Ihr flüchtet zum Nachsten vor euch selber, -- says Zarathustra, -- und möchtet euch daraus eine Tugend machen: aber ich durchschaue euer "selbstloses". "Das Du ist heilig gesprochen, aber noch nicht das Ich: so drängt sich der Mensch hin zum Nachsten". Nietzsche. "Werke", B. VI., p. 88. [Endnote "c": p. 104].

We wind up stuck in a morally empty place, in something generally corrosive of person and quenching of spirit, since only the developed "I" is the bearer of the spiritual principle, and I stress in particular, that in ethics we have to admit not only the primacy of the "I" (of the person, the spiritual individuality), but even we have to admit this "I" as the sole element of ethics. And then the old question about the relationship between "egoism" and "altruism" will receive a bit of new light.

In essence, this opposition between "egoism" and "altruism" is quite vulgar a matter, and in philosophic ethics it ought to have no place. Upon the word "egoism" lies a seal of moral opprobrium, whereas upon the word "altruism" lies the seal of moral approval. Why? As regards its philosophic meaning, "egoism" derives from the word "I" [Latin "ego"], and "altruism" from the word "other" [Latin "alter"]. If we recall what we established previously, as basic for ethics, the distinction between the empirical "I" and the spiritual "I", between the sensory and the moral-reasoning nature of man, then this whole misunderstanding dissipates. Our genuine "I", that "I", which possesses absolute a value, which we ought to affirm and to realise, and the rights of which we ought to struggle for, this -- is the spiritual ideal "I", that of our moral-reasoning nature. To be an *ego*-ist in this sense means also to be a moral man, to be a *person*. But in everyday life what is understood as egoism is chiefly the pursuit of one's own lower cravings, a slavery to the empirical nature, and ethics condemns this sort of egoism, as an impediment to the truly human, the spiritual "I" in its struggle against the capricious empirical "I"; to defend per se the human person does not mean to defend all its manifold empirical content, i.e. the bare fact is that in this empirical content there is much that is radically contradictory to the very idea of person, much that is ugly and vile, and all this is foreign to our "I", all this belongs to the sidelines. In man there occurs a tortuous process of the liberation of the "I" from the lower slave-like impulses, -- this represents also a forging of the person, moral developement, which obtains through an higher spiritual energy. We shall look at what "altruism" itself represents amidst suchlike a setting of the question.

Eudaemonists often defend altruism and say, that the happiness of another man mustneeds be put higher than one's own, and even to sacrifice one's own happiness in the name of someone unknown. Yet all this line of judging matters is bereft of any sort of ethical meaning. Every "I" possesses the selfsame right to happiness, as does also the "thou", and here there are no sorts of apparent preference, since together with this both "my" happiness and the happiness of an "other" are alike non-ethical concepts, as was shown above. If "altruism" demands, that a man should sacrifice his spiritual "I" in the name of the happiness of an "other", then this demand is positively immoral, since my spiritual "I" has absolute a moral value, and while the happiness of an "other" is indeed sometimes beautiful, it still is of no sort of moral value. If however altruism demands, that one man should sacrifice the lower instincts of the empirical nature in the name of the spiritual, of the moral-reasoning nature of another man, in order that he not infringe upon his inalienable rights and should enable his growth by way of conjoint working at an awareness of human culture, then this first of all is a demand by one's own spiritual "I", and at this moment there enters in a struggle for one's own moral person, and therefore the word altruism here is nowise proximate. Man sometimes has to sacrifice his life, in order to save his spiritual "I"; herein the sacrifice and death once again are manifest as paths of moral self-realisation and only therefore justified. In general *person* (the "I", the spiritual individuality) with its inalienable rights stands higher than "altruism" and "egoism". This trendy opposition has only one accurate sense: the establishing of various qualities in the person or, as they usually are wont to say, a distinguishing between the higher and the lower demands, between those, that morally elevate man, and those, that degrade him.

It is long already time to abolish this ethical fiction of "thou", of the "others", which but impedes a correct setting and resolution of the ethical problem. The relation of man to man is ethically derived from the relation of man to his own self; obligation ought to be inferred from rights, from a right in positive a sense, where obligation is naught else than as a demand, that a right should be acknowledged, wherein a man is obligated not only to respect a right, but also to assist in its realisation. To recognise and to respect in an "other" a man, to relate to him *humanly*, this means to see in him the "I", i.e. the value, like to one's own "I". To be *human* means to be a man, i.e. to develope in oneself the spiritual person, since not to be *human*, not to admit in each "I" an unconditional value, means to be a beast, i.e. not still to have reached in growth to that condition, which we call the human person. And higher a moral consciousness demands, that each man should relate to each other man not as towards a "thou", out of sympathy whom he ought to sacrifice his own "I" or to sacrifice, in accord with the demand of "others", but rather as towards an "I", to the selfsame purpose end of his own towards himself, as also he himself. An higher humanness demands equality of correlation, which still is not there in the superficial "altruism". The unconditional respect for the human person, for its autonomy, for its right to self-determination -- here is the basic feature of the ethical perspective advanced by us. That spiritual individuality, in the name of which all life's struggle is waged, on which the whole social movement finds justification, towards which gravitate all the progressive strivings of mankind, -- this sort of individuality however for positivism in general and in particular for hedonism and societal utilitarianism simply does not exist, it is offered up in sacrifice (in the sphere of theoretical thought) out of societal benefit, historical adaption etc. The moral liberation of the human person demands the acknowledging of the following, and in our view elementary, truth: the moral problem is not a problem of some herd-like group, as regretably, not only reactionaries are wont to think, but also many progressives, and it is decided neither by the state, nor the societal process, nor by the law-courts of people, this rather -- is an inward individual problem of the human "I", striving towards an ideal perfectness.

V.

We have come to this conclusion, that the moral good consists in the affirmation of the "I", its self-realisation, and this leads us to the idea of the normatively "normal" developement of the person. Not every affirmation and developement in the person itself is a moral good, but only that rather, which leads to a perfective completeness, to the ideal spiritual condition. From ethical a perspective, the realisation of the "I" itself and the attainment of the ideal perfective completeness, are identical concepts. But the tragic aspect to the moral problem consists in this, that the absolute ideal of moral perfective completeness cannot be concretely expressed in experiential terms and empirically can never be fully realised. All the entirety of our moral life, all the moral developement of the separate man and of all humanity presupposes suchlike an absolute ideal, and without it life would be bereft of all meaning. That tormentive *searching* for the higher moral good, which comprises the most valuable content of the life of mankind, presupposes, that there is indeed suchlike a good, that it is not a mirage, that man *ought* to come nigh it. The idea of *moral developement* is meaningless without the idea of a supreme *purposive end*, which ought to be realised by this developing.

We can formulate the absolute (in its significance) condition of the realisation of the moral good thus: this is an acknowledging for the human person of an unconditional value and the right to self-determination, acknowledging it as an end-in-itself, and not as a means, and together with this the admitting also of the equal-value of people. Hence there result the principles of humanness and justice, for which over the course of history there has been the striving to find all more and more perfect an expression. But that content which is absolute of value, that higher good, which ought to be fulfilled in the life of man, and acknowledged as an end-in-itself, -- within the empirical actuality proves impossible, never will it become existent, it is an eternal call for unending growth, for a supreme spiritual energy, bursting asunder beyond the limits of every human range of scope. Every attempt to more precisely define the absolute good, of what ought to be the content of the life of man as an end-in-itself, inevitably leads us beyond the bounds of the experiential world. The idea of the realisation of the "I" by way of attainment of an ideal spiritual condition is set within eternity and infinitude, and herein for us are revealed the limitless perspectives. The human person, unique and individual, in its strivings towards perfective completeness always gravitates towards one and the selfsame point, towards the Supreme Good, in which are unified all values. Infinite power and might, endless knowledge, eternal beauty and harmony -- all this enters into the realisation and developement of the "I". The final stage to this long path, in which the empirical world is but a small slice, we have to consider as an unifying of the individual "I" with an "I" universal, i.e. of man with God. Wherefore the Divinity is not thought of as something foreign and external for the human "I", to which the "I" has to be subordinated, but rather as its own ideal of ultimate fulfillment.

Metaphysics, to which ethics indubitably leads, unites within the concept of the Supreme Good the individual spiritual "I" with the universal spiritual "I". On all these positions, which can be developed only in a tract upon metaphysics, teleological criticism casts unique a light. The supra-individual consciousness is manifest in the subject, the bearer of universally-binding norms, logical, ethical and aesthetic, and therefore the moral developement, which transpires within the human person, for it and through it, is a triumph of the normatively "normal" consciousness within the empirical, i.e. a victorious coming about of the universal "I" or, in terms of ontology, of the world spirit. The starting point of view for ethics can only be the individual, and the moral problem is a problem of individualism, a problem of the *person*, but the individualism mustneeds be metaphysically surmounted to arrive at the universal, or more accurately, individualism and universalism have to be harmonically unified into a single worldview. I regard it possible simultaneously to investigate both a consistent ethical individualism, and also no less a consistent ethical universalism. To this important question we shall now turn our attention.

VI.

In the "Preface" to my book mentioned previously, Struve contrasts his ethical individualism against my ethical universalism. I think, that herein there cannot be any sort of opposition. Individualism and universalism are involved in differing planes, answering to various sides of the ethical problem and are completive each towards the other. I can with full justification say, that Struve is an universalist in my sense, and I an individualist in his sense, our ethical differences of opinion are only inconsequential and lay exclusively within the sphere of gnosseology. From all my exposition it is sufficiently clear, how much I share in the ethical individualism of Struve, and now we shall examine, why individualism inevitably transitions over into universalism.

We have seen, that the basic idea of ethics is the idea of "person", the idea of the "I", which ought to become realised and whose sacredness ought to be admitted. But in admitting the ideal, the "normative" character of this "I" and the universally obligatory aspect of the moral law inherent to it, we surmount both the ethical empiricism, as well as solipcism.[1] Person, the "I", the individuality from the ethical point of view -- is everything, but namely because, that within it we think of universal a

[1] Solipcism both in the theory of cognition and in ethics, in my view, collapses together with the collapse of empiricism. Ethical solipcism is based upon the seeming impossibility to emerge beyond the bounds of the individual consciousness, but the individual consciousness, as an empirical fact, still does not provide a basis for the idea of the person, of the individuality, which can be conceived of only spiritually.

spiritual content. Man is sacred and inviolable not in the name of his chance empirical content, he is sacred and inviolable, as the bearer of an higher spiritual principle. Within the "individual", within the human person, we reference the "universal", i.e. the singular spiritual nature, variated and individually manifest within the empirical world. In the man who is an other, man shows reverence towards God. Ethical individualism without universalism would be bereft of its *raison d'être*, fatally it would be transformed into empiricism and in such manner would enter into a contradiction with the very idea of individuality and morality. It can be said straight out, that the moral level of the human person can be measured by the degree of its penetration into universal life and universal interests. Man tends to actualise his spiritual "I", only by emerging beyond the narrow sphere of his individual experiences in the particular sense of this word, and entering into the broad arena of world life. He finds his own "individuality" by developing in himself the "universal". Struve likewise admits an ethical universalism, when he postulates a "moral world-order". To acknowledge a "moral world-order" means to admit, that the world has meaning, that individual life is situated in an inseparable moral connection with universal life, with a world-order.

Suchlike an harmonious unifying of individualism and universalism leads to the following resolution of the ethical problem. The moral contradiction between what ought to be and what is, between the human "I", striving for an ideal perfectness, and the empirical actuality, allows for two paths, which in the final end tend to align: the path of the *individual* and the path of *universal developement*. The individual thirst for perfection, for the realisation of the spiritual "I", which also comprises the essence of the moral problem, is alleviated by a boundless individual developing, set upon spiritual immortality, and a boundless universal developing, i.e. by a progress of culture.[1] Along these two paths man makes his way towards the Supreme Good. The free spirit raises the banners of revolt against the surrounding world, against the empirical actuality, which oppresses him; he strives to set the seal of his praeternal freedom upon the outer world and to create its culture, making use of the

---

[1] With Struve the idea of progress, possessing a paramount significance for ethics and for metaphysics, is left in the shadows, and he says almost nothing about it. This, in my view, leaves a large gap in his profoundly interesting and worthwhile "Preface".

necessary material means for ideal purposive ends. Progress from a philosophic and ethical point of view is first of all a liberation of the human "I" from the external paths.[1] Kant provides almost no sort of indications relative to how the moral law can and should be realised within human life.[2] In this regard the philosophy of Fichte, Schelling and Hegel was a large step forward, since the question was advanced concerning the realisation of the moral good within history. The positing of this question leads to a philosophy of progress, which in Kant was rarely mentioned. In such manner the individual moral problem becomes transformed into a social problem.

VII.

Society, societal developement is a necessary instrument in the moral growth of the human person. To the person however belongs an ethical (not sociological) primacy over society, and the evaluation of society always is made by the person on the strength inherent to it of the autonomous moral law, independent of society, and every societal form demands justification from the perspective of an ethical individualism. But the moral law is embodied into the life of mankind by way of societal progress, wherein the human person developes and works out his individualness by way of multifarious interactions within the societal medium, within the social-psychological communing of people.[3] First of all, for there to be a spiritual culture, the bearer of which is the person, whereby it can open forth into the empirical history of mankind, it needs

---

[1] The scientific-sociological perspective is altogether different and investigates societal developement, discerning the laws underlying what is happening.

[2] This is noted by Mr. Novgorodtsev in his book cited by us and, in getting out of this gap in the philosophy of Kant, leads to a very instructive parallel with the philosophy of Hegel.

[3] Sociology looks at individualness, as the result of the intersection of varied societal circles. This scientific truth nowise contradicts however the ethico-metaphysical theory of the person.

also a material societal basis. We therefore tend to demand economic growth and we welcome improved forms of production. And then, in order to guarantee the natural rights of the person, the external relations of people ought to have official regulation, i.e. in the state and governing structure there ought to be realised freedom and equality, which should demand and provide sanction for the inner moral autonomy of each human person. A governing and political progress involves naught else, than the realisation and guarantee of the absolute *natural rights*[1] of man, which should not be needful of any sort of historical a sanction, since this right is an unmediated expression of the moral law, a given prior to anything experiential; the entirety of economic progress, from a sociological point of view comprising a *conditio sine qua non* for every culture, from an ethical point of view remains always only a means for the triumph of natural law and the person. And therefore the societal side of the moral problem, first of all is rooted in the demands of the "natural law". Every modern form of the societal aspect, -- the modern form of production with its corresponding social organisation ought to be evaluated and seek justification, as a *means* for the realisation of an ideal *purposive end* -- of the natural rights of the person and of freedom and equality, since these are basic instances in the

---

[1] After the revival and deeper study into the philosophy of Kant, the arguments of the historical school concerning rights and that of the evolutionists against the theory of "natural right" tend to weaken. The phrase "natural right" can rouse a misunderstanding, since upon it lies the imprint of the out-dated XVIII Century with its faith in a "natural" order of things, to which was adapted the appeal to "nature" by J. J. Rousseau and many others. For us the concept of "natural" is identical with the normatively "normal", i.e. corresponding to ideal a norm. The historical mutability and relativity of law cannot be an argument against "natural law", since "natural law" is what ought to be rather than what is, and this is a"norm", which ought to be realised within the historical growth of law. Vide *Nogorodtsev*: "Kant and Hegel", p. 146-156. Vide likewise *Stammler* [Rudolf, 1856-1938]: "Wirtschaft und Recht", "Das Recht des Rechtes". Towards a natural law inclines also *Prof. Petrazhitsky* [alt. Petrazycki, Leon; 1867-1931] in his "Notes on Philosophy of Law", although in a philosophic regard he tends to fumble. Vide likewise *B. Chicherin* [Boris, 1828-1904]: "Philosophic Laws", 1900.

realisation of the natural law.[1] But the natural rights per se of the person are not yet still subject to any sort of renegotiation, whether from some perspective of societal utility, societal welfare, societal adaption etc, -- rather it is absolute a value. It is impossible, for example, that there should be taken away from a man his right to freedom of conscience on the grounds, that by majority vote this be admitted as useful. The person in its "by nature" rights is something sovereign, and only under the pressure of brute force can it be made to cede these rights. There is nothing ethically that can justify an infringement upon the natural rights of man, since in the world there is no such purposive end, in the name of which should be infringed the sacred strivings of the human spirit, to distort the principle of the human person as an end-in-itself. We repudiate the ethico-governing principle of the "people's sovereignty" and oppose to it the principle of inalienable personal rights. From whence issues the moral imperative: to fight for the natural rights of man, not to allow infringement upon them. To fight for his own natural rights is a matter of honour for each man, and the same thing also a matter of his conscience in relation to the natural rights of other people. In the concrete historical setting, the struggle for the "natural rights" of man assumes the form of a struggle against oppression and exploitation. In modern society, for example, it assumes the form of a struggle for the rights of the toiling masses.

The struggle over socialness, i.e. for a form of societal collaboration, is ethically always to be subordinated to the struggle for "humanness", i.e. the struggle for man, amid the proper sanctioning of such for him, but it is impossible to strongly enough to feel disdain for those, who out of their higher humanitarian considerations come nigh to a preaching of social-political indifferentism. This comprises first of all a misunderstanding. Philosophic and ethical idealism ought to inspire and ennoble the social-political struggle, ought to breathe into it a living soul,

---

[1] This relates likewise to socialism. Liberalism, in its ideal essential form, posits purposive ends: the growth of the person, the realisation of natural law, freedom and equality, whereas socialism uncovers only the modern means for a more consequential scope of these eternal principles. Tendencies towards a social-economic collectivism might be noted, as useful or even a necessary means, but an ethical and in general spiritual collectivism ought not to be connected with this and is overall a terrible evil.

but it should nowise lead to passivity in regard to the surrounding world, to a foreboding in contemplation of coercion and violence against man, against his spiritual nature. I have yet to turn to the question concerning the relationship between morality and freedom, and therein I shall attempt to point out all the sophistry underlying the assertion, -- that if there be inner freedom then needless is the demand for outward freedom. I should want to set a mark of shame upon those, who impudently and fecklessly conjoin within them the ugly contradiction -- an admitting for the human spirit as of an unconditional value, on the one hand, and a justification of oppression, exploitation and a trampling upon the elementary rights of man, on the other hand. That spirit, which idealism bears within it, is a spirit of freedom, a spirit of light, it summons forward, towards the struggle for the rights of a mankind endlessly aspiring to become perfected. Only a total darkening of thought would suggest, that the radical idea itself of an absolute "what ought to be" should be understood only but spiritualistically, thereby connecting it with an adherence to the most vile, the most reactionary forms of what exists. An absolute "what ought to be" is impossible to expect for whatever the consolidated form of empirical being, and the "imperative ought", about which the spiritualist speaks, is indeed worthy of this name, and is an appeal for an eternal struggle against the presently existing, in the name of all higher and higher forms of life, and this idea never and nowise permits of an appeasement.

VIII.

It is impossible at present to write about the moral problem, not having said anything concerning Fr. Nietzsche, and the point of view, which I above have attempted to develope, especially impels me to do so. In time, that "immoralist", that denier of morality -- Nietzsche, will be ranked among the most significant moral preachers, proponents of a new, a positive, a free morality. His agonised image stands straddling the boundary line between two eras and he combines within him the most extreme contradictions. Nietzsche is profoundly religious a soul, and through everything, that he wrote, runs an intricate threading of anguish over the loss of God. "Hear ye not? -- cried the madman in the "Gay Science", -- how already clamour not the grave-diggers, who do but bury God? Do ye not sense the smell of the decaying Divinity? -- and God indeed is become decayed! God is dead! Remains dead! And we have murdered Him! Murderers from murderers, in what shall we find consolation? The most sacred and mighty, as ever the world hath had, has bled to death 'neathe our knife!"[1] Towards the moral problem Nietzsche related with a passionate intensity and suchlike an acumen, not often met with amongst "moralists". The tormenting search for an absolute, an higher good and all the grief over the spiritual losses for Nietzsche poured forth in the form of a passionate protest against historical morality, against the morals of altruism, of societal utilitarianism, of hedonism and evolutionism, a protest in the name of the sovereignty of the "I". The "final man"[2] is that selfsame one, who has invented happiness, whilst in his historical morality he has forgotten about this "I". The whole prevailing modern morality seemed to Nietzsche to be craven, slave-like, herd-like, a morality purely negative, police-like, since at the basis of it lies a shrunken "I", degraded. The critical work of Nietzsche possesses enduring value, and comprises his immortal merit. The protest of Nietzsche against philistine morals along with those ethical theories, which would seek higher a moral sanction not in the "I", but rather in societal opinion, societal well-being, adaption to the average etc, -- all get swept aside and the soil cleared for a more correct and deeper setting of the moral problem, forgotten by the "final man" in his pursuit of trivial virtues and trivial well-being. "They are astonished, -- says Zarathustra, -- that I have no intent to concern myself over an unmasking of their lustings and vices; but, indeed, I am not of a mind to declaim against pocket robbers!" "I go amongst these people and I marvel: they *have changed* and they are become all still smaller: -- *and are reduced to this by their teaching about happiness and virtue...*" "Virtue they name that, what makes one tame and meek: already in such manner they have managed to transform the wolf into a dog, and man himself -- into the finest of domesticated animals". "They indeed in their virtues are also meek, since they seek for well-being. And with well-being can be reconciled only meek virtues". "They are all smooth, polite and decent -- each to the other, smooth like grains of sand, polite and good one to another". "Meekly to snatch at a little happiness -- this is what they call

---

[1] Vide "Nietzsche's Werke", Band V, p. 163.

[2] Ibid., B. VI, p. 19-20.

a "yielding to fate", and amidst this they already meekly squint at the consequently small happiness". "In the majority they desire one thing only -- that no one should cause them suffering. Here is why they first run up to you and do you good". "And this -- is the *worry*: barely also is it to be termed virtue!" "And I cry out to all the four corners of the world: ye are all become small -- ye diminished people, ye are crumbled tiny, -- ye lovers of well-being! And I yet so see, how ye perish from your innumerable little virtues, from innumerable petty grovellings!" "Too pitiful, too submissive -- is your earthly domain!..." "In order for a tree to grow up into a *grand* tree, it mustneeds enmesh strong rocks with strong roots..."

Nietzsche strives towards a *positive* morality: not towards a negation and curtailment of the "I", the cautioning against pickpockets and limitation of appetites, but rather towards an affirmation of the "I".[1] It is not a matter, expressed symbolically, of swiping someone's handkerchief from a pocket -- this is a truth, that no one will dispute, and all this but involves essentially outward and delimited matters of morals, as Nietzsche himself tended to understand. But it would be demeaning for a man to see in this the total essence of the moral problem, for the moral problem lies far deeper, and if it only begins when already it ends it would be only a cut and dry matter, the morality of a drill exercise, a police-sort hygienic morality for the well-being of life. Nietzsche had a sense of this depth of the moral problem and he was appalled by those teachings on morality, which see it as outward measures set against the human "I" on behalf of the "others", on behalf of "society", on behalf of its "opinions", on behalf of "societal opinion", measures in the interests of the general well-being. But Nietzsche himself did not address the moral problem nor get entangled in it.

What is the negative aspect of morality, what does it seek to limit? It is negative regarding any infringement against the "I", it shields against any manifestation of disrespect towards its rights. But what does it affirm? It affirms the "I", its right to self-determination, to endless growth, its thirst

---

[1] This is very deftly noted by M. Nevedomsky in his "In Place of a Preface" to the translation of a book by Lichtenberg [Georg, 1742-1799]. With Mr. Nevedomsky one tends to encounter original and interesting thoughts, but he quite fumbles matters in the philosophic regard. A clear example of a lack of philosophic insight is in his attitude towards the moral philosophy of Kant.

for power and perfection. In such manner we seem to have many a point in common with Nietzsche. But for us, morality is a problem inward and positive, not exteriour and negative. Morality is not some measure against hunger and cold, which loses all its meaning with the removal of the evil, on the contrary rather, this is a positive value, which extends off into infinity parallel with the negation of evil.

Everything, that Nietzsche tends to say about the altruistic morality of pity and sympathy, includes within it a terribly profound psychological and ethical truth. All this sort of morality still does not surmount the opposition between slave and master,[1] between the weak and the strong, and it therefore cannot be a morality for the future. I think, that it would be shameful to the dignity of man for a morality to be constructed upon a revolt of slaves, of the weak and afflicted, who would bear with them a demand for limiting and curtailment of the "I", i.e. they would infringe upon the very essence of life and the spirit. "Woe to all those loving, -- says Zarathustra, -- and not knowing anything more lofty, than their sufferings!"[2] And in actuality to relate to a man only with pity and sympathy means not to see in him a man equal in value to oneself, means to see only a weak and pitiful slave, and ultimately, this means to become oneself enslaved by the sufferings and weaknesses. There is more lofty a morals, which would correspond with more lofty a degree of developement of mankind, which would be grounded upon an upsurge of human strength, rather than upon human weakness, and which would demand not pity towards a slave, but rather respect towards a man, in regard to him as towards an "I", demanding the affirmation and actualisation of every "I" and consequently not the quenching of life, but rather uplifting it to its utmost spiritual condition. Only such a sort of morality corresponds to the lofty awareness of human dignity as should be appropriate for that portion of modern mankind, at the forefront of the great liberation movement. The moral law demands first of all, that a man never be a slave, even though it were a slavery concerning the suffering and weakness of someone else amidst one's own pity for him, in order that a man never quench his own spirit, disdaining his rights to the potency of life, to boundless growth and

---

[1] I am not employing the words "slave" and "master" in the social sense. Nietzsche himself never reflected the social point of view.

[2] Vide: "Nietzsche's Werke", B. VI, p. 130.

perfectability, even though this be a disdaining the well-being of other people and of all society. The human "I" ought not to bow its haughty head afront anything, except its own ideal perfection, its own God, before which only is it answerable. The human "I" stands higher than the judgement of other people, than the judgement of society or even the whole of being, since the solely unique judgement is manifest by that moral law, which comprises the true essence of the "I", which this "I" freely admits to. The demonic protest of the person against external morals, against societal opinion and even against all the outward world, to many indeed quite many seems "immoral", but from our point of view this is a profoundly moral revolt of the autonomous moral law, of a law, opening to man infinite perspectives, against the push on the part of the given objective actuality to convert man into a mere means and tool. This is a revolt of the strong in spirit in the name of spiritual strength and therefore it possesses an inner moral justification, against which all the surrounding world is morally impotent. In the "immoral" demonism of Nietzsche there are elements of that higher morality, which the ordinary and established morality tends usually to condemn.

Man not only has the right, but even a duty to be rendered into a "supra-man", since the "supra-man" is a path from man to God. "*I am come to preach to you the supra-man*, -- says Zarathustra to the throng gathered around him, -- man is something, that has to be surpassed. What have ye wrought, in order to surpass him?..." "All beings, as there have been up til now, have given birth to something grander than themself; and would ye to be an ebbing back away from this great surging wave and, perchance, prefer to return to the condition of a beast, merely so that man be not surpassed?" "What suchlike is the monkey for man? A laughing-stock or a shame and vexation. And the same would become man himself for the supra-man: a laughing-stock or a shame and vexation..." "Hearken, I do preach to ye the supra-man!" "The supra-man: this is the meaning of the earth. Let also your will proclaim: *let there be* the supra-man as the meaning of the earth!"[1] But further on Nietzsche enters upon false a path.

The idea of the "supra-man" is an idea religio-metaphysical. Zarathustra is a religious preacher, and Nietzsche gets off track in a biological perception of the "supra-man" and towards his exalted idea he instead flops into the earthly dirt; the dirt of the exploitation of man by

---

[1] Vide: "Nietzsche's Werke", B. VI, p. 13.

man. Nietzsche is a dreamer, an idealistic soul, poisoned by naturalism.[1] He well understands the inconsistency of all the positivist theories of morality, but he nonetheless still remains upon the soil of a naturalistic positivism. He fails to understand, that the affirmation and actualisation of the "I", its thirst for infinite might and perfectibility, not only is impossible to be thought of biologically, in forms of a Darwinian struggle for existence and selection, but also in general empirically, in the sense that herein it is impossible to postulate a supra-empirical ideal world. The beastly attitude of the "supra-man" towards man would be only a slave-like consequence of natural necessity and would take us instead from the heights of ethics down to the lower aspects of zoology.[2] At the summit heights of ethics an aristocracy of spirit (of the supra-human) can itself only be present in the form of a spiritual guide for people, not in any manner of physical, economic or political coercion, but rather as the prevailing of a spiritual excellence, knowledge and beauty. Carlyle with his "cult of heroes", despite its Old testament sort of tendencies, was in this regard more far-sighted, than was Nietzsche.

That selfsame "I", for which Nietzsche undertook gigantic a struggle, can prove to be a very typical empirical fact with all its ugliness; yet neither is this "I" within the narrow bounds of the positivist-biological perception of life. Upon this path we can meet up with the everyday vital egoism of the typical bourgeois, but there is not therein that ideal self-actualisation about which Nietzsche dreams of in his preaching of "individualism". In certain of his positive constructs, upon which lies the impression of "immoralness" and fierceness, Nietzsche gets himself off course onto a naturalistic evolutionism and even hedonism, against which he so often protests. If one were to regard the "I", as a chance empirical cluster of sensations, if one admit of only the sensory nature of man, then concerning an ethical individualism there is nothing to be said, and we risk

---

[1] In the greatest of his works, in the "Zarathustra", Nietzsche recourses to that idealistic spirit, which he displayed earlier in "The Birth of Tragedy", but he has come to serve as a fierce retribution for all the deficiencies of XIX Century thought.

[2] This was finely noted by Struve in his "Preface" to my book. With him generally can be found very nuanced critical remarks concerning Nietzsche.

falling into the web of a very crude hedonism and again we shall have to construct a morality not from within, but rather from the outside, i.e. to subordinate the person to the external criteria of "usefulness", "adaptability", etc. But in such an instance, how indeed does the "I" for Nietzsche rise up in revolt and provide such a brilliant critique to all the philistine morals and all the positivist theories on morality? All, that in Nietzsche which is of value and beauty, everything, that veils him in the name of unfading glory, is based upon one presupposition, needful for any ethics, the presupposition -- of an ideal "I", a spiritual "individualness". And by this philosophically is abolished the "immoralism", as an extreme misunderstanding, and Nietzsche can thus extend the hand to his enemy Kant. They both struggled for the moral autonomy of the human person, for its sacred right to self-determination. Kant provides the philosophic groundings for ethical an individualism, for acknowledging man as an end-in-itself and of unconditional a value; Nietzsche surmounts the philistine elements of the Kantian practical morals and prepares for the free morals of the future, the morality of a strong human individualness.

If opposite to the morals of Nietzsche be contrasted -- a Christian morality, then in it would be found that selfsame ideal essence. The central idea, which Christianity has introduced into the developement of the moral self-consciousness of mankind, is the idea of the absolute value of man, as in the image and likeness of God, and the moral equal-value of people before God. Along with this, Christianity conceived of the moral problem, as a problem inward, a problem of the relationship of the human spirit to God. This was a tremendous step forward in comparison with the moral consciousness of the ancient world, which did not admit of an unconditional value for man, it subordinated the person to the state and demanded external sanctions regarding morality. The modern idea of the person is incomparably more developed than that imperfect idea, which obtained some two thousand years back, but the Christian spiritualism provides an eternal sanctioning for that ethical individualism, towards which we strive, and which was dear also to that "immoralist" Nietzsche. Christianity, as an ideal (in non-historical a sense) faith-teaching, never resorts to a police-type understanding of morality, while that respect for the dignity of man and his inner freedom, which comprises the unfading moral essence of Christianity, and which cannot be undone by modern hypocrites, such as have the brazenness to veil over their spiritual nakedness with spiritualistic words, from which all content of value has shrivelled.

The Christian preaching of an inner goodness and kindness in the name of an ideal perfecting of man, approaching nigh close to God, and all the beauty and charm of this inner morality, are beyond the conceptual abilities indeed whether by the official statist sorts, or by the societal utilitarianists, with their crude external criteria. Regretably I have not the possibility, for reasons of external consideration, to tackle this question in all its entirety.

IX.

I have already said, that upon practical ethics sits the seal of triteness, insulting for a thinker. The sole means for hoisting ethics above the pettiness and triteness, -- is to view the moral problem in connection with the basic problems of metaphysics, which I have also attempted to do. The "accursed questions", which have tormented the some whatever sort Ivan Karamazov -- moreso correspond to addressing the heights and the depths of the moral problem, than all the commands and prohibitions of the shallow worldly morality, such as seek to train man into a being fit for life generally. Some whatever Leonardo da Vinci or Goethe get frowned on by every moral mediocrity, such as are proud of their own shallowly "useful" virtues, compared to those immoral ones, but who of these judges is of a condition to measure the depth of spirit of Goethe or Leonardo da Vinci? We say, that one of the basic tasks of morality is the struggle against philistinism, against the quasi-intellectual shallowness, a struggle for the spiritually aristocratic aspect of the human soul. And this is possible only by way of a consciousness of vivid individuality, which has the wherewithal to defend its human visage in all its uniqueness from all the attempts to obliterate and level it. Philistinism and the moral shallowness provide quite much an insight into the mode of life of progressive mankind, and ethical individualism ought especially to contend against this evil.[1] On this point, philosophic ethics declares war against the everyday traditional morality, for in this sort of morality quite often it is compelled to see an enemy to the human individuality and, consequently, an enemy to true morality. The human "I", at the basis of which for all people lies one

[1] This can be said also for the working class. In its progressive social-political strivings there still mustneeds be introduced an ideal moral content which, certainly, cannot be that of "class".

and the same spiritual essence, within life is arrayed in flesh and blood, it has to be unique, to have its own nuance, its own say, to be an *individuality.* Man is a "many-sided being", and he ought not to have to endure a levelling down, to have to protest against attempts to drill him into fitting a single stereotype, to render him into a "chorus-girl", to turn him into useful an exemplar for the herd, whatsoever the "societal benefits" these infringements accrue. There is no single non-personal capability of realisation of the moral good, these capabilities are manifold and individual. Equality, which rests upon the moral equal-value of people, in the social regard cannot and ought not to go further than an equality of rights and the removal of classes, and as a condition for the factual realisation of equality before the law, and in the psychological regard, it cannot and ought not to go farther than a semblance of those basic spiritual features, which are there also of each man. I think, that a spiritual aristocracy is possible also within a democratic society, although within such it would have nothing in common with any social-political oppression. To such an aristocracy namely, standing above every societal class and group morality, ought to belong the initial impulses towards utmost a progress, lest there obtain a domain of stagnation amidst the herd. The great moral imperative proclaims, that man ought always to be himself, and this means to be true not only to his spiritual "I", but also to that individual path, by which it is activated. Man has a sacred duty freely to follow his own "calling", and this calling cannot be for him bound up merely with any sort of collective empirical unit.

By a path free
Go thou, whither the free mind doth attract thee,
Ripening the fruits of beloved thoughts,
No reward demanding for effort noble.
They be within thee thyself. Thou thyself -- thine highest judge.

from Pushkin sonnet "To the Poet".

The greatest moral crime is the loss of person, the betrayal of one's own "I" under the pressure of external forces.

And "duty", they tell us, whither should go this "duty", which comprises the basis of morality? I already have said, that duty, the imperative ought is first of all a formal idea, gnosseologically in opposition to what exists, i.e. to being. Now we can speak about the content of duty.

The moral duty of man is a matter of self-actualisation, the developing of his spiritual "I" towards an ideal perfectability; to follow out one's duty and to follow out one's own moral-reasoning nature are identical concepts. Only a philistine sort of morals understands duty, as something external for man, attached from the side, hostile to him. The consciousness of duty, or the same thing, of the moral law is a consciousness of one's own true "I", of one's own lofty human destiny. To cripple one's own "I", to cripple one's own human individuality in the name of duty -- here are words, which for us do not possess any sort of meaning. We confess the morality of an absolute duty, the fulfilling of an higher spiritual good, but the word "duty" does not possess for us an unacceptable historical twist. An opposition of "duty" and the "I" from an ethical point of view is absurd, since "duty" is inherent to the law-giver "I".

Here is a man of austhere duty, we often hear, he never follows his own cravings, he constantly struggles with himself and coerces himself, he always proceeds as duty bids him, and not as he himself would want. Here is the everyday psychological view on duty. Philosophic ethics has to lift itself above this everyday understanding of duty, it can even be sharply disdainful towards such a "man of duty", can state that in him is an absence of some bit of a developed self-consciousness and even consider him lacking in morals in his fulfilling of duty, if this sense of duty extinguishes his human "I" in the name of traditional dictates from the outside, as though he were not "human".[1] "Humanness", i.e. the actualisation of "man" in himself and the respect towards "man" in someone other is higher a duty, and the degree of its realisation is first of all a measure of moral level. Within man there always occurs the struggle of good against evil, of the lofty against the lowly, the struggle of the spiritual "I" against the chaotic content of the empirical consciousness, in which are quite many sides, not human and not humane an admixture. Along this course is wrought the "person" and moral developement accomplished. But morally lofty and fine is not that man, who does good through clenched teeth, limiting and curtailing his human individuality, but rather the one who, in doing good, is joyfully conscious of this self-actualisation, in the affirming of his "I".

---

[1] In this regard quite exceptional of interest and characteristic is the image of Brand for Ibsen.

Kant interpreted in too old a fashion the idea, that human nature is sinful and corrupted, and he arrived at a whole series of false ethical positions, at the root of which is denying of the *Dionysian* principle in life. He was correct only in this regard, that he considered the moral law as a law of the will, and not of the sensory. But we should want to set free the life of the senses, as a life unmediated. Sensory nature itself per se is not evil, it is ethically neutral, it becomes evil only then, when it obstructs the developement of the *person*, when it obscures the higher self-consciousness and self-realisation. Said more clearly: the purely elemental play of powers within man possesses enormous an ethical value, and as regards ethics, this play of powers is not condemned by ethics. Instincts per se are neither moral nor non-moral, but a man without instincts would be lacking for flesh and blood, and in the aspects of experience he would not be alive. The human "I" developes by way of an augmenting of life and therefore the old adage "to live life to the full" never loses its significance. Within man there is a mad thirst for a life intense and vivid, a life of power and might, even though it have its evil, if not good. This is an extraordinarily valuable thirst and granted it is better to intoxicate a man with it, than for it to be absent altogether. This is the god Dionysos providing the wherewithal to know, and to whom Nietzsche raised such a fine memorial in all his works, and who commandingly summons to the elements in life, to its growth. The moral task consists not in a limiting of this thirst, but in its conjoining with the affirmation and growth of the spiritual "I". Without this moral self-awareness of "making a mountain out of a mole-hill", even the Dionysian thirst for life would be slaked exclusively by that wantonness, in which it would be impossible to find anything more. We bow before the beauty of all the mighty vital impulses, we affirm life to the extent of infinitude. Life in all its capacity, but for all this, in order that life actually be powerful, extensive and boundless, it has to be filled with *valuable* a content, i.e. within it ought to be a growth of *spiritness*, in it ought to be actualised the ideal God-manly "I".

X.

I now move along to a perchance very important question -- the relationship of the moral problem to freedom. Kant constructs all his ethics upon the postulate, upon the positing of freedom, and for him the moral problem is first of all the problem of freedom; he presupposes a dualism between the realm of freedom and the realm of nature (necessity).[1] The moral law by its origin and by its nature belongs to the realm of freedom, not to the realm of necessity, and it demands the autonomy of the human person. Only a free fulfilling of the moral law elevates man: freedom is also the moral nature of the human "I". All the arguments against the realm of freedom, taken from the arsenal of the realm of necessity, are alike naive and inconsistent, based upon unproven and unprovable presuppositions, such that the scientific-cognitive point of view on necessity be considered the sole and final point of view, and that experience, which is the offspring of only one side of our consciousness, should be considered the sole and ultimate instance. We well know, that within the bounds of experience it is impossible to breach the gaps in determinism, that here there cannot be a greater or lesser degree of necessity, but we also cannot set freedom in opposition to determinism in the sense of a mutual exclusion, rather it is that we admit of a parallelism betwixt the world of freedom and the world of necessity.

Freedom is a self-determination of the person, the imprint of freedom rests upon everything that is in accord with the "I", that issues forth from its inner existence. Freedom is not a negative concept, as bourgeois thinkers tend to assert, and for whom it is only the absence of constraintive circumstances; rather, freedom is a positive concept, it is the synonym of all the inner spiritual creativity of the human person. But to be free does not mean to be determined by the empirical "I", with its fortuitous content derived from experience; rather, freedom is the self-determination of the spiritual "I". From Kant's perspective man is free, when he is determined not by his sensory, but rather by his moral-reasoning nature. And I think, that it is possible to posit a sign of identity between the inner moral freedom and that spiritual "I", which we have set as the basis for ethics. From the gnosseological point of view freedom is the defining of the person by a "normative consciousness" (i.e. by ethical

[1] Vide Kant: "Grundlegung zur Metaphysik der Sitten", p. 74-77.

norms) in opposition to a determinative defining by fortuitous empirical motives.[1] And this leads us to a triumph of freedom and morality. The triumph of the moral good is a triumph of the "normative" consciousness, of the spiritual "I", i.e. the triumph of freedom. If morality is naught else, than a self-actualisation, then consequently it is a liberation. The individual and the universal moral growth is a triumph of the realm of freedom within the realm of necessity, i.e. the growth of that self-determination of the human person, when all human creativity is subordinated to the spiritual "I". And now we can ascertain the worthiness or not of that overreaching assertion, that the "ethical norms" and the "absolute moral law" tend to infringe upon the freedom of man. The demand of an absolute moral law is the demand of an absolute freedom for the human "I". The fulfilling of the moral law, as a violent assault upon the "I", is a *contradictio in adjecto*, for this fulfilling is always autonomous. But there are certain, perhaps, who will tend to say, that from this the empirical person will wind up suffering, in talking about its freedom. Regretably, the concept of the empirical person is not only indefinable, it is even altogether unthinkable, and from it there is no pathway towards the realm of freedom. To be a "person", to be a free man -- means to be conscious of one's own moral-reasoning nature, to fashion out one's own "normal" ideal "I" from the chaos issuing from the chance empirical interweaving of facts; but this empirical chaos itself per se is not yet still a "person' and inapplicable to it is the category of freedom. And to bow down afront the empirical fact -- represents idolatry at the altar of necessity, rather than a divine-service at the altar of freedom.

Of what sort is the relationship of an inner freedom to external freedom, of a freedom moral to a freedom societal? I have already said, that the moral problem inevitably gets turned into a problem societal, since the human person can develope and find fulfillment by manifold a content only within society, in psychological an interaction with other people, in the process of forming a common culture. Is it possible to reconcile the inward self-determination of the person, its moral freedom and of the admitting for it an absolute value, is it possible to reconcile this against outward oppression, against its exploitation by other people and by the goals of groups, with the mocking of its human dignity by societal institutions? How can those people and those groups, who finally have

---

[1] Vide Windelband: "Präludien", p. 239.

become conscious within themself of the dignity of man and the inalienable "natural" rights of his person, how can they put up with the resorting to violence and lawlessness? To these questions there cannot be twofold answers, here any sort of wavering would be shameful. What sort of intellectual justifications can be offered in defense of the outlook of reactionaries and obscurantists, the pagan-priests of violence, that can lessen their terrible guilt afront the human spirit and ameliorate a just retribution? Herein perhaps consists an historical explanation of societal evil, but there is no moral justification.

Ethics clearly and definitely demands the realisation of the "natural rights" of the human person and does not permit in this regard any sort of compromises, and by this it demands a guarantee of the rights of the citizen; ethics likewise together with this unconditionally condemns class antagonisms, as quite large an obstacle to the growth of man. From an ethical point of view are justified all the efforts, directed towards a winning of that minimum of rights, amidst which only is also possible an existence worthy of man; from an ethical point of view it would be shameful for man not to insist upon these his rights, which appear necessary a condition of ideal self-actualisation. If from the point of view of natural necessity it be shown, that violence, injustice and oppression of man ought to be increased, that freedom is an unrealisable daydream, then still the imperatives of ethics would therein also remain in full force, and evil would be no less repulsive, merely that mankind would still have to fall into a struggle against it. But the assertions of the reactionaries tend to shatter also from the perspective of necessity.

People struggle within society by way of joining into groups, and thus within history we meet not especially with the struggle of individual people, but rather a struggle between societal groups. The modern societal groupings reveal broad perspectives, conditional upon necessity, and grounded upon which the human spirit both can and ought to create a better, more free future. The creativity for the future is always overshadowed for us by not only the light of natural necessity, but likewise by the light of our moral freedom. Now we, it would seem, can boldly say, that on our side is displayed not only truth, but also power.[1]

---

[1] In this regard it is impossible not to admit the tremendous merits of Marxism, the realistic side of which we have to admit.

Reactionaries have become accustomed to contending against a materialistic grounding to the justification of the liberation strivings, but quite stronger and more intense would be the appeals of idealism. Idealism lays bare the total spiritual poverty of every reactionary ideology -- amidst which a Christian would preach a beastly violence against people, and the spiritualist drags every manifestation of spirit into a police station.[1] Spiritualism, acknowledging the unconditional value of the human spirit, cannot be united with a justification such as is external, often directly physical a manner of violent coercion against this spirit; spiritualism cannot manifest itself in an official capacity and preach the ugly lie, that a free spirit ought to feel wonderful in a slave society. That modern idealistic current, to which I proudly account myself, tends to infer the necessity of the liberation struggle for "natural rights" from the spiritual hunger of the intelligentsia soul.[2]

We insufficiently appreciate and insufficiently still understand the profound significance of that critique of the existing order, which Lev Tolstoy undertook from the point of view of a Christian idealism. After Tolstoy, for many it was impossible still to consider matters so indifferently, as were earlier considered, and the voice of conscience hence more persistently demands a pondering morally over life, to remove the monstrous moral contradictions, which among the representatives of power assume criminal a character.[3]

I conclude my article with the basic, it seems to me, deduction: the person mustneeds exist and his right to the image and likeness of God ought not to be traded off for any manner of benefit in the world, neither

---

[1] "The National Question in Russia" of Vl. Solov'ev -- is a classic sample of an idealistic critique of the reactionary-nationalists, but Solov'ev did not think it through to the end nor did he make all the necessary deductions from spiritualism.

[2] This thought was mentioned by Struve in an article, the "Supreme Value of Life". Beginning with this inconclusive article within Russian progressive literature, all the moreso is provided a basis towards a constructive idealistic current.

[3] "Tolstoyanism" with all its negative sides has long ago already lost all significance in the life of the Russian intelligentsia and therefore the positive merits of Tolstoy can now be objectively evaluated.

for the happiness and contentment of his own nor even for that of all mankind, nor for the tranquility and approval of people, nor for power and success in life; necessary also is the demand for the recognition and guarantee for one's own human right to self-determination and the developing of all one's spiritual potentials. And first of all for this there has to be asserted on firm foundations the fundamental condition of respect for man and spirit -- for freedom.

Endnote "a" [p. 61]:

Two things fill the mind with ever new and increasing wonderment and awe, the oftener and the more steadily we reflect on them: *the starry heavens above and the moral law within me.*

Kant. "The Critique of Practical Reason".

...Man and generally any rational being exists as an end in himself, and not merely as a means to be arbitrarily used by this or that will, but in all his actions, whether they concern himself or other rational beings, must be always regarded at the same time as an end.

Kant. "Groundwork of the Metaphysics of Morals".

I go amidst these people and keep my eyes open: they have become smaller and smaller and smaller: such however their doctrine of happiness and virtue doth do...

Too much gentle, too much yielding: that is your soil! But that a tree should grow mighty, it has to enmesh firm roots around the hard rock! ...

Oh, that ye would understand my word: ultimately do what ye want -- but first be such, as one that would want to!

Nietzsche. "Also sprach Zarathustra".

I teach the supra-man. Man is something, that shalt be overcome. What hath ye done, to overcome him?

Nietzsche. "Also sprach Zarathustra".

Endnote "b" [p. 74]:

This principle of mankind and of every rational nature in general, is that as of *an end in itself* (which comprises the supreme limiting condition of the freedom of action of every man), derives not from experience, firstly, because it is universal, extending as it does to all rational beings in general, and no sort of experience is capable of determining anything about it; secondly, because it does not present humanness as an end for mankind (subjectively), i.e. as an object, which one actually oneself adopts as an end; but as an objective end, which must as a law constitute the supreme limiting condition of all our subjective ends, whatever they should be what we may consider; it must therefore spring from pure reason. And namely the grounding of all practical legislation *objectively* lies in the rule and form of universality, which (in accord with the first principle) also bestows it the character of a law (in any case the character of a law of nature), rendering it (on the first principle) subjectively however -- into an end; the subject of all the ends is however each rational being as an end in itself (on the second principle); and hence follows now the third practical principle of the will, as the supreme condition of its accordance with the universal practical reason: *the idea of the will of every rational being as a will, of universally established laws.*

Kant. "Groundwork of the Metaphysics of Morals". [2nd Section].

Endnote "c" [p. 78]:

"Ye flee afront yourself unto the next, -- says Zarathustra, -- and wouldst make it a virtue hence: but I do see through your "selflessness". "The Thou is spoken as holy, but nowise still the I: thus doth man push himself downwards towards the next".

Nietzsche.

A Critique of Historical Materialism

(1903 - 108)[1]

I.

A critical reconsidering of the doctrine of historical materialism at present seems to me especially important and timely, since particularly with this doctrine is tied in a large portion of the disputes and discord, both the theoretical as well as the practical, foisted by Marxism onto the surface of intellectual and societal life. The theory of historical materialism, very interesting and remarkable as to its role in the history of societal ideas, advocates a whole series of false sociological and historico-philosophic presuppositions and even outright superstitions, which stand in the way of the developement of social and philosophic thought and hinder explanation of the most urgent questions, and which impede agreement and cooperation on whatever the common task, alike near and dear for each of the disputing sides.

The materialistic dogmatics, by which quite many are still infected, needs to be torn up by the roots, and at the root for the majority is a faith in the dogmas of historical materialism and in particular the so-called "class" point of view, which in the hands of a large portion of its adherents is wielded as a weapon against the humanly-general logic and the humanly-general ethics, and therefore excludes the possibility of any sort of logical or morally obligatory arguments. And amidst this, quite little still has been done by way of a critique of the very core aspect of historical materialism, almost little the same, as regards its groundings. In the disputes between the "critics" and the "ortodoks-orthodox"[2] some likewise themself perceive

---

[1] KRITIKA ISTORICHESKOGO MATERIALIZMA. Article was originally published in the monthly journal "Mir Bozhii", S. Peterburg, oct. 1903, p. 1-30.

[2] I employ this admittedly conditional terminology, although it fails to characterise the current as to its content of idea, and soon indeed it will

the falsity of certain dogmas of Marxist sociology, while others perceive it as the indubitable truth, and therefore the disputants quite often wind up seeming to be speaking different languages and appear like the proverbial "barbarians" brawling amongst themself.[1] "Bourgeois" in the true sense of the word, the criticists on behalf of Marxism and historical materialism have but intensified the position of the class theory. Their crude lack of understanding and ugly insinuations have fed off that superstitious sort of feeling, which up til now impedes free mental creativity, and dogmatically divides science into the bourgeois and the non-bourgeois, amidst which as bourgeois a science is viewed not an intended defense of the bourgeoise, of bourgeois society and bourgeois ideals, such as might be totally just and allowable, but instead there is smeared without basis any scientific and philosophic work, which does not confess all the class dogmas of the ortodoks-orthodoxy. There gets carried out a particular inquiry to discern a "bourgeois" material basis via a very intensive truth-interrogation, in its very passionate thirst for justice. In such manner, at one stroke of the pen there gets excised and disallowed any free and progressive work of thought, any idealistic search for new paths; it is excised and disallowed not by way of arguments and demonstrations, but rather in the old manner, inherited from Catholicism, by way of an "excommunication"; whereby it seems sufficient but to indicate, that whosoever deviates from the "class" point of view and engages in clear contradictions to Marx, is adjudged a rotten heretic, a "bourgeois".

I have tended to show a great deal of deference and even disdain towards such a sort of polemics, insofar as it was directed against me, and I do not see in it any sort of a decidedly theoretical value, -- this in regard of ideas is a *quantite negligeable*, and as such herein a matter cannot be expressed in essence, since the in essence aspect itself tends to get replaced

---

become completely out-moded and will assume more expressive a note. The "critics" not only criticise, but likewise promote a positive worldview.

[1] The true-believer economic Marxists regard as "barbarians" all who think differently, all who are insufficiently pervaded by the proletarian "class" psychology.

by "polemical niceties".[1] But the matter is not all so simple, and the core issue here is not in the tendency of these or some other personages displaying not altogether correct polemic mannerisms, with snipings and insinuations, rather it involves the basic character of their worldview, of their dogma, which many believe in so sacredly, so selflessly and confidently, that involuntarily one might overlook their nasty polemical pranks and instead yield to that pure idealistic source, from which issues the thirst for justice, though also it get mixed in with false theoretical ideas. An idealist by nature does not expend his whole "faith" upon trite crumbs of the good, upon all the tiny tweakings, nowise a part of some sort of a common great idea; he can instead only but move on towards a new "faith", one that is still higher and likewise coherent and widespread, but this process is not without worry and, in any case, is continuing a matter. In the "ortodoks-orthodox", in my opponents, always dear to me has been their passionate desire to defend the integrity and purity of their ideal, since within this I see an ineradicable idealism of the human soul, which bursts forth nonetheless through the materialistic trappings. But this idealistic demand, enlightened and expansive, can find itself a genuine satisfaction only in a new "faith", over the conceiving of which we now have to work. In order to clear the soil for a new world-concept and outlook, it becomes necessary to shed a critical light upon the fundamental positions of historical materialism, which are all still considered beyond doubt. The "non-bourgeois" critiques of Marxism up til now have done this relatively by way of a series of particular sociological questions, but they have turned attention insufficiently towards those basic presuppositions, upon which rests the *class* point of view and the materialistic exposition of the *ideology*.[2]

---

[1] I have in view that polemic directed against me on the part of the "ortodoks-orthodox", whilst I was deprived of the opportunity forthwith to reply.

[2] Within Russian literature I cannot fail to mention the very valuable article by B. Kistyakovsky entitled, "The Category of Necessity and the Category of Justice within Investigations of Social Phenomena".

II.

In entering upon a critique of historical materialism ,we first of all have to take note of its total methodological and gnosseological naiveté. Among the adherents of this teaching there exist extremely muddled views upon the character of this discipline, to which their "materialism" is to conform. Is this discipline historical, sociological or historico-philosophic? A definitive answer to this important methodological question is impossible to receive from the economic materialists. The Marxist "materialism" is a gnosseologically-naive mishmash of concrete positions on history, of abstractive-scientific positions from sociology along with metaphysical ideas from the philosophy of history. Insofar as historical materialism preaches monism, it constructs a theory of progress and applies towards the social process the presuppositions of a general philosophic sort of materialism, and promotes into a sort of quality the philosophy of history, which is purely a metaphysical discipline. The materialistic philosophy of history tends to get defended by those, who most of all hold dear the totality of their worldview, and they tend all the more readily to recourse to the term "dialectical materialism". For such an adherent of the materialistic understanding of history as a philosophic world-concept we have first of all Engels himself, and then the populariser of Engels, N. Bel'tov. But historical materialism aspires likewise to formulate a science concerning society, it sets itself the goal more especially to discern abstract sociological principles, investing such indeed with scientific a value, as laws of natural science. A total methodological clarity of this purely sociological task is grasped by almost not a single one of the representatives of historical materialism, with this methodological mishmash being one of the dogmas of orthodox a sort, but in any case historical materialism makes a pretense at forming a sociological theory and advancing a science relative to society. Suchlike are all the attempts to establish constant correlations between differing sides of the societal process, which are methodologically isolated and are the result from the empirical chaos of concrete history, and suchlike purely is the sociological theory of the struggle of societal groups and of societal differentiation. And finally, overall and most simply -- this conceiving of historical materialism, whether as purely an historical theory, or as a remarkable attempt to gain an orientation within concrete history, chiefly dwells upon the history of the bourgeois-capitalistic era. And suchlike primarily is the historical focus within the greater part of the works of Marx himself. Kautsky however is inclined to devote to "materialism" more narrow an historical emphasis, for him historical materialism is not so much a philosophic worldview or abstract teaching about society, as rather a method for the interpreting of concrete history.

The constant jumbling together of primarily different tasks, -- the philosophic, the sociological and the historical, -- leads to a very vague sort of teaching, which variously gets termed as "historical", "economic" or "dialectical" a materialism. This mishmash aspect hinders opponents from catching sight of important truths, concealed within this teaching, and the orthodox proponents are in turn compelled to defend positions of obvious nonsense. By way of a critique of the groundings of historical materialism, I shall all the while be indicating this confused medley of varied tasks and various disciplines. The inference from my criticism would be this, that the greatest significance would nonetheless accrue to historical materialism, as purely an historical theory, aware of its limitations, and that for sociology it can provide important material, although it can neither be nor can be spoken of as a materialistic sociology, and finally, that historical materialism least of all should be considered a philosophy of history, since the latter is possible only upon the basis of an idealist metaphysics. I begin with a critique of monism, which rests at the core of a materialistic conception of history and comprises as it were an original sin as to this understanding, since monism in all its forms is inadmissible not only in sociology, but in general in whatever the science.

III.

All the empirical actuality, all the objects of scientific cognition, given us within experience, by nature both organic and inorganic, the human soul and the history of mankind strikes us by its extraordinary diversity, in the world is such an abundance of colours, all so individual and so difficult to get orientated with this palette of colours, in this multiplicity of hues. Science first of all dissects and analyses within this empirical chaos, it rests wholly upon the principle of the isolation of a certain group of phenomena that obtain via experience within the chaotic diversity. Scientific knowledge begins strictly only then, when an analysis has been performed separating out from the "all", from the "totality" which we term nature, the world etc, separating out a whole series of more or less alike qualities, e.g. phenomena that are physical or chemical, biological or psychological etc. Only through such a manner does the knowledgeable mind become oriented within the empirical world and come to scientific generalisations, it establishes affinities and differences, discerns typical correlations which, in having discovered characteristics obligatory in common across all time and space, are termed laws.

It is not my intention here to go at depth into purely gnosseological questions, and for me the only important point is to establish the following basic gnosseological position: science, every science, by its very essence and purpose, by the character of its objects and by its methods for knowledge -- is *pluralistic*, in it there cannot be nor ought to be talk of monism, of everything equally materialistic or somehow otherwise; monistic attempts always appear as the result of an uncritical confusing of the tasks of positive science with the tasks of philosophy and metaphysics. A number of times already it has been pointed out, that for sciences in general, for science concerning the world as regards the "end-purpose" -- does not exist; suchlike a scientific discipline not only factually but also logically cannot be, since it would be in contradiction to the initial starting point of all the positive scientific cognition -- it would be an ascertaining from the totality, from this multiplicity a typical common series, in which could be found abstract correlations. Science begins only then, when it has determined its limits, its particular object and its particular methods, and this is corroborated by all the history of science. And hence there exist only individual sciences with their specialised tasks, and therefore we know only the laws of physics and of chemistry, of biology and psychology, and we strive also to find the laws of sociology, but we know nothing about laws of some sort of a non-existent universal science, concerning an end-purpose. It is typical, that concerning monism, many talk only as it applies to non-specified sciences, not yet having separated out their tasks from the instead metaphysical tasks. Concerning a monistic astronomy and a monistic physics nothing is heard, comparatively little is said about a monistic biology, yet rather moreso about a monistic psychology and to an extraordinary degree about a monistic sociology, but here the question about monism hardly involves the basic question of the sociological science, as rather that in its triumph many see a guaranteed future via this woesome science.

And actually the question about monism appears to be a very hot question for contemporary sociology, but only in one sense: sociology renders itself scientific only then, when sociology catches on to the fact, that in science there cannot be monism, that the task of sociology is to discover the laws unique to sociological phenomena, rather than trying to interpret the historical process from some sort of single principle, some singular source. Sociology ought literally to have involvement indeed only by philosophers, in order to conceive of all the differences between scientific sociology and the philosophy of history, the differences between positive science and metaphysical philosophy. The obvious sign of the absence of philosophic a spirit among the sociologists -- is their obstinate desire to scientifically provide sociological answers to purely philosophic, metaphysical questions. Upon this defective reasoning is based the dream about a monistic sociology. And in actual fact, what can be indicative of monism within sociology?

Monism strives to interpret everything, all the world from a single source, a single principle, -- all the very diverse qualities it seeks to infer back to some sort of initial quality, it cannot be content with any sort of multiplicity, it consequently cleaves to one and disregards along the way everything individual, all the diversity within experience. The monistic striving for the oneness of unity is a verymost deep and ineradicable demand of human reasoning, and all the greatest philosophers were, in a certain sense, monists. But in what manner can there be possible a sociological satisfying of this monistic demand? Sociology, just like with every science, starts with a distinguishing of sociological phenomena, of societal phenomena, from out of the whole of nature, from out of all the diversity of the empirical world. The "social" is acknowledged as a particular quality, empirically indissoluble, and within these limits there results the possibility to find the necessary correlations. In distinguishing the societal, the "social" aspect, from out of all the aggregate of the world totality, sociology starts an inner analysis, with a methodological isolation of the various sequences within the societal process, as e.g. the economic, the legal etc, and in such manner it establishes abstracted correlations which, even if not now, then eventually will assume that overall obligatory character, which permits terming them, these abstracted correlations, as sociological laws.

If sociology begins to seek a singular, an original and finalative aspect within the societal process, then it is only through inconsistency and an half-fast approach that it can stop short within the societal phenomena and assure itself that the admitting of suchlike a singularly original and finalative aspect is indeed the same thing as the "social". A consistent monism would demand a going beyond the bounds, separating society off from the remaining nature, it would lead sociology dealing with the worldly aggregate, and its erudite task and purpose, to construct a science regarding society, would be plunged into the waves of infinitude. Herein begins, at higher a degree, a whole series of captivating and important philosophic problems, but sociology, with its more modest and specialised scientific tasks, gets to be forgotten entirely. How does one adapt a materialistic monism, which though rather ill-suited yet in any case is purely a metaphysical theory, -- how does one adapt it to sociology, to the social process? Since materialistic monism teaches, that the singular original and finalative basis is matter, and from it proceeds all the diversity of the world; then from this perspective the consequent conclusion in its application to the social process ought to eliminate the boundary, separating society from nature and ought likewise to reveal within all the diversity of society that selfsame singular matter, which is revealed within the diversity of nature. N. Bel'tov quite consistently also says, that in the impossibility of a purely mechanical interpretation of history is lodged a weakness of dialectical materialism, and he refers to the incompleteness of other sciences in this regard. But the strength of historical materialism rests entirely upon this its weakness, its strength consisting in this, -- that in pursuing the resolution of purely a metaphysical problem by means of a materialistic monism, it nonetheless along the way expresses sociological values and historical thoughts. Everything, such as is true and vital in historical materialism, is in direct contradiction to the monistic tendency to drown all the social nuances within the bland sea of the singular sort worldly matter.

But there can still be an inconsistent application of materialistic monism to the social process, and suchlike are all the attempts to find a single, initial *social matter* within the social process. Suchlike a social type of matter is avowed by economics, as the productive powers. Particularly in this form is the monism for a large portion of the economic materialists. But the transference of monism into a specific science, into a partial sphere of empirical phenomena -- this is an evident gnosseological absurdity, a sort of neither this nor that, neither science, nor philosophy. Science does not come nigh to the singular and the initial in that group of phenomena, with which it happens to deal, it does not posit a finalative sort of questions and does not provide that sort of understanding and explanation, which can only be provided by philosophy, whereas philosophy goes quite farther and seeks for the singular and original not in suchlike partial an area, as the societal aspect, but rather in the essence of the world, revealed in all actuality in general and the social process in particular.

The concept itself of matter regarding social life (economics, productive forces) is established by sociology by way of isolation, by determining a certain sequence from the aggregate of social phenomena, -- this is the offspring of the "pluralistic" method[1] in sociology, and not "monistic". Everything that is of value in historical materialism, bears upon it the imprint of scientific pluralism and has nothing in common with monism. The valuable aspect consists in this, that methodologically there is distinguished a material side of societal life, there are established necessary correlations within this sphere (economic laws) and correlations between this side and other sides of the societal aspect, as a developing of human culture (sociological laws). Monism is not there at either the initial nor at the concluding point of the sociological investigation, since the sociological investigation involves a distinguishing apart of the societal aspect separate from all of nature in its diversity, and by way of this methodological isolation it establishes various sequences within the societal process and discovers in them and between them necessary abstract correlations, i.e. sociological laws. There are certain who still conceive of monism as an application of the principle of causality towards all phenomena, i.e. a consequent involvement of scientific determinism, but this is a misuse of terminology, since monism is an ontological teaching. This principle of causality obtains as obligatory amidst the scientific investigation of all the phenomena of the world, and this is a truth, which at the present time not a single adherent of philosophic dualism tends to deny. It is known likewise, that for psychology there are such determinists, as e.g. Wundt, who seek to establish a principle of an inner psychic causality, distinct from the outer physical sort. Yet for social phenomena a physical causality likewise seems unsuitable, since determinism still fails to lead to monism.

---

[1] Suchlike a special method, certainly, does not exist, and I employ this conditional expression, in order to highlight the baselessness of a "monistic method".

Monism answers a metaphysical thirst of the human spirit, which also can be satisfied only upon the basis of metaphysics. The monistic tendency in our cognitive aspect as regards the historical process is satisfied only by the philosophy of history, which is part of metaphysics, and not of scientific sociology. And here is where idealism loudly declares its rights. If Marx did much for sociology, then for the philosophy of history Hegel provides even moreso. Only upon the basis of a metaphysical idealism can one surmount the empirical diversity, to conceive of it as a visible manifestation of a singular spiritual beauty.[1] But sociology has to be both positive and realistic, as with any science, and therefore historical materialism ought to jettison its monistic pretensions, and only then from this teaching can be extracted the valuable givens for sociological science.

IV.

I now move on to a critique of another no less important basis of historical materialism. Proponents of historical materialism tend to regard their teaching not only as the most perfect form of monism, but likewise also as the most perfect form of evolutionism. It is against this sociological evolutionism, which has pushed to the extreme all the blunders of a quantitative mechanical theory of developement, that I intend to direct my criticism. A quantitative mechanical evolutionism is inconsistent the same and unscientific the same, as also is monism, and to it ought to be opposed a different, a new theory of developement. The evolutionary theory of the second half of the XIX Century, so characteristic as a subject of pride of the positive outlook of minds, rests upon completely false philosophic foundations, and it is time already finally to admit, that we do not have as yet a satisfactory theory of developement, that what we have are only separate bits, valuable in themself, but as altogether united, is a false hypothetical theory. And amidst this, the fact of developement is a very enormous, a very great fact both of human life, and the life of all the world. At the present time there can no longer be disputes between proponents

---

[1] Even in metaphysics a pure monism is insufficient and unsatisfactory, since it does not resolve the problem of the "individual". The future, rather, would seem to belong to a sort of metaphysical mono-pluralism.

and opponents of the theory of developement, and whereas not to be an evolutionist is impossible, to defend evolutionism in general against an anti-evolutionist has become an anachronism. The dispute can only be about this or some other understanding of evolution, since there can be various theories of developement.

The conventional evolutionism, taken on faith by all the economic materialists in the capacity of an irrefutable dogma, desires as though to monopolise the denial of miracles, but in essence it permits of a "miracle", as its basic presupposition. Faith in the transition of a simplistic quantity into a complex qualitative capacity -- this is a basic article of faith of the quantitative mechanical and essentially materialistic evolutionism. It is a faith in a miracle of miracles, in a miracle of the birth of qualitative spirit from out of unqualitative matter, of life from the non-alive, of society from nature, in which there are not its proclivities, and then too the capacity for knowledge and morality from something absolutely distinct from them, including within it not even an hint of the capacity for knowledge and morality. Solving the secret riddle of the birth of all the qualitative capacities in the world is not bestown evolutionism, which operates only with simplistic quantities. That laboratory of evolutionism, in which are prepared all the higher qualities, all the most complex manifestations of spirit from out of simple quantitative combinations, is a laboratory of alchemy and positive alchemists work miracles in it.

Quite much is said about developement, about adaption etc, but amidst this they forget about one small detail, they forget about who it is that developes and adapts, i.e. the subject within evolution. And they decided, that the subject of developement is likewise the product of developement. And thus for example, adaption is recognised not only as a factour in the developement of life, for Spenser and other biological evolutionists life itself, that life which is developing, is naught other than an adaption of the inner relationships towards the outward, it is a product of developement. But every "adaption" with logical an inevitability presupposes that, what adapts, in the given instance -- life, as the subject of developement, and also presupposes that, to what the adaption proceeds, in the given instance which is qualitatively as such distinct from the life in nature. But with the evolutionists the concept of "adaption" swallows up all the remaining moments, especially the inward moment, and therefore developement is left hanging up in the air, since it does not have a substrate. For such, and in order to posit a theory of developement upon correct and singularly possible a path, it is necessary first of all to admit the following basic position for any evolution: in every developing there is presupposed that, what developes, the subject of developement, as something initial and inward, and the theory might then show, how in the world there developes all its qualitative manifestations, while being unable to regard the inner qualities as merely the mechanical product of developement. Thus, for example, the theory of developement would uncover the factours in the developing of life, but life itself in its qualitative uniqueness would be presupposed, as something from the start, not merely analysed and deduced from the absence of life, from the physico-chemical processes of inorganic nature; it would uncover the factours in the developement of the societal life of people, but the societal aspect itself, i.e. a certain quality underlying the interaction of people, deriving from an attribute of the human spirit, would be presupposed and not merely deduced from its absence, as though issuing from inorganic and organic nature etc. Quite literally, against quantitative a worldview we resolutedly contrast a qualitative worldview. Against faith in evolutionary miracles, in an alchemy, by means of which from out of the elementary quantitative combinations of matter and its singular energy there happens everything in the world, resulting in all the higher and complex qualities of human culture, -- against this we contrast our opposing point of view, by which the qualities, discerned only in the higher stages of human culture, are seen as initially lodged within the spiritual, inner nature of the world and as such are non-inferable from the quantitative. This involves those subjects or substrates of developement, which are revealed and open forth through interacting sequences. But only the basic qualitative capacities of the human spirit are initial and stable, around them form fluid psychological strata, all the social forms, all the content of culture unsteadily is apparent only by means of discerning the primal qualities. Developement namely is also a revealing, an unfolding forth, in it there is something initial and inward that is rendered outward, receiving thus its greatest expression. And we ought to recognise, that what receives its greatest rich expression and discovery in the spiritual culture of mankind, its highest knowledge, highest morality, highest religion and art, -- all this is lodged within world life, as a seed, as a qualitatively non-dissectible substrate of developement.[1]

---

[1] This theory of developement presupposes metaphysical pluralism

There thus arises a very interesting and important philosophic problem, which demands either this or some other metaphysical resolution. But no single science with its specialised tasks comes nigh to a resolution of this philosophical problem, since such a science ought to be aware of its limits, which the evolutionists too often overstep. In the task of biology little the same there tends to enter the question of the essence of life, about its initial birth from something, just the same as also with the task of physics and chemistry where there tends not to enter in the question about the issuing forth of matter and energy and about the ultimate nature of the world. In the task of sociology, which for us at present is particularly of interest, there does not enter in the question about the final emergence of society and its relationship to the world totality. To bring together the various sequences of phenomena, investigated by the social sciences, and to conceive of them as a single whole, is a task of metaphysics, and not of science. Sociology likewise presupposes the physical interaction of people, directed towards the combined supporting of life and developing of culture, a presupposing also all the initial qualities of the human spirit, the cognitive mind with its *a priori* forms and its striving for truth, as also the moral will with its striving towards the good and right, sensation with its demand for beauty, the religious consciousness, uniting all the functions of the soul in a singular striving towards God etc. Amidst a superficial empirical viewpoint what hits the eyes, for example, is that initially there was a state of ignorance, and then ensued enlightening, and that what enabled this was a series of social factours. But the enlightening was rendered possible only because there were inner capacities within the human spirit, there was a demand for knowledge and the light, but it could not take form from ignorance by merely a mechanical path. Sociology does not possess any sort of right to regard the product of social developement as comprising the higher functions of the human soul and accounting them as the higher benefits of spiritual culture, for this is outside of its competency. Quantitative evolutionism in sociology is inadmissible and absurd the same, as in all the spheres of knowledge, indeed an effect of metaphysical materialism.

What suchlike comprises a materialistic evolutionism in sociology? This is the attempt to infer all the qualities of human society and human

---

(spiritualistic monadology) and tends towards the Platonic teachings about the Ideas.

culture, its valued beneficial aspects, such as knowledge and morality, religion and laws etc, to derive these from an unqualified social sort of matter -- economics. With such, everything seems a product of social developement, with no sort of subject of developement, besides this or some other quantity of societal material. The concept of causality gets applied to the relationship between economics and the other sides of social developement in the most arbitrary sense of this word. A mechanical understanding of causality is totally inapplicable to sociology, and this often already has been sufficiently made clear. All the qualitatively independent sequences of world and social life can be brought to unified an approach only within a metaphysical conceiving of the world substance, which for science has no significance. Materialistic monism and evolutionism within sociology seems an approach insufficiently positive and empirical. Let us consider more attentively, what sort of conclusions can be made in regard to historical materialism and to its central idea -- an ideology by way of economic explanation -- from our understanding of evolution in general.

V.

The combining of materialistic monism with materialistic evolutionism leads to this position in sociology, that the sole reality and final source of all the social life of people, of the totality of human culture is made manifest by a social sort of matter -- economics, the material forces of production. The light of human life, all ideology, all the spiritual values of culture -- is only but a reflection of economics, the "construct' over material a "basis". The ideal developement of mankind is explained from the material aspect, is deduced from it. The immanent growth of the material forces of production creates all the diversity of societal life and culture, --i.e. according to a strict sense of a materialistic understanding of history, the accumulation and combinations of quantities of social material -- economics -- of itself creates the diverse ideal qualities, and increase with the developement of mankind. Consider for example such an ideal quality, as morality. Societal science declares factual the growth of morality within the historical process. Yet what ought to be the correct attitude of sociology to this fact? Sociology ought first of all to take morality, as an *a priori* presupposition, as an initial quality, non-inferable from any other quality, and in following it out along the line of moral developement it cannot allow of an interruption, a not-morality, some peculiar quality of the human spirit, it ought rather to think this line on out to infinity, vanishing off into the distance of world life. Yet this line of moral developement issues forth from the ideal side of human nature, which as such is initial and cannot be deduced from anything external and foreign to it, and in this line of the developing of every moral quality, it is begotten as moral a quality, is the result of its growth from within. For metaphysics, causality is an inner creative work of spirit, but the science of sociology is called to reveal only that functional dependence, which exists between the growth of morality and the growth of all society.

Societal developement creates the basis for the external manifestations of the inward moral principle, and this external manifestation of morality within the societal life of people often is termed "morals", which indirectly enters in as an object of sociological science. Sociology herein tends to state the connection between the level of moral developement and the level of societal developement in general, it looks at societal developement as a condition, amidst which only can develope within the life of mankind a moral principle which can become crystalised into laws. Sociology thus can establish a whole series of necessary correlations and can thus come nigh to a working out of sociological laws.

Literally, the immanent moral developement, issuing forth from the ideal nature of man, undergoes social frictions, the social material proves favourable or unfavourable condition for the revealing of a moral moment in the life of mankind, for the birth into higher an human culture. Yet what seems a question on the ultimate source of morality and its essence, is not the affair of sociology, it is a question for philosophic ethics. But historical materialism has an approach quite otherwise, it transfers a defective materialistic metaphysics into science and transgresses the bounds in substituting metaphysics for science. The consequent economic materialism denies a qualitative autonomy for morality, it strives to deduce it from something on the outside, from social a material, which by miraculous a manner begets all qualities: to it remains only to increase its quantity, to combine it thus or otherwise, and apparently there results law, and morality, and cognitive knowledge, and religion, and artistic creativity, and all whatever.

However, judging matters thus would only be by a consistent economic materialist, for whom this theory appears to be an entire philosophic worldview, while someone less rigidly partisan and bestowing the theory more limited an historical significance, e.g. Kautsky, would be in agreement in admitting the basic traits of human nature, as premises, with which the materialist understanding of history is reckoned to occur. That which we have said concerning morality, can apply to whatever side of an "ideology". As regards the central question for historical materialism concerning the relationship between economics and ideology, between the material and the spiritual culture, we should establish the following basic positions. Social materia (economics, the forces of production) is not a given within the object for sociological science, as a singular substrate for the social process, it is a methodological aspect worked at separately from all the whole diversity of societal life, and as such appears very fruitful for an acceptance by sociology. All the aspect of ideology, all the spiritual culture issues forth from the ideal sides of the human spirit, which also is manifestly the true subject of historical developement: all sides of ideology presuppose non-dissectible qualities of the human soul and are rooted in them. Between the social materia, the economic and the spiritual cultural, the ideology, there exists a functional interdependence, a constant correlation, which can be formulated thus: the material social developement creates the basic soil, the condition for the ideal developing of human culture, and there is a necessary correspondence between the degrees of economic and ideological growth, but by no means is it a begetting of the ideological line by the economic lineage. The conjoint struggle by people for supportive life creates a material culture, and this points back to the social-economic phenomena, without which is impossible the spiritual growth of mankind. But the science of sociology ought to look at economic developement, as independent an aspect, not to be deduced from the ideological developement; this aspect has its own particular criteria within economic expediency and productivity. One mustneeds admit the great merit of historical materialism, in that it has pointed to the tremendous independent significance of the material economic developement and as such has ceased to seek for the causes of this developement within the ideal impulses of the human person, which themself cannot create the social materia and sociologically depend upon the material forces of production. The free human spirit creates ever higher and higher forms of culture, creates law and morality, science and philosophy, art and religion, but in its creativity it rests upon the material societal developement, the aggregate of social materia, which appears necessary a tool the same, for the accomplishments of mankind, as in general external nature is for the spirit.

From all what has been said, we can rightly make the conclusion, that historical materialism can have significance in the capacity of a limited historical theory, it can shed light upon the concrete history of mankind, and then from it can be derived a series of valuable positions for a sociology of the future, but as a philosophy of history, as a system of philosophic materialism, reducing to the extreme all the deficiencies of quantitative evolutionism and its inevitable wont for transitioning into a denial of the qualitative autonomy and the true reality of all the spiritual benefits for human life, all this has to be radically rejected. It is impossible to seek for a material sub-foundation, a material substrate for ideal developement, for all the ideal constructs, since the "ideal" is empirically just as real, as is the "material", and their intersecting towards singular a substrate is already in context a metaphysical theory, and as such is already assuredly idealistic and reckons upon a substantiation of spirit amidst the visible aspect of matter. The philosophy of history regards historical materialism as relatively correct, but makes thence deductions directly the opposite to any materialism. A philosophy of history, possible only upon the basis of a metaphysical idealism, has to construct a theory of progress, since the question of progress issues from the sphere of sociological science, and perceives of "economics", as the material means for the ideal ends of human life. The meaning of the historical process can be sought only within an ideology, howsoever much we might have said concerning the significance of economics and material developement; from philosophic a point of view, the ultimate substrate of the historical process, the primal source of all values, growing amidst progress, is manifestly the living spirit, it is the subject, the creator and end-purpose of the historical progress.

I resolutely repudiate all monism and the current mechanical evolutionism in its application to sociology, but in the philosophy of history, in the metaphysical understanding of the historical process I tend to be an adherent of a spiritualistic monism and idealistic theory of developement. Vl. Solov'ev provides quite more for the philosophy of history and the metaphysical theory of progress, than do all the economic materialists taken together.[1] Possible only is an idealist understanding of history, only by it is satisfied the monistic tendency of our cognition and our demand in the theory of progress, such as should ponder our life and our struggle for a better future. A series of almost banal truths in historical materialism, at the basis of which lies the obvious fact of the coarsely lived materialism of the mass of humanity, overwhelmed with trite everyday interests, -- all this is impossible to deny, and is indicative of the need for enlightening by philosophic efforts in thought. And thereby the relative veracity of the Marxist interpretation of concrete history and the Marxist sociology can live harmoniously with the absolute truthfulness of the idealist philosophy of history, with the idealist ethics and metaphysics. Needful is a synthesis of the realistic sociology of Marx and the idealistic philosophy of history in Fichte and Hegel. In such manner might be resolved the constant problem, left unsolved by Kant, of the relationship between the ideal norms, inherently present to the human spirit, and the objective streaming of the historical process, in which the social materia manifests itself with such crushingly quantitative a force. After Marx we can already no longer be economic reactionaries and utopianists, for we have had some fine schooling in sociological realism and have absorbed certain truths, unsettling in their significance. We give a nod of respect likewise to the toiling of Marx, a relentless materialist and realist, for his idealistic thirst for justice on earth, in which is a reflection of eternal truth. Therefore, despite our decisive criticism and sharp rejection of certain positions of Marxism, we offer a mark of respect and marvel at one of the greatest people of all time. And now we move on to the sociological theory of the struggle of groups and classes, to this most important inference of materialistic monism and evolutionism within sociology.

---

[1] Vide: "The Philosophic Principles of Integral Knowledge". This is a little-known and under-appreciated but nonetheless profound and original a work by our remarkable philosopher.

VI.

The Marxist theory of class struggle has tremendous historical significance. This is, first of all, an historical theory, and it borrows the concept of class from a concrete historical era, the capitalistic era, and as such it is a reflection of a very noted and immense fact in the social life of the XIX Century, the fact of acute class antagonisms and class struggles, which is not only a matter of blind prejudices and pre-conceived ideas. But in this perspective of whatever theory of class struggle that Marxism preaches, it still cannot make a pretense to sociological a significance; in order to be received as a sociological theory, it would need to arrive at positions, having an abstract significance, independent of some concrete historical time-frame and dimension. Upon the Marxist theory is too powerful a stamp of the modern era with its live struggle, in this is its strength on the one hand, yet on the other -- in this is its sociological weakness. But the historical theory of the struggle of classes can be transformed into a sociological theory of the struggle of groups.

Historical materialism was the first to have clearly noted a truth, important for societal science, -- that people struggle for life against nature and against one another not only alone, but also by way of combining into groups, that within the social process we always find it not a struggle of people, as rather a struggle of groups. It established, that a social grouping occurs upon the basis of this or some other redistribution of the social materia, comprising forces of production. This methodological inference of the sociological concept of grouping is highly important for sociological science and to it mustneeds be ascribed an abstract sociological meaning. And thence under grouping we shall understand not only "class", in that sense, in whatsoever this word was applied to society in the XIX Century, -- classes per se were not at the first stages of societal developement, and in justice to Marxist belief, classes will not be there at the higher stages; rather, the group is the base, the elementary sociological unit. When we think about the societal aspect, we are already thinking not about the separate isolated man, who for sociology does not exist, -- but rather about a particular segment of interacting people, a social grouping of people, and we take this social grouping of man and then investigate the relationship of the person to the group and the relationship of groups to each other. The concept of the social group, i.e. an external mutual interaction of people, applied to a material basis of social life, is a basic social concept.

Sociology considers the totality of the social process, in terms of mutual interaction and the intersecting of various social groups.

For the philosophy of history, for philosophic ethics there exists first of all the human person, as a spirit, which creates the higher good of human culture, as an end-purpose of history. But sociology, in accepting the ideal basis of human nature in the capacity of non-analysible premises, does not make this the object of its investigation; it is not interested in the inner nature of the human spirit, nor ideal values, but rather in the outward relationships of people, which also are termed social in the particular meaning of this word. It does not set itself the absurd goal of deriving the entirety of spiritual culture from material a basis, but instead sets itself a moreso specialised task: to discern the external relationships of people and to establish the necessary correlation between the outward social grouping and the social materia, and to reveal this sociological truth, that the outward dimension and mutual interaction of societal groups arises upon the basis of material economic developement. The societal dimension of labour is a very general sociological fact, giving rise to all the diverse societal positions, but it leads however to the developing of the person by way of the conjoining of groups. In the prevailing position of Marxism, that the "economic factour" is the foremost in defining the developement of social relationships, there is a remarkable dollop of truth, but this mustneeds be understood critically. The economic factour cannot play any sort of constructive role in the ideal developement of mankind, it does not construct any sort of ideals, any sort of spiritual values, but instead plays only a basic role in the outward social grouping of people, in the developement of the "societal aspect", which always is merely a necessary condition, a necessary tool for the developement of "spirituality", for the inner ideal developing of mankind. In such manner, we remain convinced, that the teaching about the dominance of the "economic factour" can hold paramount a significance for history, and be very important for sociology, and yet hold no sort of significance for the philosophy of history. I once again stress, that sociology does not deal with the inner man, but deals rather only with the outward man, with man, insofar as he enters into outward social interaction with other people. Sociology is incapable to make inferences about the inner man, with his ideal content, from its scope of the outward man with his interaction in social groups, and any like attempt at such is a basic lie from the Marxist philosophic world-concept. But sociology should establish the correlation between the outward social man with the social group, to consider the social man in his diverse interactions with various social groups and discern these or other group influences upon the developement of the person (in the purely sociological sense). And upon this basis we arrive at very important insights.

The person, the individuality, from sociological a point of view, is the result of the intersecting of various social groups, in it there become united diverse social influences, and the degree of its developement and the richness of its content is directly proportional to the degree of social differentiation.[1] Ordinarily this would be formulated, that the person is a product of the "social medium". But this mustneeds be understood in a limited, specialised sociological sense. Sociology lacks the authority to assert, that the inner ideal qualitative capacities of the person are created by the outer social medium, and this question is not put to it, since it is concerned only with the external societal strata, that influence the growth of the inward nature of the human spirit and the forming of the outward societal man. Sociology deals only with the outward groups of man, upon which lies the impress of the outward levels of the social process. Only the philosophy of history, of ethics and metaphysics all deal with the general-human aspect beyond these groupings of man. It can be said, that sociology deals not with man, but only with his surroundings. And therefore sociology ought not, as is attempted by historical materialism, to look upon the social process as upon a laboratory, in which to get man all prepared satisfactorily, for man cannot be created by the outer material social medium, howsoever great be its influence; man is spirit, he is in the image and likeness of God and supposedly as such for sociology a given. Sociology attempts to discern only, how from beneathe the external social trappings man proves himself to be, and how in the struggle of groups there arises the human in general.

Under the influence of a particular historical moment and warring vital concerns, Marxism has heightened the group antagonism, the opposition between classes, it has entrenched between the groups an impassable abyss. The conjoining of all the societal groups within its interaction is formative for a given society, which has its own general-culture supra-group interests. Societal developement indicates a drawing

---

[1] A format for such a purely sociological investigation might be the work of G. Simmel, "On Social Differentiation", though with him there is too strong a strain of philosophic scepticism.

together between the societal groups, a weakening of the abyss, a strengthening of the societal fabric. The downfall of slavery will be made possible only then, when there is lessened that abyss between the grouping of slaves and the grouping of masters, which has hindered the slave to conceive of himself as likewise a man. The present struggle between workers and capitalists becomes possible only then, when the impassable gulf dissipates between the group man from among the workers and the group man from among the bourgeoise, when the worker has the possibility to realise, that he likewise has rights, as does the capitalist. We can set the following paradoxical in its form position: the class struggle itself, the growth of its strength and awareness is possible only thanks to a weakening of class antagonisms, only thanks to a closer proximity between the various societal groups. The working person developes only insofar, as has the group to which he belongs, in its interaction with other groups, in the proximity with them, insofar as there has weakened his group limitedness and whereby he this receives influences not only from his own narrow group, but rather from all the conjoint societal attitudes, from the most diverse manifestations of culture. The same can be said for the person from the group of man from the third estate, it developed in the past, insofar as it got over its acute difference from the aristocracy, and at the present time it can yet develope further only insofar, as it gets over its difference from the representatives of the working class. The person cannot become developed, as long as its singular and defining vital influence derives from the attitude of its economic group towards some other economic group, with which it is directly connected. Only a broad circle of societal and cultural life can provide the materia needful for the developement of person. If a worker were to know only the factory and the capitalists, with which he wages daily a struggle, he still cannot become developed as a man, the potential of his developing consists in this, that he recourse as possible to moreso diverse societal circles, with the needful for him influences from diverse cultural sources, needful contacts, pursuing purely idealistic aims. The person sociologically is nourished not directly by the social materia, but rather by the societal relationships of people, by the intersecting and mutual interaction of all the societal groups and the various cultural strata, though the person remain attached to his own social group, with its basic imprint upon life, and upon it first of all lies the seal of limitedness, as primary a social stratum. The constant drawing closer and intersection of various societal groups in the direction of the predominance of democratic groups weakens group limitation and leads to a gradual distinguishing of the all-human aspect from beneathe the thick layers, obscuring his ideal nature. In this is lodged the developement of the person and the democratisation of society.

I shall now move along to a most important part of the article, to a critique of "class ideology" and the Marxist class perspective in general, since I repudiate the class point of view even in an application to political ideologies, and I see in it an enormous hindrance not only for the resolving of theoretical questions in sociology and philosophy, but practical questions also.

VII.

The idea of a class ideology, of a class perspective upon life with its struggle, upon the historical process and even upon all the world -- this is the point, at which Marxism ceases to be a science or philosophy and becomes instead a religion. That indignation and irritation, which gets expressed by economic materialists at every attempt at criticism of the class point of view, shows that here we are dealing with seemingly sacred a matter, evoking towards it religious an attitude. I say this not in jest, for me this is a vivid indication, that the religious demand is not to be eradicated from the human soul, and that, if it be not satisfied normally by religion, then -- it will be satisfied by something other, assuming religious a form, wherein science and the social struggle become a religion. But a class sort of religion is a transitory condition and a surrogate, which ought instead to transition into a true all-human religion.

Historical materialism details this general position, that every ideology derives from economics and is merely its reflection, and it regards the concept of social class as the connecting link between the economic and the ideological aspects. There results the following judgemental aim: the material forces of production create the defining class struggle of society, the social-economic position of each class creates the defining psychology of its representatives, and amidst this specifically class psychology the economic actuality gets reflected in the ideology, the inward spiritual man becomes explicable from the outward economic man, from the social materia, as the primal source. Basic for Marxism, this precept of a class psychology contains within it an undoubted dollop of truth, and this is first of all not even a theory, as rather a stating of fact. Within every society, as represented by its mutual interaction of social groups, and in particular the complex class society of the XIX Century, we tend to be struck by the fact of the group limitedness of the typical representatives of these or those groups. In that the representatives of the bourgeoise, as a class, in a stifling majority of instances are inveterately bourgeois with extremely limited a group perspective, and that there is some other group limitedness to be encountered among the petite bourgeoise and again some other amongst the nobility, all this is true, which mustneeds be admitted as something almost banal. Upon human nature lie layers of social strata and this can be most mightily manifest by those, who are rooted within a group segment of any society. Each historical man of himself represents an admixture of an ideal all-human nature with its potential possibility to create truth, together with a group societal psychology with its inevitable limitedness, with a narrowness of social horizons. The human spirit by its nature strives for freedom and the light from beyond the narrow frameworks of every group and its in general empirical limitation, but along the way it likewise encounters the accumulated age-old group traditions, the preconceived social thoughts, feelings and aspirations.[1] Yet of what sort however is the relationship of this group limitedness, of this "class psychology" to an ideology, to the ideological developement of mankind, to the creativity of more perfect forms of culture?

Here, obviously, there cannot be causal a relationship. The class limiting factour of the bourgeoise can distort science, but as such cannot construct it, it can distort the ideals of social justice, but all the same cannot construct them. The class peculiarities of the representatives of labour include within them perchance a lesser degree of group limitedness in regard to certain truths of social science and to the ideal of social justice, their group setting can perchance be more favourable for truth and the right, than suchlike amongst the bourgeoise, but here also no sort of group particular traits can create either scientific truths, or social ideals. Historical materialism with a striking critical deficiency confuses the cause with the condition. Such a negative condition, as group limitedness, which

---

[1] Human nature, which we contrast opposite the social strata, tends itself to be twofold and has evil residing in its spiritual depths, but the consideration of this problem lies quite beyond our present task.

can only be more or less favourable, cannot create something suchlike positive, as truth within the context of our cognition and justice within our ideals. It moreover is obvious, and one can say, that the search for truth and the creativity of ideals tend to become influenced by social issues, and therefore results quite many a lie within human theories and many an injustice in social aspirations. On account of group limitedness, on account of the "class point of view", there can obtain only a distortion of ideology, whereas every true and just ideology is an appeal to the ideal sides of human nature against the group limitedness, and every step in the ideal developement of humankind is a victory of man in general over the class-limited man.

We have already said above, why ideology cannot be derived from economics, as its primal source, and why the ideal cannot be a reflection of the material. Hence from this it follows, that an external fact of this or some other class social position cannot explain the inner process of human creativity. Ideology has its source not in the social materia corresponding to a social group, but in rather the ideal nature of the human spirit, and it is always a surmounting of the group limitedness, an attempt to rise above it. The word combination "class ideology" is inwardly contradictory and absurd, for there can exist class interests, class prejudices and preconceived notions, but class ideals, class truths, class justice there cannot be. The ideal and inspiring aspect to Marxism is naught other, than an attempt to rise above every group sort of limitedness, amidst which is also the limitedness of the working class, by way of an ultimate doing away of classes with their special interests and constraining outlooks. The real material for every ideology is manifest by all the accumulated social actuality, the mutual interaction of its social groups, but the living spirit issues forth from the ideal side of man, conveys him into all-human a life, by which and for which is created the whole of culture with its ideal ends.

The class perspective includes within it a notable bit of truth, to which we have already alluded, it accurately stresses the fact of group limitation, points to the favourable or unfavourable influence of group interests and preconceived notions in the seeking of truth and justice, but as a socio-philosophic worldview, as a religion, it ought to be decisively discarded, since at its basis lies a crude mishmash of the all-human, of the spiritual existence, together with the outwardly grouped man. The class perspective upon ideology is a completely false deduction based upon a whole series of false premises, of a false monism and evolutionism, upon a false view on the relationship between economics and ideology, and upon a false understanding of the sociological theory of the struggle of groups. On the bazaar-like squares there is current the absurd notion, that critical philosophy is perchance a manifestation of bourgeois an instinct for self-preservation, that philosophic idealism is reactionary and the handiwork of the governing classes, that in each philosophic construct there needs to be sought out the suspicious material-class underpinning. This is a prevalent, albeit by no one and never proven idea, used by people incapable of thinking for themself, and it is time finally to put a stop to this ugliness. Normal logic gives no one the right to search out and detect material class underpinnings within philosophic ideas, especially when such in essence nowise include in them anything of the "material" or of "class", instead manifesting a selfless search for truth and directly and consciously defend justice. It is impossible to be an ideologue of class; it is possible for one either to belong to a given class, to be pervaded by its interests, to stand up for them, and then the word "ideologue" proves misplaced; or, in not belonging to a class, nor future interests, one can defend the justice of his demands, but this means being an ideologue for truth, to provide guidance for a supra-class ideal and therefore here the word "class" becomes out of place. In order to ultimately make apparent my own point of view, I move on towards an analysis of a legitimate political ideology and, in part, towards an explanation of the role of the intelligentsia in the creativity of social ideals. These are tremulous questions, bringing us nigh close to practical life, and will comprise the concluding segment in our critique of historical materialism.

VIII.

That there exists a connection and correlation between the economics of a given society and its legal-state structure, -- is a fact noted even by those who are not economic materialists. All thus are obliged to think, that the economic aspect appears as a premise for the legal and political aspects. Every political programme, evidently, is a reaction to the economic actuality and it inevitably tends to reckon with the real redistributionist forces, with the social grouping. Historical materialism sees in political ideology not simply a reflection of the economic actuality, it regards it as the offspring of this or some other social class, it admits of only a class political ideology and only class politics. At the basis of this assertion lies that dollop of truth, that upon political ideology incomparably moreso than upon any other, sits the seal of group limitedness, and at each step it becomes perverted by its own selfish group interests, which only with difficulty are able to rise above the narrow horizons of its everyday life with its trite interests. The theoretical blunders of historical materialism find their explanation and justification in the immense and it can be said basic fact of the social history of the XIX Century, in the fact of the ugly distortion of political ideals by the limitedness and avarice present in the predominant bourgeois group, a distortion, approaching a total obliteration of the human visage. The shameless oppression of man by man, the unprecedented cynical influence of exclusively material interests, the crude political materialism, stifling the ideal wellsprings of man, all this naturally would have to tend to lead to the result, that the oppressed and those thirsting for justice will have lost faith in human nature, that they will no longer see the possibility to discern the shameful aspects of the bourgeoise a man, since the man in whom lives the moral law, cannot suck human blood and regard matter as higher than spirit. And while the protesting forces in the society of the XIX Century inevitably seemed garbed in a class attire, beneathe it also was hid an ideal stirring for truth and justice, a thirst for the restoration of the human visage, the surmounting of class man in the name of all-humanity.

Well having understood those motives, which have led Marxism to a class point of view, we all the same have to admit it as a false theory and even at present harmful not only in the areas of philosophy, science, art, morality, religion, but also in the sphere of politics. The concept of a class political ideology is unthinkable first of all, because in general a class ideology is unthinkable, as we have attempted to demonstrate above, and we shall now attempt to take closer a look, at how a political ideology is created. We have already said, that social grouping occurs upon economic a basis, and each social group has its own specific economic interests, its own limited social task, issuing from its relationship to other groups. Thus, for example, workers struggle against the capitalists for improvement in their material position, involving a series of special group interests and tasks, which are decided upon by a progressive workers politics. Immanently, from the economic position of the workers, from the workers movement, there results only a purely professional narrow-group politics. The workers movement, insofar as it remains strict a group, insofar as it results from the relationship of workers to capitalists, is first of all, a trade-union movement, and from it immanently does not result still any sort of political ideology, it does not still set itself an ideal task transitioning to higher forms of human culture. A general class interest, the unity of striving within a given class -- this is no more than a fiction, as brilliantly demonstrated by the English labour movement. Each group has a mass of their own particular interests, such as cannot be a general social-economic "idea" of the fourth estate, for it comes down to a whole series of separate strivings, varying within the bounds of a given group. From the economic position of whatever the class and its relation to another, it remains impossible to as yet derive any sort of political ideology; every political programme rests upon an analysis of the mutual interaction of all the classes, upon their relation to all the society and culture, i.e. it presupposes a surmounting of class limitedness. The state even from a strictly realistic point of view cannot be an organ of some whatever class, it is the product of the equal interplay of all the societal forces. It would be sociologically absurd to isolate the working class from within a democratic state and in a destructive capacity to use it in opposition relative the state powers, since the working class is a creatively-constructive societal force and an organic part of the democratic state and its legal formats.[1]

The social-political ideal, put forth by Marxism, does not necessarily derive from the economic position of the workers and their group struggle. As with any ideal, it gets included into the group movement from along the sidelines, as something rooted within the ideal sides of the intelligentsia soul and as such it aspires to rise above the aspect of group limitation, to raise up a professional movement to the extent of being an all-human social and cultural movement. At the present time the Marxists themself often admit this, although in doing so they betray one of the basic aspects of their theory, according to which every social-political ideology is the product of immanent economic developement. And indeed, what sort of meaning can be invested in the assertion, that social-political ideals are in essence the products of an immanent economic developement of a definitive class? Herein is possible twofold an interpretation. It is possible first of all to say, that the political ideal directly issues forth from a given class, immanently results from its economics. This is the moreso crude

---

[1] In general the Marxist concept of "class" can be interpreted only nominalistically, and not realistically.

sense; economic materialists tend to understand, that social-political ideals never become the unmediated product of the class itself, that rather the ideologues of a class engraft them during the immanent process of developement. Therefore they suggest different an interpretation: class ideology is a reflection of the social-economic position of a given class, an ideal sort expression in testament of its thoughts, feelings and aspirations. But here we meet up with an indisputable misuse of words, with a very uncritical dealing with concepts.

The "idea" of a fourth estate, as an ideal of an all-human truth, is rooted in the ideal depths of the human spirit, having been revealed within the creativity of the great idealists, and by its very essence it is an attempt to surmount the group limitedness of the workers movement, it transforms interests into ideals, and introduces a moral principle into the social-economic movement. Every legitimate ideology is the application to a given social actuality of an ideal principle of natural law, which not only cannot be inferred from the economic position of whatever the group, but also in general neither from the empirical actuality, since it is of transcendent a nature, it appeals always to an eternal justice and absolute truth, and it discloses within a given empirical actuality new capacities for the realisation of this ideal task. Natural law is an independent self-sufficing quality, not inferable from economics, and it is an authentic grounding for every political ideal. The bearer of this ideal legal principle, and consequently also basic in its social-political ideal is the developing intelligentsia soul, rising above group limitation, i.e. the all-human aspect. Consider liberalism for example, a quite immense political and legitimate ideology, yet together with this, the most suspect in purely its class economic source of origin. To the point of triteness, everyone tends to repeat the stock sort of formula, that liberalism is a bourgeois doctrine and arose for the material interests of a growing third estate; even to the opponents of economic materialism this seems highly plausible. Yet the whole misunderstanding here is based upon a confusion of the ideal essence of liberalism, of its indeed eternal ends, with those temporal means, which were utilised within a certain era, along with those distortions and that inconsistency, which real historical forces tend to evidence. It is quite easy to point out the bourgeois and reactionary aspects of the German "national-liberals", the inconsistency and half-fast aspect of the "free-thinkers", likewise as it would be possible to point out, that the social-democrats tend to appear the solely genuine and consistent liberals, since they bear the standards of freedom and equality, of the "natural rights" of man. It is not difficult likewise to point out the bourgeois aspect of an economic individualism, rendering the "historical" right to property into a "natural" right. But it is impossible to prove as bourgeois the eternal moral essence of liberalism: the idea of person with its inalienable natural rights, the idea of freedom and equality, and these are fundamental aspects in the realisation of the natural rights of the person, the idea of a guarantee for all the inalienable rights of person within the state structure. Only an impermissible violation of human logic and intentional moral blindness can lead to the wild assertion, that the right to freedom of conscience, that spiritual wellspring of every freedom, is but a "bourgeois" right and therefore cannot especially rouse one. It is possible to seek out the class material underpinnings for an explanation as to the limitedness of historical liberalism, for those distortions, caused on the part of these or some other societal forces, it is possible to recognise as bourgeois those means, which were utilised within a certain historical era for the realisation of the purposive-ends of liberalism, but the ideal principles of liberalism issue forth from the depths of the human spirit and are a revealing of eternal moral values. The "idea" of a fourth estate has completely the selfsame ideal moral content, that liberalism also has, and it only instead proposes new methods,[1] corresponding to the modern moment of social developement, for a more consistent dealing in life with all these eternal principles hoisted above every social activity and social grouping, and now the modern societal forces are grouping for a resolution of this age-old task.

Marxist ideology tends to be eclectic and half-fast, in a middle position between the interests of the group man and the ideals of the all-human. Marxism is nothing quite more, than an expression purely of the group, of a professional workers movement with its limited realism, and nothing less, than that all-human ideal of truth, which ought to uplift people to an high degree of culture. This is therefore a purely transitional ideology, not distinguishing yet to a sufficient degree the real tasks of the group movement and the ideal tasks of the all-human movement. In Marxism the all-human with its ideal visage, negating every class limitedness, every oppression of man by man, morally only becomes roused somewhat, and our task consists in this, to provide it a full

[1] Such a method, e.g. is economic collectivism.

expression. And for this there is needful a surmounting of the "class" point of view, to depart from its narrow and limited aspect, since it is only partial, whereas the totality is evident only from "all-human" a point of view.

The bearer and fashioner of political ideology is the inter-class, or more accurately the supra-class intelligentsia, i.e. that part of mankind, in which the ideal side of the human spirit has won out over the group limitedness. The "intelligent" does not have any direct connection with this or some other economic group, for this is a man of utmost inner freedom, he lives first of all with interests of reason, of intellect, and spiritual hunger is his prevailing passion. Each man ought to be an intelligent, but group social influences present enormous an hindrance, ages in the making, and herein creates a whole series of gradations. Marx himself was suchlike a supra-class intelligentsia sort, looking upon the labour movement and its relation to societal developement from up afar, which more and more ascends over the limitedness of group strivings. His inspired interests were an acknowledging of the social process and directed towards a realising of social justice. The human spirit in the person of its finest representatives freely creates the legal and political ideals of truth and justice, but it realistically relies upon the mutual interaction of all the societal groups, upon all the progressive forces of society, transforming the limited aspirations of the professional groups in the ideal task of modernity, awakening man from his limited group existence. The ideal of justice produces an accounting of real group interests, acknowledging some of them as just, and others unjust. The injustice of the group interests of the bourgeoise and its extreme group limitedness renders this group in modern European society as reactionary and makes difficult any orientation towards human nature for its representatives. The group, representing the labour principle in modern society, in this regard is set in incomparatively more favourable a condition, since upon it does not lay the blemish of an oppressor and it has no interest in maintaining the existing evil. But the transition also to an higher culture, to a more just social order can be the result only of a complex interaction of the most progressive of groups, and nowise the activity of a single group. The paths in the future are diverse and there cannot here be some whatever sort of precise sociological foresight, since there are no historical laws, by which the ideal for a better future will arise from fatal a necessity. There always very much still remains the provenance of the freedom of the spirit. It is not given for science to grasp the mystery of human creativity, since the paths it traverses are not within the realm of freedom.

In suchlike a manner the supra-class intelligentsia, starting from the itself unconditional significance of the idea of "natural rights", from the eternal ideals of freedom and justice, would outline the progressive task, in common for the many real groups, and unite the parallel series of group societal movements into an all-national activity worthy of human existence. The intelligentsia would rise above the narrowness of each of the societal groups, perceiving its liberalism in the genuine and idealistic meaning of this word, but together with this it would utilise all these groups, as a real basis. For example, it might be possible to bestow a tremendous significance to the Zemstvo representation, to have an influence upon it and rely upon it in a certain historical aspect, not contaminating it with the group limitedness of the average landowning gentry, which chiefly tends to have been represented in our zemstvos. A class movement can only be part of a general liberation movement, it has its own limited professional goals and therefore ought to be subordinate to the all-human task, of positing ideal questions for the human person, in strongly demanding its rights.

It ought not to be thought, that we are but rehabilitating the old utopianism and returning to "subjectivism", of which we ourself earlier indeed had been critical, and only philosophic an ignorance could elicit suchlike an accusation. We quite well understand all the significance of material societal developement, which cannot be created on mere impulses of the intelligentsia soul. In recognising the developement of the material forces of production and the corresponding social grouping, as a real basis, we have to focus on social-political justice and spiritual culture, since it immanently of itself will not arise from the social materia, since the social materia is not a cause, but rather a condition, not an end, but rather only a means. Our practical programme ought to account for both a realistic sociology and also an idealistic philosophy of history, the latter aspect pointing to the purposive-ends, which for us has actually to do with people, while the former points but to the means, which thus do not render us sterile utopianists.

There is need to discern the grain of truth, contained within historical materialism, and to discard the false materialistic metaphysics, distorting everything, such as is true within this teaching. We shall thereupon have valuable a method for historical an orientation, amidst a series of important positions for sociology and realistic directions for social politics. But the theory of a class ideology, of a class science and morality, of class politics, bearing within it only relative an historical truth, in the capacity of a worldview, in the capacity of a religious sanctity, ought to be ultimately repudiated. In the form in which the class point of view now obtains, there results harmful a bias, bedeviling the free creativity of the human spirit, and it hinders the discerning of the ideal all-human nature, which ought finally to unfold into all its excellence and abilities and thus create a domain of truth. The illusions however of a "class" sort of truth are formed by the temporal and transitory evil in life, of which nothing ought to remain, since the universal truth is one and eternal, and has to win out.

The Political Meaning of the Religious Tumult in Russia

(1903 - 109)[1]

From the supreme heights of the intelligentsia (in the person of the national hero of thinkers in Russia -- Lev Tolstoy) all the way down to the Populists, it (Russian society) constructively and deliberately creates culture, working at resolution of the utmost of its tasks -- the religious, intent upon working them out just like it was with the Christianity of the first centuries and the Reformation of more modern a time both in connection with problems moral and social. To this peculiarity of our time -- an attentive effort of the people's awareness over the religious problem (an effort, which is not simply a tormentive misunderstanding, as was the Schism) we bestow enormous a significance: in it is evidenced for us a clear sign of the cultural maturity of the Russian people in its entire and auspicious prognostication of the broad extent of a national culture. Howsoever burdensome be those conditions, in which occurs the process of creativity of a national culture, we are ready with joy of heart to repeat the classic words of von Hutton [Ulrich, 1488-1523]: *Die Geister sind erwacht: es ist Lust zu leben*! ["*The spirits are awakened: it is a joy to be alive*!"]. Yes, they are awakened! In various locales, under various latitudes, upon that immense expanse, whence has spread the Russian tribe, culture is being created and the human person is being created, amidst original thought and suchlike an advancement of personal and social life.

P. Struve. "In What is indeed the True Nationalism".

There occur periods in the life of a people, when every fact of spiritual culture, the most it would seem, the most remote from the political

---

[1] POLITICHESKII SMYSLRELIGIOZNOGO BROZHENIYA V ROSSII. Article originally published 1903 in publication "Osvobozhdenie" in two-part installments: № 37 p. 218-220, and № 38 p.242-245, per the Klepinina Berdiaev Bibliographie. However, our Moscow Kanon+ 2002 text edition, from which we translate, indicates 1903 issues № 13 and 14 of P. Struve journal "Osvobozhdenie" ["Liberation"] without the pagination.

evils of the day yet assumes acute a political sense, when every vital manifestation of culture, every spiritual pursuit of the human person stands under the standard of a national political liberation and the very fact of its existence demands freedom and truth. Our native land is now entering upon an era of an as yet unprecedented rousing of the people's powers amidst the discrepancy between pertinent enquiries pushing for the freedom of the person in contrast to our despicable state order, and the impudent political governance has reached an extreme intensity. The question on the political liberation of Russia, on the creation of an order based on law, guaranteeing freedom, has become a question for the utmost worthy existence of the Russian nationality, and all our national spiritual culture requires political a freedom, as an elementary condition of its utmost course. In the consciousness of all the Russian people, not ultimately bereft of conscience and honour, there has to be an awareness of this unquestionable truth, that without freedom Russia is threatened by ruin and by spiritual death. We intent to point to this in context of the religious tumult, which in our eyes has an immense symptomatic significance. On the pages of "Osvobozhdenie/Liberation" we shall thus look at this tumult neither from a theological nor philosophic perspective, but rather from a political point of view.

The ugly and stifling fact of the Russian autocracy has constricted the awareness of the forefront representatives of the Russian intelligentsia and has distorted their perspectives. Under the influence of this grievous nightmare of Russian life, our vanguard intelligentsia has become too "monistic" and similarly their concepts of the social-political movement, the complexity and diversity of liberation tasks has tended to fade, and in their perspective nowise has entered in any enquiry of the religious consciousness, has been no awareness of the enormous significance of a religious reformation,[1] in very close a manner connected with the political liberation of Russia. Howsoever we might regard Orthodoxy, Christianity

[1] Under religious reformation we understand here not a transition to Protestantism, but simply religious renewal and deep-rooted reform of the organisation of church, which at present is connected with Caesaropapism and therefore in no manner can remain the same in a free Russia. We have no intention in this article to imagine, of what sort religion in the future might comprise, nor to express our personal religious convictions.

and religion in general, it would be absurd historically not to think, that in Russia, freed from the burden of autocracy, that there would be no sort of religious strivings nor any sort of free embodiments of a religious consciousness. That Constituent Assembly, which would be convened to create a free Russia, would not be empowered to administer religion, but it would and should set religion free, to proclaim and to guarantee freedom of conscience, in accord with the quite indelible paragraph of the "Declaration of the Rights of Man and Citizen" and, in such manner, provide the possibility for the Orthodox Church to become transformed from a state ministry of confessions subordinate to the Russian tsar, into instead a free religious organisation pursuing its proper religious aims. The religious movement will therefore indubitably have for us a political significance and will assume its own place within the complex and diverse liberation struggle. Politically in opposition would be not only the free religious searchings of our intelligentsia and the sectarian religious movement amongst the people, this itself is quite clear, but also the Orthodox Church itself, if it recovers from the "paralysis" about which Dostoevsky spoke ["The Church in Paralysis since Peter the Great"], and becomes again pervaded by a vital spirit and conscious of its Christian vocation.[1] And in its capacity of witnesses from beyond we have to admit, that upon the basis of Orthodox Christianity is possible a movement, directed against autocracy, a movement declaring its own concerns: freedom of conscience, freedom of the Church from oppressive interference by the state, and the demanding of a Christian politics. In the person of Pobedonostsev is embodied not so much the spirit of Russian Orthodoxy, as rather the spirit of Russian autocracy, and in this has been the profound inner reason for the disdain of sincere representatives among the clergy towards the running of the Church under a civil ministry of the Russian tsar. By truly a Christian logic, it is already long since time to expel from the holy temple of God the money-changers, making a shameful business off the religious conscience in the interests of the police, in the name of some other god, a god of state violence and oppression. Upon the banners of the Ober-Prokurator of the MostHoly Synod in the person of Pobedonostsev, and of the historical Orthodox Church, insofar as it cringes before him, is inscribed the ideal of a churlish state positivism, and not religio-Christian an ideal.

---

[1] This was finely noted in the pages of "Liberation" on the articles, "Orthodoxy and Autocracy" (№ 5-7).

Catholicism fell, because that within it the church was transformed into a state, the church wanted to become master of the earth and rendered the state into a weapon for its earth-dominating ends. Catholic clericalism is based upon a resorting of the church to the state with its materially coercive methods of activity, and this downfall of a church was expressed in the bon-fires of the Inquisition. But in any case, Catholicism played an enormous creative role within history, and the psychological traits of Catholicism can be sensed even within modern socialism. The Orthodox Church however has not played similar an independent role within Russian history, it has been a tool of the state, and religion was set into an abasedly subordinate position to the autocracy. Sincerely and deeply religious natures, who see in Orthodoxy the singularly true religion, have to admit, that the Orthodox Church is still not as it should be, and it remains for them to dream about the ideal type of clericalism, in which the state gets converted into the church and the coercive police union gets replaced by an union of love.[1]

When Peter the Great in his Spiritual Regulation established the Holy Synod, in doing this Peter boldly declared: "The Collegium to do naught without His assent", -- the Orthodox Church therein ceased its independent existence and was transformed into a civil ministry of confessions, and Caesaropapism, acknowledging the tsar as head of church, ultimately triumphed. The degradation of church, its readiness to be a reactionary weapon in the hands of the state, evokes hesitant an attitude towards Orthodoxy amongst the finest representatives of the Russian intelligentsia. That intelligentsia, which justly sees the "politically suspect" as contrast to its own lofty moral duty and its own historical mission, does not regard the Orthodox Church as a dangerous enemy, it well understands the impossibility of clericalism upon Russian a basis, and its terrible foe is the absolute tsarism, whereas Orthodoxy elicits towards itself only but hesitantly indifferent an attitude. If the Russian intelligentsia, religious by

---

[1] Suchlike was the clericalism of Dostoevsky, suchlike was the theocratic ideal of Vl. Solov'ev, a profoundly religious Orthodox mystic while at the same time an enemy of historical Orthodoxy with its presently existing organisation of church. Suchlike also was the clericalism of the finest of the Slavophils. Whether it be correct to term as "Orthodox" an indefinite historical form of Christianity, is a question, not for us here to touch upon.

nature in the best sense of this word, has for long a while been imbued with religious an indifference and has been alike foreign to matters, both as an active religious negation and in active religious construction, then the responsibility for this falls upon the Russian governance, in contriving to transform religion, this highest manifestation of spiritual culture, into something loathesome and repulsive. And perhaps one of the most terrible transgressions of Russian governance will be admitted that through its vile activity, it has inspired in the finest part of the Russian intelligentsia, which has had to undergo a crucifixion for truth with a spirit of religious indifferentism and a suspicious attitude towards every religious searching, as towards something politically unworthy of respect. For this crime, the Russian governance merits before the judgement-seat of God the "fiery Gehenna" anathema by the Orthodox Church, insofar as it represents the mystical Church of Christ.

Russian great literature -- is the most religious in the world. The creativity of two of the greatest Russian geniuses -- L. Tolstoy and Dostoevsky, bears preeminently a religious character, and there is a kernel of truth in the Slavophil idea, seeing in this a reflection of our national spirit. The religious aspects of our philosophic searchings, and the religious spirit has garnered notice even in our atheistic journalism. It is an indication of the chief symptoms of the religious tumult, which is of note in recent years.

It is admitted by everyone, that the instigator of the religious tumult in Russia was L. Tolstoy, -- he breached the gap within the religious indifferentism of the Russian intelligentsia, and thereby brought issues of a religious awareness to the centre of attention. For this he found himself excommunicated from the Church, namely for his religious searchings, since people who are simply among the indifferent do not find themself excommunicated from the Church. We do not consider as especially lofty the religio-philosophic views of L. Tolstoy, but the significance of Tolstoy for the developing of our religious awareness and for our liberation is so immeasurably great, that it is impossible to overstate it. L. Tolstoy with a stroke of genius revealed the ugly contradictions and hypocrisy within historical Christianity, he pointed out the anti-Christian character of our historical Orthodoxy. Only after the preachings of L. Tolstoy, by the power of which we shall see hence not as some sort of denial of religious metaphysics, but rather the sense that towards questions of religious an awareness, it becomes impossible to relate with a passive indifferentism, and that to set free the religious conscience is possible only amidst a positive and active attitude towards religion, and that to overcome the historical Orthodoxy is possible only by an active religious striving. L. Tolstoy with an extraordinary mightiness has set before us the ideal of service to God by way of the embodiment of the religio-moral principle in life. In the Tolstoyan idealistic anarchism there is a grain of great and undying truth. And it is characteristic, that among us especially ardent and active defenders of freedom of conscience there have appeared such religious people, as the Slavophils and Vl. Solov'ev, and to them belongs a visible place within the Russian religious movement, for they alike rose up against both the passive irreligiosity of the Russian intelligentsia and against the official religiosity by dictate of state power amongst so-called Orthodox Christians.

In recent years one can point to a whole series of facts regarding religious life in our society. One such was the rousing speech of the Orlov nobility-head M. A. Stakhovich in defense of the freedom of conscience, and another such was the sermonising and publishing activity of the priest G. S. Petrov, essentially little of interest yet characteristic in this, that he emerges as a representative of the clergy, from whom we had been accustomed to hear nothing except dogmatic dead stuff and cringing afront the Russian governance. Very characteristic likewise the rousing of interests and questions of religious awareness among a number of representatives of our vanguard publicists, and yet while coming from Marxism, seemingly foreign to all religious interests, nonetheless religious in essence. But here we also propose taking a closer look at an event, very characteristic in this regard, yet insufficiently known to Russian society and not as yet having received proper an appreciation: we have in view the Peterburg "Religio-Philosophic Gatherings", the protocols of which were published in the journal, "The New Pathway" ("Новый Путь").[1]

In these "Religio-Philosophic Gatherings" we see a phenomenon as yet unprecedented in Russian life. Representatives of literature and representatives of the clergy join together for a free discussion on religious questions, with the Russian literary figures sitting alongside Bishop Sergei, Archimandrite Antonii, Protopresbyter Yanyshev among others, and they

---

[1] *trans. note*: Vide the chapter , "The Meetings and Encounter", in the Fr. Alekandr Men' book, "*Russian Religious Philosophy: 1989-1990 Lectures*", in our 2015 (frsj Publications) English translation.

dispute about freedom of conscience, about the excommunication of L. Tolstoy from the Church, about the attitude of Christianity towards the flesh, about the relationship between the intelligentsia and the Church. True, the greater part of these literary figures are not of the popular sort -- Merezhkovsky, Rozanov, Minsky etc, but they sometimes spoke on matters, which no archbishop had ever happened to hear. We know, that for us it is customary either to bestow a kiss to the hand of some high spiritual personage and proper to cringe before him, just as he in turn has cringed before the Russian governance, or even to be with him in the same room we considered impossible; we have not been accustomed even to think, that the representatives of our clergy were capable of speaking on their own, expressing their own whatever thoughts, and for us it was wild to imagine, that with them it was possible to dispute on life-shaking questions and freely in front of them express our own thoughts. And suddenly freedom of conscience and freedom of speech momentarily is asserted in a small corner of Peterburg, by the so-called "Religio-Philosophic Gatherings", with the Russian clergy happening to hear very bitter truths from the Russian intelligentsia, who moreover up til then had not seen it as their moral duty in an open proclaiming of suchlike bitter truths. These gatherings indeed have undoubtedly a political significance, as a symptom of profound political unrest, penetrating even into such corners, as seemed completely hopeless in this regard. In Russia such happenings are possible only in an era of an as yet unprecedented "time of troubles", when the troubles become an all-national concern -- and our journal "Liberation" ought to be able to bring some light into those corners, which will have their own place in the push for liberation. We are not therefore inclined to overstate the significance of these Peterburg "Gatherings" and we are well aware of the limited political concern of almost all the participants. We consider this aspect as a symptom and want better to determine its objective meaning. And its objective meaning is great, in what it here consists.

Every religious quest, every sincere religious renewal and construct, every spiritual craving and spiritual creativity rests inevitably upon one issue, in which come together and unfold all the nodes of Russian life -- in the Russian autocracy, and an objective logic would demand the removal of the autocracy, though this be not readily apparent. Upon the basis of autocracy and its caprice becomes impossible not only political activity, not only economic activity, but also in general anything constructive, and nothing it would seem, in a political regard by way of cultural work, impossible would be spiritual creativity within religion, in science, in literature, in the enlightening of the people. Every cultural creative work, howsoever remote from politics, demands freedom of conscience, freedom of speech, freedom of the press, freedom of association, demands the independent activity of the person, the free creativity of the human spirit and therefore presupposes a guarantee of the rights of the person. In the autocratic police state, spiritual culture represents a sort of contraband, and by its very existence it only goes to prove, that there is in fact a limit to the police oppression even by a very powerful and very reactionary government, that it is impossible to ultimately quench the spirit, that it nonetheless will rise up and make declaration concerning its rights.

The Russian autocratic state cannot alleviate the material hunger of the Russian people, nor the spiritual hunger of the Russian intelligentsia. The Russian people is wont to satisfy its spiritual religious hunger not in the Orthodox Church, soiled by its subservience to that enemy of the people -- the bureaucratic governance, but rather in the free sectarian movement. The Russian intelligentsia also will render its spiritual religious hunger into a deliberate weapon in the struggle against oppression by the autocracy. All levels of Russian society have to recognise, that the Russian autocracy has entered into that final and liquidating phase of its existence, when it can only wickedly and inhumanly be negative, to be negative towards everything -- with the gallows, prison, the knout, the shedding of the people's blood; it remains able to create nothing, in any single sphere of life. Our government is nihilistic in the genuine sense of this word, it is ultimately bereft of shame nor does it seem to know the decreed laws of God and man. There is no religion, worthy of the name, which can justify the actions of Mr. Pleve [alt. Plehve, Vyacheslav; 1846-1904; imperial chief of police] and be his confederate, and if the Christian religion has not yet ultimately gone to ruin, then it ought to make known its existence and rebirth by a protest against the crimes of the Russian government and with a demand for Christian a politics, which is possible only amidst freedom and an unconditional respect for the human person. Vl. Solov'ev attempted to do this, but it was insufficiently definite and without consequence. Now the finest of the Slavophils ought to be rendered revolutionaries, if they intend not to repudiate their ideal nature. We shall now take a closer look at the discussions in the "Religio-Philosophic Gatherings" and upon them trace our basic point of view.

In the first issue of "Novyi Put'", a journal which chiefly devotes itself to questions on religion, is an article by N. M. Minsky, under the title "Concerning the Freedom of the Religious Conscience". "I personally regard, -- says Mr Minsky, -- freedom of religious conscience to be of the greatest good in life and hence for a corresponding change in legislation -- for utmost reform, on which moreso than anything else, depends our future. But the attitude towards this question on the part of the intelligentsia seems to me inaccurate and superficial".

We are ready to agree, that the attitude towards this question is superficial, and we think, that the positivism of our intelligentsia, which is held by all still its greater portion, also is unable to look deeply into this question. But how so deep is Mr. Minsky himself, in considering himself an idealist. He, certainly, defends freedom of conscience, which is very praiseworthy on his part, but he defends it by means of arguments, which do not seem to us particularly profound nor idealist. Mr Minsky submits an appraisal on freedom of conscience, he weighs the arguments of the churchly representatives that are against freedom of conscience, and as a result of these considerations he makes a deduction in favour of freedom of conscience. This is the old, the utilitarian method in positivism, in the given instance of a religious positivism, and herein is weighed the usefulness or harm of freedom of conscience for a triumphing of the Christian religion. Mr Minsky on this basis decides the question -- on the usefulness of freedom of conscience, while Archimandrite Antonii, against whom he disputes, -- is against this freedom. It is fine, that he openly raises the question, disputes about it on the side of Orthodoxy as rather a matter within, but his arguments in a religio-philosophic regard are superficial, while in political a regard they show an elementary lack of understanding and insight. We shall attempt further on down to provide our own setting of the question of freedom of conscience.

Mr Minsky concludes his article with the words: "For us the intelligentsia and the Church ought not to be in a position of warring sides. These "returnees", about whom I speak, these fighters and creators in the sphere of religious ideas await from the Church something better than a rebuff of censuring violence. They await an active and positive assist and good-will. They are hopeful, that in the bosom of the Orthodox Church will be a religious reformation, similarly with state reform, to be realised not as in Europe, -- happening not from below, but rather from above, not by way of fighting, but rather by way of love, not through conquest, but through blessing". In the drama, which the sincerely religious Russian intelligentsia tends to experience, Mr Minsky fails to mention the chiefly active player -- the Russian autocracy. The autocracy oppresses not only the Russian intelligentsia, but also the Russian Church, the religious conscience, and therefore a free relationship between the intelligentsia and the Church, the awaiting from the Church of "assist and good-will" is possible only amidst the "vanquishing" of the autocracy, amidst the construct of the Church set free. To expect religious reform from above, whilst keeping to the existing state structure, is in the best instance naive. We have been waiting for a shamefully long time and have no right to expect anything more, than that the religious reformation itself has to be made from below by revolution. We await a blessing, but this "blessing" will come only amidst liberation, which will liberate the intelligentsia and the Church itself and put it in suchlike a condition, that if it retain still its creative powers, will allow for the possibility of a "path of love".

How indeed is to be resolved the question about freedom of conscience and the attitude of the intelligentsia towards the Church within the Religio-Philosophic Gatherings? His Eminence Sergei, Bishop of Yamburgsk, says in his opening statement: "A genuine, serious, actually durable unity is something we shall attain only in that instance, if we express each in front of the other, and in order that each should see, with whom he has to deal, what he can accept from him and what he cannot. Without this indispensable condition our accord would be a mistake, and our combined work -- impossible. We desire truth and sincerity; and therefore everyone, who sincerely strives towards the same, although his approach be from completely different a side, and although to the extreme gone astray, still all the same this searching for truth and the desire to assist the matter of our unity, is heard from our side with all respect and all cordial in intent. And by such an approach we shall get to know each other better, and perhaps, reach an accord". In such manner, His Eminence Sergei to a certain degree guaranteed freedom of conscience within the bounds of the "Gatherings" and by this itself acknowledged, that freedom of conscience is already needful, in order to debate the question on the freedom of conscience.

At the gatherings were read a series of papers on pertinent themes. Thus there is, for example, the paper of Mr Ternavtsev: "The Great Task facing the Russian Church". The author, evidently, is a conservative and Orthodox, and therefore they will take an especial interest in his speaking thus: "The supreme power, religious by its origin and anointing, the bearer of the greatest faith-confessed hopes, operates through a bureaucracy, whereby these hopes are not being accommodated whilst being irreparably indifferent towards the well-being of the governed, and with a detached sense of responsibility in its matters". Mr Ternavtsev accords merits in due order to the Russian intelligentsia and he does not blame it exclusively in its age-old issues with the Church. The only way out from the grievous position, in which Russia is now situated, in Mr Ternavtsev's view is: "in a revealing from the churchly side of its implicit "truth also about the earth", the teaching about the Christian state and the religious vocation of the secular powers".

In the 3rd Session was read a paper by Mr Merezhkovsky under the title: "L. Tolstoy and the Russian Church". Within the attitude of Mr Merezhkovsky towards L. N. Tolstoy there is much that is inaccurate, but all the same towards the end of his paper he posits the following question: "To what extent also are the actions of the Church dependent upon government promptings? To what extent was the former spiritual Collegium a genuine, not only historical, but also a mystical representative of the Russian Church? But herein again arises the question earlier posed by me, concerning the actuality of that "paralysis" in which, according to the opinion of Dostoevsky, the whole Russian Church has been situated "from the times of Peter the Great", in consequence of its outward mechanical subordination to the state. What, particularly, has happened: is it a matter of a paralysis healed, in accord with the words of the Lord, to rise up and lift the hand in self-support, or is it a matter of all still laying there in paralysis while someone else standing there lifts the withered hand of the paralytic, in order to strike at the other's own enemy?" "And indeed here again arises and suddenly worsens to the extreme the unresolved, the merely postponed by Peter I question on the relationship of autocracy and Orthodoxy..." This question was thus posited so directly only by Mr Merezhkovsky, but in essence, this was a question basic to all the debates in the "Religio-Philosophic Gatherings". And if it was not stated there even still more sharply and directly, then it was only -- through oversight and fecklessness.

L. Tolstoy was excommunicated from the Church by the Russian state, excommunicated via the police motives of the Holy Synod, and not from religious motives of the Church. In this ugly fraud and brazenness of an excommunication, which ought to rouse the indignation not only of free-thinking people, intent merely with their own individual religious concerns, but also of sincerely believing Christians, who as such are not blind nor forgetful of state methods of force, who would yet tend to see in the Holy Synod and Pobedonostsev authentic representatives of the Mystical Church of Christ. Orthodox Christians, confessing their faith not through a dictatorical principle, could tend to defend the excommunication of L. Tolstoy from the Church in a free Russia, amidst the existence of the Church having its freedom, but not now, when we have no freedom of conscience and no church in the true sense of the word.

A very distasteful figure at the "Religio-Philosophic Gatherings" -- was a Mr Skvortsov, an official of the special commissions under the Ober-Prokurator of the Holy Synod, redactor of "Missionary Oversight", conducting its vile harassments of sectarians. Mr Skvortsov appeared at the Gatherings in his capacity of being an agent of the autocracy, sitting there somewhat fastidious and oblivious. "The Synod in Russia, -- says this gentleman, -- is a form and arrangement quite excellent. It is not a component of the secular power, but rather as at a council. The tsar is the embodiment of the will of the people. His participation in the affairs of the Synod is, in essence, a participation in these affairs by the people itself". To Mr Skvortsov other participants speak many caustic and unpleasant truthful remarks.

In the 7th Session is read a paper by Pr. S. M. Volkonsky: "Regarding a Characteristic of the Societal Opinions as to the Question concerning Freedom of Conscience". This paper per se represents a *decisive* defense of *freedom of conscience* and can be characterised, as a voice, issuing forth from the upper and conservative strata of the Russian nobility. "Everything, -- says Pr. Volkonsky (the speech concerns Mr Stakhovich and the attacks against him), -- that has appeared in the pages of the "Moscow newspapers", under the signatures of the Rozhdestvenskys, the Znamenskys, the Simanskys and others, with a series of objections, published in the "Orlov Messenger" and reprinted in other newspapers, all this is a matter of chancelry theology -- somehow logically defective, reflected in the *unctiously-blind churchliness under the auspices of political reliance*. (Italics ours). This final aspect is so strong, that it smashes its way through any other sort of argumentation, and clambers forward, and now already not only every churchly, not only every theological question on theological a basis, but even every philosophic question on theological a basis is transformed into a police-political question; this is some sort of a closed circle, from which no one can indeed escape, and into which inevitably they want to drag everything". Pr. Volkonsky here comes nigh to the most basic question, and evidently, not without being influenced by Vl. Solov'ev. The Orthodox, under the guidance of Mr Pobedonostsev and the exalted motives for a Russian unlimited tsardom, seeking to support it all upon the commands of Christ, tend to be hindered in the ability of discernment of the political connivance involved. Against this ulcerous sore within Russian life there ought, ultimately, to be raised the outcry not only of those who are indifferent to the religion of the people, including the strugglers for political freedom, but perhaps even moreso the outcry of the Russian people, for whom particularly has to be repulsive the transformation of the Church into a police accomplice, in which it is dragged along, but in which no one still wants to have do with in their inner heart. Such outcries are beginning to spread forth by reason of one of the most outstanding of Russian people -- Vl. Solov'ev, and people, struggling for religious freedom and for religious renewal, ought consciously to join in with the mighty liberation movement, outside of which is not possible religious freedom, nor of any other sort freedom. Impelled by a religious awareness, and thirsting for an embodiment of Christianity in life, one cannot but be in a sharply negative attitude to an anti-Christian autocratic state and towards the existing arrangement of the Church. Historical Orthodoxy, humble and cringing before the government, propped up by a numbing ritualism, gets sustained by the religious lack of awareness by the people, by the indifferentism of the intelligentsia, by a weakness in spiritual hunger.

The replies by representatives of the clergy to questions concerning the relationship between the Church and the state, of the role of the Holy Synod, on whether the Christian religion should recourse to the means of state coercion in questions of religious conscience, tend to strike one by their duplicity and broadness. Archimandrite Antonii, one of the chief spiritual orators of the "Gatherings", was able to demonstrate, that Orthodox Christianity is the absolute truth and therefore it is exclusive of every other faith and belief, and that the representatives of Christianity have to employ spiritual forceful means over human souls in the name of their salvation, but only just how the matter involves the employing of state coercion, the one making the argument gets off track, and he begins to speak as a representative of the autocratic state, and not of the Orthodox Church. The literary defenders of the freedom of conscience, having won the point of the idea over the clergy, then decided not to push matters by dotting the "i".

Bishop Sergei goes on to say, -- "The principal deliberations, about whether Christianity allows for freedom of conscience, seems to me not possible. There are certain words of the Saviour: "no one can come unto Me, if the Father in having glorified Me, doth attract him not", i.e. the turning to Christ and the fidelity to Christ is as such an inward and heartfelt act, which only God knows, as well as the man himself. Christ in His life showed us the fulfilled example of freedom". It thus would seem, that the principle of Christian freedom possesses unconditional a significance, and that it is impossible to hem it in with utilitarian conditions, but at the point where Bishop Sergei and others get around to the Russian reality, the commands of religion are momentarily forgotten and get replaced instead by state-utilitarian considerations, as though pursuing the interests of lesser-claim brothers. They want to persuade us, that the religious conscience gets abused in the name of love for the people, which can lead to the perishing of one's soul by a falling away and heresy. And here for the bishop stands up the official of the Holy Synod Mr Skvortsov and emphasises to him, what it is necessary to do in practice, in the practical aspect -- this is his field, he instead is the master here and, if it is impossible to do what Christ teaches, then still he quite firmly knows, what Mr Pobedonostsev, in having sent him, teaches. A certain speaker accurately notes: "What a shocking duplicity there is in the talks of all the spiritual orators. Each begins with the assertion, that Christianity is inseparable with freedom of conscience, each puts this freedom into the red corner, and having incensed it in good measure in a cloud of fragrant smoke, pulls over it a veiling of sanctity and he begins to arrange it, as though for this sanctity it should be altogether hid from the light". The causes behind this duplicity are from thus the concepts -- that it is impossible to go unpunished the serving at the same time of two masters both God and mammon, both Christ and the Russian state, propped up at each step not only by the Christian commands, but also by a most elemental human sort. Nothing can be more hideous and repulsive than this dual serving of two gods. "In principle, -- says Mr Philosophov, -- freedom is admitted, yet *de facto* it is denied. That which is proposed as at the basis of Christianity, what appears as an indisputable element for the utmost developing of the Christian teaching -- is repudiated in the name of an accommodation to life". Mr Merezhkovsky says: "When indeed namely has the state been religious, actually Christian in principle? You have pointed to the autocracy. I think, that in the autocracy there is a grain of the religious, but this however is only potentially, not really. We cannot now religiously and fully sense, that "the tsar -- is a father", this for us is only a legend from former ages. When the Church recourses to coercive force, this then is not of Christ and not from a Christian state, as might be possible in future".

Concerning Mr Merezhkovsky, it mustneeds separately be said, that he is a talented man and he raises many interesting questions, and his book, "L. Tolstoy and Dostoevsky", tends to be read with great interest. He sometimes says some very harsh truths to the representatives of the clergy, but he could exhibit some shame, in flippantly asserting, that "in the autocracy there is a grain of the religious". For Mr Merezhkovsky the conflict between Orthodoxy and autocracy is as though a conflict of the "God-Man" and the "man-god", and this is that selfsame problem involving Christ and the Anti-Christ. In such manner, the autocracy, if it be shown to have evil to it, then the evil is heightened mystically by its nature.

In the Russian autocracy there is nothing of the mystical or the demonic, nor to render about it a judgement based exclusively on the person of Peter the Great, as Mr Merezhkovsky is inclined to do. Our police autocracy rests upon a cult of brute force, upon most shameful a materialism, known only to history, and this gets confirmed by each action of the Russian government. The romantic dream of the Slavophils about an ideal autocracy has nothing in common with the historical and actual autocracy, and this harmful and absurd daydream was shattered by that expresser and interpreter of the real autocracy -- Katkov. Katkov discerned the nature of the Russian autocracy and demonstrated, that at its basis lays the principle of state positivism, a police officialdom, and not the religious and idealistic. Not for nothing did Vl. Solov'ev term Katkov the historical Nemesis of Slavophilism. And for Mr Merezhkovsky there is no reviving of the errant Slavophilism, long since already consigned to the archives of history.

The only positive and constructive work, to which the Russian government has shown capable, has been in the encouraging of industrial developement. The most visible representative of the government, Mr Witte (who is in any case moreso a positivist, than a mystic), has attempted to be an economic progressive, a fashioner of the material culture of the land, and at the same time a political reactionary and thereby himself a quencher of spiritual culture. Mr Pleve (alt. Plehve), some several times already having deployed religion in the name of his bureaucratic career, is already bereft of any constructive plans, he is a nihilist and materialist denier of everything cultural, everything vital, everything of creativity and foremost of all the spiritual, since it presupposes the freedom despised by his police soul. For indeed religion, mysticism and every idealism presupposes first of all the admitting of the rights of the human spirit, of its creativity free from material-policing oppression, and there cannot be admitted as religious and mystical that which is directed exclusively towards a quenching of the spirit, chaining it down to its earthly aspect, and with all its glib and materialistic being it denies spiritual freedom and creativity and knows no other paths to take, except that of the police and the gendarmes, prisons and the knout, the gallows and bloodshed. Mr Merezhkovsky ought loudly to declare, that the first actual manifestation of a mystical Orthodoxy, of a reborn Christianity, cannot but be a clear and decisive demand for the abolition of the police autocracy and the dispelling of the principles of state positivism and utilitarianism, of every police sort direct sort physical oppression in the name of the mystical rights of the human spirit. The genuine and sincere mystic, if he denies the political logic and fails to understand the significance of legal guarantees, can only be an anarchist. The mystic, if he is not merely peddling his mysticism and instead relates to it seriously, has the right to contrast against a liberal or socialistic state only an anarchistic clericalism, and nowise an autocratic state. And we think, that an anarchistic dream is the singularly worthy idealistic dream concerning a free society of people, since the idealistic anarchism would be an ultimate triumph of the inward over the outward, of freedom over force, of the human spirit over the natural and social materia.[1] But the path to this realm of freedom is remote, and upon this path ensues in its own right a political logic, which demands, as a concrete task, the construct of more free and more competent an organisation of the state structure, such as

---

[1] An anarchistic utopia is the consequent and ultimate inference from the principles of liberalism. Socialism is only, conditional upon a certain historical era, a method of the realisation of liberalism in the direction of the anarchistic ideal.

would most greatly guarantee freedom and the rights of man. Rendering the dream concrete will also demand from us not only the idealistic positing of the tasks, but also a realistic attitude towards their fulfilling.

On the conscience of Mr Merezhkovsky is still another issue, his twofold attitude towards aristocratism and democratism. He rightly protests against a diminishing of the Christian religion down into the semblance of an altruistic morality. We are likewise inclined to think, that at the basis of Christianity is rooted love towards God, which we are commanded to love moreso, than our very self, and hence already is inferred love for people, whom we can love to the extent of our very self. Upon the love for God, and consequently, for what is right, for truth and the good, which mustneeds be loved moreso than people, moreso than their well-being, -- is based the supreme dignity of the human person, and as such is an expression of its metaphysical nature. But in what regard does all this stand to democratism? Within Christianity is rooted the historical and logical groundings of the modern democratic culture, though too it is more complex and more extensive a matter, and the political and social democratism mustneeds admit the unquestionable moral axiom, expressing the unconditional significance of man and the equal-value of people afront God. As such, to this democratism there cannot be set in opposition an aristocratism upon mystical a basis. Yet a spiritual aristocratism can and should be defended, with the profound differences of spiritual individualities and diverse spiritual cultures, but this aristocratism and these differences cannot be tied in with social inequalities, the spiritual qualification is not created by a material qualification. This has to be admitted ever and again. The value underlying the considerations of Mr Merezhkovsky mustneeds be admitted in the positing of the question concerning the relationship between the spirit and the flesh. In the "flesh" for him becomes symbolised the whole of mundane culture, science, art, the state, marriage. And the Christian religion can have a future only, if it sanctifies the "flesh" -- the human culture. Herein arises a very important problem. Mr Merezhkovsky, evidently, regards himself Orthodox, which however does not prevent him from roundly criticising the historical Christianity, which in his view has tended towards one-sided and directly false an ascetic direction, which as such preaches the Christianity of a Second Coming.

The final sessions of the Religio-Philosophic Society were devoted to the question concerning marriage, an essential side of the general question on the "flesh". This -- is a specialty of Mr Rozanov, and on this question he finds there to be an "heretical" tendency towards the Old Testament and with this quite befuddles the representatives of the Orthodox clergy. But an overview of the marriage question is outside our present task.

At the 13th Session, Mr Merezhkovsky at one point is given to declare: "We have come together here, in order to help one another in seeking truth, and to dispel from each other the inevitable pangs of doubt. For me it goes against the grain in those instances, when I meet up with some pretension to a possessing of absolute truth". This in effect is a proclaiming of freedom for religious hunger and it was thus unpleasant for Mr Skvortsov and others like him to hear such things, in their desire to monopolise absolute truth and speculate upon it for very mundane ends. John of Kronstadt (Kronshtadtsky), that limited representative of a police-type Orthodoxy, denounced "Novyi Put'" and declared it "inauspicious". In such manner, he a thousand times over asserted, that on the basis of autocracy there can be no sort of religious thought and no sort of religious movement, such as can be sanctioned as positive, only the grovelling.

All this is new against the backdrop of Russian life, but this is only the first sproutings of a conscientious religious movement, which will present to the Russian autocracy its ultimatum and by this it will fulfill its historical religious duty. In conclusion we want to say why, in our view, the arguments of Minsky, of Merezhkovsky and others in defense of freedom of conscience are incomplete and non-idealistic, and how the question about freedom of conscience ought to be put.

Idealists and mystics namely cannot produce positive utilitarian arguments either in defense of freedom of conscience or against it, in the name of some whatever positive religion or in the name of its demise. Freedom of conscience is an absolute value, a good itself per se, the right of freedom of conscience is an inalienable natural right of the human person, an unmediated expression of its metaphysical essence, and nothing on earth is of such value, in the name of which can infringe on this right, can banish it, whether by will of the tsar or by will of the people. Nor even such purposive-ends in Heaven, since the Kingdom of God is a realm of freedom, and the path towards it lies through the developement of mankind towards freedom and the natural rights of man, which have become embodied within society, manifest first of all by a pointing to the higher and heavenly nature of man, and they -- are the gift of God, and for the defending and growth of this gift upon the earth -- man will have to answer before God. For us alike ought to be disdained an earthly utilitarianism, considering the rights of man from the point of view of state benefit,[1] And so also with the heavenly utilitarianism, infringing upon human rights and freedom in the name of positive religion, in the name of the forced salvation of people, of their benefit for the next world.[2]

In freedom, bestown you, is your well-being, the salvation of mankind and the true humanness. Ruination threatens only from the trampling down of freedom, from the disdaining of the rights of man, and in this is a spiritual death, the death of religion and culture, in this -- is the impossibility facing society itself, and the struggle for freedom and rights is a struggle not only for the absolute values of life, but also for life itself, for the elementary benefits of life. For us, as Russian people, it is needful to clearly and resolutely perceive our great responsibility in the face of history, in the face of the future of our native land and to direct all our efforts and thought towards our national-political liberation, the liberation indeed of all our nations, in which a religious liberation ought to occupy its proper place. The historical hour has already struck, the powers of the people have arisen and no one can now refuse their political duties and political rights.

---

[1] The present representative of state utilitarianism is Mr Pleve and those like him, and to us it seems a monstrous theoretical defect of insight, when to this perspective there happen to stray people of rather different aspirations, people thirsting for freedom.

[2] At the basis of the positive Christian religion lies freedom and therefore the argumentation of the representatives of the Church are inwardly perverse.

On the Modern Russian idealism

(1904 - 111)[1]

"And how do Russian boys up til now act. Some that is? Here, for example occupying a foul tavern, here they also gather, seated in a corner. All their whole being before they did not know one another, and they then leave the tavern, and again in forty years they will not know one another, well and indeed what, about what will they judge, while they've caught a moment at this tavern? About the worldwide questions, naught else: does God truly exist, is there immortality? And those that do not believe in God, well, they instead talk about socialism and about anarchism, about the refashioning of all mankind into a new state, and thus indeed one feature becomes apparent, all the selfsame questions, only with different an ending. And a multitude, a multitude of very original Russian boys also only do thus, in what they say about the age-old questions such as we have in our time. Is it not so?"

Dostoevsky.

I.

The growth of idealistic searchings and idealistic trends in philosophy, in literature and in life can be regarded as a basic fact of the Russian spiritual culture of recent years. Herein beats the pulse of modern thought, passions play out, evoking misunderstandings and irritations for some, and expectations and hopes for others. Our journalistic sort of positivists, evidently, have lost the capacity whatsoever to take an interest, except to discredit the latest idealism, and they breathe menacingly, as though mankind be threatened by ruin from an outbreak of idealism, as though different an enemy, old and in common to both us and the positivists, smiting at each step with coarse power, lurks in the background. Granted we be happy dreamers and we quench a fantastic thirst, -- yet the

[1] O NOVOM RUSSKOM IDEALIZME. Article originally published in the journal, "Questions of Philosophy and Psychology", 1904, № 75, p. 683-724.

dreams and phantasms have seemed to our opponents stronger and more dangerous than any real enemy. And how many a misunderstanding and lack of knowledge is discovered here, how many terrible and pitiful defects of reasoning, how uncultured the polemic modes and primitiveness of construct! I intend to speak in my article on this Russian idealism, set now at the centre of attention, and to somewhat dispel certain misconceptions.

First of all it mustneeds be said, that with us there is no defined, no clear and entire worldview, as might be held in common by all the so-called "idealists", and none of us, involved in the idealist current, make any pretense to this. What unites idealists is not so much a definite and single-form positive worldview and faith, as rather a searching and negative attitude towards the limitedness of positivism, its insufficiency for the cognitive spirit. Within idealism there exist many shades and factions, and its representatives have not yet arrived at the fashioning of a worldview: since ahead there open many paths. Now already might be defined, in extreme measure, two factions of idealism: the one is decidedly metaphysical, with its emphasis upon a transcendent religion, the other is ethical -- gnosseological, plying its way within the flow of the Kantian transcendental idealism. The very word idealism, perchance rendered a war-cry, is quite indistinct and has to evoke many a misunderstanding. Through various sorts of non-philosophic associations this expression has received some sort of a repute of grandeur and occasions quite blind demands and misplaced witticisms. It is possible, certainly, not to dwell on this and furthermore that idealism, as a philosophic current, nowise makes pretense to some special sort of loftiness and idealness. We have never attempted to infringe upon the lofty virtues of the positivists, we merely pointed to their philosophic weakness, the simpleness and primitiveness of their worldview, the contradiction between their idealistic constructs and their theories. But the word idealism can evoke misunderstandings also from purely a philosophic point of view.

Quite a bit of confusion is evoked by the term idealism within the theory of cognition, and here quite readily are tempted people, little familiar with philosophy. The matter consists in this, that idealism within the theory of cognition is unreceptive to metaphysics and in the majority of instances leads to phenomenalism, or the same, to positivism, whereas realism within the theory of cognition, certainly, is not naive, it opens the doors for metaphysical knowledge, and manifests as it were a gnosseological justification of metaphysics. Contemporary gnosseologists, transcendental idealists in all its shades, deriving from Kant, arrive in the final end towards a confirmation of positivism. Reality, being, the truly existing is declared a fiction and there wins out a quite genuine illusionism. The idealistic theory of cognition, in essence, tends all towards ideas and categories, behind which is emptiness, and which possess no bearer; it cannot find a way out from the vicious circle of concepts nor find paths to reality, in the depths of being. The pure and characteristic sort of transcendental idealist Cohen [Hermann, 1842-1918] is a resolute foe of metaphysics and a very genuine positivist, and only upon firm and rational groundings (ideas, *a priori* categories) does he construct a positivist edifice of our cognition and our morality. The riddle of being in its bottomlessness and mysteriousness gets completely abolished for such idealists and particularly because, that they are idealists, that for them it all comes down to the ideas of reason, to a system of concepts.[1] Windelband [Wilhelm, 1848-1915] affixes the objective reality to the normative reason; he does not emerge beyond the categories and concepts, the ideas and the values, to the actual scope of being, the existent; his final recourse -- is the supra-individual reason, as the source of objective norms and values, but this reason is not endowed with life, and is not being.[2] The sharp-witted and nowise bereft of profound thought underlying the school of immanent gnosseological monism, with Schuppe [Wilhelm, 1836-1913] at the head, leads to its logical end and discloses the basic defects of almost all the German gnosseology. This is the pale spectre of Hegelian Pan-Logism, ultimately consigning us into the grip of the illusory; completely impossible here becomes any transcendence towards being, since all being is declared immanent thought, as identical with it, and everything is resolved via a "consciousness in general", in a contentless tautology.

[1] The closest one in mentality to Cohen, Natorp [Paul Gerhard, 1854-1924], in his interesting [1902] book, "Platos Ideenlehre. Eine Einführung in den Idealismus", makes a characteristic attempt to wipe away from Plato all the ontological elements and to explain the Platonic Ideas in a spirit of the Neo-Kantian teaching about categories. Plato however can hardly be transformed into a follower of Cohen.

[2] The talented and sharp-witted student of Windelband, Rickert [Heinrich, 1863-1936], still moreso defends the resolving of all the objective reality within the normative reason.

One of the most remarkable positivists and empiricists, Laas [Ernst, 1837-1885], is likewise indeed an idealist within the theory of cognition, and likewise he denies the real, he transforms the world into a spectral what is seen, into negative phenomena without substrate or bearer. Idealism and positivism herein pathetically align each with the other and in the final accounting they uphold one and the same philosophy baselessly. All these gnosseological directions are hostile to metaphysical cognition, since in it either there gets altogether ignored the problem of reality and the concepts of being go unanalysed, or else it is that our profound consciousness of the transcendent reality, the consciousness of being outside of concept, is declared a fiction, the seemingly so, and everything is admitted as immanent thought with its categories, affixed to ideas without bearer, without an existent.

In the grandiose and majestic testament of German Idealism, in the Pan-Logism of Hegel, there occurred as it were an ultimate uniting of gnosseological and ontological idealism, the given idea was life, the idea was conceived of as being, and being -- as idea. But this grandiose idealistic system lacked the wherewithal to overcome the illusionism, hid within the very nature of the abstract rationalistic idealism. With Hegel there disappears the distinction between being and non-being, and the absolute idealism leads to an absolute nothingness. Beyond the universal logic there has not become apparent true being, the living individual existent, from the gloomy prison chaining us to concepts there was no pathway towards being; this is an innate defect of abstract rationalism, its attempting to grasp the world by way of deductive concepts from reason, abstractly cleaving apart our spiritual nature in the name of its ratio-judgemental side. We have to restore the rights of living experience, not the abstract and semi-conditional experience of the empirico-positivists, but rather that experience, in which we are in unmediatedly in contact with true being, with the living soul of the world. We ought vitally to protest against rationalistic attempts to kill insights by means of concepts; Schopenhauer perceived this as profound a necessity, and he was perhaps closer than others in approaching the true path of metaphysical knowledge. Schopenhauer was one of the few trans-rationalists in the history of philosophy and in this he is nigh close to us.[1] It might be bold

[1] Vide the fine [1901] book by Volkelt [Johannes, 1848-1930], "Arthur Schopenhauer". The irrationalism of Schopenhauer is connected

a thing to say, that the fate of metaphysics, the fate of all the philosophic thought of the future is connected with the surmounting of two strongholds, standing in the way: Kant and Hegel, gnosseological idealism, rationalistic in spite of all its critical aspect, which has infected the entirety of contemporary German philosophy, and the absolute abstract idealism, even moreso rationalistic, yet now by many haplessly forgotten, but reflects that final point, at which we hit a dead-end; upon this path everything tends to have vanished and new paths to search are needed. Hegelians in their searches for a substrate, the underlying existent, in their desire to escape the stifling atmosphere of abstract concepts, have transitioned over to materialism, and in this attempt a firm relying upon matter reflected the profound inner logic. To uniquely original Russian philosophic thought, which we still have not begun sufficiently to appreciate, there belongs a very profound and very brilliant critique of Hegelianism and of all rationalism in general; it all gravitates towards a metaphysical realism, towards a concrete spiritualism, towards a restoration of that wholistic experience, in which unmediatedly is given the existent.[1] I see in this a seed, from which will grow Russian philosophic thought, called to have its say within world culture.

---

with a pessimistic teaching concerning the irrationality and blindness of the world will, but is not a trans-rationalism.

[1] The first Russian thinker, setting out upon this path, was Khomyakov. He was clearly aware of the inconsistency within the rationalistic paths of European philosophy and he provided a deep-minded critique of Hegel. In him was grounded already the basic features of that which can be termed a concrete spiritualism. Vide the "Collected Works, A. S. Khomyakov", tom I, p. 263-348. The Slavophil tendencies of Khomyakov and the fragmentary and haphazard character of his philosophic works have hindered a proper appreciation of this outstanding thinker. The work, begun by Khomyakov, was brilliantly continued by Vl. Solov'ev, whom they are beginning all more and more to appreciate. Likewise needful of mention is the remarkable work of L. M. Lopatin [Lev Mikhailovich, 1855-1920], entitled "The Positive Tasks of Philosophy". This book stands higher than many of the acknowledged German philosophic works and ought finally to be appreciated as to its worth.

Here is why in the theory of cognition it would be more correct for us to term ourselves as realists; transcendental realism -- here is a gnosseological point of view, towards which the metaphysical faction of idealism tends to gravitate. In metaphysics the expression idealism likewise is not altogether fine, and better would be to term ourselves adherents of spiritualism or panpsychism, since at the basis of being we posit spirit, and not idea. Moreover the term idealism might be adopted in ethics, insofar as we admit of absolute values, but this also regretably would be inaccurate to term it as idealism for ethics, which rests upon metaphysics, upon ontology, and sees the basis of the good not in transcendental ideas, but rather in the transcendent nature of spiritual beings. In general, many so-called idealists moreso confess ontologism, than idealism, and at the basis of their worldview lies not concepts, not ideas (gnosseological and ethical), but rather metaphysical being. We again ought to admit the primacy of being over thinking, although not at all in the sense, in which the empiricists and materialists tend to admit such. And this certainly demands further explanation, which I in time hope to present, but for now I merely want to point out the ambiguity and lack of conciseness of that conditional term "idealism", which we ourself tend to esteem, amidst the mockery of others. We shall for the moment continue to use this general catchword "idealism" in the interest of simplicity and convenience.

II.

To certain of our opponents it would seem, that the contemporary idealism is the idle chatter of a bunch of the literary sort, who now suddenly have begun to indulge in phantasies. Others accuse us of simply rehashing recent German booklets on philosophy. But a rightful judgement ought to be rendered, recognising the roots of idealism as lodged deeply within the earth, and that it is to an utmost degree national whilst together with this it is universal. These roots lie within the depths of the Russian national spirit and they are readily apparent in the Russian great literature. It is impossible to deny this, that literature is both an expression and a reflection of the national spirit. In literary creativity is expressed our innate nature, a very intimate and individual side of our national existence. The most universally human poets along with this have also been the most national, as for example, was Goethe. Russian literature -- is our national matter of pride; it is a singular contribution by us to world culture and within lies concealed the greatest of prophecies for our native land. It would be quite interesting and instructive to draw a parallel between Russian and European literature.

The most recent idealist trend was predicted by the entire history of Russian literature: in it was lodged verymost profound philosophic and religious yearnings, and perhaps, the tasks of Russian philosophy and its publicists involves an elaboration of the motifs of Russian literature. Already more than once it has been pointed out, that no one has shown such interest in the ultimate philosophic questions on being, as the Russians, and only our cultural youthfulness, the still weak developement of an intellectual culture can explain the insufficiency of systematic philosophic thought. I, however, am not lacking in hopes to show, that the tasks of Russian philosophic thought are qualitatively higher than with contemporary European philosophy, in decline and fragmented, and for us is lodged the possibility of an independent and fruitful philosophic creativity.

Let us shift our gaze first of all towards Pushkin, to this miracle within Russian history, to the authentic fashioner and initiator not only of Russian literature and the Russian language, but also all our spiritual culture. We lack the ability to appreciate him fully, we relate to him in too school-like a manner and do not give him proper credit for his greatness and depth, in his significance even for our time. Pushkin was properly appreciated only by Dostoevsky in his remarkable speech at the Pushkin festivity. By his own genius, akin to that of Pushkin, he perceived the all-human, the universal character of the creativity of Pushkin and in this all-human aspect he discerned our national trait.[1] Pushkin first depicted this eternal wanderer of the Russian earth, an every-man with a restless and weary soul; he foresaw the history of the Russian intelligentsia of the XIX Century, in him already were those deep elements, which in

---

[1] "To be a genuine Russian, -- says Dostoevsky, -- to be fully Russian, perchance, also means only to be a brother of all people, a man of all, if you will". Vide "Diary of a Writer for Year 1877". Dostoevsky often points also to this national peculiarity of the Russian intelligentsia: the fellow is a fiery patriot of the West, since the West for him is a dream about all-humanity, and not the grey actuality, not the tedious dullness, as it is for European man.

subsequent stages were revealed in the creativity of Tolstoy and Dostoevsky.[1] The question about the meaning of life, the tormented religious, philosophic and moral searchings all the moreso pervade the creativity of our artists. In this regard, a vivid example is in the tragic fate of Gogol. The Russian melancholy regarding the meaning of life, -- here is a basic motif of our literary writers and here is what comprises the very obscure essence of the Russian intelligentsia soul, restless and wandering about, in agitation dwelling upon the accursed questions, which are rendered for him questions of one's own individual fate. In this is our chief difference from the philistinism of the European intelligentsia, buried under thick portions of a bourgeois positive faith in the meaning of life and search for God. How is the Russian intelligentsia man depicted in the creativity of Tolstoy and Dostoevsky? Pierre Bezukhov, Prince Andrei Levin, Nekliudov, Raskol'nikov, Ivan Karamazov, Stavrogin, Kirillov et al all live an incessant inner working away at the question about the meaning of life, about God, about good and evil, they are in search of religion; their individual fate is narrowly focused, inseparably caught up with the final questions of human existence. The Dostoevsky heroes are writhing in torments, the tragic aspect reaches in them an as yet unprecedented extreme and all because, in their divided soul the Devil and God are at war. Tolstoy, who had all sorts of earthly goods, fame, wealth, familial happiness, was on the point of going out of his mind and wanting to do away with himself, in that he was unable to resolve the question of the meaning of life. How does this compare with the Western European man, who is accustomed to end it all by suicide in case of some whatever immense misfortune to his personal life's career? This profound inner agitation, this languor over the loss of God, this thirst for the supreme meaning of life was sensed already in Pushkin, Lermontov and Gogol. In Gleb Uspensky, a writer still little appreciated, in the creativity of whom they are accustomed to see only populist-citizen motifs, it is possible to find a religious philosophic core. This is quite characteristic of Russian literature, that in it questions social and on citizenship are tightly intertwined with questions moral, religious and philosophic. This thirst for an utmost harmony in Uspensky is a religious thirst, a search for God, and it will not dissipate over the simple desire for social improvements.

[1] Very accurate remarks on this can be found in the book by Mr Merezhkovsky, "L. Tolstoy and Dostoevsky".

The same thing in our contemporary Chekhov with his "A Dreary Story" [1889]. Yes, in our literature we ought to seek out for the source of our national pride, rather than in the other sides of our unique history, sides infamous and murky.[1]

The European man of the XIX Century in his bourgeois novel was depicted otherwise. He tenaciously pursues his social medium and strengthens his living position; in him there are not these searchings, this religious agitation. In the social opposition to bourgeois society likewise are downplayed the spiritual concerns, and it thus has failed to create its own literature, its own spiritual culture, totally sundered from the philistine realm.[2] The Fausts and Manfreds have vanished from the bourgeois European culture and as it were have instead gotten embodied over into the heroes of Dostoevsky and Tolstoy. God is dead, and interests have so slackened, that there has not remained an authentic searching for the meaning of life. The solitary individuality of Nietzsche (minus the Nietzscheans) looms over the European culture and impresses one by his purely Slavic religious yearning. In the most recent trends in art is seen a crisis, varied searchings, a revolt beginning against an all-engulfing philistinism, but here also amidst purely a psychological refinement get drowned out the ultimate questions on human existence and there is no creative might, -- the school of a philistine positivism and naturalism have too much split the soul.[3] Modern European literature has not gotten to

---

[1] Mr Volynsky [Akim, 1861-1926] has expressed the quite accurate thought, that the Russian critic has seemed incapable of evaluating all the Russian great artistic literature. There were historical reasons for this, but now already the time has come, a challenge facing the Russian idealist movement. Vide Volynsky's book: "Russian Critics" [1896]. Volynsky expressed many an accurate and valuable thought, bold at the time when his book appeared, but regretably, he botched it by the absence of historical a perspective.

[2] By this, I certainly do not want to diminish the social significance of this struggle against the bourgeoise.

[3] The decadent and modernist trends in literature and art -- are matters very complex and interesting. Herein is a profound inner crisis of modern man, and it has not yet merited proper investigation and study.

higher a point than Tolstoy and Dostoevsky, and it will long still learn from our philosopher-artists.

The same features of the Russian national spirit are expressed also in the history of our publicists and critics, as well as our societal movements. The Russian publicists and critics were imbued with philosophic searchings; the most remarkable of our publicists were thinkers and teachers of life. The glorious era of the 1840's, which for us again seems nigh, was predominantly philosophic a period. The publicists and critics, both from the Slavophil and the Westerniser camps, tended to decide all the questions of life in connection with the fundamental questions of philosophy, and the spiritual atmosphere was pervaded by German Idealism, by Schelling and Hegel. The Slavophils decisively constructed their own worldview upon principles of philosophic idealism and displayed even philosophic an uniqueness. The most significant theoretician of the Slavophils and one of the most remarkable of Russian minds -- was Khomyakov, a genuine philosopher, and in him already are to be noted original features of concrete idealism, distinct from the German abstract idealism, which afterwards was assimilated into an entire philosophic system by Vl. Solov'ev.[1] But Hertsen and Belinsky likewise were tormented by philosophic problems; in them the philosophic idealism led to a deep rift and they arrived at their social radicalism, like a religion, as a result of their philosophic and moral searchings. They were passionately national; they were unable to let anything calm them. The 1860's were an era of a disdaining of philosophy and the triumph of a very elementary and naive sort materialism; but here also was expressed the idealistic and philosophic nature of the Russian intelligentsia. Upon materialism and atheism both Chernyshevsky and Pisarev set almost a religious seal; all the same accursed questions tended to disquiet them, and their publicists in the final end were philosophic in spirit: they sought to study the meaning of life. In the 1870's Lavrov and Mikhailovsky were genuinely philosophers on the questions that tormented them, and which they attempted to solve. Already more than once it has been pointed out, that all our subjective sociology has been a clumsy attempt to resolve on the basis of positivism the instead purely metaphysical problems. In the 1890's when Marxism arose among us, it then at once assumed philosophic

---

[1] Khomyakov undoubtedly anticipated Solov'ev's critique of abstract principles.

an aura: they connected it with the Hegelian dialectics, and then with Kantianism, and it satisfied all that selfsame religious thirsting of the Russian intelligentsia.

And our societal trends? Social radicalism has been a religion for the Russian intelligentsia and therefore often it has led to religious martyrdom. How little in our societal movements there has been of political realism; the societal struggle for the Russian intelligentsia is not so much the pursuing of concrete political tasks, as rather the resolving of a personal moral problem. Strange is the existence of the Russian intelligentsia fellow, singular in his sort, and alongside features negative and even absurd he bears within him tasks of something higher and better, than do the people of Europe.

But why indeed among us has there been no genuine philosophy nor genuine philosophers? Here is a question, which usually undermines all the assertions about our philosophic national spirit. Philosophy, they often say, is for us like an invasive plant, appearing in bad translation from the German. This is inaccurate: in this opinion is expressed a lack of knowledge both of Russian and of European philosophy. Yes, we have not had philosophers which can compare with the great classical European philosophers; we have not had a Spinoza and Leibniz, a Kant and Fichte, an Hegel and Schopenhauer; yet in Russian philosophy there is none to compare with our Pushkin and Gogol, Tolstoy and Dostoevsky. Amidst all the depths of our philosophic searchings we have as yet very low a philosophic culture and onerous hindrances stand in the way for its developement. But if we compare Russian and European philosophy in recent decades, we shall also see, that Russian philosophy is nowise lower, and qualitatively even higher than the European and that it is fully original. European philosophic thought is situated in a condition of decline, fragmented and shallow; positivism has wrought too great a devastation. In France there is almost no philosophy, in England is weakly only an effort towards knowing the Neo-Hegelian current.[1] Flourishing the most has been philosophy in Germany, and the philosophic culture there is actually quite lofty. But whither has there gone the great philosophic spirit of the past, and how shallow the thought of modern academic philosophers in Germany has become. They all write gnosseological tractates, sifting

---

[1] Green [Thomas Hill, 1836-1882], Caird [Edward, 1835-1908], Mackenzie [John Stewart, 1860-1935] and others.

their way through all possible shades of criticism, somehow or other attributed to Kant, with a scientific painstaking precision they investigate isolated questions and remain unable to emerge into the perview of philosophic creativity. In modern Germany there is not one genuinely consequential philosopher, excepting perhaps a certain von Hartmann [Eduard; 1842-1906].[1] Even with Wundt amidst all his breadth and many-sidedness there is no genuine philosophic creativity, nor boldness and profundity. Certainly, in Windelband and Rickert, in Cohen and Natorp, Schuppe and Avenarius one can find many a clever and refined thought, and can learn much; but even with the best of these the quality of philosophic inquiry has become diminished, and there is sensed a powerlessness to create, to construct the philosophic thought of the future. German philosophic thought is experiencing an undoubtable crisis; this likewise is transitional a condition, similar to recent trends in art. It is necessary to set out upon a completely new path, in order to go farther, it is needful to surmount both Neo-Kantianism, and the immanent school, and the empirocriticism, for in general all this is but a refined positivism or a positivist idealism, leading to an hopeless illusionism, to a negation of being. All the variant hues of positivism and criticism, suffer one and the same sickness of spirit -- in the disintegration of the interests of everyday life, everyday knowledge and everyday morals there is shown as lost the problem of God, the problem of man, as an existing being. The disintegration and the fragmentation on all sides of culture, of philosophy, art, the social struggle, the assigning of everything into separate compartments, the incapacity to transform it all into a single question concerning the fate of man and his relationship to the supra-human -- here are the fundamental features, which characterise the contemporary condition of European society and all its thinking.

In the as yet youthful Russian philosophy there are tasks of more healthy and correct a developement of philosophic thought; to a greater degree also the great philosophical traditions of the past are being preserved in us. First of all I would point to two immensely significant philosophers, who by extent of thought, breadth of perspective, profound insight into the history of philosophic thought tend to stand remarkably

---

[1] In the recent past there can be considered only Lotze [Hermann, 1817-1881], a genuine metaphysician, rare within German spiritualist philosophy.

higher than the contemporary German philosophers, -- I speak about Boris Chicherin [1828-1904] and Vl. Solov'ev, both whom Russian intelligentsia society knows so pathetically little of. Chicherin was the less original and less close to us: he was too much the rationalist and doctrinaire, but here was an immense mind, a man of enormous knowledge and it is to his great merit, that he preserved the legacy of classical idealism, he defended metaphysics in an era of its philosophic untimeliness; he was an Hegelian and an Hegelian critic, when Hegel had expressed some but foppish gibberish.[1] Vl. Solov'ev -- is the most significant and most original of Russian philosophers, worthy to occupy his proper place in the history of philosophy right next after the German classics of idealism. The uniquely original and national character of the philosophy of Solov'ev is expressed in this, that he conceived of the need for a transition from abstract idealism, having attained its point of completion within Hegel, transitioning rather towards a concrete idealism, placing at the foundational basis of philosophy not absolute ideas, but rather the concrete existent.[2] Together with this he perceived of philosophy not as an "abstract principle", but rather as an integral, organic world-perception or life-understanding, in its inseparable connection with the question about the meaning and significance of life, with religion. Further on down I shall speak about concrete idealism, or spiritualism more accurately, as that philosophy of the future, which is taking shape in Russia. In any case, any whatever land would be proud to have Solov'ev, as a first-rate thinker. But though our nonetheless authentic philosophers are nowise lower than the contemporary European ones, still they go quite unappreciated. Particularly I would mention A. A. Kozlov [Alexei Alexandrovich, 1831-1901], to whom belongs a very refined gnosseological defense of spiritualism, or as he preferred to express it, panpsychism. I regard it as a great service of Kozlov, that in an era of positivism and Neo-Kantianism, an era ignoring the problems of being and denying every ontology, he instead posited in primacy of place a gnosseological analysis of the concept

---

[1] Concerning the merits of "The Philosophy of Rights" by Chicherin, and about his resolute defense of natural rights, -- this is an idea fundamental for us, needing to be addressed more specifically.

[2] Vide: "Critique of Abstract Principles" and "Philosophic Principles of Integral Knowledge".

of being and decisively defended the idea of substantiality, and proceeded along the path of gnosseological justification of the extra-temporal and non-spatial existence of spiritual substances.[1] Likewise talented and notable philosophers are our contemporaries, L. Lopatin [Lev Mikhailovich, 1855-1920] and Prince Sergei Trubetskoy [1862-1905]; in them one can notice the same original features of Russian philosophy -- concrete spiritualism, and a metaphysical teaching concerning the existent.[2] Amidst the growth of our culture and our philosophic learning we can expect a flourishing of philosophic thought in Russia, and a thought that is original. These unique aspects of Russian philosophy, as a philosophy of the future, are lodged within Russian literature, within our national spiritual composite.

In Russian spiritual culture deeply rooted is an unique idealism, which at present is consciously worked at by the most recent Russian philosophers and publicists, -- this is what I want to point out. The recent Russian idealism, despite its brief history and indefinite character, is national in the best sense of this word; it is not the product of idle thoughts from a bunch of the literary sort. Behind us and for us is the whole history of our own culture and within this is lodged our correctness and vital capacity. We are profoundly aware of our spiritual oneness with Tolstoy and Dostoevsky, who are marveled at by all the world.

---

[1] Vide his "Conversations with a Peterburg Sokrates", included in his book, "One's Own Word" ["Своем слове"]. These "Conversations" ought to occupy a visible place within the history of Russian philosophy: and indeed worthy of honour with the German gnosseological literature. An enormous significance obtains in that distinction between consciousness and knowledge, which Kozlov attempts to establish: by this is opened the path to the affirmation of transcendent being, along with the removal of harmful rationalistic presuppositions. Kozlov can moreso be termed a Neo-Leibnizian. Nowadays it is quite the thing and useful to oppose Kant with Leibniz, but a Leibniz, purged by the fire of criticism from the old rationalism.

[2] I have already mentioned the remarkable work of Lopatin, "The Positive Tasks of Philosophy". Kozlov in context of his gnosseological views, negating the reality of space, time and matter, tends towards more definite a spiritualism, than does Lopatin or Solov'ev.

Since I will be subjected to an accusation of Slavophil and national sympathies, all possible misunderstandings here need to be eliminated. The Slavophil teaching, once glorious and attractive in many of its features, has gone dead; worse indeed, than dead; it degenerated into a Katkovschina, as expressed by Mr Katkov, into an human-hating nationalism, into a reactionism of the purest sort, into the "Russian Assemblies". Nothing has remained of the idealistic spirit of the old classical Slavophils; all their romanticism with faith in the great mission of the Russian people and the innate love for freedom has gone to rot into an official patriotism, the worshipping of an official state crudely material power. And this served as a chastisement for that fateful mistake, which the Slavophils had permitted in their teaching about nationality. By their fiery faith in the national spirit, in its unique creativity striving to realise its national imperative, they connected it in fatal a manner with an idealising of the national materia, of the out-moded economic, juridical, political, churchly and other in general remnants of life and they mistakenly sought the national spirit in our past historical existence. They thus impeded the creative spirit of the nation, and put limits to that free upbuilding, in which only can there be expressed a free national culture.[1] The Slavophils tended to idealise the obschina, the peasant commune, and also the economic backwardness and lack of culture, the state-legal forms, long since censured by history, and the stagnant material forms of religious awareness. Nation is a concept spiritual; individualism and uniqueness can only exist through the free creativity of a culture; the national spirit cannot be fenced in and strengthened by any sort of forced, material, police sort of measures -- here is an indisputable truth, which the Slavophils failed to follow out to the end. In the name of our national culture, in the name of our uniquely original creativity we first of all have need of an Europeanisation of all our societal structure, in the realisation and guarantee of certain absolute legal postulates; only this will set free our enchained and oppressed national spirit from the fetters, wrought from a metal neither national nor uniquely original, but rather from a crude sort of affairs, obtaining in common for us from the dominions of violence. The individual and the unique within the human person exists only within freedom; in coercive force everything

---

[1] This was brilliantly pointed out in the article by P. B. Struve, "What indeed is the True Nationalism". Vide "Questions of Philosophy", № 59; this article appeared in the collection "On Various Themes".

becomes impersonal and dulled. The same thing is true also for the life of a nation, which only in freedom can realise its great historical possibilities, whereas by force and oppression it loses its individualness. The official sort of state, state positivism -- here is the deadly enemy, swallowing up the romantic and mission-minded dreams of the Slavophils. If each people has its own purposive vocation in the world, then let its realisation obtain through freedom, free creativity, a constructiveness unchained, not fettered by any sort of coercive stagnant forms. Religion, literature, philosophy, moral renewal, everything from which a spiritual culture derives, and in what is expressed also the great individuality of a people, -- all this demands freedom and does not permit of forceful coercion of creative impulses, nor can all this find proper an appraisal from the utilitarian criteria of state positivism. Yes, we can and we ought to be proud of our great literature, reflecting the national stock of our soul, and see in it lodged our independent position within world literature; but a tinge of shame ought to be expressed by us with thought regarding those coercive forms, which chain down our free creativity. And therefore with indignation we repudiate the political errors of the Slavophils and especially loathe their degenerate descendants. Amidst all this, I do not want to deny the great merits of Slavophilism in positing the national problem. In contrast to an insipid abstract cosmopolitanism or a coercively violent immoral nationalism, there can be a third possibility, an idealistic perspective on nationality, positing the national spirit not in the tasks of statecraft, but rather in an unique and creative realisation of universal all-human tasks.[1]

The most recent Russian idealism has its roots not only in our national culture, but also in the millennia-long history of philosophic

---

[1] A very accurate and profound, perchance singular not only in Russian, but also within European literature, is a resolution of the national question as provided by Vl. Solov'ev, -- that of developing only the finer aspects of Slavophilism and most of all doing away with all sorts of fanatical nationalism. Vide likewise the book by S. Bulgakov, "From Marxism to Idealism", in which there is a decisive repudiation of the negative sides of Slavophilism, while to nationalism gets opposed not a stale cosmopolitanism, but rather an idealistic understanding of nationality and a warm faith in the vocation of Russia, in its enormous significance for world culture.

thought, which the modern positivists tend to ignore. Philosophic creativity can only then become fruitful, if it is connected with the past, -- the greatest revolutions in the sphere of thought have their precedents within history. We would want to invoke a remembrance of the philosophy of the classical past, in our bland and compulsive positivist era. There is a need to conceive of for real new values, but we do not believe, that this creative task can be achieved without an orientation to the eternal values of the past. But now we shall move on to the theoretical groundings of the modern Russian idealism, such as they seem to me. And thus, the interpretation of the idealism will to notable a degree be individual.

III.

There are two problems -- the problem of the person, the individual fate of the human soul, its rights and its values, and the problem of progress, the fate of humankind and the world, the ends and the meaning of history; in these tend to intersect quite abstract theoretical, and yet also very concrete and vital matters of interest for us, and amidst this all the most recent Russian idealism has concentrated upon an attempt to posit and to solve these questions. All the so-called progressive and advanced aspirations of modern mankind, in which pride is taken, rest upon these two core ideas -- the idea of the person and the idea of progress. To transform the fate of the human person and the fate of human progress into a single fate -- is a theme of modern history, worked at tirelessly and tormentedly. In philosophy, which deals with themes related to human life, this finds expression in tendencies towards universalism and individualism, towards monism and pluralism, and the great difficulty of every philosophical construct consists in a combination of these as it were contrary tendencies. An enormous error in a large portion of philosophic systems was in an exclusive predominance of universal and monistic tendencies. And in this was expressed a basic fault of the old philosophic thought, the flaw of rationalism, inherited also by the whole of positivism.

Positivism in all its hues and shades cannot construct either a theory of the person, nor a theory of progress; it cannot even conceive of these problems, nor is it able to posit them, and it lives merely by those crumbs, which fall to it like contraband from the metaphysical table. The very concepts of the person and progress, without which positivism cannot dispense, since its adherents -- are living people, striving to think about life, find this impossible merely upon the basis of positivism, and are hence thoroughly imbued with metaphysical presuppositions. This also is the starting point for the "idealists", wherein they arrived at the conclusion, that these concepts, by which the positivists so unconsciously operate, and towards which all our existence comes down to, everything in our life that is of value and uplifting, -- the conclusion is hence that these concepts are thoroughly metaphysical, and that by their existence and by their significance for us they already tend to topple the positivism. What sort of meaning would be had by all the social movements, the upbuilding within history, the struggle and toil, towards which they summon us, if the human person is merely an empty sound, a chance combination of energy and matter, a playing out of sensations, and if progress -- be a progress without actual ends and meaning? The struggle and toil can drown out in us the tormenting question about the meaning of life, can weaken the spiritual thirst, but this is a shameful and humiliating way out. L. Tolstoy was a thousand times right, when in his "non-activity" he challenges us to take a break from this meaningless and harried activity, in order to look about, ponder the question concerning the significance of all this work, and think instead about life. Work ought not to be some narcotic, which numbs the conscious consideration of the problems of life.

Idealists are often mocked as being reactionaries, and accused of being detached from life, dithering in abstractions remote from the genuine tasks of the time. But from what sort of heights do the positivists themself tend to employ to do this, in the name of what, and issuing from what sort of values? In the name of our indeed idealistic values, clambering up our indeed mountain, -- like contraband ye have made use of our indeed metaphysical concepts. You swear to be for the rights of the down-trodden and oppressed human person, you appeal for a struggle for progress, you make a genuflection to freedom, but ye lack the ability to openly admit the metaphysical character of all these sanctities. When you begin nobly and exaltedly to reproach us, we know beforehand, that you will give us a thrashing for our own good, eh, that there is nothing deceptive about you, that it is impossible for you to deceive, and all your hot anger we again as always have taken as an indication of your moral zeal combined, regretably, with a rather low level of philosophic awareness. We already have long understood the psychological mystery, that it is possible to be an atheist out of a need for religion, to be an immoralist out of a need for morality, a materialist out of a metaphysical need, a cosmopolitan out of a national need. This often becomes noble, but sometimes not particularly clever. No, you have never been deceptive in anything and you do not deceive suggesting, that we had no basis to see in this a contraband pilfering of our positions. Ye would be fine people, if you had not in you this tendency towards pilfering; but we understand, that you need something to live by, that ye risk dying from a spiritual hunger, that one cannot sustain oneself on the laws of nature and statistics, on the abstractions of biology and sociology, and we stand ready to supply you with sustenance; you have been flattered to be possessors of these theoretical matters despised by you, and in practical matters the same way you are fond of the ideas of the person, progress, freedom etc. But it is time to be done with this bad habit of seeing a fine progressive-positivist tone within a vulgar shouting, ridicule and accusations by way of addressing an incomprehensible idealism. And now we shall move on to a philosophic consideration of the problem of person, of individuality.

The problem of individuality is a fundamental problem of our times; it is connected with our verymost profound experiences; it pervades the entirety of modern art, on it arises also every struggle for rights, every morally considered setting of the social question. There is no question, so needful of philosophic insights and attention, as this question concerning the individual. Positivist science tends to remain perplexed at the mystery of individuality; it is interested instead only in the laws of nature, only in the general, the typical, the featureless; for its specific ends it is too involved maintaining an economy in thought, keeping it from dealing with the individual. And positivist science is right. Under the touch of scientific cognition, everything alive and individual dies away, everything concrete gets transformed into an abstraction.[1]

All the so-called scientific experience, based upon the conditional opposition between subject and object, does not bring us to true existent being, to the real; in it are given merely the conditional signs of real being. Elsewhere I attempted to provide justification to that gnosseological point of view, under which all the materials and fundamentals for a working out of the concept of being, this basic philosophic concept, which we grasp

---

[1] Vide the 1902 book of Rickert, "Die Grenzen der naturwissenschaftlichen Begriffsbildung". This is one of the finest books on the theory of knowledge in contemporary philosophic literature.

from an unmediatedly direct given conscious awareness, -- is the conscious awareness of a live transcendent, rather than merely our gnosseological subject, which creates and conceives of the so-called "nature". This is a fundamental defect of every rationalism, and likewise the modes of criticism, deriving from Kant, as well as the positivistic empiricism, even though they might disavow the rationalism, -- and which tends to reckon, that the gnosseological subject, thinking in context of his categories, grasps hold of being and by this fully encompasses it, thus makes impossible any transcendence. This defect is based upon a confusing of consciousness with knowledge, with the subject, with reason, reduced to judgemental an act, upon an interpretation of every cognition, as logical and already artificially considered.[1] Rationalism cleaves apart the human spirit, creates an artificial opposition between that, what is from "reason", and that, what is from "experience", whereby both reason and experience are alike delimited and restricted. Needed is a restoration of the unity and integral wholeness of our cognitive existence and to construct a theory of the metaphysical experiential, accounting for both the conditionally experiential, and the conditionally rational cognition. The perception and intuition, finally, ought to be set free from the constraint of "concept", weighing also upon the so-called experience. The unmediatedly given, the pre-found[2] is not the subject, nor judgemental thinking, but rather the consciousness[3] in its boundlessness, and here we fully come in contact

---

[1] Very profound remarks in this regard can be found in Kozlov's "One's Own Word". Vide likewise N. Lossky's "The Fundamental Teachings of Psychology from a Perspective of Voluntarism", p. 107-136. This is a fine book, uncommonly excellent within Russian philosophic literature.

[2] I deliberately employ the term of *Vorgefundenes* by Avenarius [Richard, 1843-1896], since Avenarius likewise set himself the task to deal with gnosseology at a point prior to the typical opposition between subject and object. Vide his "Der menschliche Weltbegriff". Regretably, he stumbled along the old positivo-naturalistic path and adopted too many rationalistic "presuppositions".

[3] There is no best word in the human language, nor will anything be gained, if its literal or conditional sign be replaced.

with the very core of being, with the existent. It mustneeds assiduously bear repeating, that all being is transcendent to the thought process, that it is not confined and locked up within the concept, and together with this it is immanent to our integral nature, to our metaphysical existence, since there is possible, I would say, a transcendent metaphysical experience, infinite motion within an ocean of consciousness, in which we come nigh in contact with existent being, and not only the conditional so-called scientific experience and the deduced concept from reason. This comes very close to the gnosseological theory of a mystical apperception by Vl. Solov'ev, but there is a certain distinction. First of all we would object against a total identification of philosophic knowledge with religious faith. Experience (the unmediated apperception), which provides the material for the metaphysical knowledge of the existent, is obligatory for all cognitive beings and only through the intellectual flaws of rationalism does it fail to find itself an accurate interpretation and thus often remains unperceived.

A very important result similar to gnosseology would be the especial construction of the concept of being. All being that involves consciousness, every living and individual being, i.e. every being is a concrete spirit, a living and individual *substantia.*[1] Spiritualism is justified by the first stages of gnosseology; gnosseologically it would be absurd to view the concept of being as though it had no meaning except that, which derives directly from a construct of the life of a spirit. The category of "substantia"[2] is a basic category of metaphysical knowledge in regard to

---

[1] The distinction, which Vl. Solov'ev establishes between being and the existent, is very sharp-minded and profound, vide his work: "The Philosophic Principles of integral Knowledge", Ch. IV in Tome I of his "Collected Works". But as regards terminology it would be preferable to keep the word "being", interpreting it as the "existent".

[2] The now in vogue "energetism" trend is completely displacing the category of substantia from the scientific perview and destroys the phantom of the substantiality of matter. This is very useful for us also, but it represents naive and pitiful attempts by the energetists to present it as a complete metaphysical system. With the substantiality of spirit, energetism cannot come to anything and remains completely unable to provide a teaching regarding being: its competency is purely scientific. Vide "Philosophy of Nature" by Ostwald [Wilhelm Friedrich, 1853-1932].

being; it is employed by the metaphysical "great" reason in dealing with matters of the unmediated living consciousness. But what sort of a concept of being is provided us by positivism, by criticism, rationalism? Positivism is simply uninterested in the truly existent, in real being; it explains it as either a fictitious concept or unconceivable, or it inclines towards a naive and absurd materialistic concept of being, about which at present it is neither discussed nor upheld. Criticism as a trend in this regard comes very close to positivism and only the more involvedly and better presents its position. For certain factions of Neo-Kantianism being is likewise a fiction, while for others it is incomprehensible, and a third variant akin to Kant, postulates a spiritualistic concept of being, not having any sort of grounds for this in their theory of cognition. Rationalism in all its shades attempts to find being by way of deductive concepts, to derive being from reason and in the final end comes nigh to Pan-Logism, to an understanding of being, as an idea, and it attempts to reduce everything down to logical relationships. All the possibilities of empiricism, criticism and rationalism become depleted, and their inability to work out a concept of being, fundamental for gnosseology and metaphysics, mustneeds be considered beyond doubt, despite the partial correctness of these points of view. Being as such is not there whether in the fluid experience of the empirico-positivists, nor in the categories and concepts of the criticists, nor in the ontological ideas of the rationalists. And the question concerning being is the fundamental and in the final end singular question of philosophy, and only in connection with this or some other understanding can there be decided, as posited by us, the problem of the individual.[1]

In the torrent of empirical phenomena there are nuances and distinctions, there is an endless diversity, but there is no individuality, not the person as such, if one hold to the positivist point of view. A constituative sign of the concept of individuality defies analysis, its substantial uniqueness, is non-deducible as to the nature of this individuality from on the outside, from its non-individual nature, its singularity. Individualness involves being-in-itself, the initial being and all

---

This book is very interesting and instructive in scientific a regard, but philosophically very naive.

[1] Still once again has to be pointed out the great merits of the reposed Kozlov in the analysis of the concept of being.

its conditions, its creative acts, its interactions with others presuppose this its inner metaphysical nature: it cannot be the product of externally fluid processes. The rationalists have worked out an abstract concept of the person, but a living, concretely unrepeatable being in all its uniqueness for them does not exist; they subsume being to thinking, for them there is only life within concepts. And here the entire current of criticism, a very characteristic manifestation of the German idealist movement, attempts to posit the problem of the individual: I have in mind Windelband, and in particular Rickert and Laska [alt. Lask, Emil; 1875-1915].[1] This current admits of the irrationality of the individual and admits of value to the individual. Scientific cognition obliterates the individual; concrete diversity dissipates into a worked-out conceiving of general concepts; thus is fashioned "nature" with its laws and it rests upon generally-binding norms of reason. Besides these norms, of the general, of "nature", there is still the individual, the irrational, not subsumable to rational conceptualisation, hence "history", under which Rickert regards everything that is concrete and living. This likewise is positivism, avoiding the metaphysical setting and deciding the problem of being in general and of individual being by dwelling on the details; but it is a positivism of higher a quality, since it persistently addresses the great problem, ignored by the vulgar sort positivism. This current does not want to allow, that besides the scientific cognition for which there is nothing individual, there can be still moreover a metaphysical cognition, which has only to do with the individual aspect, since it desires to know being, the existent.

Positivists regard individuality as a biological concept, they see in it biological a form. Many currently consider the core aspect of individuality to consist in the biological instincts and the psychological responses. But indeed instincts, biological traits are common in general both to man along with animals, with nature, and all this is namely that, what makes him most similar with all, the hence non-individual or more accurately sub-individual, and still does not lead to that condition, which we term as the person. From the biological and in general naturalistic point

---

[1] Vide the already cited book by Rickert, "Die Grenzen der naturwissenschaftlichen Begriffsbildung" and the sharp-minded 1902 book by Laska, "Fichtes Idealismus und die Geschichte". In Laska it is possible to find those metaphysical crumbs, which are particular to this semi-positivist current.

of view it is impossible even to state the fact of individuality, impossible to catch hold of it, and the positivist at most can regard this fact as standing outside the competency of scientific cognition, and hence something of a mystery. If man is merely a speck in the vast waves of natural being, if he is only a snippet of the natural process, a chance product of necessity, then he is not a person, not an individualness, he is simply nothing. Whatever the theory we might cleave to, we nonetheless live by that unmediated awareness, that man is a metaphysical being, and that the roots of the individualness mustneeds be sought more deeply than with biology and psychology. Psychological individualism tends to get strongly preached by the contemporary trends in art; it is very much in vogue and close to the heart of modern man, though through a sort of misunderstanding, a crude intellectual mistake. If psychological experiences and moods have no bearer in a living unique spirit, if our psyche be not understood as a substantia or spiritual monad, but the rather as a temporary snippet of the necessary process of nature, taking form outside any involvement of emotional conditions, then all our individualistic pretensions will float off into the air, and all the titanic dreams about the might of the human individuality, which modern man speculates about, will prove to be a pitiful self-deception. Individuality is not of the moment, but rather in eternity. And an understanding of the soul as substantial not only will not contradict the actual, but rather even will presuppose the consequent hence active process, the free creativity, in the soul-emotive acts and conditions as are necessitated in the bearer, on the inside, in an unique unity.[1] When we consciously say "I", we then are already declaring the substantiality of the soul. The great individualist Nietzsche best of all in his way demonstrated the impossibility of a biological and psychological understanding of individuality; the whole of Nietzsche is an outcry lament of immeasurable languor over the loss of metaphysical individuality. I know, that it is generally accepted to regard the individual under empirical a guise, and the metaphysical in context of the general and in

---

[1] Nor likewise is it possible to talk about an interpretation of substantia in the spirit of Herbart [Johann Friedrich, 1776-1841], as a stationary mathematical point completely cut off from the emotive processes. This is purely a rationalistic mistake. For us, substantia is a living spirit, in which all the active processes organically are inseparable from its bearer.

common. Even Schopenhauer decided not to consider non-temporal and non-spatial being as the individual aspect and by this he tended to contradict the profoundest tendencies within his metaphysics. But for me this truth is very basic, very important.

An enlightened approach is possible only amidst a thorough reworking of the theory of cognition, which posits at its basis the problem of reality with an analysis of the concepts of being. We unmediatedly have *conscious an awareness*, and thereupon also we conceive of ourself, as being, as spiritual a substantia, as an "I", defying analysis, not derivable from "nature", but the rather one and singular. This is an aspect of every being, which otherwise is impossible to be conceived of as an "I", as individual, alive and spiritual. For metaphysics an undoubtedly large role is played by voluntarism, which ultimately is affirmed by modern psychology and likewise leads to the struggle against rationalism.[1] We live and move at transcendent a depth, and these transcendent experiencings are moreso immanent to our existence, than are the conditional, the other-sided and indirect, in conceiving of the world of experience, of nature. In general, it is necessary to protest against the rift between the immanent and the transcendent, which comes from Kant, with a need rather to admit the immanent aspect of the transcendent and to open the door for metaphysical experience. All this needs further justification and developement; but never and no one in authentic a manner has toppled this directly conscious awareness and cognitive knowability of our substantial "I", not indeed gnosseological as such, but rather the ontological "I", the source to all true being.

Gnosseology always begins with the opposition between thinking and being, of subject and object; but this is still not the beginning; still prior to this opposition we find a direct given, which admittedly is termed consciousness, and our reflective reason ought not only to turn itself thither, whence all is conditional, where all gets transformed into the concepts of our thinking, yielding scientific experience, but also to turn itself hither, wherein is given unconditional being, wherein is revealed transcendent experience and there becomes possible metaphysical cognition. Herein opens before us an endless path in a recognition of conditions, in their transition to true a knowledge. If there is an immutable truth in philosophy, then it is this, that every being is substantially and

---

[1] Vide the already cited book by N. Lossky, "On Voluntarism".

spiritually so, that every being -- is an individual "I", that the world is a complex system of the interactions of spiritual substances of various orders, higher and lower. Concrete spiritualism is the solely possible metaphysical system and the solution to the problem of the individual, the sole justification of the very setting of the problem of the person. Panpsychism is connected with very ancient and very profound human beliefs and feelings, and this ineradicable conviction regarding the spiritual grounding of the world cannot be snatched away from us by impotent positivist-rationalistic theories of knowledge. Consider how the painter Böcklin [Arnold, 1827-1901] calls us to a faith in the soul-emotive life of the world, to its inhabitation with living spirits. And this has nothing in common with the stale pantheism, as such swallowing up everything individual and thereby resolved by purely literal and tautological assertions. The uniquely original manifestations of Russian philosophic thought gravitate towards spiritualism and bear an anti-rationalistic character. We, perhaps, approach closer than does the modern European philosophy to the innate question, to the problem of reality and the problem of being, and we thereby seek the way out from the sickness-like crisis of modern thought.

All the positive assertions, connected with the problem of the person, are pervaded by this metaphysical premise, that the person is a free, self-defining, spiritual substantia. Only a living and concrete spirit, timeless and non-spatial as regards its nature, can be endowed of unconditional a value, to it only can be inherent unconditional inalienable natural rights, only its individual fate can have profound meaning and only over it so strongly can be plotted out modern history with its basic motif -- the working out and affirmation of individuality. Militant positivists might retort: and if the human spirit is so free, if in its value can be no doubt, if its rights be absolute and inalienable, then why struggle for freedom, for rights; such a spirit cannot suffer oppression, to be oppressed would be merely an empirical mirage. This represents either a misunderstanding or else solipcism. The substantial spirit is not something remote and completely separate from the man living upon the earth, a man oppressed and struggling; we resolutely protest against any such sort of dualism. The spiritual nature of man is given to revolt in the name of its birthright; it contends against lower powers, those restricting and oppressing, in the name of an ultimate liberation, both individual and universal. Mere bits of matter, a chance plaything of sensations cannot inscribe a declaration of its rights, cannot of itself stand in opposition to meaningless nature and crude power. The struggle for freedom and rights from logical a sense of obligation presupposes struggle, for a freedom in accord with one's inner nature and inner being by a conscious awareness of one's absolute rights. Prometheus was a great spirit of divine descent and he waged a titanic struggle in the name of the recognition of his lofty nature. The lower nature cannot regrow itself into its proper products; everything higher has to have a different and uniquely original source, since never can necessity beget freedom, and the conscious awareness of absolute rights can never be inferred from factual a lawlessness, and the struggle against violent coercion has to have an inward source, opposed to all coercion.

The spiritualistic monadology confessed by us understands the world, as consisting of a mass of spiritual beings of various orders, defying analysis in its individuality and striving towards a free self-determination, towards a destruction of necessity, towards an abolishing of the downward pull by matter, of that seeming aspect of being, which is created by the lower, the elementary and simple beings by nature. This philosophic concept can be termed a metaphysical pluralism; in it are found expressions of tendencies towards multiplicity, towards the individual, lodged deeply within our perceptive nature and which do not find sufficient expression in the greater part of rationalistic and monistic systems.[1] The world reflects multiplicity as to its existing composite; every being is individual. Too many philosophic currents tend to stray, in that they ponder various acts, as though comprising a process bereft of any substantial bearer; the world is presented as a drama with action, but without actors, and in such manner being gets transformed into a phantasm, an illusion. The modern theory of cognition ought deeply to think about the category of substance and recognise it as basic and irremovable in working out concepts of being. In pluralistic a spiritualism is situated a metaphysical reflection of our individual strivings, our struggle for the rights of the person, for freedom, and there thus obtains a semblance of meaning in our tortuous interest towards the basic question of human life, the question concerning the fate of the individual, with which is connected a profound tragic aspect, unknown by the positivists. The theory of the person is finalised by a philosophy of immortality, and here we pass over to a

---

[1] Among the great philosophers, pluralism was best of all expressed by Leibniz, but was still impaired by the flaws of rationalism.

completely different pole of thought, to the question concerning the purposive-mission of mankind, its collective calling, i.e. to the problem of progress.

IV.

It is possible to regard the metaphysical character of the idea of progress as incontestably established, and I have no wish to repeat an hundred and a thousand times over, that progress presupposes a purposive-end and meaning to history, that it leads to the idea of a moral world-order, that positivism in essence ought to repudiate the idea of progress and admit of merely a process, of evolution, of movement without aim and without meaning.[1] I am here merely pointing this out. If the problem of the person inevitably leads us to the acknowledging of spiritual a substance, to a spiritualistic pluralism, then the problem of progress just the same inevitably leads to a single, utmost high substance, to the good as a potential, to a spiritualistic monism. Ineradicable from our consciousness is that the fact of the meaning of human life and human history is based upon the premise, that besides me and everyone else, besides man and humankind there is yet a third, still higher, than me and my neighbour, there is the solely One, and it is in relation to this solely One by the multiplicity of all -- that the riddles of being, the metaphysical basis of movement in the world, transpires.

More than once already has been pronounced harsh judgement against progress from the point of view of the tragic fate of the individual human soul, its hopes swallowed away, its life beset by failure, with spilt blood and tears. Dostoevsky with trenchant a pathos renders a judgement upon progress as regards the individual fate, in the remarkable words of Ivan Karamazov about the tiny tear of the little child. This has been assumed to call attention to the problem of theodicy and rather unsuccessfully. It is impossible to justify God by the world, on the contrary, we seek to justify the world with its evil and sufferings on the basis of God, we seek to find meaning and a way out from the tragedy of the world within the MostHigh. Here likewise there stands before us the

---

[1] Vide the article by S. Bulgakov, "The Fundamental Problems of the Theory of Progress".

question concerning a justification and meaning to progress with its terrors and sacrifices, with the perishing and suffering of the individual -- of man, admitted as an end-in-itself.

The idea of progress is imbued with a dream of the perfect, the higher, the utmost-human condition of people, in which triumphs an ultimate harmony, with no blood and tears, in which the supreme might gets combined with the supreme good. The proposing of such a lofty condition, as a goal, is a sign of the concept of progress. Concretely within the history of mankind this dream assumes various forms: in socialism it gets embodied in the idea of Zukuftsstadt [state of the future], which the believing socialist awaits the same, as a believing Christian awaits the Second Coming. Many an utopia has been born from this demand to think of the summits of progress, the luminous dazzling sun of human perfection and might. Consider for a moment, that mankind does clamber its way up the lofty mountain, that it enters into this realm of desired harmony, all wonderful, beautiful and happy. This small bunch of people, happily arrayed upon the heap of our corpses, upon the soil moistened by our tears, -- such cannot be attractive to us, cannot be our purposive-goal, cannot redeem the individual ruination, cannot answer to the accursed outcry of nary a single lost human soul, cannot make sense of the tragic terror within human life. The progress of the positivists is a very ugly, very inhuman idea; progress thus ought to be dumped, if positivism is correct: it is impossible morally to accept it, it is impossible a price to pay. Why ought future generations be set higher than those of the present and the past, why for their future contentment and arrangement ought I to work, to suffer, to the perishing of myself and others? It is necessary, is the single reply, which we hear from the positivists; this is demanded by the growth and increase of life, which we worship, as utmost a sanctity; and you will perish, as the unfit, if you will not serve our progress. This pitiful reply clearly shows, that for a consistent positivist there furthermore does not and cannot exist the problem of progress, just the same like with the problem of the person; he ceases to understand, in what is the question here, he stifles in himself the voice of his immediate human nature. The idea of progress, just like the idea of the person, can be defended only by idealists, and on this the positivists have no sort of standing; they can in the final end defend only the laws of nature, this fetish for modern inventions, and to insert all the views and forms of the word "life", -- life indeed, as taken from the pamphlets on biology and presenting therein concepts quite empty and bereft of content. We are fully ready to subscribe to the hymns of life, which the poets of positivism do compose, but this says nothing about our agreements, nor about our disagreements, since generally this means nothing.[1] We indeed shall live, to deepen and broaden life, but we shall not do it by misemploying biological metaphors!

But the problem of the justification of progress, of the redemption of its sacrifices, the relationship of progress to the fate of the person has to be decided, and without this a conscientious man cannot participate in the work of progress, cannot serve this meaningless idol -- this bunch of the future happy ones. A spiritualistic metaphysics, the mono-pluralistic interpretation of being can bring us nigh to a deciding of this problem, whereby the individual man, creatively participating in progress, creating a better future, works for himself, creates his own future. The utmost high mountain of progress is the Kingdom of God, in which will enter all individualities, in which will be redeemed every tiny tear of the little child and become transformed into joy. That which is on the empirical scene presents itself as extended along chronological a pattern, in temporal a sequence, whereas in the metaphysical, being which is extra-temporal extends instead along a single line and in this single line appear all the spiritual substantiae of the world, all the human generations as we tend to say. Only this aspect makes possible a joyful and meaningful participation in progress, with the eternal creativity and perfecting, amidst the tormentive and grievous, in the liberation of humankind, connected wit the liberation of all the world. The individual human fate herein aligns with and intersects with the universal fate of mankind and the world, and herein the universalistic monism is understood, as a finalative completion of the individualistic pluralism, since the multiplicity is situated in the sole Unity not to its negation, but rather the fullness of its assertion. People in the XIX Century wanted to replace belief in God with instead a belief in progress, but it would seem, that having cast aside God, it becomes needful also to cast aside progress, since it is bereft of meaning and cannot be

---

[1] In this regard, very characteristic is the positivist collection entitled, "Sketches of a Realistic World-View". The entire philosophy of this anthology tends towards purely literal type exercises on the concept of life and gets resolved in such tautological assertions as -- the good is a maximum of life, beauty likewise is a maximum of life, progress -- is the growth of life etc.

justified. And let the positivists not get too puffed up with pride over their progress and their progressiveness: in their useage this is nowise more significant a word; and that they love life, well, so who does not love life. We shall attempt further to shake apart one of the fondest ideas of the positivists, the idea of service to mankind, as some higher end of life; we find here a new confirmation, of just how impossible it is to construct a positive theory of progress.

The aim of progress and the higher criteria of progressiveness devolves for positivism into aspects of the concepts of man and of humanity, and it leads to a religion of mankind. The important thing for us is to shake apart this fictitious and nominal concept of mankind and to demonstrate, that with the positivists it is presented uncritically in place of the supra-human, which inevitably would presuppose the admitting of unconditional values. The innate lie of the philosophy and religion of mankind consists in this assertion, that my neighbour should have greater a value, than I myself, that the "many" are qualitatively of greater value than some single "one", that future generations are of more value than those of the present and the past, that within mankind there is something greater and higher, than in individual a man. We seek the true instinct for something higher, than man, and only upon this higher aspect do we consider it possible to base an evaluation and define the relationship of man to man. Upon the individual man, as a factual given, it is impossible to construct anything, from him, as a fact empirical and fortuitous, it is impossible to gain the fire for human progress, and at this point the positivists begin to add up these null zeros and transpose them chronologically forward, and from this they worked out the concept of mankind, beckoning and powerfully crying out "forward", whilst failing to note that psychologically this concept was pervaded by elements of the supra-human and metaphysical, while logically nominal and fictitious. Let us examine this more closely and approach it from completely personal a side.

There is a man, the "I", and there is another nigh close, the "thou". From the point of view of positivism what unites them is the biological concept of the human form and the sociological concept of human society. Yes, they share one and the same "nature", and by its "laws" they devour each the other; they share the selfsame "society" and by its "laws" they wage mortal a combat each against the other. This is the necessity, which the positivists so staunchly defend against us in the name of their freedom, and this necessity is thus boundless a void; it is impossible even to find in it a basis for the establishing of value and in it there is no telling right from left. In the name of what indeed can there be unity between the "I" and the "thou", in the name of what indeed does one see in another a man and a brother, in the name of what indeed do we admit to each another as of unconditional a value? It is in the name of something farther off, in the name of a third, higher than the "I" and the "thou", above the human, in the name of that most lofty nature, which we both reflect, which we bear within ourself, as one's higher destiny and as an awareness of one's own birthright, which we do not surrender in exchange for a pot of porridge sort of human happiness, for a general well-being and the other things dreamt up by the positivists. In the positivist concept of mankind there is no larger a qualitative content, no greater values, than in the individual man, comprising as it were a simplistic complexity, and in effect this does not call for formation of values and qualities. Man cannot and ought not, if he wishes not to lose his human visage, to serve merely himself, as positive a fact, or to serve his neighbour, the selfsame fact, or that sum total of the neighbour, which is signified by the ponderous word, "humanity". Humanity, composed of my neighbours, is as it were a tedious flatness without a single high point; to love it and to serve it "I" cannot, and if there is no third aspect, nothing higher, than this or that man, no trans-human and lofty height, such as is needful to uplift us all. Egoism and altruism, between which all the positivist theories vacillate, are alike paltry, desultory and insipid, and alike they fail to reach the awareness, that the human person is higher than egoism and altruism, higher than "my" and "others" interests, that it represents a call to serve a third something, individually and universally to embody the trans-human aspect, which it is impossible to attain by any sort of summations, by any sort of adding up quantitative combinations. Upon this third, not me as an human, nor someone else as an human, rests the higher dignity, the absolute value of every human "I". A man can only take pride in himself in that he gets an uplift in his own eyes, in what leads him from the natural condition to the trans-human.

Simply to love one's neighbour is impossible, and it is impossible even to admit in him a kindred human nature; "I" can love in him only some third aspect, which is higher than us both and which we each manifest in individual a form; the pathway from man to man is only through the sole Unity, only the sole unity can be loved, only thus can each man be loved. To organise the mutual relations of people such, that man be not a wolf to his fellow man, but rather a brother, is possible only upon trans-human a principle, in the name of the sole Unity, the MostHigh, and suchlike organisation presupposes supra-natural purposive ends. This has been recognised most profoundly by Christian philosophy.

For everything said above, it is quite possible to find purely psychological illustrations. Whatever the theory, even the most positivist, whatever a man might hold to, there is some third and higher aspect, higher than himself and his neighbour, that lives within his soul, though it have quite various names. When a man serves some whatever "idea", be it socialism, progress, science, art, truth or justice, he posits this "idea" as higher than himself and his neighbour, higher than man and humanity; it becomes for him an expression of the trans-human, a third element in contrast to him and everyone else. This third aspect is what Nietzsche so tormentedly thirsted for, when he said, that it is needful to love the remote, moreso than the nigh close things, and phantasms moreso than people, when he fashioned his image of the trans-human, the beyond-man. But if this beyond-man be only a biologically perfected man, advancing forward with time, then the insignificance of the result does not correspond to the grandiosity of the quest. It would be a pitiful consolation to be satisfied merely with that man adds on bigger muscles. The supra-human for Nietzsche, not by intent but via realisation, is human all the same as with the positivists, but with poetic an artistry. The proud dream of the man-god, so dear to modern mankind, can have one only worthy meaning -- the meaning of movement from man to God, upwards from nature. A naturalistic man-god is a fabrication signifying nothing. I do not want to be used as a mere means, a tool of other I's that are the equivalent of me, and all humanity, comprised all the same as I am, nor also the supra-man, merely moreso strong but not moreso of value, as this would contradict my dignity, my integrity. The supra-man of Nietzsche and the future happiness and harmony of mankind in the positivist religion cannot compel me to forsake my own "I", to pass over to something other, to share in a collective progress: all this is too human and insipid, all sham values.

The free human spirit, substantially unique, cannot place its duty and its vocation in a nature external to it, to an external social end, termed as humanity; this innately contradicts the individualistic tendencies lodged within us and there would thus triumph only a mechanical universalism that is in effect alien to us; the dignity and purposive vocation of the person rather is in this, to admit of the higher and trans-human inwardly, as immanent to our nature, a sort of spiritual substantia, with which each person is inwardly connected by the verymost intimate and individual threads, in the name of which only is it possible also to discern the brother in a fellow man and unite thereby in an harmonic accord; mankind ought to become organised not from the outside, not by coercive force, not by forced drills and manipulation of the human person towards human a society, but rather from within, freely, by way of self-initiative, from the very depths of man seeking fulfillment in the trans-human life. The metaphysical connection between the substantiae, on the effect of which they comprise the world totality, -- the cosmos, can be only within a singular and utmost high substantia, in which obtains the fullness of every being and towards which all the multiplicity of the world, all the individualities gravitate, as towards the ultimate perfection and power, towards its ultimate assertion. Herein the individual and the universal cease to be antagonistic principles.

The positivist theory of progress thinks in terms of an endless perfecting, absent an end within time; in this movement all will quantitatively grow, but never will there be created a "new heaven and a new earth". An authentic and a good infinity would be, not in an absence of an end-point in time, but rather in the surmounting of all time and every end, in timelessness. There cannot be a convergence with eternity in this paltry perspective with its tiny improvements. This is one of the innate contradictions in the positivist theory of progress.

V.

We have seen, that the problem of progress can be posited and decided only metaphysically. Progress presupposes a sole unitary, -- a trans-human, such as is higher in comparison with man and other people, -- higher than humanity, and then this third, in the name of which man becomes for his fellow man not a wolf, but a brother instead, amidst which becomes possible the communing of spiritual individualities, with this comprising the aim and the source of values. But for the defining of the true meaning of progress we mustneeds turn towards a basic idea of the recent idealism, which we attempt to be characteristic of, the idea of freedom. In an analysis of freedom we once again have to point out the inconsistency of positivism and the need for metaphysics.

The philosophy of the future ought to be termed a philosophy of freedom. Freedom is alike both a religio-metaphysical and a socio-political idea, and a true philosophy will be a philosophy of liberation. It was not the positivists that worked out the idea of freedom both in philosophy, and also in the political sense of this word.[1] The positivists in practice often become boundlessly devoted to freedom and are ready to lay down their life for it, but theoretically this is always for them an empty sound, and they are unable to conceptualise the tasks involved in human life and human history, as regards liberation; for them it is all a victory over nature, the social organisation of people, happiness and contentment, all everything that suffices, but freedom leaks thru for them in merely contraband a manner. Positivism is powerless to attain such heights, as to admit, that freedom is higher than happiness and contentment, higher than the strong underpinnings of life, higher perhaps than life itself, and that freedom -- is God, that *God* -- is *absolute freedom, as existent.* Positivism never will grasp, that the task of humankind, its worldwide mission, -- is not the building and organising of life for the well-being of people, but the rather liberation, since man ought to serve not his own contentment nor the contentment of his neighbour, but rather freedom in the name of the MostHigh, in the name of absolute freedom; the strong edifice, in which mankind is arrayed, is merely a temporal means. Herein the enormous distinction.

A genuinely consistent positivism ought to discard from its lectionary the word freedom; it can nowise stand fast in opposition to necessity, to nature, to external violence. Positivism and semi-positivism, under which I include Neo-Kantianism, fought over how to save freedom, since they sensed, that without it would vanish all the beauty in life, but nothing came out of all this. The gnosseological attempts to provide purely a negative explanation to freedom, as the opposite to necessity, can satisfy no one and have merely a methodological significance. And here, just as generally also with philosophy, there is felt the urgent need to resort to ontological a perspective, to discern those metaphysical premises, which are lodged within the idea of freedom. We cannot be satisfied by either the negative and illusionistic teaching concerning freedom by the

[1] Now too often it tends to be forgotten, that the "Declaration of the Rights of Man and the Citizen" was inscribed under metaphysical a reasoning.

Neo-Kantians, nor by the old Kantian teaching about its mentally-grasped character. Particularly distressing are all these police-like, purely external arguments in defense of freedom, as something needful and useful, without which falls asunder the distinction between good and evil, and is smothered the voice of conscience, and is lost the significance of punishment, etc; such a path of proofs is not worthy of philosophy. It is time already to pass over to a positive understanding of freedom, -- of freedom, as being. It would not be difficult to show, that freedom is closely connected with an admitting of spiritual substantiae, such as are nowise inferable nor individually further reducible, by the creative energy at the core of their developing. Even if freedom can be set in opposition to nature and empirical being, then still in any case it is impossible to set it in opposition to the substantial being of spirit. Freedom is substantial might, the creative power of spiritual existent being, of itself creating the future. This understanding of freedom is connected with a particular theory of causality, with a purely metaphysical teaching on causality, as causation, the creating of the consequent by an actual spiritual substrate. Thereupon is established the close connection between the categories of freedom, causality and substantiae.[1] All this would nowise contradict the conditional scientific understanding of causality, as a functional relationship, and the sharp-minded attempts by Ernst Mach to ultimately banish from scientific knowledge the metaphysical pretensions, connected with causation, can only clear the soil for metaphysical knowledge.

But freedom is an irrational power and it can make for both the good and also evil, both the reasonable and also the unreasonable; it is thinkable only amidst a voluntaristic and also alogical, supra-rational understanding of being. For the rationalist, including also the positivist or metaphysician, in reducing everything to rational experience or to the rational "small" reason, -- for such, freedom is ungraspable and a strange mystery. The rationalist always attempts to attach freedom to necessity; he is afraid of freedom, of that dark depths of being, from which is born in the

---

[1] In modern philosophic literature the best investigation on the question about causality and freedom can be found in L. Lopatin's "Positive Tasks of Philosophy", Tome II. Vide likewise the interesting article of S. Askol'dov [pseudonym of Sergei Alekseevich Alekseev, 1871-1945], "In Defense of the Miraculous", in the journal "Questions of Philosophy and Psychology".

world not only good, but also evil. The rationalist and the positivist never will comprehend, that a required good has no value, inwardly it is contradictory and even repulsive, and that only a free good can be admitted as of the highest value, only the good, having traversed all the worldwide tragedy, having passed through the free falling away and negation, in the attaining of the Kingdom of God.

But the freedom of the individual substantiae is relative; they are connected with the multiplicity of other substantiae of a lower nature, and the progressive destruction wrought by this of necessity and through violence fills all the history of mankind. The meaning of freedom consists in suchlike a self-determination and creativity of spiritual substantiae, whereby from the world is formed the cosmos, rather than chaos, for otherwise the individual spirit would fall into a forced dependence, bound to it. *Liberation is the abolition of dependence upon the multiplicity of the unique substantiae comprising for us "nature", and it is attained by suchlike a directing of our inner freedom, amidst which from the world is created the Kingdom of God.* The relationship is of a connected multiplicity to a sole unity, and towards this tend all the points of being, and the liberation of all the multiplicity gets resolved in the form of the absolute freedom of the sole Unity. This metaphysical liberation finds itself a reflection in that residue of being, which we call human history; this history is filled with signs and symbols of a metaphysical liberation of being, of metaphysical tragedy, in which there act, fight and suffer spiritual beings of various gradations.

We thus come nigh to an understanding of the historical process, as a liberation, possessed of a meaning both metaphysical and religious. Mankind by its creative power ought to liberate both itself and the world. The freedom of the human person, and its rights, has an absolute and transcendent significance. The struggles for freedom and rights are embellished in the light of eternity; in freedom we "come in contact with an other world". Freedom stands higher than happiness, higher than the projects of life, higher than the world, for this is a boundless value and can be nowise surrendered, since the sole Unity MostHigh comprises absolute freedom. The positivists and utilitarians of all shades desire to organise humankind, to render it well-off, to create a realm of everyday matters and by this they think to bypass the tragic aspect in life, lodged within the metaphysical essence of the world, within the relationship of the multiplicity to the sole unity. Their understanding of progress is therefore insipid; they are chained down by their philistine limitedness; for them freedom does not possess any innate value in itself: it becomes only a means for well-being, and from the perspective of positivism it is impossible to raise any objections against this, in bartering away freedom for whatever the edifice wherein dwells the promise of human happiness.

For us, the freedom of the person is the supreme principle of life in general; the rights of the person have as their source not ultimately in positive legislation, nor the state, nor the collective societal entity with a power to grant and take back again, but rather in the metaphysical existence of man, since freedom and the rights of the person cannot be calculated in accord wit utilitarian and state formats, and cannot be disdained in the name of some other god, a god of violence, and not of freedom.[1] No sort of solid state and societal arrangements, aimed at creating human contentment and security, can be set higher than human freedom. Many, far too many tend to reason, the way that Dostoevsky's Grand Inquisitor reasoned: they know the method, how to render people content and happy, how to arrange things for them on earth, equally for all, whether this method be Catholicism, socialism or some other system of tranquility, and here they are ready to crucify someone, who comes forth to them with word of boundless freedom; they are afraid of an ultimate freedom, they often swear by it, but then curse it, if it disturb the warmth and cosy edifice set up by them for the happiness of mankind. Thus it becomes necessary here to make ultimate a choice -- freedom or contentment; progress, as a growth of freedom, transcending all the bounds of our experience, or progress, as the arranging and tranquilising of mankind, for a growth of everyday happiness. And still further the choice: to admit of the rights of the person, as inalienable, absolute, not merely conferred from the outside, from collective a will, or the rights of the person, as merely a means, supporting utilitarian a consideration, having as its source the social totality. Those struggling for the rights of man, for human freedom ought finally to admit, that the ideas and rights dear to

---

[1] This point of view, basic for us, leads to a rejection of all forms of state positivism, of all the state-based theories of rights and towards the assertion of a natural-law theory of the state. At the very foundations of society, for us, rests the rights of the idealist meaning of this word. Vide the article of Pavel Novgorodtsev [1866-1924] that is included in "The Problems of Idealism".

them -- are thoroughly from the metaphysical plane and ultimately freedom ought to take precedence over the pursuit of happiness, and rights -- over social and state utilitarianism.

Social-political freedom in quite inseparable a manner is connected with metaphysical freedom, it indeed rests upon it and is presupposed by it. If man is not free by the metaphysical nature of his existence, as unique a spirit, if he be merely a chance snippet of the processes of nature, if he derives entirely from natural and social means, this then can concern his adaption to the medium, which seeks to complete his organisation, his education for the social totality, which seeks to increase his well-being, but it remains impossible to speak then anything in the language of freedom. Once and ever again it is needful to cease the talking about that paltry illusory freedom, which is the product of necessity, -- it is impossible to call by the great name of freedom the simple absence of external constraints, which has to appear as the result of the adaptability of people to life in general. The struggle for freedom, to thirst for freedom, to see in it the supreme value -- can only be by a being free as to its inner nature, as to its destiny and vocation in he world, with the image and likeness of an higher free being, which it can set in opposition to that which is external for itself, connected to natural being. Freedom can enter into our inter-connected world only from a free source, only from spirit, in which is lodged the greatest potency of freedom, as a power, and the coming of freedom into the world rests upon a power absolute, in the image of that supreme freedom, in which the world is to be transformed into a free harmony. The delimited ideal of in general life for us can only be the ultimate removal of attitudes of domination and violence between people and in place of this, an ultimately free and inner unity. The practical aspects of the positivists are infinitely higher than their theories, and we should wish, that their theories be rendered worthy of their practices, and that the great struggle for liberation should correspond to a philosophy of freedom.

VI.

In my article I have made an attempt to characterise in its basic features the essence of the recent Russian idealism; but this has been done individually, in accord with my own personal understanding. The following conclusions obtain: our idealistic movement is entirely national and unique; it is an attempt to resolve on the basis of traditions, inherited by us from the history of philosophic thought, the problem of person and the problem of progress, and to lead to a philosophy of freedom and liberation. I think, that it would not be baseless to term our young and nowise still strong idealistic movement an uniquely original Russian romanticism, closely aligned with the liberation strivings of our era. Romanticism can assume quite varied forms and certain features of romanticism from times past are forever dead and buried; but in romanticism there is also something of the eternal: in it is recognised the tragic essence of human nature, in it are found poetic expressions of our ineradicable religious strivings and expectations. We would wish to preserve and to pass on to the future these our national features of restlessness and anxiety, this tenacious work over the accursed questions, this incessant search for God and the impossibility to become reconciled with whatever any sort of system of insipid tranquility, with whatever any sort of philistine contentment. Romanticism -- is healthy a phenomenon, insofar as it is a reaction against a purely rational culture.

But we have learned much and we have forgotten nothing, since we cannot repeat the mistakes of the old romantics. We are not opposed to the trends in positive science and realistic politics, on the contrary, from our perspective both positivism in science, and realism in politics ought to be strengthened, since in scientific and political utopias we do not regard it possible to seek God. That slander against the idealists, that they would deny science and forsake the severe struggle impending for the earth, ought finally and ultimately be put to rest. We never split heaven and the earth; we think, that the so-called earthly life all involves the metaphysical nature of people; we stress especially, that the transcendent for us is not remote, foreign and cut off from the entire course of our life, but on the contrary, is nigh close, innate, present in each act of our life. We but only want to defend the mission-like expectations, both the national and the all-human, connected with the struggle for freedom, to set forth the meaning of freedom. And historically it is remarkable, that these our aspirations have coincided not with the decline, but rather with the societal ascent of our native land, with the growth of hopes for a better future.

A. S. Khomyakov as Philosopher

(For the Centennial of His Birth)

(1904 - #110)[1]

The theoretical head of the Slavophils, A. S. Khomyakov, ought justly to be acknowledged as one of the most outstanding of Russian minds. The enormous mental abilities of Khomyakov were esteemed by his opponents of the time in the Westerniser camp.[2] A man extraordinarily many-sided, a philosopher, a theologian, historian, a publicist and poet, Khomyakov was a conspicuous figure of the Decade of the 40's, deeply endowed with brilliant talents. But amidst all this, Khomyakov is now neither known nor read, he is forgotten and without esteem. Whole generations of the Russian Intelligentsia since Khomyakov's time had noted his Slavophil errors, which historically have been associated with very grievous impressions for us. Certain sides of the Slavophil teaching of Khomyakov were appropriated by unclean hands, and from their subsequent touch was destroyed the messianic dreams of the lofty vocation of the Russian people; faith in an unique national culture, in our national duty was turned round into a preaching of the hatred of man and violence. A romantic and an idealist, Khomyakov in horror would have turned himself away from these "Russian gatherings". His precious worth redeems this great man, so unreservedly loving his Russia and believing in its great creative future, and his sin afront the future Russia -- was his idealisation of backward forms of life, trying to link the creativity of the national spirit to these stagnant forms. Overlooked in Khomyakov was everything remarkable and of value, and actually prophetic for our national culture. I intend within my jottings to give an appraisal of Khomyakov exclusively as a philosopher.

---

[1] A. S. KHOMYAKOV KAK PHILOSOPH. Initially published in the monthly journal "Mir Bozhii", July 1904, p. 17-22.

[2] By Hertsen, in his "The Past and Thoughts" ("Byloe i dumy").

The philosophic articles of Khomyakov, despite their fragmentary and non-systematic character, are indicative of extensive interests, and nothing can justify the ignoring of Khomyakov within the history of our philosophic thought.[1] The philosophic world-view of Khomyakov was put together in the spiritual atmosphere of the classical German Idealism, and his thought repeatedly elaborated upon the philosophies of Schelling and Hegel. The grand system of Hegelian panlogism was a limiting factour in the development of German Idealism. It was impossible to go further, and the collapse of the system of Hegel was a serious crisis for philosophy in general, and herein Khomyakov busied himself over themes rooted in the defects and contradictions, which had brought European philosophic thought to complete ruin. Khomyakov indeed made a brilliant and profound critique of Hegelianism, a critique of rationalism, of this as it were original sin innate to almost all the European philosophies, and he clearly perceived the impossibility of a passing-over from abstract idealism, wherein being is rendered into nothingness, a passing-over towards a concrete spiritualism. These conceptions of a concrete spiritualism make of Khomyakov a progenitor of an autonomous Russian philosophy, such as later was brilliantly expounded by Vl. Solov'ev. Solov'ev ought justly to call Khomyakov his direct predecessor.

Let us look at, first of all, how Khomyakov critiqued Hegel. "*Being*, -- says he, -- has to be completely put aside. The concept itself, in its fullest abstraction, has to beget everything from its own loins. Rationalism or the logical reason had to find for itself an ultimate crown and Divine sanctification within a new consciousness of the integral world. Suchlike was the immense task, with which the German mind concerned itself in Hegel, and it impossible not to be astonished at the audacity, with

---

[1] The most important philosophic articles of Khomyakov are located in the first volume of his Collected Works: "Regarding Humboldt" ("Po povodu Gumbol'dta"), "Regarding Extracts, Found in the Papers of I. V. Kireevsky" ("Po povodu otryvkov, naidennykh v bumagakh I. V. Kireevskogo"), "About Contemporary Appearances in the Area of Philosophy" ("O sovremennykh yavleniakh v oblasti philosophii"), "Letter Concerning Philosophy to Yu. Ph. Samarin" ("Pis'mo o philosophii k Yu. Ph. Samarin"). The theological works of Khomyakov comprise the second volume of his Collected Works, but I do not propose to touch upon them.

which he set about for its resolution"[1] "The logic of Hegel consequently might be termed *the en-spiritising of abstract being.* Such would be its fullest, it seems, never yet expressed definition. Never has man set himself so fearsome a task, so bold an undertaking. The eternal, the self-begotten creation would be from the loin of the abstract concept, not having within itself any sort of essence".[2] Khomyakov thus formulates the point, at which the philosophic movement in Germany had halted: "the reconstruction of the integral reason (i.e. spirit) derives from the concept within rational-judgement. How soon though the task defined itself in suchlike a manner (and particularly suchlike a sense of Hegelian activity), and the pathway had to end: any sort of advance became impossible".[3] And further on: "the common mistake of the whole school, still not clearly discerned in its originator -- Kant, but often characteristic of its end figure -- Hegel, consists in this, that it constantly appropriates the developing of the concept within personal understanding as something identical with the developing of the actuality itself".[4] "It would be impossible to initiate a progression from this substrate, or better said, from this absence of substrate, from which Hegel set out; from this there come a whole series of mistakes, the jumbling together of personal laws with the laws of the world; from this likewise there is a constant confusing of the developement of the critical concept in mixing it up with the developement of the world of appearances, despite the opposition within them; from this also is the flaw of all this titanic work. The rest of the errors generally of Hegel lay within the error of the whole school, appropriating the judgemental-reason as integrality of spirit. The whole school failed to notice, that in taking the

---

[1] Vide "Sochineniya Khomyakova" ("The Collected Writings of Khomyakov"), vol. 1, p. 267.

[2] Ibid., p. 268. The honour of this profound insight into the spirit of Hegelian philosophy mustneeds be shared by Khomyakov together with I. V. Kireevsky, whose philosophic thought he draws upon from the discovered extracts of his papers.

[3] p. 291.

[4] p. 296.

concept as the unique ground for all intellection, it destroys the world: since the concept inverts for it all the underlying actuality into a pure, an abstract potentiality".[1] Khomyakov understood profoundly the impossibility of an utmost development along the path of the rationalistic and abstract judgemental-reason, since this path leads to an absolute nothing, it transforms the world into a mere ghost of a shadow. It is necessary to exit from this inescapable conceptual circle, towards being, to seek a substrate, the real. Hegel made a grandiose attempt to breathe living spirit into abstract ideas, but therein was shewn the impossibility to create the real world through the rationalistic deduction of concepts.

Khomyakov explains excellently the fatal inevitability of the transition of Hegelianism over into materialism, which in fact occurred within German philosophy and which was an indicator of the malady of its crisis. "The criticism realised only: the complete bankruptcy of Hegelianism, striving to create a world without substrate. His disciples did not understand this, that in this consisted the whole aim of the teacher, and they very simplistically imagined for themselves, that what was needed was merely to introduce into the system this needed substrate, and the matter would be in harmony. But from whence to get this substrate? Spirit evidently did not suffice, first of all, since the very task of Hegel forthwith expressed itself as a search of the process, creating spirit; and secondly, also since the very character of Hegel's rationalism, in the highest degree idealist, was not at all spiritualistic. And herewith the most abstract of human abstractions, -- Hegelianism, -- forthwith grasps after materiality and so passed over into a purest and most crude materialism. Materiality would be the substrate, and then the system of Hegel would be preserved, i.e. the terminology is preserved, and to a large part are preserved the defined intellectual transitions, the logical modi etc, preserved by word alone, by that which might be called a fabricated process of the Hegelian mind. The great thinker did not himself survive until suchlike a shame; but perhaps, his disciples would not be ridiculed in suchlike a shaming of the teacher, had not the tomb hidden his dread visage".[2] This is a very interesting page in the history of human thought.

---

[1] Vide: "Sochineniye Khomyakova", vol. 1, p. 299.

[2] p. 302.

Thus was constituted "dialectical materialism", at the present time having a grip on many a mind, or more accurately, hearts, -- this strange and logically bankrupt collection of ideas, simultaneously exclusive one of the other. Dialectics presupposes panlogism, the dialectical logic of things is unintelligible under the concept of a material thingly substrate, and this would be a monstrous logicisation of matter, which indeed makes materialists similar to rationalists, and also idealists, and it points to the impossibility, the inner insolvency of materialism. Khomyakov understood all this better than many of the people of our time, pretending to the calling of philosophers. "The whole school, of which Feuerbach serves as a lustrous centre-point, reckons itself Hegelian, yet amidst this look at its relationship to the basic tenets of Hegel. Kant says, that *it is not possible to know things-in-themselves,* Hegel says, that *the thing-in-itself does not at all exist, and exists only in conceptual-idea.*[1] For him this position is not fortuitous, not appended, but rather it is rooted in and is directly connected with the very foundation of his philosophy; and thus his whole system is naught else, than the possibility of the conceptual-idea, unfolded under all the manifold of activity and completed by activity of spirit. And here for his students the *thing* appears altogether as a general substrate, and the *thing-in-itself* namely, is not a self-limiting concept nor even the object of the concept, but is namely its actual self. You see, that I was right, saying, that the new-German school, seemingly Hegelian, took from the teacher only, so to speak, the fabricated process of intellectual and terminological schemata, while being already at this time altogether alien to his spirit and perception. The conceptual-idea without substrate, or a potentiality to be concept, transitional in activity apart from something comprehended and something comprehending, was likewise an aim of Hegel, and in general concerning it Schelling tended to say, that this is thought, but in which nothing is thinkable. For the realisation of the whole system, although understandably with its complete distortion, was introduced a new principle -- the thing, as a thingness in general. Would there, ultimately, be removed that accusation, which fell upon the original head of Hegelianism, i.e. is there indeed a thought received, in which there is something thought?"[2] "When the school in its final Hegelian development came to its

---

[1] This is now reiterated by the so-called Immanentist school.

ultimate denial of any sort of substrate, it is understandable, that its final disciples, in order to save the floundering teaching, with which they had been challenged by all the wonts of mind, they decided to introduce into it a substrate very tangible indeed, very contrary to that abstraction, from which the system of the teacher had come to ruin, and they were not concerned to question for themselves, whether the concepts be reconcilable with each other, which they by force had set free".[1] Materialism tolerates not the slightest scientific criticism; but in the face of pure rationalism it possesses an apparent advantage, in that it proposes some sort (although also imaginary) of a substrate and by this it satisfies an inner demand for action, which resides in the soul of man; both indeed, both pure rationalism, and materialism also, are nothing other, than two sides of one and the same system, which I cannot term otherwise, than as a system of *necessarianism*, of non-volition".[2]

I made the many foot-noted quotations from Khomyakov in view of the great interest, which his thoughts present also for our time. Khomyakov in this regard is not at all out-dated: we too face matters laden with philosophic problems, we likewise live with a sense of the bankruptcy of rationalism with all its visages and forms, though they be under the guise of criticism or empiricism, and we likewise seek a substrate, -- the truly existing. The difference merely is in this, that we criticise now not so much Kant, as rather the neo-Kantians, not so much Hegel as rather the neo-Hegelians, and we have lived through a greater number of disappointments. Khomyakov anticipated the theory of the "mystical perception" of Solov'ev and his "critique of abstract principles", and likewise also the most recent searchings of gnosseological points of view, surmounting rationalism, empiricism and criticism. "The whole German critique, -- says he, -- all the philosophy of the Kantian school, has remained yet at that level, at which Kant set it. It has not moved beyond judgemental-reason, i.e. that analytic faculty of reason, which is conscious of and investigates the given, received by it from the integral reason, and dealing only ever with concepts, it is never able to find within itself the

---

[2] Vide: "Sochineniye Khomyakova", vol. 1, p. 303-304.

[1] p. 308.

[2] p. 312.

criterium for definition of the inner and the external, since it deals only with that, which already is perceived, and consequently, is rendered inward. You remember, striving in part to expound on this great step which was made by our too soon deceased a thinker, I. V. Kireevsky, namely -- about reason's acknowledgement of the integral reason, which perceives the actually (real) given, given over for examination and the conscious judgemental-reason. In this area only does the given yet bear within itself the fullness of its character and tokens of its origin. *In this area, prior to the logical consciousness and filled with a living consciousness, needing neither demonstrations nor proofs, man is conscious of what appertains to his mental world and what appertains to the external world*".[1]

Both rationalism and empiricism abstractly dissect the living consciousness and conceal from us that *experience,* in which is immediately given real being, the existent. I am not taking into account philosophically the felicitous terms "mystical perception" or "faith". This experience, wherein converges our existence with the existent whole, rather than merely with the analytically rationalistic, is binding upon all, and it towers over the conditional contradiction of the rational and the empirical, it manifests itself as the source of *metaphysical* knowledge and fashions the metaphysical reason.[2]

Russian philosophic thought stands now in disrepute and it is imperative to remember, that this is upon paths coursing through and leading into the wilderness. Suchlike is the path of rationalism, the path of Kantianism, with a fateful inevitability leading to Hegelianism, propped up upon nothingness or an illusory materiality. For us there is only one pathway, leading to the consciousness of the existent, -- the path of spiritualism, cleansed from all the sins of rationalism and abstraction. Our philosophic thought enters upon this path, and at the moment of its departure it does not hesitate to remember about that first Russian thinker, pointing out the true path for our autonomous philosophy -- A. S. Khomyakov.

---

[1] I put an italic stress on this as especially important for the gnosseology of Khomyakov and its immediacy for us.

[2] Intellectual errors often hinder the veracity of explanation of this experience.

N. K. Mikhailovsky and B. N. Chicherin

(On Person, Rationalism, Democratism, etc.)

(1904 - 112)[1]

This year [1904] has carried off two impressive men, who occupied a visible place in the history of our thought and our community, -- N. K. Mikhailovsky [† 10 Feb.] and B. N. Chicherin [† 3 Feb.]. The fate of these two men was quite different, opposite to the point of strangeness: one of them was a "masterful mind" for some several generations of the Russian intelligentsia and all his life flowed by in noisy journalistic fights; the other one never enjoyed popularity, he was little read and his work of powerful thought transpired somewhere afar off, and did not coincide with any of our prominent intellectual and social currents. But all the same it is possible to find something in common between these oppositely situated men, who never and nowise met. They both of them were finely chopped out of a whole block of granite, with a firmness inspiring the greatest esteem they went forth with their faith throughout all their life, they grew strongly into their soil and they sincerely scorned everything hesitant and wavering, everything not in accord they forthwith set aright with persuadings. This catches the eye -- the psychological similarity between people in the social regard so very opposite, and yet it is possible to continue on with the comparison. Both Mikhailovsky [1842-1904] and Chicherin [1828-1904] were typical rationalists, although the first proceeded from Comte and affirmed rationalist positivism; the second -- proceeded from Hegel and created a whole system of rationalist idealism. They both, whether Mikhailovsky, bespeaking the mind and strivings of our democratic intelligentsia, or Chicherin, lordly despising anything of democracy and infected with bourgeois biases; both had their own pathos, inspiring for each their jottings, both in one and the same -- with the idea of

---

[1] N. K. MIKHAILOVSKII i B. N. CHICHERIN. Article first published in St Peterburg monthly journal, "Novyi Put'", oct. 1904, p.278-295.

the supremacy of the person, its self-worth and self-integrity. Each of them in his own way loved freedom, but amidst all the opposing contrast of philosophic basis and social conclusions both of these deceased thinkers confessed a purely rationalistic individualism, and thus were profoundly foreign to the irrational individualistic strivings and skirmishes of the rebellious spirit of our own day.

The strength of Chicherin was in a philosophic basis for individualism, in a remarkable philosophy of rights, in a consciousness of the metaphysical nature of liberalism, taken in its ideal, its meta-historical purity. From out of this flowed all the meaningfulness of the juridical publications of Chicherin, in that they also imparted a demand for rights, issuing from his sourcings, and upon the rights he bestowed an absolute metaphysical significance. The strength of Mikhailovsky -- was in democratic deductions for individualism. In his brilliant journalistic writing he connected the gist for inquiry in the intelligentsia person with the current of masses of the people, and an entire era of our public grew up closely familiar with his name. Why was Mikhailovsky so popular, and Chicherin so unpopular? The answer to this question would find characteristic several peculiarities of Russian life.

First about Mikhailovsky, more closely akin to us. We belong to that generation of the decade of the 1890's, which was motivated by a new and powerful social freeness, and which entered into an antagonistic struggle with all the old tendencies. The struggle was conducted with the brusqueness and mercilessness of green youth, with the consciousness of growing vigour, and we wildly believed, that the future belonged only to us. And in particularly strident and heated a manner we were wont to debate with that veteran of the old current, its last major representative, -- N. K. Mikhailovsky. In the heat of polemic we were often unjust and even rude in regard to this remarkable man. And we did not understand this, that "we were opponents, but very strangely so. We had *one* love, but *not identical*. And we, like Janus, or like the two-headed eagle, we looked in varying directions, at a time *when our heart was one*".[1] We had the same love for freedom, it was one heart that beat within the Russian intelligent fellow, and even more closely than the common love one common hatred bound us together... And at present our country stands at such a turnabout,

---

[1] Words of Hertzen as to the relationship between the Westernisers and the Slavophils.

that there is this overall and common somehow especial sense and especial desire to place a wreathe at the tomb of our opponent, friend and father -- N. K. Mikhailovsky.

With the death of Mikhailovsky there as it were passed from the scene an entire era in the history of our intelligentsia, dear in memories there was torn away from us a part of our being, of our intelligentsia nature. And each of the Russian intelligentsia ought to feel to the quick this death and ought to ponder at the grave of N. K. over the intelligentsia's historical past and its obligations in facing the future. When during the days of early youth we were all absorbed with Mikhailovsky, he awakened our youthful thought, he put questions, he gave guidance to our wakened thirst for social truth. Later we departed our original thinker, we outgrew him, but we also up to the present thrashed about over the problems posited us by him, so closely involving philosophy and life. This was very characteristic: Mikhailovsky was never the philosopher in his manner of resolving various questions with his lack of philosophic erudition, but it was philosophic questions in particular that troubled him his whole life, and at the threshold of his consciousness he already rose up in revolt against the limitedness of positivism. In this he was typical of the Russian intelligentsia, filled with philosophic outlooks, but deficient in philosophic schooling and enmeshed in the biases of positivism. We loved and we love Mikhailovsky for that spiritual thirst, which so sharply distinguishes the Russian intelligentsia from the philistinism of the European intelligentsia.

With Mikhailovsky we formerly parted ways over different understandings of the social developement of Russia and various social programmes. And here there flared up very strong emotions. But now much has abated and we can more calmly evaluate the social contributions of Mikhailovsky, a democrat deep and sincere and a struggler for the sense of the person, although just as before we have negative feelings towards Populism and we accept the legacy of Marxism, albeit only critically under examination. One thing beyond doubt: both populism, and Marxism alike grow pallid in their opposition amidst the great historical task for the establishment of law in our life. And now we rather moreso might reproach Mikhailovsky, in that he lacked foresight to provide a juridical formulisation to social demands in his journalistic articles. Populism always lacked in its weak political consciousness of law and in the decade of the 1870's this even led to a sense of political indifference. But with disappointment it is likewise necessary to note, that the Marxists also, historically having set about with wholly other political frames of reference, have themself not always appreciated the tremendous significance of the demands for laws.[1]

I draw attention here to one of the central points of the literary activity of Mikhailovsky, to this, what I have termed his pathos, to the idea of the person, to his individualism. Herein will be evident at once both our kinship with Mikhailovsky, and also our deep divergence from him, perhaps moreso than that, created by the social programmes, since what is said here goes to the very holy of holies. The philosophic position of Mikhailovsky was veritably tragic and inescapable. He led an idealistic struggle for the sense of the person, he set human individuality in opposition not only to nature, but also in opposition to society. We are prepared to welcome this with all our soul. But this suchlike *sense of person*, from whence does it draw its power for opposing the surroundings by its *individualness*?

Alas! For the positivist the sense of person is only a biological concept, and for the rationalist the person does not possess individuality. The "person" of Mikhailovsky is a biological abstraction, some sort of impersonal biological normality (the maximum of the physiological diversification of labour within the individuum). With an accuracy of instinct, Mikhailovsky protested against the pretensions of Darwinism, he hit upon the basic sin of naturalistic evolutionism -- the ignoring of *that, what* it is which adapts and developes, the failure to include this inner creative activity into the process of developement. From the point of view of philosophic idealism he was unable to do this and he attempted to create something akin to a biological idealism. But this however was merely a self-deception. The person, with the creative energy inherent to it, if posited from the perspective of positivism and naturalism, becomes wholly decomposed into a social and natural means, and the individualness is rendered a chance playing out of biological and social forces. Here there is nothing that remains, nothing to posit in opposition to the external world. The most terrible test for any positivism (not only in its extreme naturalistic form, but also with all the psychological correctives and with all the newest refinement of criticism) -- is in the entire inability from this

---

[1] I have in mind some of the sad biases of the orthodox-sort Marxists, although in general I very highly value the socio-political significance of the movement, connected with Marxism.

perspective not only to establish a grounding for the idea of person, but even simply to assert it. It is impossible to find that organising centre, which forms the unity of person, it is impossible to find the bearer of all the psychic conditions and creative acts. A philosophically acknowledged individualism is completely incompatible with positivism, and in the individualistic mindsets and impulses one mustneeds recognise a psychological refutation of positivism, a challenge to it. The philosophic theory of person presupposes the existence of an extra-temporal and extra-spatial concrete spirit, non-derived from "nature" and society and not subject to becoming dissected into some simplest elements. Only an existing individual spirit, free and endowed with creative energy, and not merely some temporal socio-biological form, not some fragment of the process of nature and not some chance play of sensations, can rise up against the external world and oppose to it its absolute rights. With Mikhailovsky there was an undoubtable gravitating towards metaphysical individualism, but the spiritual atmosphere, in which he emerged, did not permit him to break with the traditions and biases of positivism. He was likewise undoubtedly a rationalist, and herein there formed an abyss between us.

I shall return again to the rationalist teaching about person, when I speak about Chicherin, but also as regards the rationalism of Mikhailovsky it is needful to say a few words. Mikhailovsky, just like any rationalist, all his life defended a sense of person that was impersonal, colourless, abstract, generalised, he defended a biological abstraction, bereft of individualness, and this was an irony of fate concerning this "struggler for individualness". Like any rationalist, he took human nature not in its mystical, trans-rational integrality and fullness, he instead appropriated it abstractly, he dissected it rationally, and in such manner he killed the living immediacy of life, which brings us in contact with the mysteried world.[1] The plenitude regarding the experiential human person is inaccessible for the rationalist, and only this plenitude brings us into connection with "other worlds", and only herein do we discover our own individualness, essentially irrational, and unrepeatable in its uniqueness.

Rationalism is too apt to fight against everything dark, mysterious, problematic in human nature, everything that can frustrate its felicitous arrangement, its wont to set out human persons in rows, to normalise all

---

[1] Vide my article, "On the Modern Russian Idealism".

and everything. For us the human person is not a biological or ethico-gnosseological abstraction, but instead a living concrete individual spirit, in its supra-intellectual fullness made contiguous with the inner essence of the world. Rationalism deals with the matter always from a secondary, rationalised, abstractly-dissective approach, and hidden for it is the path to the consciousness of the primal, living, experiential total plenitude of being. Rationalism therefore, having set out under the guise of empiricism, acknowledges only the conditional, the rational, the as it were locked up in a spatial-temporal prison sort experience, an experience hedged in to the utmost degree by the categories of reason. And it fights against having to gaze at the directly visible experience that is transcendent, mystical, shattering all bounds and shattering all sorts of walls. In our national spirit are lodged intimations of a philosophy of trans-rationalism, of trans-intellectuality, and this is bound up in our rebelliousness, not set within any sort of limited framework, but rather in our anguish and strain for new, "other worlds". The foundations of a true individualism are contained in the philosophy and religion of Christianity. Christianity only has set love and freedom as higher than any law and the fate of the individual man is ascribed absolute meaning and significance. And we intend to discover it anew, cleansed of historical distortions. And it seems to me, that we have greater philosophic rights to declare the "struggle for individualness", since there is no degradation of person by an abstractive rational levelling-down. Mikhailovsky may be pardoned his rationalism because of his democratism, for his stubborn and incessant thinking about the people. But for Chicherin they have condoned nothing.

Justice demands that Chicherin be recognised as one of the most adept of Russian minds. His knowledge and the sphere of his interests was extraordinarily broad. But as regards taste he suited no one, in his writer's individuality there was something unattractive, something constricting and not liberative. His was an administrative mind, he dispensed orders and would not tolerate disobedience, in this mindset was something too doctorial, and in his nature something too deliberative.[1] Chicherin loved order awfully much, and in his system everything found its own place, everything was proven justified and enrolled under its certain category. Read his "Science and Religion" (this was the chief philosophic work of Chicherin, presenting a whole philosophic system), and it will strike one

[1] Vl. Solov'ev called Chicherin "a mind pre-eminently methodical".

unpleasantly, in that the religious problem is dealt with so deliberately, that God is rendered a god of good-arrangement and order, that the most decisive, it would seem, idealism does not lead to new worlds, but rather so that in the old antiquated world everything remains in its former place. His religion was of a conservative, and not liberating power. And it conserves the old economic, familial, state and other modes of life. About the birth of new forms of life he neither gets to nor speaks. Chicherin had a very diverse and strong mind, but with him there was never a grasp of creativity and he defended that form of Hegelianism, which considers truth once and forever revealed. And how oppressive and stifling it was to live in this rationalistic prison of a Kantianised Hegelianism, here where already all searchings are ceased. Rationalistic logic has appropriated everything into its own hands and has created an iron discipline, and irrational dispositions, such as might open into any sort of abyss, are not permitted. And this was an insult against the Living God.

Contemporary idealists have indicated, that they have to put Chicherin into their lineage. And to a certain degree, this ultimately is just. It is not we, who have contrived at metaphysical idealism, but rather it is thanks to Chicherin, that he defended it during a very difficult era for this tendency. But there is also a great difference. Chicherin never indeed strove towards new constructs, towards the consciousness of a new and transformed man. He created only a system of rational ideas for the affirming of a strong structuring of life, of a securely firm knowledge, morality, state, family etc. But this man never understood *tragedy*, he did not permit of it, and therefore he is foreign to us. Chicherin was essentially a conservative[1] and he was always foreign to our dearest cravings.

The strongest side of Chicherin -- is his philosophy of rights, and here we ought to rate highly his activity. Chicherin was a brilliant defender of the theory of natural rights, and the most recent idealistic tendencies in the philosophy of rights ought to esteem him as their chief proponent. Positivism celebrated its victory, and every conversation about natural rights evoked merely a condescending smile, but Chicherin bravely stood up for this old and eternal idea, to which again human thought had turned and which is at the basis of all social philosophy. Mikhailovsky was not philosophically constituted to defend the rights of the person, he ultimately

[1] I say "conservative" although he was one of the most powerful theoreticians of liberalism.

was obliged by the contradictions in his individualism to infer the rights as deriving from society, from an end-purpose external to person which instead situates and evaluates its rights. This is the fated lot of every positivism: the person does not possess an absolute significance nor rights inherent to it by nature, it becomes everything only from the outside, everything in it is evaluated in accord with the interests of a collective unity, external for it. As a struggler for individualness, Mikhailovsky was unable to liberate person from slavery to external nature and society, he did not detect that inner metaphysical subsistence of person, which it is possible to acknowledge only as unconditionally and infinitely of value and to posit in opposition to all external force.

Chicherin occupies a rather more firm position. For him, the human person was a metaphysical subsistence, not derivable from natural or social means. The rights of person are rooted not in the whims of society and not in the chance gifts of historical developement, but rather in the metaphysical timeless nature of man, and they are manifest as its unmediated expression. The demand of rights -- this is the voice of reason of an absolute, universal Reason. Man is a moral-intellectual, free entity, and his metaphysical freedom -- is the source of his rights, which ought to be recognised and crystalised within society. Chicherin's definition of rights, like freedom, is essentially accurate and quite profound a definition. And the matter involves but this, to deduce from this all the consequent inferences. Chicherin understood the metaphysical nature of rights and the deep inner connection of political freedom with metaphysical freedom. There was deeply lodged within him an idealistic awareness of rights, and respect for person, for its rights and freedom, it constituted the pathos of his life, his religion. Chicherin was our sole theoretician of liberalism, and only he understood the deepest ideal foundations of liberalism. Where the dignity of person is still not recognised, where freedom is subjected to abuse, and subjective rights are not crystalised into an objective right, it is there that such a thinker and publicist ought to be especially revered, and his services ought to be acclaimed by everyone. Why is Chicherin so little read, why has he never taken hold in people's hearts, nor led the thoughts of our intelligentsia, rushing forth with all its being towards freedom and rights?

Chicherin all his life was an implacable foe of democracy. His brilliant and deep works are permeated with quite malevolent excesses against the social movement, and quite crude his misunderstanding. It is unpleasant to read in the "Philosophy of Rights" those places, in which he talks about socialism, and it is annoying to see, how a bourgeois limitedness distorts the thought of so fine a thinker. This great logical and ethical failing cannot and should not be forgiven Chicherin. Historical conditions have unfolded such, that bourgeois liberalism cannot have success with us. Our strivings for freedom are tinged not only in a democratic light, but they bear also a more or less social character. And it is impossible to find admittance across the broad circles of the Russian intelligentsia, if there be repeated the historical treachery of the principles of liberalism, which were effected within Europe by the liberal social forces. From of old we have fostered within ourself a sense of disdain and contempt for bourgeois society, and this justly based instinct has led us often towards a distortion of historical perspective and politics. We did not have to be real politicians and therefore we were in no condition to estimate the great political significance of the publicist activity of Chicherin. Only now does the direct force of life shove us forth onto more real a path and compel us to recognise the complexity and different forms of the struggle, the inevitability of a different kind of provisional accords and temporary cooperation of different social forces.[1] And moreso now than before it is needful that there be broken down the prejudices of the two opposing sides: the one, which considers the bourgeois as the very essence of liberalism, and the other, which assumes the principles of liberalism to be bourgeois calculations to satisfy its own class self-interests.

The word liberalism is besmirched and worthless, although it derives from the greatest of human words -- freedom [Latin "liber"]. If the principles of liberalism be taken in their ideal purity, in their metahistorical and timeless significance, then they are manifest as a direct expression of the metaphysical nature of the human person, politically formulated as the unconditional respect for the freedom of the spiritual being. The essence of liberalism is in the innate, inalienable, absolute in regard to source *rights of the person*, in freedom and equality; the realisation of liberalism is a replacing of coercive relationships between people by relationships that are free, and it is grounded upon a supreme ideal -- in the unity of people, based upon inner freedom. True liberalism sees the source of the rights of

---

[1] The above was written still during the period of the "Union of Liberation", which fell apart after 17 October.

the person not in state power, howsoever it might be, even though it be the expression of the sovereign will of the people, -- but rather in absolute values, independent of the will of separate persons, segments of the nation or of all the people. Therefore the "Declaration of the Rights of Man and Citizen" is not a declaration of the will of the people -- of the fortuitous will of the people, but is rather the discerning of absolute values, lodged within the metaphysical essence of the free spirit. Freedom and the rights of the person are higher than any power, though this be the power of the people, higher than any intents and interests, even those of the working class. The right of private property was promulgated by the fortuitous and relative will of the people (a certain social group), but the right of freedom of conscience or of freedom of speech was the disclosing of an absolute, metahistorical good. And the whole task consists in this, to educate the will of the people, the will of the creative social groups in a respect and love towards absolute values, expressed in the "Declaration of Rights". And woe to those, which be seduced by temporal goods and prefer them over eternal freedom, which subsume in value the useful and who do not grasp, that it is a matter of rights *inalienable*. A pure, a true liberalism, not sullied by contact with social forces that have betrayed freedom in the name of their own interests, suchlike a liberalism affirms for the human person an absolute significance, and its rights in principle are put forth not in dependence upon chance historical forces, and therefore it expresses the tasks of the social life of people, it posits values, it possesses an undying value. It is not possible that there should become obsolete and out-moded the idea of the natural rights of the person and their guarantee in the societal order, the idea of freedom and equality, nor becomes obsolete the understanding of the meaning of societal developement as a process of liberation, the roots of which are lodged within the metaphysical depths of human nature. Chicherin understood the depths of liberalism and he superbly connected it with an idealist metaphysics. He stands many an head higher than the ordinary liberal positivists, who defend liberalism, not comprehending its essence and significance. Chicherin in such manner set accurately in place the primary foundation within the edifice of societal philosophy. He was a first class philosopher-jurist. But further on Chicherin makes a fatal mistake.

Of what sort is the relationship of liberalism to democracy? Democratism is but one of the definitions of liberalism, its interpretation, an inevitable inference from the principles of liberalism. A non-democratic liberalism is essentially a *contradictio in adjecto*, and antidemocratic liberal tendencies, which appeared already during the epoch of the great French Revolution, were a logical and ethical distortion of the idea of liberalism in compliance with class interests, a manifestation of historical and class limitedness. Once the absolute significance and inalienable rights be acknowledged for every human person, herein then already in idea is affirmed democratism with all its inferences, and class distinctions are negated. The "Declaration of the Rights of the Man and Citizen" is the promulgation of the reign of democracy; it demands respect not only for the rights of the person (of every person irregardless of his external position), but also towards every individual will, through which there ought to emerge the creativity of new forms of life. The subsequent and sincere individualism is always democratic, since for it there exists only the individual person as such, its spiritual nature and its inward uniqueness, rather than in the socially wrought definitions of person, turning it into a mere part of the whole, effacing its countenance. To uphold social and political inequality -- means to infringe upon the holy of holies of individualism, it means to posit things higher than man, it means to promote the unique human individualness only for its things (social preferences) and to degrade others for the absence of these things. In a valuation, grounded upon social and political inequality, individualness as such vanishes, becomes obscured, the spiritually negative triumphs over the spiritually significant, wherein his outer trappings defines the attitude towards a man. This kingdom of philistine values, by which the bourgeois world lives, is deadly to human individualness. *A genuine spiritual aristocratism is possible only in democracy, only after when those domineering the historical scene cease to be powerful by their social position, rather than by their spiritual might.* Particularly since that we are individualists, that we recognise the profound spiritual varieties of individualness, that we recognise the value of the human person as such, in its inner nature, we demand a most resolute democratism and we thirst for the cessation of the domination of things over people. Let life create the person and set upon it its individual seal, and not the things appertaining to the person, impersonal things, the mighty hold of which was once seized upon by Marx with genius. But perhaps socialism is the sole reagent, by which can be manifest the manifold spiritual individualities and thereby defining each of them in its actualising uniqueness. Yet in any case there is need of justification regarding the fate of individualism in terms of its historical-relative means. This justification perchance is provided by contemporary history...

Mikhailovsky understood the connection between individualism and democratism, and this was his strong side. Chicherin did not understand this and he was unable to understand, his bright mind was distorted by class traditions and prejudices, he was riveted to the fictitious values of bourgeois society. Chicherin all his life was afraid even of purely political liberal democracy, and in order to shelter himself away from its victorious demands, he made some quite deplorable compromises with his philosophy of rights, he replaced natural rights, always radical in spirit, with historical rights, beneathe the shadow of which the ruling classes of contemporary society could calmly sense themself. The attitude then towards democracy, which Chicherin inferred from his idealistic liberalism, was also purely a logical stumbling. Liberalism and democratism -- are one and the same, and if we nonetheless subordinate the second to the first, then in effect what principally we posit is freedom higher than the people, and rights -- higher than might. But the people ought to be freed, and the free construction of a new social order ought to proceed through the individual will of all the people.[1]

The attitude of Chicherin towards the social movement was nonetheless completely shameful for a thinker. This cold, sagacious mind began here simply to be abusive and displayed a quite monstrous lack of understanding. Chicherin was a very poor economist and yet completely Don Quixote like he defended Manchesterism, at a point when it had been given up by everyone. This was done not in terms of an economic perspicacity or economic cultivatedness in Chicherin, regretably, it was done from the stolidity of his character. He never conceded a single bit to economic individualism and he was quite staunchly the old-believer, he was prepared to defend a Bastia-like bastion, at a point when everybody had long since forgotten about it. Within Chicherin were interlaced lofty features of an individual character, which would inspire esteem in anyone, together with a very unpleasant tenacity in his biases, with a predilection and lack of desire to move himself forward, to be seeking. He never doubted himself in anything, this stony, rational man. Yet we must point

---

[1] The national sovereignty can and should be limited not by some portion of the people, but by the inalienable rights of the person, by values, independent of any human will.

out this merit of Chicherin, that he was one of the first to have risen up against the populist idealisation of the obschina-collective and he gave it more accurate an interpretation. In this he can even be acknowledged as a predecessor of Russian Marxism. To refute the social-economic mistakes of Chicherin is nothing, it is too elementary. I am addressing only one very essential side of this question.

The social-philosophic failing of Chicherin, similar to that of the historical failing of the bourgeoise, was the promulgation of private property as a natural right. This was not only logically defective, not only was it a manifestation of bourgeois class limitedness and the historical relativeness of the bourgeois epoch, it was also an infringement upon the individual worth of the human person, since by this the value of a man was bound up with impersonal things, things not created by him. Economic individualism was an historically accidental predicate of liberalism and it did not get down into its true essence. The liberal "Declaration of Rights" has been adapted and enlarged upon by the contemporary social movement. For example, the German Social Democrat Party is the sole liberal party, which is actually struggling against the reactionaries in the name of freedom, and German "liberals" least of all can pretend to this title, since they have betrayed freedom in the name of social prosperity. Social democratism is only a method of the subsequent developement and embodying into life of the principles of liberalism. We ought not to forget this. If democracy is an inevitable inference from the essence of liberalism, then likewise inevitably democracy is rendered social. And the creative task consists in the elimination of the non-correspondence between the social content and the forms of the "Declaration of Rights", ideally condemning the class structuring of society. We ought boldly and fearlessly to draw the most consequential of consequences from the liberal-democratic "Declaration of Rights of the Man and Citizen", i.e. we ought to acknowledge the struggle for the liberation from social enslavement as a struggle consequently *liberal*, and justifiable by the metaphysical premises of our liberalism.

But so-called "idealists" do not attach their feelings and their paths to pre-defined methods and forms of the realisation of the rights of the person, of freedom and equality. We account these methods and means of struggle to be very complex and varied, we have no fetish-like attachment relating to things external to man, for example, for strictly delineated forms of the social struggle. We admit the inner essence of democratism, which we consider identical with the inner essence of liberalism; but doctrinaire socialism, dissipating its religious senses upon unworthy causes, affixing them to the material organisation of life, is foreign to us and represents an outrage against the higher worth of the human spirit. We are not sketching out for ourself a finite social perfection, but if an utopia be sketched out, then at its most worthy we would recognise it to be in a condition of the ultimate triumph of individualism, an union of people, based upon inner freedom and love, and not upon externally imposed organisation. And indeed, towards what the contemporary socialist movement is striving, insofar as it frees man from the allure of things, also therefore in a certain sense for us comprises a "twice two -- is four". In the social sphere there is nothing to oppose to it, only that it should do its deed, and every bourgeois reaction is powerless and defunct. But by this path it is impossible still to create the new kingdom of spirit and it is impossible to conquer that spiritual bourgeoisness, which afflicts not only the ruling, but also the oppressed classes of contemporary society. This gives me cause to cross over to the other side of the world-outlook of Chicherin.

I want to repeat once again in connection with Chicherin, what I said regarding Mikhailovsky. The individualism of Chicherin though idealist, together with this also is purely rationalistic. This philosophic declaration of rights is of an impersonal, generalised, intellectualised sort of person. For Chicherin's idealism, as also for the positivism of Mikhailovsky, there exists only the rational side of the person, and there engages it only a general intellectual nature. But indeed the irrational side of the person powerfully likewise declare their rights, which also make for the individualness. The individual human nature not only demands intellectual rights, in common for everyone, but it also thirsts to tear asunder the bounds of the rationalising world. And we desire that there should be inscribed a "declaration of rights" of the concrete individual spirit, taken in all the integrality of its nature, not dissected away rationally to survive but in a mystical, supra-intellectual experience at a transcendent depth of being. This would be as it were a challenge not only to the social, but also to the spiritual bourgeoisness of our world, an anticipation of spiritual renewal, which can be accomplished only by a religious movement. And I shall sum up our relationship to Mikhailovsky and Chicherin, in terms of which we intended to define ourself.

In the philosophic regard Chicherin is closer to us, but in the social regard Mikhailovsky is closer. Both the one and the other we highly esteem, and we are prepared to learn much from them, though they both belonged to the old currents, each of them was variously a conservative and struggled against the new tendencies. Chicherin feared the growth of democracy, and Mikhailovsky with fear and suspicion looked upon the irrational strivings, upon the mystical searchings of the new generations. We think, that the future belongs particularly to mysticism and democracy. Social democratism upon the soil of positivism would lead up to the greatest drabness, to a quenching of the spirit, but it can however create a very refined spiritual aristocracy, if it be conscious ultimately of itself as but a means for the afar off and mystical aims of human life, which our small and limited reason denies, but our great infinite reason recognises.

In our social programme we join in with the emancipative and democratic covenants of our intelligentsia, but we provide rather other a philosophic basis and we insist, in character with the moment of time currently being lived through, on a keenly correct formulisation of our social demands. The quite diverse social forces ought to come together here in the tremendous demand for rights. And this would be an historical testing for our intelligentsia. We call upon the social forces such as recognise their human dignity to concentrate their attention and their energy on the deep-rooted question regarding Russian life, but our perspectives are far set, and we could never reconcile ourself with a bourgeois society and that bourgeois spirit, which not even the most extreme fighters for a new social order have surmounted. And we should remember, that the betrayal of the principles of freedom, so impudently accomplished in Western Europe, ought to find from us a most resolute rebuff. But we ought to go even further than those, who would make ready this rebuff, we ought not to allow, that spiritual freedom and the consciousness of the ultimate ends of life be betrayed, be traded off for social prosperity, showing us to be spiritually but beggars in that hour, when social renewal comes for us. And we shall not yield up in surrender to our comrade-enemies the coming kingdom of spirit, just as we shall not yield up in surrender to the bourgeoise the kingdom of social democracy.

An Answer to Critics

On Polemics. "Idealism" and Science. -- "Idealism" and Freedom. -- The Relation of "Idealism" to the Moment Experienced by Us. -- The Grouping of Societal Trends.

(1904 - 113)[1]

Concerning the "idealists", quite much has been written. Polemics against the "idealists" appears almost the sole spiritual fodder, which certain journals for several years here already have been offering their readers. Via the polemics against "idealism", certain beginning writers have gained unique reknown. The "idealists" have provided themes to their opponents, and have prodded them onto such questions, which they of themself would never independently have thought of, thus transforming them ever so slightly into philosophers and aesthetes. And all this is exclusively in the name of eradicating the hated and harmful "idealist" current. The Marxism, presented in our journals, bears upon it the apparent traces of decline, of an out-moded trend and with shouts for grasping at straws. Suchlike a straw exists in the empirico-criticism, and in the socially harmless vulgar Nietzscheanism, and in all these vapid, purely literal hymns to life. There was once a great teaching, mighty and glorious, and we too fell under its hypnotic spell. That was the classical Marxism and within it there stirred creative powers. But the Marxism, born of a different and already by-gone historical era, has grown old and ossified, it can no longer still play a creative role in the fashioning of a spiritual culture in our time. The heirs to this teaching attempt to patch its old clothes, but these patches are made from a material completely unsuitable, altogether foreign. Whatever might be the philosophic or scientific qualities of the empirico-criticism of Avenarius {Richard, 1843-1896], one thing is beyond doubt: to Marxism he has no sort of a relationship. Our degenerate sort Marxists

---

[1] OTVET KRITIKAM. Article first published in St Peterburg monthly journal, "Novyi Put'", nov. 1904, p.361-375.

have grasped hold of a mode of philosophy, since nowadays no one goes about without a philosophy, and the old philosophy of Marxism has ultimately fallen apart. Foreign the same to the spirit of Marxism are the recent naturalistic attempts to dissolve the social tintings of colour into an energy metaphysics. There has appeared likewise a demand to embellish the grey and insipid theory of the vulgarised Nietzscheanism and even the flippantly harmless decadentism. Amidst all this, our current Marxists are already clearly lagging behind and produce quite comic an impression. The still surviving representatives of classical Marxism, the indeed knights, solid as stone in their unwavering would frown, and with hostility and vexation would glare at all these novelties. Their voices, regretably, do not manage to reach our journals, and therefore all these quasi-Marxist organs prove so insignificant, so bland. Like parasites they feed off the vital juices of "idealism" and they dissolve down these juices into a facile positivist gruel, which they eat to our destruction.

Some things need to be stipulated, in order that there be no misunderstandings. The practical movement, connected with Marxism, has tremendous tasks, it is very alive and its significance I regard very highly. The discussion however relates to and concerns the theory of Marxism, the significance of Marxism within spiritual culture, in the contemporary searches, in seeking a definition of the valuable content of life. And herein becomes obvious a total impotence and inability. We love life, we worship it, life is the highest good, the highest end, the highest criterion of good and evil, -- cries the chorus of all these representatives of current day Marxism, as they attempt to rouge and whiten the old decomposing theory. How bland and bloodless, modest and preening all this is in comparison with the vivid, intense and audacious praise of the joy of life by one of the most interesting, gifted and remarkable writers of our time -- V. V. Rozanov. There is no one infringing upon the practical virtue of the empirico-criticists and their amoralistic Marxists, but the poetry of life is not their thing.

The "idealists" have not answered their "critics", have not accepted their challenge, have not taken up the gauntlet. In vain have the critics made a fuss and agitated, attempting to provoke us into polemics. There was not some sort of a secret plot on the part of the "idealists" in this, it was instead the result of natural and innate feelings, on which quite many concurred. It would not be sporting to object to all these polemic exercises, nor would the "critics" become inspired, it would be boring even to read all this, let alone reply to it. But it has become time already on principle to speak out about polemics in general and about our polemic mannerisms in particular.

For quite some while in our journalistic literature quite fierce polemic mannerisms have held sway. In this mutual fisticuffs has been expressed all our unculturedness, and this reflected also a total disrespect towards the reader and a transgressing of aesthetic propriety, a scorning of proper manners which is so characteristic for us. To ennoble our literary dispositions, to elicit moreso aristocratic manners would be nowise of small importance as a cultural task. We well understand, that the crudeness, the impatience and the absence of an authentic inner freedom in our journalists tend to be conditioned by special circumstances: by that tense atmosphere, in which the Russian writer tends to live. The existing order of things furthers a sick suspiciousness, one act of censorship begets another, one act of coercion begets another such act, one officialdom -- begets another sort officialdom. The responsibility for this spiritual deformity of the Russian intelligentsia falls upon the dark, stifling, ruling powers of Russian society. But it is time finally to stand up for spiritual freedom, for the right of creativity free from the infringement by any sort of officialdom, of any sort of the fads, monopolising progressive thought.

Of what sort is the psychology of the polemics, what sort of emotional motives predominate within it, towards what sort of instincts of human nature does it appeal to? This question seems to me interesting and worthy of examination.

In essence, the psychology behind the polemics is vile and it appeals to the lower, and not higher sides of human nature. Just listen to the polemics in literature or in verbal sparrings. Always one is struck, as to what gets forgotten with these questions, about which the polemics started over, and to what little an extent the truth is brought to light, to what extent those engaged in the polemics are slavishly enthralled by some sort of third and foreign power, in addition to the public, each drawn to heartily wanting to win everyone over to their side. We make terrible sacrifices in the name of our listeners and readers, and the catching hold of the hearts of these little ones long since already has overshadowed for us the catching hold of truth and right. In the polemics there is always something demagogic, always it is oriented toward this or some other instinct of the masses and always behind it is hid the psychology of slavery to the mob. The aim of the polemics is directed to its side of the audience, to evoke yells and applause, and this noise rarely serves to a triumphing of truth. Who wins at polemics? Oh, this victory then is won not by deep thought, not by power of argument, not by your inwardly being right! Alongside the feckless polemics, that by its very existence invites condemnation for presuming to decide the fate of truth -- there is also the chorus, a chance element, on the sidelines, having small a role, and often understanding nothing. Our typical journalistic sort polemics always plays upon some whatever heart-strings of the reader's soul and greedily awaits the applause from the reader, but all this ultimately reflects an insipid lack of respect towards the reader. For the genuine reader, the kind dear to us, uninteresting has to be all these endless, fruitless and petty quarrels of Mr. A and Mr. B, all these personal vendettas, the suspicions and the brawls, all this polemical blazing away, amidst which gets buried the interests of the truth and likewise forgotten all the demands for clarifying the questions. And if we genuinely wish to have respect both for ourself, and for the reader, then it becomes a matter of disregarding the polemics and the polemical critics, and on our part instead to reply to the perplexity of the reader, to clarify the questions as to their essence and to ignore all the polemical tricks against us, -- literally as regards a personal polemical attack to instead reply with an impersonal critical explanation to readers, as to what is involved in the important and significant questions amidst the polemical sparring.

Already several years back a polemic campaign was waged against idealism in general and against the one who is now writing these lines, in particular, and all this criticism strikes one by its shabbiness, since it is simply vapid, simply does not rouse one to reply, and often it has been churlish and petty. People, understanding nothing in philosophy nor conflicted over the religious problem, have raised totally out of place political objections against philosophic and religious searchings. This wont for applying political criteria to the most intimate inquiries of the human spirit on the one hand, and on the other hand -- the weighing of a political credo in terms of criteria completely non-political, is an indisputable indicator of a lack of culture, of a low level both of political and mental developement. Let our polemicising and criticising journalists learn to make philosophic objections to philosophic assertions, let them admit for the human person the right to a plethora of spiritual experiences, and then it will become both possible and needful to converse with them in cultural a language. And again all the same we shall attempt to formulate, the whatever chief perplexities evoked for the reader by the polemics against "idealism".

Let it ne noted, that to begin with I myself will raise an objection. "Idealism" is an extraordinarily indefinite general catchword, and this -- is a spiritual brew, which includes within it quite varied a range of views, bearing the possibility of very profound points of contention.

"Idealism" has been under suspicion of or even directly accused of comprising reactionism, doubly a reactionism, from both the scientifico-enlightening and the socio-political points of view. Around these two points -- the relationship of "idealism" to science and its relationship to freedom -- I shall also concentrate my reply. From our religio-philosophic point of view, is scientific enlightenment and liberating progress needful? Here is what evidently rouses the greatest doubts, since towards science and politics our intelligentsia relate with religious a reverence.

On the first point we shall not long dwell, this is very elementary, simple and almost a silly question. No one ever at all had any thought to infringe upon science. The "idealists" always made a sharp distinction between the discipline of scientific knowledge as separate from philosophy and religion, and certain are possibly even quite the positivist regarding science. The might and significance of science is totally incontrovertible, its necessity obviated at each step of our life. And we delimit the competency of science only then, when it involves itself not in its own matters, when it tries to speak on questions of philosophy and religion. But then too we would likewise the same relate negatively to a philosophic or religious deciding of scientific questions. Another question is what sort of role we tend to ascribe to science, to scientific enlightenment within human culture, within the course of world history. On this we straight out have to state, that we grant for science a subordinate and serving role, but profoundly otherwise and to the final degree contrary for us is the perspective of rationalistic enlightenment. We are in an irreconcilable struggle against the rationalistic culture, such as tends to distort the spiritual nature of man, that quasi-scientific self-smugness, that shallow and doltish denial of everything irrational or supra-rational. Moreso a sort of sharp-witted and deep-thinking critics could find very firm grounds on principle for polemic against us, but not deserving of even serious a consideration is that elementary and defective reasoning, claiming as though we are against science, that we are representatives of a reaction against science. Yes -- indeed a reaction, but not against science, rather instead against rationalism, against the infringement of positivism upon the plenitude and integrity of human nature. It is somewhat awkward for even the thousandth time to be repeating, that science cannot construct a worldview, cannot be a religion, cannot be a creator of values and a guide in life, that outside of the scientific-rationalistic cognition of our limited reasoning there is still an infinitude, which the positivists and in general all the rationalists cannot and do not want to see, as to what finally from such limited a competency of science itself tends to happen. I am ready to welcome the theory of scientific knowledge of Ernst Mach, insofar as it purges the science from all the metaphysical pretensions and makes it more modest, more scientific. This nowise obliges me to concur with the limited philosophy of E. Mach, moreso the contrary. By so doing, science will be all the more scientific and positive, and by this also philosophy will be the more philosophic and metaphysical, and religion will be all the more religious. Scientific arguments against philosophy and religion are however logically impermissible, and this is an error not only of rationalistic a consciousness, but also an indicator of very lower an intellectual culture. All this can be summarised thus: we esteem science no less, than do our critics, we see the need of it and we are aware of its force at every step taken, but we are foes of a rationalistic enlightenment and we posit our pathos within those sides of the human spirit, which are situated outside the control of science, outside its purely logical veracity. And now I shall move on to another, a quite more important question.

One matter of perplexity, connected with "idealism", merits quite attentive an examination. Here we would seem to have a matter dealing with an argument most damaging to us and very dangerous, if it were not a trite misunderstanding. I have in view the typical and widespread opinion, that "idealism" admits of an inner and metaphysical freedom, but lacking in its capacity to pass over to an outward and social freedom, that it cuts itself off from the earth, from the struggle, with which such a bloody intensity is waged in the name of a better earthly future, literally to wit, that "idealism" has turned its back upon the liberation social process.

Our critics very arbitrarily and to the utmost degree uncritically tend to manipulate concepts such as "freedom", "person", "progress" etc. It is the only way for them and far easier to object to us in triumphant a pose, since they do not want and cannot themself provide philosophic a reply to particular thoughts and expressions, and thus they resort to the quite vulgar feelings of their audience. From all sides I hear those indignant, scoffing voices, which would take away from us the right to demand outward freedom, to thirst for it. But everything is fine on your merely saying-so, each man inwardly is free and no sort of force can intrude upon his rising spirit. By this same ploy, from the "idealism" is removed the right to admit to a meaning of world history, at the very point in time when most of all there has arisen the demand to acknowledge the meaning of it, to investigate it. And we see this meaning first of all in liberation, in self-liberation and the liberation of the world. At the foundational basis of our religio-philosophic teaching I would place the idea of freedom, and inseparably connected with it the idea of person, and only then can there be a sanctioning and purpose in the struggle regarding the liberative social process.

What indeed is *the person*, and what indeed is *freedom*? Our positivist critics know, that freedom is a thing beautiful and alluring, that for the person it mustneeds struggle, and still moreso they know, that we do not have freedom, and that the person is oppressed and stifled. These are all fine sentiments, but positivism in all its shades and hues is powerless to provide a grounding to the ideas of the person and freedom and hence lead to a philosophy of liberation, to a liberation world-perception and worldview. Person and freedom ought not only to be the goal and result of the struggle, but instead ought also to be the subject of the struggle, and this is what the positivists have inadequately failed to consider. Person cannot be the product produced of the impersonal -- be it nature, the social medium, the historical process; freedom cannot be the product of necessity, -- of natural developement, it cannot be commanded and ordered on demand. The world historical process is only because of and can be liberative, in that within the very nature of the world is lodged a creative freedom, a principle contending against the demands of an oppressive necessity. The person can rise up against that which externally is imposed on it, stifling it, only in the name of its own particular inner nature, only in the capacity of an inwardly free being, endowed with creative energy. Otherwise, what is it that has rebelled, who is it that has struggled? The human person, this metaphysical spirit, inwardly free, can be bound, enslaved and oppressed; it possesses an absolute value, but its dignity can be mocked. But to struggle against oppression and enslavement can only involve a free being, and not some mere crumpet of matter, not some chance droplet within the ocean of natural necessity. This they nowise want to admit. And this brings the freedom-loving positivists to a very strange dilemma: either there can desire to struggle for freedom only a being that is unfree by its nature, some mere by chance snippet of the natural and social medium, or else a being that is free by its nature, a concrete spirit, a person, that can be reconciled with slavery, oppression and lawlessness. And still further: those, that see the meaning of the world and the historical process involved in liberation, should have to deny the meaning of the struggle for freedom, whereas those, that deny any meaning behind world and historical developement, should have to see in it merely a necessary process of nature, and thereby have to admit the meaning of the struggle for freedom. And herein we encounter a sort of frightful misunderstanding. The misunderstanding in short can be expressed thus: for the free no one would aspire to freedom, to gain freedom can only be the unfree.

This sort of judgement can be demonstrated logically, if it be not apparent in the content of the concepts employed here. For us, freedom is the creative power of an individual spiritual substantia, and this is an activity inwardly, from the depths of human nature, directing the self-determinative person. The concept of person, of the human individuality is unthinkable without freedom, as an inner defining of its nature. The creative acts of the person are free, but it is connected with the creative acts of other persons and by its belonging to the world totality, whereby the person clashes at every step with "necessity", assuming the forms of oppression and enslavement. Therefore the inner spiritual freedom of the human person can and has to be in conflict with binding necessity, oppression, enslavement, i.e. external non-freedom. In winning freedom for itself and for others, the inwardly free person realises its destiny in the world, imprints upon it its own creative mark, defends its right to operate only by its own freedom, by its inner creative force, which clashes with the constrained and constraining world. Whereas in contrast would be that unfree object, which the positivists call man, himself unable to oppose anything, any sort of external oppression, any sort of non-freedom, since he is nowise creative and his resisting principle is nowise in a condition to carry through in this constrictive and servile world. Only a free, a spiritual being, whose roots reside in the fathomless depths of being, can strive towards ultimate a freedom, thus constituted to struggle for it, whereas the unfree smidgeon of nature will dwell in slavery til the end of the ages.

No, ye positivist criticist gentlemen, freedom and the person we do not cede to you, for this is our monopoly, and not yours. And indeed not to their face can one say very much to the positivists, for they are more accustomed to talk about the general welfare, about the arranging of life, about the inevitable push for new social forms etc. It is time for us finally to lay down our cards and air our differences of opinion, which are very substantial not only in philosophy, but also in social regards, in an understanding of the meaning and aims of world history.

There are two paths, the one -- is the path of the love for man, which desires to make people happy, to organise and comfort them, to build for neighbours a suitable habitat, in which they forget about their irrational and tragic freedom, and repudiate their rights to an absolute truth transcending the world. This is the path of the Grand Inquisitor, which leads to the anthill, wherein there is neither freedom, nor person. The other path -- is the path of love for God, which desires the freedom of people, which sets truth and trans-human values as higher than well-being and the organising of life. This is the path of One, Who came with words of boundless freedom and the rejoinder, that God, freedom and truth stand higher than the well-being and comfort of people. And one mustneeds choose either the man-loving path of well-being or the God-loving path of freedom. And the contrast in opposition between these two paths has to become more pronounced along the subsequent steps. Thus it would be as an open and veritable struggle, the struggle between two opposed principles within world history, the transcendent principle of freedom and the immanent principle of contentment, the struggle between God and "the prince of this world". This profound opposition is very difficult to put into context as it applies to the societal matters of our day, but if one make the attempt to do so, then "freedom", "person", and the understanding of the meaning of world history will prove out on our side, and not on the side of the two-bit smalltime grand inquisitors, as we tend to be more clearly the strugglers for freedom, and liberation moreso corresponds to our religio-philosophic teaching.

The position of "idealism" at this historical moment, which Russia at present is experiencing, is very difficult and responsible a matter. We see a profound spiritual substrate to the societal unrest, which has seized hold of Russian society at all levels, and we are very acutely aware, that the discussion involves the very existence of the entire people, and about whether we go the path of creativity and consequently freedom, or the path of negation, the extinguishing of spirit and consequently slavery. The organising of all the constructive and liberative societal forces without a discerning of their ultimate religio-philosophic worldview and furthermore their social interests, is apparent in our slogan-heavy times. We however call for action by organised societal powers in the name of a remote, and for too many an inconceivable, reign of freedom. The difficulty and the responsibility to this position I see still to be in this, that we cannot and ought not to cede away the end-purpose in the name of the means, not trade away the right to all the fullness of our spiritual experiences and aspirations, and that we cannot and nowise should want to borrow anything from the theory and practice of the Grand Inquisitor, which on the one hand would open the door towards human happiness, while on the other hand forever slam shut the door to freedom. For us, the relative, the outward societal freedom is necessary an aspect for absolute freedom, the inward and mystical. For us, needful are the societal guarantees of the inalienable rights not for a felicitous ordering of life, but rather for the discerning of religious truth, which we now find ourself hemmed in from doing by both opposing sides. The hour is nigh, when the political objections against the religio-philosophic assertions and quests will finally lose all meaning and significance, when there becomes apparent finally all the shameful wretchedness of these objections. That will be the hour of the societal renewal of our native land, its liberation. We have to be ready for this historical culmination not only as societal beings, but also as emissaries from this world. And we ought not to yield up our birthright freedom, neither to those holding power, nor to those winning power.

And now I shall move on to matters of "this world". There is a need to reply moreover still to one accusation, remote from the final sort philosophic questions, but perhaps among the most important of all. The accusation against the "idealists" as being reactionary, -- it would seem now as already removed, and thinking people cannot be doubtful of our practical "liberalism" (in the broad sense of the word), but there remains in force another accusation, namely the accusation of "liberalism" (in more narrow a sense) as a betrayal of the working classes, who have always been at the centre of our attention, and hence an accusation of social bourgeoisness.

The insinuations by the limited sort adherents and lovers of the theory of class psychology little bother us, but we very adamantly have to object to the distortions and misunderstandings, which very easily can arise in this area. In my article on Mikhailovsky and Chicherin I attempted to set forth my view on the relationship between liberalism and socialism. And now I shall attempt to provide greater detail. Principally, in writing these lines on my social perspectives the purpose is not to pick arguments with those who regard themself our opponents, since by this is not determined our real attitude towards the grouping of societal currents existing in Russia.

That societal current, which in recent years appropriated for itself the monopolised defending of the interests of the toiling masses, has fallen into a quite vile sort of utopianism and has displayed a large degree of political short-sightedness. Populism once believed, that Russia is able to overleap the capitalist era, that it did not have to respect the rights of the person and it distrusted freedom, since it might hand over the people into the hands of the bourgeoise. This was utopian and reactionary an attitude, both in the social as well as political a sense. Marxism passionately came out against this utopian reactionism. The so-called "economism" has represented a shifting towards an exclusively economic realism and has focused upon the as yet weak awareness of law. But most remarkable of all, is that namely among those, who have taken it upon themself to fight against this "economism", reflects that there is occurring a very original process of a Populist-sort reviving of Marxism. They likewise want to overleap something, while yet they likewise disdain the independent significance of legal guarantees, and from their perspectives vanishes the nearest stage of our historical developement. We have here thus an undoubtable example of a rebirth of utopianism coupled with unique a reactionism upon radical a basis, since the toiling masses constantly are in opposition to those legal demands, which as such comprise the historical trans-national task of the times. Even from a strict Marxist class point of view it can be admitted, that there occur historical moments, when quite varied social groups fulfill one common task and thereby further their own class interests. And what inspires us at present is not some definite societal and state order, nor the historically limited actuality of the bourgeoise, but rather the inalienable rights of the person, as such comprising an absolute, trans-class and supra-historical good.

And while we fervently remain in oneness with our societal liberation movement, we think, that the deep social fissures cannot destroy this unity on facing common tasks. Yet I do not think, that the subjective unity can conform to the objective unity, no, for that would be an utopian dream, but a conscious historical collaboration, in any case, is and ought to be possible, since life is more powerful than doctrine.

This is one side of the question, which also evokes talk about our "betrayal". But there is also another side. Not for one second do we forget, that the "betrayal" can actually be inculcated by the at present progressive societal forces. Our today allies will tomorrow be our enemies. We know, on what side we have to be, and have not changed the precepts, which obtained in the era of our Marxism.

Of what sort are the tasks of the intelligentsia? The intelligentsia ought to uphold the at present *unity* of the aspiration for liberation. The Russian intelligentsia by its nature is first of all a lover of freedom and in its strivings it has tended to rely upon the peasantry, then later upon spontaneous a force, then upon the workers, and then the Zemstvo. But by its nature up to the present it has not had sufficient an awareness and therefore has not possessed a genuine taste for laws. In very progressive a Marxist one can meet with slave-like sentiments, the fear to discover the innate thirst for freedom. It is time already to cast aside this servile trembling afront a doctrine and in one's own awareness of rights discover one's own true human nature.

Can there here be any talk about a treason towards the toiling? Only those can think this, who do not admit of the legitimate basis for a great interaction among all the societal groups. Within our programme we resolutely take under our defending the real interests of the toiling masses, and we are in nothing distinct in our intentions from those, who suspect us of treason. On an economic basis is clearly detected the opposition of interests and for us there can be no doubts, as to hat side is the justice, and with whom we have to combine our social fate, but on the basis of the position of law it is quite otherwise, and here we have a matter relating to the interests of all the nation.

It is needful to remember, that in the grouping of our societal trends much is temporary, connected with the historical moment. We well understand, that there can quickly arise a time, when this grouping will be otherwise, but the historical moment obliges us to support a certain sort of combination of social forces. Our impending historical task will be decided only by the input of all the societal currents and it would be a total loss of historical perspective to put all our hopes on one only societal power.

This is nowise a denial of the relative truths of class politics. The meaning of the great movement presents itself to us in quite different a light, but about this I have already spoken in the first part of this article.

The Fate of Russian Conservatism

(1904 - 114)[1]

The fate of Russian conservatism is very peculiar, and in it is to be sensed historical an irony. Conservatism holds sway in Russian life and holds in its clutches creative powers, but in literature it has died, it does not exist as a current of ideas. With us there is no conservative ideology and at present there cannot be. And this is characteristically so: not a single conservative journal can exist in Russia, every conservative journalistic initiative withers under the indifference of readers, from an absence of literary powers. A conservative journal is simply unnecessary for anyone, for it there exists no sort of tasks, no sort of questions, either theoretical or practical, posited for resolution. The indeed very gist of Russian conservatism, triumphant in life and abolished in literature, consists in this, that it distributes all questions and tasks according to various departments and appeals to those holding power for their resolution. Amidst such a point of view and such an outlook for literature there remains nothing, for it nothing to do, it can only produce inquiries and inform. And the activity of the conservative press has almost entirely now coalesced together with the activity of one of the departments, hence verymost remote from anything there would be of literary and intellectual tasks.

Look if you will at some whatever issue of the "Russkii Vestnik" ("Russian Herald"). Is it possible to find there even a single genuine writer, even a single idea, even any sort of material for literary reading? Even the most extreme conservatives prefer to read progressive journals. There was an attempt to create an aggressive conservatively-clerical journal, the "Russkoe Obozrenie" ("Russian Revue"), but this attempt suffered a most shameful fiasco. In the history of our conservative journals always there was something morally impure of fruition. And in the literary family nowise acceptable are those, from whom there might be expected any sort

---

[1] SUD'BA RUSSKOGO KONSERVATIZMA. Article was first published in St Peterburg monthly journal, "Novyi Put'", dec. 1904, p. 324-333.

of perfidy, any sort of betrayal of literature by those holding power. Veracity of idea can be acknowledged only for that literary current, which values ideas, free thought, and grants literature an independent creative significance.

But our conservatism has found itself a refuge in the newspapers, here is its realm. For a long time at Peterburg there was not a single genuine, principled newspaper and only in the most recent time, under the influence of new outlooks and expectations, did there arise "Nasha Zhizn'" ("Our Life") and "Syn Otechestva" ("Son of the Fatherland"), which tend to satisfy the demands of political organs given to ideas. And this is understandable. With us there could not but be monopolies of the so-called conservative organs of the daily press, this monopoly was created by those grievous conditions, in which our press was situated. Conservative newspapers could speak then, when others were compelled to keep silent. At a time when a journal had to have literary grants, and some particular ideas and creative tasks, a newspaper could dispense with all this, as this is regretably demonstrated by the existence of the street newspapers. And for long dark years in the daily press there reigned the "Novoe Vremya" ("New Times") and it has guided the hearts of an enormous mass of Russian philistines. It would be too much an honour to term this organ conservative, since in calling it this there would however be something of an hint of some sort of order of ideas, some sort of current. Oh, we well know, that the "Novoe Vremya" can be also liberal, can spiel forth whatever the pleasing songs, when the moment requires this, when this suffices and is profitable, and it never stands forth to take the kicks in defending conservative ideas, over which the "New Times" street would smirk. The "Novoe Vremya" is representative in Russian history as a symbol of shame experienced by us, as a vivid example of literary depravity and prostitution. The "Moskovskie Vedomosti" ("Moscow News") and "Grazhdanin" ("Citizen") are better than the "Novoe Vremya", but what does this say concerning conservative thought, which shelters itself in these organs? Russian conservativism has completely gone to ruin in the recent "Moskovskie Vedomosti" and this sufficiently indicates, how dramatic its fate is. Let us look more closely at the history of conservatism and its nature.

Once upon a time in Russian literature there was a genuine conservative ideology -- Slavophilism. This was a current of ideas comprising a very unique and interesting world-outlook, and it was richly insightful and immensely talented. Slavophilism -- was twofold, it was not simply conservatism, in it were very many progressive elements, and demands in common with the opposing Westerniser camp. In the Slavophil teaching were uniquely combined two contrary principles -- power, authority, and -- freedom, and this combination pre-decided the ultimate sad fate of Slavophilism. The old classical Slavophils were romantics, they did not love the real and positive power of rule, they did not desire it for the people and they symbolically relegated it to one person designated by God. In such a manner they arrived at a mystical justification of the rule of power and romantically they dreamed of uniting the rule of power with a free people, to which they devoted their attention and thought. The Slavophils took under their defense the rights of the person and they wanted to affirm its will for freedom without its willfullness and apart from its willfulness. This was a monstrous contradiction: it was impossible to ground freedom upon the basis of its opposite, the rule of power. This romantic aspect decayed under the later generations of Slavophilism and the principle of power ultimately swallowed up the principle of freedom. And a true romanticism, such as cannot be subject to decay within the process of history, has to seek not for a mystical justification for the rule of power, but rather for a mystical justification of freedom, it ought not to affirm two mutually-exclusionary principles, but rather instead one -- the will to freedom, and not the will to power, and ultimately, for every human being a desired non-power of rule. The Slavophils dreamed, that the ruling power desired a free people, and only such a ruling power they considered to be true, mystical, while they had heated a contempt for an historical rule of power, enslaving the people. Both theoretical considerations and historical experience teaches us, that only the will of the people itself can desire the people's freedom, and not a ruling power contrary to it. The historical progressing of mankind towards an ultimate, mystical justification of freedom can be accomplished only by way of the dissolution of the ruling power within the will of each human person, creating for himself the wished-for freedom: and by way of the delimiting of every rule of power, even the people's rule of power, is there the realising of the inalienable and absolute rights of the person.

And it is remarkable, that the diametrical opposite to the Slavophil teaching about the rule of power, -- the teaching about the people's-power, about the sovereignty of the people, likewise falls into one of the forms of state positivism and within it likewise the principle of freedom is swallowed up by the principle of the rule of power. If Slavophilism eventually degenerated into a conservative state affair, cultivating the strong rule of power and instigating repression against the thirst for freedom, so also the positivist teaching about the people's power can degenerate into a democratic governmental affair, in a reactionary cultivation of the rule of power just the same as regards freedom.[1] And we ought resolutely to oppose every sort of governmental positivism, to oppose against every cult of the rule to power the romantic cult of freedom, the cult of non-power. The problem in the relationship of the rule of power and freedom -- is a fundamental problem of human history and in very narrow a manner it is connected with an understanding of the meaning of the world process. And herein are to be discerned two contrary poles, two types of mysticism -- a mysticism of the rule of power, with its fatal inevitability degenerating into a positivist cult of the state, into a governmental affair, and in contrast to this a mysticism of freedom, shining forth with a vivid light upon the world-historical process of the liberation of mankind and guarding the romantic visions of human nature. The old Slavophils wanted to combine these two types of mysticism, to conjoin the two paths and they were fiercely punished for this, their continuators disgraced them, taking up only one half of their teaching, only the idea of the rule of power and they took it to the extent, that it became bereft of every other idea and there remained alone the rule of power, naked, veiled over by nothing, and shameless. The Slavophils believed in the great mission of the Russian people, but for them this mission had to be realised through freedom, a mystical rule of power assisting in this realisation, with a people free from politics, from concerns over the affairs of this world. In any case, for the old Slavophils the rule of power was not the sole means of the realisation of our national fore-ordained destiny. They idealised the old forms of exercising authority and onto them they attempted to forge the creative national spirit, but for them nonetheless they realised creative tasks, the resolution of which called for freedom.

---

[1] To avoid misunderstanding, it mustneeds be stipulated, that by this my stand is not against democracy, on the contrary, I acknowledge it in its most decisive forms, but I should want to construct the realm of social democracy upon other principles, basically upon the principle of the absolute rights of the person.

What happened further on with our conservative thought? It developed the one half of the Slavophil teaching, lodging within it the principle of bowing to authority and combined it with traditions neither literary nor intellectual, -- with the traditions of our governmental practice. And this bowing to the idea of the rule of power imperceptibly passed over into servility in face of the fact of the rule of power, in the face of the official obfuscation of life. The mysticism of the Slavophils degenerated in fatal a manner into the governmental positivism of Katkov, which snatched away the romantic veiling from the Slavophil teaching about the rule of power and made a mockery of their idealism. Katkov was outstanding, as regards his abilities in terms of a first class political publicist, but with him we already do not see any sort of conservative ideology, any sort of religio-philosophic sanctioning for conservatism, here already all the tasks of human life rest upon the rule of power and leave no place for freedom, and there is preached the bowing to the naked official fawning. The disciples of Katkov and those that followed after went still further, they did not possess his talents, they lost every connection with literary-idea traditions and all their literary activity but came to this, that in differing tunes they began to call for the police. They subsidised the conservative journals, they attempted to support them, but their unneeded aspect, their unliterary aspect made impossible not only the flourishing, but even the pitiful existence of these quasi-literary undertakings, in having become appendages to the corresponding departments. Of the significance for the state powers, which Katkov had, all these pitiful conservative literateurs could not have, not having even their own name, and in literature, and in the world of creative ideas there is no place for them. A conservative literaeur at the present time is almost a *contradictio in adjecto*, since the paradoxical process of our history has killed conservatism, as a fact literary and of idea, in having fortified its rule of power in life.

Along the sidelines stands only the immense figure of K. Leont'ev, having crafted a very original and profound religio-philosophic conception, justifying a quite gloomy reactionism and misanthropism. But Leont'ev was very much an individual figure, and for his ideology it is difficult to find a place within the main course of our conservatism and he was of no benefit to it, unneeded for the practical aims of the conservative official foppery, he was too much the romantic and utopian.

And herewith began the fleeing from the conservative camp of everyone alive, of everyone talented and honourable. Particularly important to mention is the fleeing of Vl. Solov'ev. The world-outlook of Vl. Solov'ev was fashioned in an atmosphere of conservatively-Slavophil traditions and their defining influence upon him demonstrated the idealistic-progressive side of the Slavophil teaching. If amongst the old Slavophils there was room for both Katkov and Vl. Solov'ev, then in the furthest fate of Slavophilism these contrary principles separated and it became friend against friend, as enemies. Vl. Solov'ev emerged as a brilliant critic of our conservatism and nationalism, he revealed the irreconcilable contradictions between the foppish official in contrast to the universal principles of the Christian religion. In the "Natsional'nyi vopros" ("The National Question [in Russia]"), Solov'ev with especial intensity pressed the point of the immorality and godlessness of the practice of conservatism, of all this misanthropic, reactionary nationalism, stifling the spirit. Vl. Solov'ev demonstrated, that to remain in the conservative camp is impossible, that the practice of our conservatism is incompatible not only with idealism, but also with whatever the sort of ideas. And this was of a tremendous service for Russian literature and for Russian society. But the principles of the rule of power and that of freedom continued to fight it out within this immense thinker and great man, and until the end of his days he did not overcome this dividedness, he could not leave hold of this tenacious idea of the rule of power. Vl. Solov'ev thus also therefore did not arrive at a definitive socio-political world outlook and his principal attitude towards liberalism and socialism remains unclear.

And having fled from the conservative camp there is still another man, very gifted and to the highest degree original, -- I am speaking about V. V. Rozanov.[1] Rozanov wrote in the conservative press, he served conservatism, but there also he was always a representative of the romantics, not of the foppish official, such as is unnecessary for an authentic practice of conservatism. The mysticism of Rozanov sought the justification and sanctification of life, in order to render life joyful. But the sanctioning of life can only be religious, and here Rozanov wants to go to the very depths and primal roots of the religious consciousness of mankind. He goes from Christianity to Judaism and ancient Babylon, he seeks

---

[1] Vide the article of P. B. Struve, "Romantika protiv kazenschiny", in the sbornik-anthology, "Na raznye temy".

a religion of birth, and not death, a religion of the joy of life, and not its gloomy renunciation. Such a man it is impossible to put into the conservative camp, and hateful for him has to be the practice of gloomy reactionism of the foppishly official, and not mystical sanctioning of life. And Rozanov had to arrive inevitably at a decisive radicalism, to arrive at a mysticism of freedom, rather than at a mysticism of the rule of power. And actually, Rozanov never was given to having definite and clear socio-political views, he remains naive, and the questions of an outward ordering of life little interest him, but in his spirit he has to be a very extreme radical and has to be concerned about this. In the evolution of Rozanov we once again become persuaded of the ultimate spiritual bankruptcy of Russian conservatism, in the impossibility that there can be with us any sort of a conservative ideology.

Conservatism can be romantic and can have authentic literary representation only in that land, wherein it does not give rise to oppression in life by its rule of power. In Russia it is only -- official foppery, and no sort of creative tasks in the state of affairs does it either posit, or decide. All the vital interests of the land find their reflection in our progressive press, all the questions are dealt with by this or some other of our progressive currents. To the lot of the conservative press falls only one task -- to hold back the course of life, to quench the positings of thought and the problems of life. But this indeed is a tiny literary task and for its fulfilling are called others, more competent and moreso the official organs.

And now let us look, at what are the theoretical grounds of conservatism. Slavophilism attempted to give a mystical justification to the conservative pillars of the state, the church, the family, it sought a religious sanctioning for the embodiment of a ruling power upon the earth. And subsequent conservatives all still covered over their spiritual nakedness with a mystical veiling, and their purely materialistic recoursing to force they justified by lofty and idealistic words. But the triumphing reaction snatched away this veil from our conservatism and displayed its genuine nature, most clearly apparent with Katkov.

The religion of Russian conservatism is a religion of state positivism. Only a state positivism can be a justification of the official foppishness and only its servants can pray to God as to the rule of power. By state positivism I understand a system, which does not see freedom and the rights of the person as absolute values and instead considers the state ruling power as the source, the distributor and the decider of all the rights and even of all the strivings of the human spirit. For state positivism all spiritual culture is created not in the person, through the person and for the person, it instead has to happen through the sanction by the ruling power and the materialistic implements of force thus weigh down upon every sort of free creativity. From a religio-philosophic point of view the question might be put thus: in what is embodied the supra-human principle upon earth, is it in man, in the person, which ought therefore to be admitted as sovereign, or is it in whatever the ruling power, standing over the person, be it in the state, in organised collective units, having appropriated sovereignty instead for themself? This is a very basic question and upon its decision depends both all our worldview, and all our attitude towards life, as well as towards the historical process.

From our point of view, a consistent mysticism can admit of only a theocracy and as such it has to deny every other sort of "cracy". And mysticism inevitably degenerates into positivism and even the coarsest materialism, if it admits of the earthly ruling power as the embodiment of the heavenly ruling power, with the state as the intermediary between the person and the supra-human principle. The principle of ruling power in its essence is material, it belongs to the natural, to the fettered and congealed being, and contending against it is the principle of freedom lodged within the depths of the spiritual world.[1] The path from "nature", the servile, locked within the grips of "necessity", to God, to the supra-natural and the supra-human existence can only be in liberation and its bearer and creator can only be the person, the source of freedom. And a true "theocracy" ought to declare an irreconcilable struggle against all forms of holding power, all the godless "cracies" and instead acknowledge the human person as the sole embodiment of the spirit of God. Upon the "earth", in the empirical and the "natural" world, there is nothing higher than the human person, this is the highest form of being and upon it falls the mission of the liberation of the world by way of the entire world historical process. The supra-human liberating impulse issues forth only from the depths of the metaphysical nature of the person, only from within, and not from the

---

[1] By this, I am not asserting that vulgar dualism, which sees in "flesh" an evil principle, and in "spirit" a good principle. The evil principle I tend to see comprising the material nature of necessity, of coercion, of being tied down. And from this perspective "flesh" ought to be liberated and transfigured.

outside, as tends to be asserted by all the state positivists, all the adherents of the earthly, positivist "cracies".

Mysticism thus leads us to a justification of decisive an individualism and anarchism, which we set in opposition neither to religio-philosophic universalism, nor to social democratism. To the state positivism we have to set in opposition a legitimate legal idealism, and in opposition instead to the mystical justification of the rule of power -- a mystical justification of freedom. All the romantic aspirations, all the intimate expectations of human nature can only herein find refuge. Conservatism however inevitably degenerates into a naked and shameless recoursing to force and to its benefit it can only put forth the most positivist and utilitarian arguments. Conservatives still can defend their theory of coercion with allusions to the welfare of people, to happiness, contentment and tranquility, in the name of which the ruling power has to deprive people of freedom, always a tragic matter, begetting not only joy, but also grief. The "Moskovskie Vedomosti" constantly appeals to the welfare of the Russian people or to its forceful salvation, i.e. to positivism either openly or garbed in religious a costume. State conservatism inevitably bears an utilitarian character and its every manifestation is a denial of absolute values, of inalienable rights, of the religio-metaphysical meaning of freedom.

But all too often currents directly the opposite to conservatism stand upon the selfsame grounds of state positivism and utilitarianism, and thus are not in a condition to provide an authentic justification of freedom, nor to construct this theory of individualism, about which we spoke above. External coercion can only be opposed by an inner freedom, and the state ruling power -- by absolute rights. It is impossible to seek salvation from one organised coercive ruling power by having recourse to another coercive ruling power, and both positivism and utilitarianism are powerless to lead us our of this vicious circle. A positivistic ruling power or an idealistic non-power -- herein is a genuine dilemma. And striking by the extent of their naiveté are certain individualistic theories of society, which would combine the sovereignty of the human person and its immeasurable freedom with a materialistic worldview.

Never yet in history has the ruling power with conservative principles, principles of a reactionary state positivism, reached so far an extent, and so oppressive of spiritual culture, as with us in Russia. All this system has been relentlessly criticised and the finest Russian people always have basically rejected it, but there is still the point of perspective, under which rarely have they looked at our practical conservatism. Our conservative system is an organised, nihilistic in the very strict sense of this word, negation of culture, the negation of religion, of philosophy, science, literature, art, morality, rights, of all the spiritual content of human life. Our conservatives have been transformed into genuine nihilists and therein they support the conspiracy against all creativity in life.[1] It is impossible to acknowledge and to affirm spiritual culture and to deny its sole bearer and creator -- the human person, with its right to free self-determination. The principle of the rule of power is nihilistic, since it always negates something, hinders something, whereas the principle of freedom is creative, it creates something or sweeps along the path that, which sustains a creative content.

Russian conservatism is impossible, because that there is nothing for it to safeguard. The Slavophil romanticism dreamed up those ideal principles, such as ought to be conservative, but they did not exist in our historical past. Our conservatism therefore has not affirmed anything culturally unique, but has been rather in denial of the creativity of culture, having degenerated into a nihilistic reactionism. Creative powers however are becoming organised, to undo the grip of nihilistic negation.

---

[1] Now, during an epoch of revolution [1904-1905], our old conservatism has ultimately become transformed into hooliganism, preaching murder and pillage. Playing the role of conservatives are the cultural and honourable "liberals" from the "Peaceful Renewal" party.

The Catechesis of Marxism

(1905 - #115)[1]

There is need finally to greet the appearance in Russian translation of the catechism of Marxist philosophy.[2] Let there now be perused the remarkable book of Engels, "Anti-Düring", which Beltov has so talentedly transposed into the Russian language. It seems almost that it is the sole dogmatic part of Marxist theology. Let us take a look at this baggage of dialectical materialism, almost the sole baggage, and then the legend concerning this great, this all radically transforming philosophic theory, ought finally to be tossed aside.

The book of Engels possesses remarkable an historical interest, but at present to seek in it for some whatever satisfactory world-concept and teaching would be simply laughable. This book is outmoded in all its parts and does not stand at the heights of the current state of science and philosophy, it does not correspond to the current social actuality, and it coarsely argues against modern trends and investigations. Our modern "manner of being" ought to beget also a modern "consciousness", yet in the name of the basics of the Marxist catechism it would be necessary to admit of its outmodedness. But for us it is inconceivable, how in former times they could find philosophic riches in Engels' "Anti-Düring".

The pretensions of Engels are sufficiently great, and no less perhaps, than with Düring himself. In critical form he seeks to provide an entire philosophic and social system and to resolve the most difficult of problems with an extraordinary quickness and levity. And first of all, in order to determine the nature of dialectical materialism, let us look, at what sort of theory of cognition that Engels presents us with.

In several words is decreed the naivo-realist theory of cognition, whereby realism is to be understood, as materialism. "If one enquire, as to

---

[1] KATEKHIZIS MARKSIZMA. Article was first published in monthly literary-social journal "Voprosy Zhizni", 1905, No. 2, p. 369-379.

[2] Regretably, the Russian translation is very distorted.

suchlike thinking and consciousness and of what sort is their origin, then we shall find, that they manifest themselves as products of the human brain and that man himself is a product of nature, which evolves in a determinate means and together with this, from what already has made itself apparent, that the products of the human brain, which indeed in the final instance manifest themselves as products of nature, do not contradict everything remnant in nature, but instead correspond to it".[1] And here it all is.

I do not suggest going about the refuting of this primitive gnosseology, indeed no one at present could stand to defend it in such bare form. But it is very important to point out a basic contradiction of dialectical materialism, insufficiently taken note of by critics, and amidst herein which particularly tend to collapse the philosophic groundings of Marxism. Dialectical materialism presents of itself a logically absurd content of concepts, since in this content is lodged a simply monstrous logicising of matter. The ultra-empirical, realist and materialistic theory of cognition reveals itself also amidst this to be ultra-rationalistic, since it bases itself upon a boundless faith in the rationality of the material world process, a faith in a thing-like logic, a material rationality. But a rationalistic materialism, the logic of matter -- is far worse, than wooden iron or a black whiteness.

The Marxist dialectic was begotten of the Hegelian dialectic and bears upon itself its fatal imprint. Engels sought to posit a dialectic with the head at the feet, but after this it ought to lose its head, since on its feet it stands on nothing. The Hegelian dialectic was idealist, and its logically binding premise was panlogism. Dialectics always is an ideational-logical process, it is possible only within Reason. Thesis, antithesis and synthesis -- this is an aspect of the logical course of an idea, this is a process of the self-revealing of an idea, a process purely ideal and it is therefore rooted within the nature of the Logos. It is obvious, that the world process can be acknowledged as dialectical only amidst the idealist teaching concerning the identical aspect of being and thought, wherein being is understood, as idea, as Logos. Only then can the world process be interpreted as the dialectical self-revealing of idea, only then within the world Logos align the laws of being with the laws of dialectical logic. And this means, that only an idealist panlogism can justify a dialectical interpretation of being, which only can be spoken of concerning a dialectical idealism, and nowise

[1] p. 29.

concerning a dialectical materialism. And Marxism would again have to stand on its head with feet in the air, if it wanted to save the dialectics and safeguard the logical outcome obligatory to every philosophy. But then would perish the materialism, there would perish all the revelations of Marx and Engels concerning the mystery of the historical process and much as is actually of value and survivable. In any case it is necessary to choose: either the historical process is a dialectical process, -- the self-revealing of an idea, and then in it there is an inexorable inner logic, or this is a materialistic process, and then in it there is no sort of logic, no sort of rationality, and alone only chaos.

And in actual fact, who among the adherents of dialectical materialism would attempt to prove this unprovable and absurd position, that within matter, by which also is created thought, is created reason itself, that there is an inner logic, on the strength of which the material processes are wrought dialectical, i.e. can become identical with the logical coursing of the idea? I made an attentive reading of Engels' book and I find striking its naiveté, -- he does not even suspect the difficulties and impossibilities, connected with this position, and upon which he so firmly attempts to stand. And all the Marxists lack any such suspicion. Engels, certainly, is an empiricist and he regards experience as the sole source of knowledge, but there does not enter into his head a single fatal question, fatal for every positivist empiricism and quite lethal for every materialism. What guarantee is there to the rationality of the experience, rendering the world measurable by laws, upon what is created the assurance, that within experience there be not given us something extraordinary, exceeding all the bounds? No sort of inherent reason is necessary for us, say Messrs. the positivists and materialists. No, please, Messieurs, for you especially inherent reason is more necessary, than otherwise would be, since the devil well knows what can happen, there can happen a miracle, and ye would not be able to put up with this, for indeed no sort of scientific prognosis would be possible, depriving you of measurable-laws.

Both all the positivists, and even moreso the materialists sacredly and supremely believe in the inherent rationality of experience, in a certain inherent rationality of the world process, in a logic to things. Everything for them is by law, everything is within the limits, and "law" indeed always is from reason, and they are all rationalists in the purest sense, but not aware of it. With the Kantians everything is demonstrable within the natural order and it is impossible to expect any sort of miracles, since reason posits the laws governing experience, but the materialist has no right to make any sort of prescribings to experience and ought instead to expect any second the most unpleasant surprises from out of the material chaos creating our experience, -- our sole stimulant. But the materialist takes the easy way out of this tragedy, for self-consolation he becomes convinced in the inherent rationality of experience, in the inherent rationality of matter, in the logic of the course of things. Suchlike is even the most simple, most vulgar materialist, but the dialectical materialist is still a thousand times more rational. The dialectical materialist somehow regards it possible to believe, that "material productive powers" (a certain mass of things) is endowed with an inner logic, that material social developement flows along a rational scheme, literally, that in the thing-ness of the world there is reason, upon which it is possible to position oneself, as upon a mountain of stone. The whole system of Marxism is purely rationalistic, Marxism naively and optimistically believes in the triumph of reason within the historical fate of mankind, everything for it is made into rational schemae, everything is conclusive, everything foreseen. And even the Marxists, who dispense with the dialectics, continue to believe in the inherent rationality of being, in the schema-aspect of developement, and in the stability of experience. In the system of Marxism with its rationalism there is tightly connected a monism, a typical companion. Marxism believes, that there is a single basis and from it is to be inferred, that everything individual is illusory. And in this monism, as also in the rationalism, all still quite alive is the Hegelianism.

And why not presuppose, that being is irrational and manifold, why not presuppose it though only for a second? A claim for this indeed would be in quite many of the "empirical" groundings. Perhaps, in a world of much absurdity, perhaps, only the individual is real and not singly one, but the rather several principles come into play within the mystery of the world-construct, perhaps, within experience is manifest to us something miraculous and extraordinary. One can more quickly believe in all this, than in the rationalistic-monistic system of Marxism.

The absurdity of dialectical materialism is quite clear for philosophic thinking, but even dialectical idealism ought to be put to the test, though concerning this teaching in its extreme measure it would be possible to speak. In a journalist jotting as regards the book of Engels I cannot go into a critique of dialectics in its classical idealist form, and my task should but be to point out the inner inconsistency and inadmissibility of combining dialectics with materialism, upon this namely, that the dialectical weave can be woven from ideas, but nowise from material things. I cite here merely a few places from the critique of Trendelenburg [Friedrich Adolf; 1802-1872], who is little known amongst us: -- "For a dialectics of pure thought there results an inescapable dilemma. Either that negation, by which is mediated in it the progressing course of the second and third moments, is a logical negation (A = not A), and then it is powerless to beget anything definite in the second moment, and in the third has not the wherewithal to permit of unification. Or it however -- is a real contradiction and then it is inadmissible by the logical path, and therefore dialectics is not a dialectics of pure thinking". "Without a living contemplation, it would be the consequence for the logical method indeed to decisively put an end to it all with ideas, -- this is an eternal unity of the subjective and the objective. But the method does not do this, being aware, that the logical world in the abstract element of thought is merely a "realm of shadows", nothing more. It would begin to seem for it certainly, that there is another, a fresh and palpitatingly-alive world, but certainly, -- not from the purely thinking". "It is appropriate for dialectics to show, that the thinking enclosed within it actively encompasses the whole entirety of the world. But the proof of this is not a given. The imaginarily-closed circle everywhere is broken stealthily, in order to admit from without, what suffices it not from within. The shut eye usually sees before it but a single phantasmagoria. Human thinking lives by contemplation and dies from starvation, when it is compelled to feed itself off its own belly".[1]

The Marxists believe however, that they have made the transition to the "fresh and palpitatingly-alive world", that their thinking cannot "die from starvation", since it is fed by experience, that their dialectics is based upon facts. But by facts of experience it is impossible to have a basis for dialectics, without subjecting the experience itself to logicisation and rationalisation, which then happens by stealth. And the point of contact of the Marxist matter has seemed deadly for dialectics. Marxism has never however been able to make the transition towards live contemplation, otherwise it would not have persisted in this error, wherein that the world is rationalistic and monistic and that living experience cannot be forced by

---

[1] Trendelenburg. "Logical Investigations", [1840], tom I, p. 61, 81, 110.

conditional schemae. I moreso than the dialectical materialists tend to believe in reason, in the cognitive power of this instrument, in this even I am closer to such of the old rationalists, like Leibniz, but I deny the rationality of experience and of empirical being.

This has been about the theory of cognition for Engels, which fails any critique and even does not make attempts seriously to provide a grounding for dialectical materialism. And now I pass on to other aspects of the book, and first of all to the teaching about freedom and necessity.

In the catechism is contained a remarkable teaching concerning a leap from the realm of necessity over to the realm of freedom, which long ago already tempted many a "student". It would seem rather strange, how one fine day suddenly "necessity" gives birth to "freedom", and certain even began to introduce corrective variants, that, perhaps, earlier either there was a bit of freedom, perhaps, or later there would be a bit of necessity. In the leap from the realm of necessity to the realm of freedom was something attractive and alluring, but amidst this also something mysterious, almost mystical. Here, perhaps, lies concealed the peculiar romanticism of Marxism, but the theory, veiling the romantic expectations of freedom, is very grey and in a philosophical regard weak.

Engels, in essence, proposes a totally rationalistic teaching concerning freedom. "Freedom of the will signifies nothing other, than the capacity of man to be in a condition to decide with the knowledge of a matter... Freedom basically consists in an understanding of natural necessity, mastery over oneself and over external nature, since it of necessity is manifest as a product of historical developement".[1]

Freedom is a product of necessity, is a conscious necessity. This again is a materialisation of Hegelianism. Freedom -- is the product of a material social developement and together with this is the result of the triumph of consciousness, of reason. How is to be posited the mystery of the transformation of necessity into freedom, if there be not the potentiality of freedom, by what miracle does matter create spirit, the mind? Not only Marxism, but also positivist evolutionism commands a belief in this. By way of chemistry they want to cook up freedom in a retort-flask, but we repudiate suchlike a freedom and do not believe in it. Neither Engels, nor the Marxists, nor the evolutionists, nor the Kantians tend to conjecture, that there might yet be a teaching about freedom, as a creative, as a constructive

[1] p. 153-154.

power, without which never will be accomplished the longed-for liberation. And the leap into the realm of freedom, a long leap stretching across the whole historical process, is admissible only under this presupposition, that freedom, as a creative capacity, is lodged within the nature of the world, within the nature of man, that it drowses there even in the initial stages of the world developement, in each of the monads, comprising the world. I would even tend to say, that necessity is a product of freedom, that necessity is only a strange for us manner of freedom. In the teaching about necessity and freedom Engels is crudely rationalistic, he has no suspicion of an irrational freedom, and in the final end he becomes aligned with a quite vulgar evolutionism. And here the Hegelian understanding of the world-historical process as a liberation, set with the head over the feet, gives grievous results, for in materialism perishes both dialectics, and freedom.

No less important for Marxist philosophy is the teaching about the transition of the quantitative into the qualitative. If there be eroded away from this teaching the remnants of Hegelianism, then we receive the typical quantitative world-understanding. Almost all the evolutionists deny the independence and originality of qualities in the world and they preach a mechanical ideal of knowing. They tend to say, that from what is pleasing can be from what is pleasantly received, the question merely but in the quantitative combination. And this metaphysics of a crude sort they tend to pass off as positive science. It mustneeds be admitted, that we still do not possess a somewhat satisfactory theory of developement, only mere pieces, only indicators to separate factours. A true theory of developement would have to reckon with the mystery of the individual and would have to admit of the originality of the qualitative. There exists already a strong movement against Darwinism, since Darwinism has lost sight of the inner creative moment of developement. Now generally there is to be noted the contention between two types of world-view, and in this contention we resolutely stand on the side of the qualitative world-view. Alongside the monistic theory, which singlehandedly sought to hold sway, there is the breaking through of a pluralistic theory, which, perhaps, belongs to the future both in science, and in philosophy, after getting free of certain of the shortcomings of rationalism. Experience indeed is pluralistic and we need, perhaps, to construct a new ideal of cognition, more closely aligning us with life and the individual. And when the conditional lie of monism vanishes, then it will become clear, that the qualitative cannot be created by the quantitative, that qualities are initial and indissoluble and that only from a combination of qualitative monads is created the world and its developement. The arguments of Engels are striking by their poverty.

From whence, in actual fact, have they taken it, that the world is monistic, that at its basis lies qualitatively one, begetting of itself various qualities by way of quantitative combinations? Such a presumption there cannot be and there ought not to be, this question can be decided, evidently, empirically, and experience already in any case speaks out the sooner for pluralism. Monism is purely a rationalistic "premise", based upon this, that what is an oneness of nature for reason creates an oneness of nature for the world, and terms it this oneness. A monistic tendency exists in thinking, but indeed from this it is nowise possible to infer it concerning a monistic aspect of being. But, through a strange misunderstanding, the ones who speak most of all about monism are those selfsame materialists, who least of all have any right to this, since they tend to deny reason itself, as the source of monistic strivings. And with the falling of the monistic "premise" falls also the theory of the transition of the quantitative into the qualitative. Engels is little in a condition to uphold this theory, just the same as for dialectics, just as for freedom. The philosophic drama of Engels consists in a contrary-nature co-uniting of materialism with rationalism and this is a drama habitual, since materialism does not possess any logical right to be rationalistic and together with this always proves rationalised. In this is the lack of thought and the impossibility of materialism.

Let us move on to the social system of Engels, though questions purely economic I shall not touch upon. Engels in general is quite unjust and contentious towards Düring, but particularly this mustneeds be said regarding Düring's critique of the theory of coercive force, very interesting and meriting of attention. I shall not touch upon the economic materialism, which Engels defends in critiquing Düring; about this much has been written, by me also, but I shall say a few words about the theory of coercive force in essence. In this theory is included a very important and profound philosophic thought, which cannot be toppled by allusions to the role of economics and economic exploitation within history. Economic exploitation never was and cannot be an end in itself, as Engels attempts to assert, it was merely he means for the domination of man over man, a domination already not economic. In the history of violent relationships of people the form of economic oppression played no small role; from economics might depend the form of domination, but the radical evil of human inter-relationships, its fall into sin, as Düring justly asserts, consists in an act of violence by one human being over another, in the will admitting of non-equivalence. Within the world struggle two principles: the principle of power, of violent force, of being tied down, and the principle of freedom. The principle of violent force is evil, the principle of freedom is godly, and therefore with the limiting condition of mankind there can only be an ultimate freedom, an ideal of non-power. Economic oppression is only one of the manifestations of this radical evil, of a primary violence. The elimination of economic exploitation is obligatory, but this is only one of the ways towards a removal of violence from human relations. Still more radical would be a denial of the sovereignty of every ruling power, even though it be of the people, but the ruling power and the forceful violence connected with it are not abolished by a simple elimination of economic oppression. Political violence sits deeper than economic exploitation, and this is a truth, which is not explodable by any relative correctness of economic materialism.

I cannot but note, that Engels ignores the philosophy of law, the basis of every true social philosophy, and for him this is -- a bourgeois metaphysics. In the book of Engels is decisively repudiated the inherent value of the rights of the person, and therein already it cannot instruct us nor give guidance for difficult moments experienced by us. Such a book might provide slogans for other times, for us however it can only annoy.

The social politics of Engels in general is very outmoded, and this is admitted by the modern German social movement, even though and vainly so certain old-believers want to transplant it onto Russian soil, in a completely different combination of conditions. We vividly have in us a feeling of the dreadful harm of doctrinarism in politics, it hinders the educating of our broad radical-democratic current, away from the promptings of our historical task. This doctrinaire aspect, evidenced in the reading of Engels' catechism, is an indisputable indicator of cultural deficiency, the inability to differentiate between the various spheres of human life. In it politics gets scrambled with ethics, and with religion, together with a demand from politics of a confession of quite limited a philosophic theory, etc.

Oh yes, theoretical thought is needful for politics, it helps differentiate our interests and helps provide a way out from that lack of thinking, which is sustained by our doctrinaire elements. We have reverent a regard for theoretical thought, theoretical interests for us are an end in themself, but they mustneeds be separate from real politics within independent a sphere, a sphere lofty. Science and philosophy are thus set free from the role of being facilitators of practical politics, and politics is set free from the deadening doctrinaire aspect. We cannot however seek our God in politics, our souls for this are already too differentiated, and our utmost pathos we put into another corner. But in politics we have to be idealistically attuned realists. Realism however demands of us the democratic bloc, into which ought to enter all the radical elements of society. And woe to any sort of catechisms, if they hinder us from fulfilling our historical duty.

We have survived difficult and responsible a time, and very burdensome now it is to be a writer, twice as burdensome. Concerning this one aspect, -- important for the given moment, they do not give permission to write; concerning the other, -- the eternally important, the moment itself does not permit to write. In acute periods of political upheaval the moment tends to overshadow the eternal ends of the creativity of culture and therefore indeed transpires more quickly all the desired. The necessity of freedom is motivated diversely, but perhaps, the greatest motive appears to be the impossibility to conceive of a spiritual culture without it. If the historical hour of freedom does not soon strike, then what threatens us instead is a quite gloomy cultural reactionism, a gruesome spiritual decay.

Tragedy and the Everyday Ordinary

(1905 - 117)[1]

We have remained alive, which by our being so has bewildered and continues to bewilder us even more, than the reposed, or less unctuously, the dead. For us everything is lost, not having earthly hopes, all is in despair, all is maddened with the terrors of life. What is to become of us? Who will take upon himself the superhuman duty to commit these to the earth?...

Socrates, Plato, the good, humanness, ideas -- the whole assembly of the former angels and saints, guarding the innocent human soul from the fallen evil demons of scepticism and pessimism, do vanish without a trace into the expanse, and man before the face of his own fearsome first enemies in life endures that terrible solitude, from which he hath not the power to carry out his tradition and heart's wish. Herein also ensues the philosophy of tragedy...

The conscience itself is beset with the deed of evil!...

The whole world and the man alone do clash, and it would seem, that these two powers are equally great...

To esteem the great chaos, the great misery, the great misfortune! This is the final word of the philosophy of tragedy.

as quoted from L. Shestov's 1903 book:
"Dostoevsky and Nietzsche: Philosophy of Tragedy"

It is difficult to write upon this theme, so intimate, so remote from all the evils of the day, so remote from the common interests of the moment. But we shall defend our right to write about the interesting and the important, though it be but for the few. I shall say nothing about the

---

[1] TRAGEDIYA I OBYDENNOST'. Article first published in the monthly St Peterburg journal "Voprosy zhizni", № 3, March 1905, p. 255-288.

trans. note: the reader should bear in mind the backdrop atmosphere of societal chaos in Russia during this period of the eventually failed "1905 Revolution".

politics, which at present so absorb our interests, and it would be difficult to connect our ineradicable and elemental political passions, our political antipathy and our political illusions, with the philosophy of tragedy. For me it is clear, that alongside our theories, alongside our very fatal doubts, our politics relies upon very bloody feelings: we find unendurable the foul stench of the coercive civil order, and on an elemental and supra-rational level we love freedom, we revere it afront the sense of honour, connected with the struggle for rights. Oh indeed, we cannot believe in the setting up of an happily contented mankind and furthermore we do not wish it, the whole mechanism of the political struggle, if comprised of suchlike triflings, would evoke in us a crushing boredom, and long since already it has sundered all the threads, tied to the religion of the progress of mankind in all its views and forms, and it all indeed turns our stomachs, when acute moments occur. To the political spite of the day our most profound and deep-rooted aspect, our transcendental feelings almost, have been precipitated downwards. And afront the lucidity of our hatred towards the harsh stench of reactionism, coercion, betrayal, exploitation, afront the crystal clear, they have become agitated by honour to forsake everything problematic, genuine, all the fateful doubts into the hands instead of everyday and elemental values. But in our attitude to the "moment" there is sensed as it were the firm and sure ground amidst something of its connection with "eternity". We can have doubts whether on the good, or on progress, or in science, or in God, in everything lofty and of value, we can even have doubt in our own existence and that of other people, but for us there remains the undoubtable foul treachery, and we shall not continue to put up with the stench from the "Moskovskie Vedomosti", and just like before we loathe the police coercion and our thirst for freedom remains insatiable. Political passions have transcendent roots in human nature, and out attitude towards "matters of the moment" is assured for us. And indeed everything they give us, is like a nightmare, all these "wicked days", this monstrous force of the "moment", this trampling down of the rights of absolute freedom and creativity in the name of rights to a relative sort freedom. Here we find ourself with some sort of twofold reactionism and twofold coercion, and in a fatal manner we are torn asunder. Under the fear of death we ought to shake off from ourself the already intolerable coercion, it draws us primarily into the struggle of the "moment", and together with this we shall arise against the force of all the techniques of the political struggle, of all the triflings and manipulations of its methods over our ultimate freedom of creativity, over our right to "eternity". In the psychology and metaphysics of the political struggle and political passions, with this constant subverting of "ends" to "means", there is still much of the enigmatic and almost mysterious. The nightmare, about which we speak, has appeared in all the revolutionary epochs and it somehow provided complex and perceptible rights to people. This twofold aspect is insurmountable and tragic, but it nonetheless remains unshakably our primal, elemental political feeling and wishes.

* * *

Human culture is twofold in its roots, but never yet has this twofold aspect been so acute, so tragic and threatening, as in our epoch. On the surface of contemporary culture everything is more or less smoothed over, everything little by little is set in place, and the healthy vital struggles continue and make for progress. Certainly, the culture of contemporary society is filled with "contradictions", which are apparent even to the naked eye, contradictions between the proletariat and the bourgeoise, between the progressive and the reactionary, between positivist science and idealist philosophy, and ultimately between a certain "good" and a certain "evil". But in these "contradictions" indeed there is nothing yet of the tragic, there are impulses to the struggle, so that life might perk the more powerfully.

Such is the sick path of history. Upon it social mankind is arrayed, and moves along upon it to an intended coming happiness. Upon this path everything becomes submerged from view, despite all the "contradictions", with all the apparent fears and suffering in life. It props itself up upon "the great path", and to it there is tacked on some sort of avowed value for it -- wherein it means to find itself a place in life and situate itself within the limits of the everyday and universal "good" and "evil". And that man, who has found his homeland upon the great historical path, for a time has insured himself against a jolting into tragedy. About what happens in the depths, within the underground realm, about that which is most intimate and important, -- they tend to say little upon the surface of the above-ground culture or else they speak in the yet too abstract, the too generalised and smoothed over, adaptive view for "historical" values.

But the subterranean rivulets begin to trickle through and bear up upon that, which foams up in the *subsurface*. And the subsurface subterranean contemporary culture has become eroded by the force of the *tragic* problems of life; there with an unprecedented acuteness has become posited the problem of *individuality*, -- the individual human fate, and therein it has festered a sick individualism, and the "good" itself was invoked in answer to the tragic ruin of the lone and solitary human "I". Within the subsurface has developed an unprecedented loneliness, cut off from the world and with an opposition of the lone man to the world. This subsurface operation is expressed in contemporary culture, in decadence, in *decadentism*, which represents a very deep aspect and cannot be accounted merely as the most recent trend within art. The complex and refined man of our culture cannot endure this dividedness, the demands, that the universal historical process should set at the centre of his intimate individual tragedy and he curses the good, and progress, and knowledge etc, and the things avowed good, if they be not inclined to come to terms with his fraying life, with his ruined hopes, with the tragic fear of his fate. In Europe there appeared Nietzsche, and we had Dostoevsky, and this was a genuine revolution, not in the outward political sense of this word, but within the very depths, inward.

Man has undergone a new experience, unprecedented, he has lost his footing and is thrown about, and a philosophy of tragedy ought to deal with this experience. The tragedy of the individual fate has existed in all times, it accompanies each life, but the deeply absorbing experience, the as yet unprecedented as to its subtlety and complexity of experiences have become acute, and anew they have posited the problem of individuality. History knows a grandiose attempt to resolve the question concerning the fate of the individual human soul, to find an exit from the tragedy -- in the religion of Christ. Christianity acknowledged an absolute significance to the individual human soul and to the transcendent meaning of its fate. Yet this -- is a religion of tragedy, and up to this present time it holds sway over souls, both consciously and unconsciously. However, the attempts to resolve with its help the modern tragedy, to save the underground man, -- the decadent, they are already wont to term as a *Neo*-Christianity. But the contemporary Christian renaissance tends to undergo the fate of every other renaissance: *the past*, the formerly great, veils off the new creativity, the new searching. And hence the tragedy of the underground writes its own philosophy.

"Question: is there hope for those people, who spurn science and morals, i.e. is there possible a philosophy of tragedy?"[1]

* * *

This is all only an introduction, but now I pass over to L. Shestov, about whom long since already there is need to write. I consider ignorance of the works of Shestov to be a deep injustice, and I can only explain it, from that the themes of Shestov and their methods of developement are superfluous for the great path of history, as these are but underground freshets, noticed and necessary but for the few. Set up as it is within its own "positivist" or "idealist" world outlook, validating itself with universalised life, it but shrugs its shoulders and is unable to comprehend, why Shestov is making an unneeded fuss over all this. Herein is the profound needlessness of the writings of Shestov, the impossibility to make of them any sort of general utility and render them in one's eyes of particular value and notice. Shestov is very talented a writer, very original, and we, in casting about in our eternal searching, are filled with trepidation, and the understanding, that such tragedy ought to be dealt with amidst the questions, which this sincere and unique man so sharply raises. I regard Shestov as of imposing a greatness in our literature, and very remarkably symptomatic of the duality of contemporary culture.

Shestov's book, the "Apotheosis of Groundlessness" ("Apofeoz bespochvennosti"), has just recently come out, but I intend to write in general about Shestov, and rather moreso about his book, "Dostoevsky and Nietzsche", which I regard as the finest of his works. It seems a pity to me, that the "groundlessness" has begun to write its own "apotheosis", and herein it has become rendered dogmatic, despite the subtitle of "An Essay in Non-Dogmatic a Pondering". Bereft of all hope, the groundlessness is transformed into a peculiar system of stasis, and indeed an absolute scepticism can likewise kill tremendous searchings, just like an absolute dogmatism. Groundlessness, a tragic groundlessness, cannot have any other "apotheosis", besides the religious, and thereupon is already something positive. The tragic motif is weak in the "apotheosis", and in this is something tragically fatal.

---

[1] L. Shestov, "Dostoevsky and Nietzsche", p. 17.

First of all concerning the "psychological" method of Shestov. "There ends for mankind the thousand year reign of "religion and conscience"; there begins a new era -- the "psychological", which Dostoevsky has revealed for us in Russia".[1] Shestov first of all and most of all loathes any system, any monism, any force of reason over the living, concrete, individual actuality. He thirsts to reveal herein the *actuality*, which lies concealed beneathe the writings of Tolstoy, of Dostoevsky, of Nietzsche, his interest is not "literature" and "philosophy", not the "idea", but rather the truth about the *experiences* of all these writers, their real soul, their living experience. Shestov has an anguished idealistic demand for truth, of truth not inconsequential, and the categories of *truth* and *falsehood* are basic for him. Upon this foundation there is further comprised an unique gnosseological utopia: the negation of the cognitive value of generalisation, of abstraction, of synthesis and ultimately of every theory, of every system of ideas, along with the unmasking of their falsehood and the striving towards some sort of new cognition of individual actuality, of unmediated experiences, the reproduction of the living experience. And he desires, that his writings be not merely literary, that in them be not some "idea", but only that which is lived through itself, the experience itself. Music for Shestov is the highest thing of all, and he desires, that philosophy be transformed with music or in an extreme measure be rendered more musical. Wherefore also he has begun to write with aphorisms, since he is afraid of any coercion over the individual coupling together of his experiences, the rationalisation of his experience.

In all this there is much of an healthy protest against the absolute dominion of rationalism and monism. The psychological method is very fruitful, but it is here also somewhat hopeless, with some sort of a colossal misunderstanding.

It is only possible to experience experiences, it is only possible to undergo a living experience, whereas everything literary, every philosophy is already a reworking of something lived-through, an experience, and hence this is completely fatal. But aphorisms likewise are artificially contrived, they likewise already rationalise the chaos that is lived-through, they likewise are comprised of phrases, which likewise reflect their own judgement, even if they be not generally-binding. There remains for Shestov to express in music this truth about his soul, towards which

[1] Ibid., p. 58.

he strives, but music long since already exists, it is prohibited for no one, and as a result it might supplant former methods of cognition, but would disclose none new. "With amazement and perplexity I began to note, that ultimately "idea" and "consequentiality" tend to sacrifice that, which most of all ought to be safeguarded within literary creativity, -- free thought".[1] But in this spot I would snare the author of the "apotheosis". What indeed is suchlike the free thought, what is suchlike a thought? This has already a certain "premise", for indeed every *thought* is already the result of a reworking of the lived-through, of the experience by that murderous instrument, which we call reason, and in it there is already a binding "consequentiality".

That which is humanly lived-through, human experiences, possesses many modes of expression, many methods or reworking. For this there is music, but there is also philosophy, which inevitably produces its own operations over the experiences to the aid of reason, of an abstract, generalised, synthesising and working out of a theory concerning our new experience. And this is fatally, this is "psychologically" inevitable, for such is the nature of man. It is possible to rise up against various rationalistic and monistic systems, and I deeply sympathise with this, but then we have to substitute for them other things, irrational and meta-rational. This can be discovered in the example of Shestov himself whose, if he pardon me, many "ideas" are often quite original and profound.

Amidst the help of his psychological method Shestov has succeeded in the revealing of new and awesome activity, concealed beneathe the works of Tolstoy, of Dostoevsky and Nietzsche, to bespeak the truth about the experience of these great writers, so tormenting for us. But all the same, Shestov has fallen into a psychological schematisation, into exactly the abstraction and generalisation so despised by him. Shestov has a certain psychological schema, which he imposes upon his analysis of the writers, and essentially there are two basic schemae. According to Shestov, within literary creativity there is almost always projected the experiences of the writers, by way of either self-negation or of self-affirmation. Thus, for example, Nietzsche suffered from the "good", and he proceeded by bypassing life, and therefore he sings Dionysian hymns of life, and he rises up against the "good". "Together with this, in order to afford himself respite, Nietzsche concerns himself with the future of all

---

[1] "Apotheosis of Groundlessness", p. 2.

mankind and even of all the universe, it (fate) hints to him, as also to Dostoevsky, a certain small and simple question -- about his own particular future".[1] "When by will of the fates there is put before Nietzsche a no longer theoretical, but rather a practical question -- what to preserve, whether the marvels of human culture acclaimed by him, or his solitary and circumstantial life, would he not be compelled to renounce his most sacred ideals and acknowledge, that the whole of culture, that of the whole world nothing would prevail, if it were impossible to alone save Nietzsche?"[2] "In his works he relates to us his whole life, that woesome life, which undermined everything great and lofty, which on account of its preserving has cast into doubt everything, which mankind has worshipped".[3] And Shestov hopes, that there will be disclosed ultimately "the truth about mankind, and not merely the disgusting and fatiguing overall human truth". Shestov thirsts for the absolute, the *meta-human truth.* The "experience" of Nietzsche embodies such -- an unsuccessful life, profound hopes, terror afront his own individual destiny -- there within the works of Nietzsche. He transvalued all values in the name of self-preservation, he cursed the "good", since it could not save him from perishing, in his phantasies about strength, in the "will to power" he negated his own powerlessness, his own weakness. This is one psychological schema, of psychological abstraction and generalisation, which undoubtedly sheds light upon the tragedy of Nietzsche and reveals a morsel of "the truth about man".

Shestov establishes another psychological schema for L. Tolstoy, about whom he expressed many profound and true thoughts (yes indeed, thoughts, for elsewise I should have nothing to term this with). The attitude of Shestov to Tolstoy is quite characteristic and discloses a certain "truth" about him himself. Tolstoy gives Shestov no peace, he simultaneously both loves and hates him, and he is apprehensive, lest Tolstoy might not be proven right.[4] Shestov, evidently, likewise denies himself in his works, he curses "morality" for hindering him to live, he bestows it its own

---

[1] "Dostoevsky and Nietzsche", p. 151.

[2] Ibid., p. 166.

[3] Ibid., p. 170.

[4] In his first book, "Shakespeare and his Critic Brandes", Shestov is still under the powerful influence of L. Tolstoy.

illusory power. Beyond the words of Shestov about Tolstoy there is revealed his own particular flesh and blood, and he gives himself away.

"But for himself the fall into the category of the fallen, to take upon himself the *capitis diminutio maxima,* to lose the right to the protection of human and Divine laws? To this he voluntarily would no further consent to this, anything is better, than this. Better to be married to Kiti, better to be occupied as a landowner, better to be hypocritical regarding the good, better to deceive oneself, better to be like everyone else -- only so as not to be cut off from people, only not to be consigned to being "buried alive". This struggle defines as such all the creativity of Count Tolstoy, in the visage of whom we have an unique example, of the genius of the man, in whom there is this as though striving to make himself comparable to the mediocre median, to render himself merely mediocre".[1] "Count Tolstoy falls into some scepticism, before him there opened up an abyss, threatening to swallow him up, he beheld the triumph of death upon the earth, he caught glimpse of himself as a living corpse. Seized by terror, he cursed all the lofty questionings of his soul, he began to learn about the mediocre, about the average, about the commonplace, truly sensing, that only from these elements would it be possible to erect that wall, which even if not forever, then still for long would cut off the terrible "truth". And he found his own "Ding an sich" ["thing-in-itself"] and his own synthetic judgements *a priori,* i.e. he learned, how they separate themself from everything problematic and create for themself firm principles, by which it is possible for man to live".[2] Here is the terrible truth about Tolstoy. Tolstoy's Christianity is indeed actually "the ideal of an organised mankind". Tolstoy's religion and philosophy is a denial of the tragic experience, as lived through by Tolstoy himself, a salvation within the everydayness from the pitfalls, from the terror of everything problematic. What an incongruity betwixt those grandiose searchings and that systematic calm, to which they led.

The second psychological schema of Shestov is similarly again very successful. With similar approaches he turns towards Dostoevsky and reveals sides in him, that up til now have not been allotted sufficient attention. Much has been spoken about the God of Dostoevsky, but even more strongly there was in him a devil, a demonic tumult. The greatness of

---

[1] "Dostoevsky and Nietzsche", p. 70.

[2] Ibid., p. 75.

Dostoevsky was in Ivan Karamazov, and not in Alyosha. And Shestov discloses within him a realm of the *subsurface*. Dostoevsky, in his opinion, -- is an *advocatus diaboli*. He attempts to solve the riddle of Dostoevsky as regards his "Notes from the Underground". "Evidently, there is no other path to the truth, than through drudgery, the underground, the subsurface... But then perhaps all the paths to truth -- are underground? And everything profound -- is subsurface. But about what is it other, if not about this, that the works of Dostoevsky tell us?"[1] Dostoevsky's "underground" man says: "Is it that either the light should shine, or for me not to drink tea". In these remarkable words the individual human fate is set in opposition to the fate of all the world, it hurls a challenge to the "light", the "light" is called to answer for the individual perishing. This -- is the tragedy of individuality, driven underground.

According to Shestov, Dostoevsky himself was an underground man and one fine day he discovered in himself suchlike an "ugly and hideous thought" -- "Let the ideas triumph a thousand times over, let them emancipate the peasants, let them establish rights and compassionate courts, let them abolish conscription -- his soul for this would rest none the lighter, nor gladder. He is himself compelled to say, that if in place of all these great and happy events for Russia there should instead befall misfortune, he would sense himself none the worse off, -- and perhaps even better off"...[2] "If sometime there should chance to transpire the lofty dreams of his youth -- then all the worse. If at some point in time there should be realised the ideal of human happiness upon the earth, then Dostoevsky beforehand would condemn it".[3] "Dostoevsky is victorious on the front of reality, and having come across idealism upon the path -- he goes it one better: all the terrors of life are not so fearsome, as are the contrived ideas of conscience and reason. Rather than shed tears over Devushkin ["Poor Folk"] -- better it would be to admit the truth: let the light shine, so that there be tea for me... They sometimes have the thought, that "truth" consoles, that it strengthens a man, builds the spirit in him.

[1] Ibid., p. 37.

[2] Ibid., p. 52.

[3] Ibid., p. 56.

But the subsurface truth is built up altogether differently".[1] I include another lengthy quotation, in which very acutely and clearly is posited the essence of tragedy: "If the task of man is to find happiness upon the earth, then it would mean, that everything always should perish. This task is already unfulfillable, since perhaps would not the future happiness would redeem the unhappiness of the past and the present? Perhaps the fate of Makarii Devushkin, whom they scorn in the XIX Century, might be better off, when they permit no one to insult his neighbour? Not only not better, but worse. No, if already in the past, so let the unhappy forever live among people, let them also despise the future Makarii. Dostoevsky now not only does not want to prepare the basis for the splendours of the crystal palace, -- with hatred, with malice, and together with this with a secret joy he is beforehand triumphant amidst the thought, that always there is to be found some gentleman, who is not prone to settle the earth in contentment... Dostoevsky does not want universal happiness in the future, he does not want, that this future should be justified by the present. He demands another justification and he supposes it is better to beat one's head on the wall to the point of exhaustion, than to be becalmed in the human ideal".[2]

In the opinion of Shestov, Dostoevsky "all his life contended against theoretical apostates from the "good", though in all world literature there was but one such theoretician -- Dostoevsky himself". Dostoevsky fought with himself and for this he invented Alyosha, and Starets Zosima, he wanted to save himself from the tragic terror of the subsurface, preaching to other people the religion of Christ -- the old experience of a way out from tragedy. He strove to hearken to his own loudly preaching voice and to comfort himself, to justify himself. Shestov in such a way attempts to disclose the truth about Dostoevsky, the subsurface truth. Too much has been spoken about the religion of Dostoevsky, about his prophetic significance for Russia, and it was necessary to show the reverse side. But Shestov contrives to oversimplify the complex individuality of Dostoevsky, and throws away too much by way of a "digression".

"The devil fights with God, and the field of battle -- is the heart of people", -- says Mitya Karamazov. For the heart of Dostoevsky there was most of all this centuries-eternal battle. I am prepared to agree with

---

[1] Ibid., p. 96.

[2] Ibid., p. 98.

Shestov, that in the creativity of Dostoevsky rather more strongly is everything problematic, revolting, "diabolic", and rather more weak is the totally positive, the reconciling, the "Divine". But betond the creativity this is concealed most profoundly, and down to the ultimate limit is the imputed division of human nature. In the heart of Dostoevsky there lived also God, and therefore so terrible was his tragedy. Below I speak further about this, to wit, that every true tragedy presupposes not only a "no", but also some ultimate "yes", for the very essence of tragedy lies beyond this side of a "+" or "-".

But I wish also to reply to Shestov concerning his psychological schematism, I want instead to come out on behalf of psychological individualisation. Whether in Tolstoy, or in Nietzsche, or in Dostoevsky, Shestov contributes aspects that are of himself and he tells us very interesting things, but these writers are indeed far more complex, more multi-faceted, and ultimately, replete with the "truth about man" here, and perhaps it should be considered altogether impossible a matter to strive at. And it mustneeds be considered, that there exist tragedies, which people have experienced by completely different paths, other than Shestov's. For Shestov the tragedy of modern man is always the result of some sort of fright, a terror afront life, an impotence, a falling. But, I would think, the creative powers of life beating their way forth through the limits can also lead to tragedy, amidst too great a boldness, and a positive thirst for the supra-human and supra-natural, stirred by the will for immeasurable and boundless freedom. Upon this ground likewise can appear a non-ordinary, such as I would say, transcendent experience. Shestov ties everything into one type of experience and by this he himself falls under the power, hated by him, of the tendency towards monism.[1]

* * *

---

[1] Shestov sometimes falls into an harsh tone of suspicion and as it were of accusation. In such a tone is written, for example, his article about D. S. Merezhkovsky, in which sharp and shrewd remarks are to be met with. This is a defect within the "method" of Shestov, rather than that of his person, an aspect in his writing temperament.

In what is the essence of tragedy? Tragedy begins there, where the individual human fate is torn asunder from the fate of all the world, and it indeed always is torn asunder, even for the very ordinary people, not comprehending the tragedy, it is sundered by death. But indeed life itself is filled with dying, human hopes die, feelings die, abilities perish, and sicknesses unexpectedly crash down upon our heads. Objectively every human life is tragic, but subjectively are only those that sense the tragedy of life, consciously and acutely faced with the question about their individual fate and who have hurled forth a challenge to all the acknowledged universal values. *The downwards falling into that place, in which are interwoven the individual and the universal, -- here is the essence of tragedy.* The "I", the individual living human being, I perish, I die, the "I", a being with limitless questions, a pretension to eternity, to immeasurable power, to an ultimate perfection of self; and they console me with this, that there is the "good", which we ought to serve, whether it be "progress", which prepares for a better, more joyful, more perfect existence for the future generations, but not for me, nor for others, nor for strangers afar off, or which is "science", which provides universally-binding knowledge of the laws of nature, of that very nature, which is a given for me so mercilessly. But the "good", "progress", "science", all the values of the world, of the remote world, are powerless to save me, are powerless to return to me even but my one swallowed-up hope, powerless to avert my death, to reveal for me eternity, to render me, every given "me", empowered. People, unacquainted with tragedy and wanting to screen it off with everydayness, prefer to transfer the infinitude of the strivings of the human spirit from the person to instead the human race, they presume to affix themselves to the historical fate of mankind. They tend to say: mankind is immortal, mankind will be rendered powerful and perfect, and only within this is the future for each one.

"Is it a matter of either the light to shine, or for me not to drink tea? I say, let the light shine, and always in order for me to drink tea". -- Thus speaks the man of tragedy. Worse still, is that what constitutes the "good", "progress" etc, I summon them to a responsibility for *my* fate. And most important of all to realise, is that what is spoken of here is not about everyday "egoism", as when a man prefers his own interests over the interests of strangers. It is not about the ordinary "egoism" which is encountered at each step and which has enclosed within it no sort of tragedy, and even often ensures itself against it. Egoists, preferring "tea" for themself over "tea" for others, usually manage to connect their own individual life together with the life in-common, universal, historical, they manage to affix themself to acknowledged values, and they often become useful, necessary people. Here the question about "tea" -- is philosophic, ethical and religious, yet this "accursed question", has tumbled into the underground realm. If each individual human being is not to live eternally, if there is not readied for him the utmost joy, power and perfection, then accursed be the coming joy, power and perfection of the impersonal world, -- of the future mankind. This -- is the problem of individuality, the fundamental problem of human life, the root of all religion, the problem of theodicy, as they often term it.

This likewise is the fundamental problem of Shestov. He hurls a challenge to the "good", because it is powerless, because it saves not, and he perishes alone, having lost hope, a dying human being. The most wicked enemy for Shestov -- is the apotheosis of the moral law, of the Kantian categorical imperative, of Tolstoy's "the good is God". Shestov pronounces *a moral judgement against the good*, he calls it to answer for the sacrifices, with which this "good" has strewn history. "It (idealism) is furnished with the categorical imperative, providing it the right to reckon itself an autocratic monarch and legally to see in everything, refusing it obedience, as unsubmissive a rebel, meriting flogging and execution. And the categorical imperative has manifest such refined cruelty each time, when its demands were transgressed!"[1] "All the terrors of life are not so terrible, as are the contrived ideas of conscience and reason". "Conscience" compels Raskol'nikov to stand on the side of the transgressor. Its sanction, its assent, its sympathies are already not from the side of the good, but from evil. The very words "good" and "evil" already do not exist. The expressions "ordinary" and "extraordinary" have replaced them, and the object of the former is conjoined with representations about the commonplace, the worthlessness, the uselessness; and the latter aspect however becomes synonymous with greatness".[2] "Conscience as such has taken upon itself the deed of evil". In the opinion of Shestov, "the true tragedy of Raskol'nikov is not in this, that he has resolved to transgress the law, but rather in this, that he recognised himself incapable of such a step.

[1] "Dostoevsky and Nietzsche", p. 7.

[2] Ibid., p. 106.

Raskol'nikov is not a murderer; there was no sort of transgression beyond for him. The history with the old money-lender and Lizaveta -- was a fabrication, a slander, a false accusation". "His (Dostoevsky's) thought wandered the wastelands of his own soul. And from whence it brought forth the tragedy of the underground man, of Raskol'nikov, of Karamazov etc. These are transgressors *without transgressions*, these are stings of conscience *without guilt* and they comprise the content of the numerous novels of Dostoevsky. In this -- is he himself, in this -- is the actuality, in this -- is the genuine life. Everything remaining -- is merely a "teaching".[1] "Pardon, still it helps to be concerned with good deeds and in such manner to calm a troubled conscience! But Raskol'nikov at a mere thought about the good flies into a rage. In his ponderings already there is sensed that burst of desperation, which later prompted Ivan Karamazov in his terrible question: -- "Why know this *diabolical* good and evil, when it costs so much". The diabolical good and evil, -- you realise, is what Dostoevsky infringes upon. Indeed further than this human boldness dare not venture. Indeed all our hopes, and not only those, which are in books, but also those, which are in the hearts of people, have lived and have been adhered to by faith, that on account of the triumph of the good over the evil it is not terrible to make the sacrifice".[2]

The *devilish* good and evil, -- and herein Shestov posits a striving for God, just like did Nietzsche in his "Beyond Good and Evil", he rises up against the "good" in the name of something higher, than the good. Shestov demands a "declaration of the rights of the underground man", he demands the replacing of *the morals of everydayness by the morals of tragedy.* But the immoralism of Shestov is based upon a misunderstanding. He indeed spurns only a certain "good", a good in quotation-marks, a good of the "everydayness", in the name of another good, without the quotation-marks, of an higher, authentic, *the tragic good.* And this quotation-marked "good" he repudiates, it becomes rendered for him *evil.* I would say even moreso, that Shestov -- is a fanatic for the good, his "immoralism" is the product of moral zeal, of an aggrieved conscience. Shestov is likewise an humanist, and out of humanness he defends the underground man, he wants to write a declaration of his rights, and he is, perhaps, even secretly inspired by the

---

[1] Ibid., p. 108-109.

[2] Ibid., p. 121.

religion of Christ, and perhaps, Christian rays of light shine forth in him. Christ taught love and spoke forth to people of tragedy, He spoke nothing about the categorical imperative and morals. The voice cracks and quivers for the author of the "Apotheosis of Groundlessness" when he pronounces the name Christ.

With Shestov there is his own philosophy, his own ethics, pardon to say even his own religion, even though he has told us, that "ideas are unnecessary". For Shestov the philosophy of tragedy is *truth*, a righteous-truth and a righteous-justice. The philosophy of everydayness is a lie, its truth is false, its "good" immoral. Positivism speaks about this "good" openly, it wants to organise mankind, to create a firm foundation (both in theory, and in practice), and to banish from life everything problematic. But in idealism, especially Kantian idealism, it strives to consolidate the everydayness, it creates a system of idea and norms, with the help of which to organise cognition, morality, and human life in general.

"The philosophy of tragedy is on principle hostile to the philosophy of everydayness. There, where the everydayness pronounces the word "end" and turns itself aside, it is there that Nietzsche and Dostoevsky see a beginning and move forward".[1] "The philosophy of tragedy is far removed from seeking popularity and success. It is in conflict not with common opinion; its genuine enemy -- is the "laws of nature".[2] "No sort of social restructurings can dispel the tragedies from life, and evidently, the time has come about not to deny the sufferings, as a certain fictitious activity, from which it is possible, like the cross with the devil, to be delivered by the magic word "Begone", but rather to accept them, to recognise them, and perhaps, ultimately to understand them. Our science up to the present has tended to turn itself away from everything terrible in life, as though it did not at all exist, and oppose to it an idea, as though the idea be also the genuine reality".[3] "And only then, when there remains neither actual nor imagined hopes to find salvation under the hospitable blood of the positivist or idealist teaching, do people abandon their eternal fancies and emerge from that half-light of their limited horizons, which up to now has been termed with the tremendous name of truth, though of itself

---

[1] Ibid., p. 242.

[2] Ibid., p. 239.

[3] Ibid., p. 240.

it indicate only the unconscious fear of the conservative human nature before that mysterious unknown, which is called tragedy".[1] "Philosophy however is the philosophy of tragedy. The novels of Dostoevsky and the books of Nietzsche only but speak also, about the "most unseemly" people and their questions. Nietzsche and Dostoevsky, just like Gogol, were themself most unseemly people, bereft of everyday hopes. They attempted to find their own place there, where no one ever goes, where according to common conviction, there is not and cannot be anything, besides the eternal darkness and chaos, where even J. S. Mill himself might presuppose the possibility of uncaused acts. There, perhaps, each underground man means as much as all the world, there perhaps, people of tragedy also find, what they have sought for... Everyday people do not want to enter into pursuit of such an incredibly "perchance" fatal devilish path".[2]

Here Shestov as it were opens before us new horizons, some sort of glimmer, the possibility of a new creativity, of tragic truth, of tragic good, of tragic beauty. There is already a revolt against the ordinary, and the struggle for the rights of the underground, tragic man. First of all and most of all this is a revolt against "nature", against its "laws", against necessity. It is impossible for man to bear this weakness, this dependence upon "nature", of inevitable death, of the inevitable dying within life. Everyday "ideas" only increase the weakness of man, they come to terms with dependence, they quell any "revolt", which might hinder the ordering of mankind, and set it to rest. Moral "idealism", proclaiming the sovereignty of the "good", is itself a vivid manifestation of the power-loving everydayness.

I see the immense merit of Shestov in the sharp and profound psychological criticism of every kind of positivism, of every kind of everyday assertion, though it be under the guise of idealism. Alongside this, Shestov provides a psychological justification for transcendent searchings, he is a metaphysician in all his impulses. "Metaphysicians praise the transcendent, but assiduously they shun contact with it. Nietzsche hated metaphysics, he praised the earth -- and he always dwelt within the transcendent region".[3] Shestov despises the metaphysics of the

---

[1] Ibid., p. 241.

[2] Ibid., p. 245.

[3] "Apotheosis of Groundlessness", p. 132.

rationalists, with metaphysics as a created categorical opinion, with a deduction of concept, but he acknowledges the metaphysical experience, he senses those things lived through, the transcending towards which means its renouncing forever any kind of positivism. Another merit of Shestov that I see is in the dethroning of the idea of the sovereignty of the "good", in discovering the powerlessness of the "good". "Immoralism" is, certainly, a mistake, but the "moralistic" world outlook ought to be overthrown, and the most refined people of our time sense this. Shestov's psychology of tragedy implies for itself a transition from the powerless, everyday "good" to instead that of a transcendent power, i.e. to God. Only transcendent a power can settle the account with the individual tragedy, not impotent "ideas", not any sort of taming down for everyday "norms". In philosophic language this ought to be denoted as a transition from "morals" to "metaphysics". Life is needed not in the moral, everyday sanction, but in the metaphysical, the transcendent, and only such a sanction can hold fast afront the judgement of an individuality in revolt, of the tragic experience. It is impossible to justify the tears of a tormented child by the existence of the "moral law", and perceptive people begin to understand already, that it is shameful to speak about "ethical norms" for the human being, driven mad by the tragic fear of life. I would even say, that it is immoral to speak about the "good" in the face of tragedy, and here already there is needful something higher, than the "good".

But Shestov ought to have acknowledged, that every tragedy in a certain sense is a "moral " tragedy. Indeed, outside of good and evil in the higher, the transcendent meaning of this word, outside of "yes" and "no" there cannot be tragedy, but at most -- an everyday drama. And Shestov stands not on this side of values, he demands only the revaluation of values within such a tendency, which puts at the centre of the world the solitary human individuality, its fate, its tragic experience. The talk of Shestov rises to a moral pathos, when he demands a "declaration of the rights of the underground man". Moralism ought to be toppled by way of a revolution in morals.

We resolutely join with Shestov on one thing: philosophic tendencies mustneeds consider their relationship to tragedy. Every philosophy, which emerges from tragedy and reckons with it, is inevitably transcendent and metaphysical, every philosophy however, ignoring tragedy and not comprehending it, is inevitably positivist, even though it call itself idealism. Transcendent metaphysics is a philosophy of tragedy, and it ought to cast away the schoolish rationalism and recourse to the experience of Nietzsche and Dostoevsky as the most important source of its utmost cognition. Positivism in all its views and forms is an everyday philosophy, it always attempts to create a sturdy structure for human cognition and human life, but it tends to topple over by the very fact already of the existence of tragedy, afront which shatter all its armaments. Both the rationalistic and Kantian idealism -- likewise are indeed positivism, likewise are philosophy of the everyday. This sounds strange and paradoxical, but it gets to the core of the matter. Idealism in such manner creates a system of rational ideas and norms, which are alleged to strengthen the order in life and settle the everyday effect. All these rational and "critical" idealists do not understand tragedy, they are afraid of the underground kingdom, their "ideas" shut off the remote horizons, they become shut in within their limited world, and they impede all immeasurable striving. All true rationalists, though they call themselves metaphysicians and idealists, in their intimate essence -- are positivists. I would even suggest suchlike a definition of positivism: *by positivism is to be termed such mental-constructs, under which is placed a limit to human striving and experience and by this limit there is created strength and stability*. From this point of view as positivists can be shown not only many idealists, but also certain mystics, insofar as their religion tranquilises and limits. Transcendent metaphysics -- the philosophy of tragedy -- is the denial of every boundary to human strivings and experiences, of every system of an ultimate repose and ultimate stability. That, what can be termed the demonism of cognition, -- is in a denial of any boundaries in our solving of mystery, the acknowledging, of what is not forbidden, of what is not unnecessary and unuseful in our sundering from the tree of knowledge, -- this also is the basis of a transcendent metaphysics.

Shestov ought to acknowledge, that tragedy by the actual fact of its existence lifts the veil of eternity, that the new, for the everyday dread experience there opens up infinitude. The conditional, the rational boundaries collapse, and with Shestov himself there pierce through rays of the other-sidely light. It is sad, that this free-spirited, intelligent, original and audacious man either does not want nor cannot pass over to a new creativity. Creative capacities are indeed likewise tragic, are not of the everyday ordinary, and least of all can they be considered tranquil. Destructive and creative moments are always interwoven, there are creative moments also in Shestov, but I fear, that he would not be quieted with an ultimate, a non-rebellious scepticism. I do not suggest that Shestov should end "with morals" and declare that, "despite" the spoken above, everything is more or less fine, and is all about naught. Let him climb further "along the narrow places, difficult of passage, lying over the tropic precipices", along those mountain paths, which be *nur für die schwindelfrei.*[1] Let him discover new places, lest he risk getting trampled at one and the same spot. Once more I repeat: I find it a pity, that the "philosophy of tragedy" has been transformed into the "apotheosis of groundlessness", no less. And not because it is sad, that the "groundlessness" incites fear, no, but because it serves as an allure to a ground infinitely more deep, lodged within the very bosom of the earth.

Philosophic scepticism is quite the mode, and I want as though to rise up against this mode. We all begin with a psychological scepticism, with fatal doubts, with a certain chaos of experience and we strive to harmonise our life of soul, to transform it into a cosmos. Philosophy is a projection of our life of soul, the attempt to give it order and harmony, and with a greatness of reason it refashions our lived-through experience. No sort of philosophy can totally abolish the psychological, our primal scepticism, for only religion has the capacity to do this, but philosophy can be and ought to be that part of our soul life, in which disharmony is transformed into harmony, chaos transformed into cosmos. In music there ought not to be disharmony, in music everything is harmony, though the world be filled with sounds of disharmony. Thus also philosophy can be of the realm of reason (of the great and not the less sort, not the judgemental), though our world of soul be filled with non-rationality, with irrationality. It is characteristic of human nature to philosophise, and against this passion which for some is so basic, powerful and fateful, it is thus as little able to get confuted, as it would be against a passion to create a musical harmony in sound. We cannot forego creating philosophic hypotheses and theories, and in philosophy we inevitably are not sceptics, but rather dogmaticians, "critical dogmaticians". And yes, I have determined to undertake the defense of the so slandered and despised philosophical dogmatism. Philosophy has its own very important destructive side, and all its deductions in a certain sense are problematic, but philosophic scepticism presents itself to me as an absurd word-combination. Philosophy is naught

---

[1] ["only for the giddyness-free"], "Apotheosis of Groundlessness", p. 219-220.

other than the attempt to overcome the scepsis of our experiences by the creative power of the metaphysical reason, and philosophy exists insofar as scepsis is overcome by thought, and therefore scepticism is always a returning from philosophy to those lived-through experiences, which within philosophy we attempted to work out. Closer to me and more understandable is a religious scepticism, and unacceptable is too quick a readiness for faith. The philosophic teaching about God still does not lead to the religious faith in God, and upon this ground can arise quite terrible a tragedy. Though, from the other side, every genuine religion has its own dogmatic metaphysics, already the result of the workings-through of the religious experience by the metaphysical reason.

Least of all can it be said for Shestov, that he is indifferent towards truth, on the contrary, he fanatically seeks it and does not lose the hope, that it finally will be uncovered, if we look straight into the eyes of the new "decadence", the subsurface, whence tragedy transpires. True, Shestov to the point of an affliction hates "synthetic judgements *a priori*" and he denies everything "generally-obligatory". There glimmers herein for him the hated Kant-Tolstoy stolidity, the consolidation of everydayness, and he keenly, and sarcastically perhaps, with a certain bias terms the *a priori* as a [the Tolstoy character] "Nikolai Rostov". In denying the gnosseological generally-obligatory, Shestov pronounces a judgement (his discourse likewise indeed consists of judgements), which pretends to a psychological generally-obligatory, but where the psychologism lies deeper than the gnosseologism. The psychological metaphysics of Shestov, which he developes via Nietzsche, Tolstoy and Dostoevsky, inevitably and fatally makes pretense to persuasion for both himself and for his readers, although he persuades not by way of logical proofs, and outside any system. Even an apotheosis of groundlessness is impossible to write, without pretense of introducing anything into consciousness, without persuading even himself of the veracity of this "apotheosis". Shestov says accurately, that a writer most of all and first of all wants to persuade and justify himself, and this indeed presupposes already certain means of persuasion and justification and truth, but this is all however an old and eternal truth. Shestov rises up in revolt against "nature" and its "laws", this is his chief enemy. But together with this he finds himself under the hypnotic spell of Kantian idealism, which sees in "reason" the source of nature conformable to laws. Therefore and only therefore does Shestov hate reason as the enemy implying nature. The everyday philosophy values the "measures of law", the strength and stability of experience; the philosophy of tragedy desires and awaits instead miracles, its whole hope is bound up with this, that the rivers will flow backwards. Meanwhile, while "nature" rules and is sanctioned by "reason", the terror of death and dying holds power over human life. Yet actually however, all our hopes, the hopes, lived-through in tragedy, are connected with the immaculateness of "nature", with the possibility to undo the "measure of law". The overcoming of death, the basis of all tragedy, is also the overcoming of nature, its transfiguration.

Kant produced too strong and too heavy an impression upon Shestov. The apparition of Kant hounds Shestov, alongside the apparition of Tolstoy's "good", and he leads a tortuous struggle with them, a struggle within him himself. Yet it is needful to struggle with Kant. Kant is very dangerous, in him is lodged the seed of a very hopeless and together with this very strong everyday sort philosophy. The offspring of the Kantian spirit attempt to organise mankind upon rational grounds, they affirm a rational morality, a rational sort experience, in which forever to block away any transcendence, any passage to infinity. But Kant himself was twofold, and his "truth" was not so powerful and insurmountable, as would seem to Shestov, and the challenge to him is still not a challenge to truth.

Philosophy is always involved with the "problematic". Not every theory of cognition and metaphysics is invariably rationalistic and monistic, and the denial of rationalism and monism is still not a denial of philosophy, as Shestov evidently seems inclined to think. The theory of cognition can reestablish the rights of intuition and reconsiderations of concepts that have predominated up to the present; metaphysics can acknowledge its own source within experience and not merely in the limited, conditional, rationalising, but in an experience that is transcendent and unbounded. Philosophy can be non-monistic and pluralistic, it can recognise metaphysical existence and metaphysical meaning for the individual, for the concrete manifold of being. Here in the judgements of Shestov once again is expressed a certain schematism, he makes an inaccurate "generalisation", that every metaphysical idealism invariably is rationalistic, invariably monistic, invariably "Kantian" and "moralistic". Shestov gives us only the "psychology" of tragedy, but this "psychology" can be transformed into the language of philosophy, and thereupon we shall have already the philosophy of tragedy. This philosophy will not be rationalistic, to calm and settle us down upon the earth, and it will not be monistic, stifling and subordinating the individual into a single totality.

For such a philosophy, a philosophy of the future, the problem of *individuality* will be basic, a starting point and referent. All our philosophic and moral world outlook ought to be restructured such, that at the centre there should be the question concerning the individual human fate, and therein that our intimate tragedy should be basic, of moving an interest. Though this be but the world outlook for a few, it will not lose therein its veracity. It is long since time already for us to get to the perspective of a *transcendent individualism*, unique to the philosophy of tragedy, and not to everydayness, and in accord with this to revalue all moral values.

*　　*　　*

I might be modest in my positive assertions and regard my final conclusions as problematic, but one thing indeed is beyond doubt: tragedy, acute and absorbing in terms of the problem of individuality, means something other than a value of the world, other than "progress", "good" etc, and if there exists the immortal, if there be possible a transcendent affirmation of individuality, then it is only under this condition. The positivists and indeed the idealists tend to think the reverse, they desire faith in progress, in the universal value of the good, as a substitute for faith in the immortal, in the individual life as eternal. But when the time for the philosophy of tragedy has ensued, such a substitution is already rendered impossible. The human person henceforth consents to recognise as it were the value of world life, only if for it [the person] there be acknowledged an absolute value, a transcendent meaning, and only if the perishing of the temporal hopes of individuality be redeemed by its eternal hopes. "I", as an unique, and in the world an unrepeatable individual being, ought to be able to participate in the realisation of worldly and universal hopes, of absolute perfection, yet I can never foreswear my own thirst of an ultimate power, of ultimate freedom, of ultimate knowledge and beauty, -- otherwise, let the world itself perish. And each individual "I" ought to be able to participate in the *purposive-end*, *in the name* of which only be acknowledged value. Let there be "light", only if "I" can thus drink "tea", otherwise the "light" possesses no sort of value. The light, the world is transformed into a function, if it stands not on the point of view of the individualistic and consequently pluralistic metaphysics. To affirm the *world* and its *value*, to realise the fullness and perfection of universal being is possible only, with the affirming of the *transcendent individuality*, fulfilling its *own* predestined lot in the world. In denying the extra-temporal and extra-spatial being of individuality, we would in fatal a manner arrive at the denial of all being, arrive at illusionism, at nihilism.

Shestov in all this should agree, that this is only the obverse side of the philosophy of tragedy, of philosophy already, and not only psychology. *Tragedy indeed in its final reckoning is the fear of non-being, but in the very revolt against non-being there is included a certain aspect of being, a certain affirmation, creativity.* The tragic, the transcendent problems would never have been posited, if a certain existential experience had not been brought into it, and in this experience, it would seem, there is already included the acknowledgement of transcendent being. The immanent everydayness would have triumphed totally and tragedy would never have been able to raise a transcendent rebellion against it, if the positivist nihilism were correct with its fictitious values, its everyday "good", "progress" etc. Then everything would have been immanently suitable, everything would be arranged without tragedy, and nowhere would there be a falling into the other-sidely. Tragedy by the fact of its experiential existence not only demands the transcendent, but it also demonstrates its being. Shestov is not certain of immortality and he does not want to build upon this basis any philosophic theories, but he is bound to recognise the connection of tragedy within his understanding also of the transcendent being of individuality, otherwise the setting of the problem by him is deprived of all content. I do not intend to demonstrate the immortality of the transcendent individual being, I wanted only to establish this for me undoubtable and quite elemental truth, that with the fate of the transcendent individualism there is inseparably bound up the acknowledgement or denial of worldly values, that the "good" ought ultimately to be cast down, if in the face of individuality that eternity be not revealed, that "progress" too is unendurable, if it be not wrought in the name of that child, which hath shed the tear. And individuality, its value and significance, ought not to be understood abstractly, rationalistically, as do the "idealists" with this. The old rationalistic, normative, yet all the same coercive "morals" ought to be overthrown, and this demands the regeneration of all our culture.

For philosophers it is very tempting to rationalise the good and in such manner to posit moral laws, laws of universally binding ethical norms.

This temptation is well-known to me.[1] And individualistic ethics also tends to err from this rationalising tendency. Thus, for example, Kant managed to render ethics completely logical and transform that which was healthy in its essence into a scholarly formalism. There was introduced into the moral problem a logical normativeness, and in the search for a formal "lawfulness" there was killed its intimate essence. All the Kantians, the critical positivists, the rationalists get bogged down on this spot, all want to construct morals from upon reason. But philosophy ought radically to break with all attempts to rationalise the moral problem, to affix the good to reason, to establish ethical norms by analogy with logical or legal matters. Behind all these rationalistic and moralistic attempts lies concealed the deep philistinism of modern society, an obtrusive and quite smug everydayness. Kantian ethical norms, so very inspiring for German professorial idealism, are plump with the spirit of philistinism, this specifically German philistinism. From the faculty of reason of the philosophising philistines it is possible to create a morals of everydayness, but *the moral problem begins there, where tragedy begins, and only the people of tragedy have the inward right to speak about good and evil.* In opposition to Shestov I would say, that "everydayness" is situated "beyond good and evil", its "norms" morally are boundless and have need but for a favourable setting, whereas "tragedy" is inseparably bound up with the problem of good and evil, it involves a tormentive moral dividedness, a moral experiencing, and therefore it courses within the bounds "of good and evil". And I think, that the experience of tragedy is a primary and basic material for moral philosophy, and only in taking account of tragedy can there be constructed an ethics. Nietzsche therefore had a greater understanding of these questions, than did Kant, and he had a greater right to speak about the actual problem, which obtains only within the modern experience. Ethics is possible only as part of the philosophy of tragedy, and its source ought to be not reason, but experience. The scope of morality is trans-rational and does not possess a law-measure, the problem of good and evil -- is an irrational problem. Kant contrived out the "practical reason" and by this he wanted to mask his rationalism, his deep ignorance of those experiences, in which is revealed the moral problem. And all these Neo-Kantians, all the idealists, expounding on ethical norms,

[1] Rationalistic formalism held me still enthralled in my article, "The Ethical Problem in the Light of Philosophic Idealism".

about an universally-binding moral law, lack knowledge of the moral experience, since that this experience is there only in tragedy, in the living-through of the problem of individuality. The moral problem is also the problem of individuality, and this is altogether that tragic question about the individual fate and the individual foreordained destiny of man. In moral torments man seeks himself, his transcendent "I", rather than upon the path towards the regulation of life and the mutual everyday relationships of people, as these rational moralists would affirm. And therefore the moral problem can be decided only individually, and beyond this decision man is not responsible before anyone, for that judgement can only be supra-human. The good is an intimate relationship of the human being towards the supra-human principle living in him. The good is absolute, and for each one it is included in the fulfilling of his individual and unique in the world foreordained destiny, in the affirmation of his transcendent individuality, in the attainment of an absolute plenitude of eternal being. And the absoluteness of the good does not impede, but rather the sooner makes it obligatory to deny identical moral norms for all. There are as many ways of deciding the moral problem, as there are individualities in the world, although by these ways there is realised one and the same absolute good -- the plenitude and freedom of the transcendent being. And it mustneeds especially be emphasised, that the good is not a law of reason, but rather the will of a living being, always individual. In moral experiences always occur transgressions, since this is already an irrational area, and always the everyday limits are transgressed.

The task of embodying the good in one's life is purely a *creative* individual task, it is necessary to *individually* create the good, and not mechanically fulfill a decree, whether of reason, or of something else. The embodiment of good is not duty to a "law", given from outside, or to "norms" etc, this is rather self-affirmation in an utmost transcendent sense by way of creative and free abilities. Yet in such an instance if everything is permitted, in such an instance chaos will ensue, cries out the alarmed moralist. I would protest first of all in the name of the actual worthiness of the good against such a police-like setting of the question. If the truth leads to chaos, then let there be chaos! Of everything I have said, nowise does it follow, that everything is permitted, on the contrary, the duty of nobility and chivalry is proclaimed in the individual human being, man ought individually to create the good, fulfilling his own unique foreordained destiny under the fear of losing his own individuality, the perishing of his own "I" (not the empirical such, certainly). This is a weighty obligation, though not in the ordinary everyday philistine sense. But in the view of the moral police and the prosecutor there is a need to regulate, to hypocritically dress up in the uniforms of the positivists, the idealists, the religious etc, whereas the tasks of the *good* do not require to be props for order, and calm, prosperity, safety and such, of everyday blessings. For this there exist other institutions, other powers.

The new, the supreme morals, the morals issuing forth through tragedy, ought consciously to posit *individuality* at its centre of the world, its fate, its rights, its unique value and destiny. This obligates to something far greater, than the rationalistic, the abstract acknowledgement of the unconditional significance and self-worth of the human person, as proclaimed by the Kantians, the idealists etc. This indeed means to reframe all the content of the world in another, a new perspective, to revaluate everything. Transcendent individualism can provide the foundation for democratic politics through a philosophy of rights, but nowise for a democratic ethics. Democratic morals denies the individuality of each in the name of an illusory individuality of all the others, or more accurately stated, for it there is no individuality as such, there is no vital history of the human soul. Democratic morals inevitably results in a self-smug and power loving philistinism, in boorishness, in not knowing acuity of soul and refinement, in its artificial drills and standardisation. After the acceptance of the tragic morals of the transcendent individualism, it would be impossible already to scorn the underground man, it would be impossible already to deny the value also, perhaps, of the significance of people, such as whom usually are regarded as "superfluous" and "useless". There are needed new experiences, which would render factually impossible the avoidance of human individuality, as serving but as means for ends outside itself, howsoever lofty, and there is needed an unprecedented appreciation for the inward human freedom, for the unique destiny of each individual being. And chiefly, rather less to judge neighbour, rather less to demand an accounting, rather less to obligate, rather less to set norms. *And to reverence the mystery, hidden in the soul of each, the mystery of individuality*. And there should be acknowledged beauty as no less equal in value to the good. It ennobles. An abstract aestheticism, perhaps, is less harmful and in any case less intrusive and despotic, than an abstract moralism. Indeed, only God can be posited higher than both beauty and the good, as the absolute plenitude of both the one and the other. But upon what sort of a basis is it that the "good" reckons itself somehow the chief, the basic thing, governing value, commanding beauty and truth and everything in the world! For an autonomous good there can only be the everyday, the positivist and utilitarian basis. From the religious and metaphysical point of view the path of beauty is no worse than the path of the good, it likewise leads to God, and even more truly, more directly. I would wish to hear a justification that is non-positivist, not in the interests of felicity, but rather religious and metaphysical, for the especial significance and the especial role of "morals" in the world. Let there cease being regarded as "morally" the best people those most useful, most capable, the builders and creators of everyday life, and let there enter finally into their own rights the superfluous, the useless for everyday day, but still beautiful and of value for the affirmation in eternity of the transcendent individuality. Each one has his own foreordained destiny in the world, and individual aims are impossible to calculate from the point of view of the generally useful. There cannot and ought not to be the everyday, the all too human intermediaries betwixt the individual soul and God.

Then, perhaps, will be born a new love, the affirmation of the utmost fullness of the transcendent being of individuality, but about this love I here cannot speak. With many of the moralists and fanatics of the "good", is there an actual interest and attention to the mystery of the individual soul, to the underground psychology, from which grow so many, hateful for them, "blossoms of evil"? The guardians of the "good" have interest and attention only in the universally binding norms, which they apply to misfortunate people, for not being generally useful and generally capable. But -- knowing another, a new, a dark and together with this illuminating experience, the guardians can only despise, in their acting with such imperfect implements, as "norms". I say this not against the Kantians only, an inconsequential group, but rather against all the zealots of *the everyday good*, against all those, that offer bloody human sacrifices upon the altar of utilitarianism, the positivist arranging of life, etc, etc. Let there be set free the human individuality from *obligatory good*, from norms, from the prescripts of reason, from subjection to the *foreign*, abstract aims, and then only can there be truly posited the moral problem and be initiated a true creativity of the good, which then would not be abjured, nor fade, nor be cursed afront the terror of tragedy. *There has ensued a time not for the judgement of the "good" over people, but rather the judgement of the human over the "good", and this is a Divine judgement.* The good ought to be justified, but the everyday sort good, the power bestown us, evidently, cannot be justified, and it ought to yield way to the tragic good, not the good as God, but rather God as the good. It ought to yield "morally", since nevertheless the "factual" everyday good, creating its own unjust, hypocritical judgement, still long will reign, perhaps, til the end of the ages. It -- is the "devilish good", that of "the prince of this world". Everydayness -- is immanentist and positivist; tragedy however is transcendent and metaphysical. And thus there transpires the struggle between the two principles of worldly life: the intensifying and transforming into the everyday the felicity of the given world, with death, with the perishing of individuality, with ultimate non-being, -- in contrast to that of liberation, the affirmation of a new world, with the eternal being of individuality. This struggle has to be expressed also in the collision of the two moralities, between the everyday and the tragic, and the most terrible enemy ought to be considered the everyday morals, donning a mask of eternity, and fighting whilst using the words of the religion of the transcendent. And religious positivism, bypassing the abyss, not experiencing the tragedy of individuality, often becomes a strengthener of the everydayness. The most fateful question remains: how to render the transcendent immanent, how to bear forth in the world the new truth.

How to consolidate and build human society upon such disorganised and problematic foundations? I think, that to regulate human relationships can be *right*, wherein beyond which there lies concealed a transcendent sense of respect. It is possible to deny ethical norms, but to recognise the juridical norms, which call for the guarding of human individuality. Right also is that side of morals, which can be rationalised. Democratic ethics -- is horrible nonsense and at root it is a contradiction to individualism, but the democratic social structure is deduced from the basis of individualism. Let there be repose -- is the right, likewise divine and transcendent in its nature, and let there not be chaos, defend against it by force. Raskol'nikov then will not murder the old woman, the police, not the moral but the real ones will prevent everything, and it will be unnecessary for the man of tragedy to commit an everyday criminal transgression. The terror of Raskol'nikov consists in this, that he wanted a new experience, transcendent in its significance, he wanted an exploit, but he emerged instead with a very ordinary criminal history. The revolution in morals not only does not threaten the ruin of the "Declaration of the Rights of Man and the Citizen", but on the contrary, it affirms it all the more. I know not, how to strengthen and build up the edifice of human happiness, but I believe deeply, that the new morals would have a liberating significance, it would bring with it freedom, bringing us closer to the new world. Freedom is a value of the morals of tragedy, rather than of everyday morals, undoubtedly. And how to be saved from the deep-rooted fragmentation, from the "double book-keeping", I know not... There can be a new love, coming from another world, and it can save and bring about creative freedom...

In conclusion I want to say: it is necessary to read Shestov and reckon with him. Shestov -- is a warning for our culture, and it is not so easy to justify regarding him the most lofty, but nonetheless everyday sort "ideas". It is necessary to accept the tragic experience, which he recounts for us, to live through it. To bypass the precipice is already impossible, and beside this dangerous path everything is deprived of value. Amidst the ignoring and belittling of that, about which he relates, about which long since already the so-called decadence anticipates, amidst the "idealistic" bravado -- there threatens an explosion from the underground. We say to Shestov our own "yes indeed", we accept him, but we go alone farther along the heights, in order to create.

Culture and Politics

(Towards a Philosophy of Modern Russian History)

(1905 - #118)[1]

More than once already have they pointed to this, that Russia is the most strange, the most fantastic and wondrous land in the world. Within it co-dwell the deepest contradictions: both an utmost and religious lifestyle, and a cultural lack of lifestyle, barbarity. This indeed is the land of Dostoevsky, and in him was mirrored our most intimate, primal elements. Only in Russia could there be interwoven: a profound and extreme religiosity together with an as yet unprecedented religious indifferentism and negativity, the greatest literature in the world together with a barbaric contempt for all literary creativity, a wildly fanatical conservatism together with revolutionism, brought in the tither that swept Europe.

I want to speak about the strange and tragic fate of Russian culture. Long ago already there occurred a sort of fatal rift between the creativity of culture, between the religious searchings, based upon philosophy, art, literature, even science, and our vanguard intelligentsia. The creators of culture and the strugglers for liberation, the creators of good and of values and the negators of evil and of injustices do not know each other, often they suffer from a mutual indifference, and sometimes from a mutual contempt and hostility. And there is yet still one other tragic rift: in that our so-called democratic intelligentsia long since already has fallen in love with the people and made heroic attempts to become one with them, but it has become sundered from the roots of national life, from the element of the people. The going forth of the intelligentsia out to the people was to a remarkable degree something mechanical, it quelled the conscience, but it proved fruitless in a national-cultural regard. In such manner, the vanguard intelligentsia, considering itself the salt of the earth, became cut off both from cultural creativity, the spiritual life of the land, and from the national

---

[1] KUL'TURA I POLITIKA. K philosophii novoi russkoi istorii. Initially published in monthly journal "Voprosyi zhizni", 1905, №. 4/5, p. 320-334.

element of the people. The intelligentsia bears upon it the weighty burden of an elementary sort of liberation, and history will raise it a memorial, but its lack of culture and barbarity ought to take aback the man, who loves culture, who esteems creative thought and beauty.

The rift between the creativity of culture and the political current of the vanguard intelligentsia became clearly expressed particularly in the decade of the 60's, the era of the militant rationalistic and enlightenment nihilism. Therein clearly evident are the roots of this barbaric attitude towards culture. Cultural values of value in themself, spiritual goods were subordinated to values utilitarian-political. Pushkin, that first creator of a Russian culture, was spurned as superfluous. And up through the present the creativity of beauty, and selfless knowledge for its own sake, and the searchings for religious truth, are devalued in accord with utilitarian criteria. Philosophic and artistic currents get critiqued politically, and not philosophically nor artistically, and a profound lack of culture is expressed in this inability to differentiate betwixt the various spheres of life and creativity.

Within human activity there is arithmetic and there is the higher mathematics, and there are two types of attitude towards life: the one, is directed towards a dealing with the old, already elementary ideas, the other -- towards the creativity of the new, the higher ideas, towards the search for the as yet untrod paths. Across the extent of the whole historical process are interwoven these two forms of human activity, the leveling, the arithmetical, and the creative, the uplifting, demanding of an higher mathematics. And there exists the old hostility between those discovering and creating, striving upwards and in depth, in contrast with those dealing on the surface, the levelers, the popularisers. The first -- are revolutionaries as regards their spirit and they cannot live off anything whatever merely preserved, but the second are wont to be regarded as more just and through a fatal misperception as the more progressive, though the spirit of conservatism and ossification often deadens their souls and renders the admitted friends of freedom into the foes of a free searching and a free creativity. The strugglers for justice, those for dealing with the arithmetical sort of truths and elementary type goods tend to regard with a sick disdain the right to embody in life the truths of the higher mathematics, to create beauty always uplifting and revealing of other worlds. Those ardent over the lower schools and mid-level education tend to fight the transition to the higher education, wherein the arithmetical begins to accuse the higher mathematics of being insufficiently enlightening in character, almost indeed reactionary. People, having assimilated arithmetical ideas and having situated their life dealing with them along the human level, fanatically revolt against the integral and differential calculus, which they do not understand, since they have not yet made the transition from middle school to the higher.

The whole enlightenment and democratic rationalism, amidst all the radicalism of its social-political perspectives, is naught else, than arithmetic, than a dealing with a most elementary sort of ideas, and it fails to include a creative ascent within it. This limited faith of our era never will grasp the integral and differential calculus of the new mystical searchings, of the eternal creativity of beauty, the creativity of culture, developing amidst the unbounded.

The Russian progressive intelligentsia in its arithmetically disposed phantasm has ignored the Russian great literature, it did not acknowledge Dostoevsky as its own, because that he was not given to the mere repeating of multiplication tables, to addition and subtraction, and hence it assumed a posture of armed neutrality in regards to the creativity of culture, to the creation of the spiritual life of the land. It looked backwards, to the extirpation of "evil", and not forwards, to the creativity of the "good". The whole of our psychology for a long time has defined itself as purely negative, with our hatred for oppression and gloom, and to our disgrace also our pathos has been chiefly negative. And creative outlooks, the glimpses of the remote seemed to us inopportune and even dangerous.

Genuine creativity, higher mathematics, the searchings and creation of the lofty values of culture we see in Pushkin, in Lermontov, in Gogol and most of all and foremost of all in Dostoevsky and L. Tolstoy. There was something creative and of a revealing discovery with certain of the Westernisers and Slavophils in the generation of the 40's, with Hertsen, with Khomyakov. It was there in Vl. Solov'ev, it is there in V. V. Rozanov, in D. S. Merezhkovsky. With the so-called "decadents" there is also the thirst for creativity, and the agitated searchings and love for culture.

Chernyshevsky, Pisarev, Mikhailovsky were talented and remarkable people, and it is possible to discern in them glimpses of something greater, than an assigned arithmetic. In them was reflected the twofold nature of the Russian intelligentsia soul. We cannot but love these people, cannot but be eternally grateful to them. But their descendants, the children of their spirit, ultimately reduced everything to the arithmetical, ultimately renounced all creativity, they spurned the values of higher culture, and wallowed in quite hopeless an utilitarianism. In Russian Marxism, when it was young, it tended to excite, it was more cultural, it added complexity to mental inquiries, it accustomed one moreso to think and to read and to become weaned from the old nihilistic pitches, but within its utmost growth it again fell into our intelligentsia barbarity and lack of culture.

Let us look more closely, as regards the 60's generation of the Russian vanguard society and its teachers for culture, to all the creative efforts, in what spirit the finest part of our youth was raised. With the mother's milk we sucked in a scorn for culture, for literature, for art, philosophy, religion, for beauty in life, for refinement and complexity of existence. Those, who wanted to free us from the thousand-year oppression and slavery, not only did not implant in us a love and respect for creative freedom, for the fullness of life, but frequently themselves quenched the spirit, they demanded a deadening of cultural creativity, abstaining from a whole series of inquiries, and they practiced a peculiar positivistic asceticism. And the souls of too many of us were rendered emasculated, vulgarly simplified, restricted to the elementally necessary and useful. Herein is a curious contrast.

The *nihilism* of the 60's was a young, an healthy protest, it was a "*Sturm und Drang*" with all the extremities and awkward aspects of suchlike eras. It was strong and noteworthy by its negativity towards our historical, predominant, demonically-dark "nihilism", of our old, oppressive "non-being". But then too it itself, this positive, progressive, this non-reactionary nihilism contained within it an ascetic attitude towards culture, towards creativity, towards the fullness of life and therefore it bore with it likewise the spirit of non-being. And our decandentist movement was a young protest, likewise a "*Sturm und Drang*", but with a sickly vigour it has struggled for culture, for freedom of creativity, for refinement of existence, for the fullness of being. It was a revolt likewise indeed against our old, historical, deadening life of nihilism, but the revolutionary character of the decandentist movement has escaped the notice of our progressive nihilists. In the relationship between nihilism and the decandentist movement we see a vivid mirroring and as it were symbolisation of the oldly existing for us relationship between politics and culture. With the "nihilists" and their children and grandchildren we see a spirit of being, its affirmation within politics and an asceticism, the spirit of non-being within the creativity of culture; while with the "decadentist movement" and those akin to them in spirit, just the opposite, -- an asceticism, the spirit of non-being and its affirmation within politics, and the spirit of being within the creativity of culture. And this is remarkable.

Many an example can be offered of the nihilistic and ascetic attitude of the teachers of the intelligentsia and of our intelligentsia society towards culture, towards the creativity of values. And this is first of all expressed in the traditional attitude towards Russian literature. The self-sufficing significance of beauty and of the creative word was irrelentlessly spurned and there was adopted a purely utilitarian outlook upon literature. Pisarev, the most brusque and most sympathetic of the teachers of our youth, spurned Pushkin, excluded him from the history of Russian culture. Later on more moderate continuators of Pisarev's work tended to find, that this was extreme and going overboard, and they mercifully admitted for Pushkin the right to existence. But all the same Pushkin remained spurned, he was unneedfully splendid, they did not read him, did not understand him. And this more or less likewise was repeated with all the greatest Russian writers, their fate immeasurably sorrowful. The religious torments of Gogol remained under suspicion and he was valued only as a societal satirist. L. Tolstoy and Dostoevsky were acknowledged as world geniuses and teachers in Western Europe, while our vanguard criticism castigated them for whatever the petty faults, it gave them reprimands for insufficient knowledge on arithmetical ideas and anathematised all their significance for Russian and world culture, everything, that in them which was cataclysmic, religious and prophetic. For the vanguard Russian criticism, utilitarian and emasculate, Russian literature has remained an unknown land, some sort of wondrous world, and herein is expressed that sickly alienation of the vanguard intelligentsia from the national roots of cultural creativity. The true appreciation of Russian literature has begun already in a completely different pole of thought, with people of a different outlook, it can be met with in Vl. Solov'ev, Rozanov, Merezhkovsky, Volynsky etc.

Quite the same barbaric attitude has always been there amongst us towards philosophy. In the 40's they esteemed philosophic thought, but in the 60's there began the positivist obscurantism. The ascetic abstemption from philosophic searchings, from thoughts over the ultimate problems of being is regarded as hardly more than a sign of societal decency. The right of a philosophic creativity was spurned in the high tribunal of a societal utilitarianism. We had an outstanding and original, an altogether unique philosopher -- Vladimir Solov'ev. Are there many that have read him, that know him, that have appreciated his philosophy? On one's fingers can such be counted. For a long time this extraordinary man regarding himself did not evoke anything, save for a dull sneering, and he was hopelessly alone. Russian vanguard society is unable to appreciate the most national heroes of its cultural creativity, and there is herein something strange and pathetic. With us there were also other efforts in the sphere of philosophic thought, as e.g. Kozlov, Lopatin and moreover certain others, no worse than the [Alois] Riehl's, the Windelbands, the Cohens, but who indeed has read them, who even has heard of them? Are there many of us who have read "Voprosy philosophii i psikhologii" ["Questions of Philosophy and Psychology"], an original philosophic journal, more alive spiritually, than the greater part of our fat journals, bereft of all creativity? In recent years the so-called "idealists" have generated an interest in philosophy, have brought attention to it, though also not very favourably, but as regards purely utilitarian considerations, only because that they earlier were Marxists and now have attempted to connect philosophy with politics.

But with us nothing is so scorned and so ignored, as is art. In this area of novelty, the lack of culture and coarseness of tastes of the Russian vanguard intelligentsia tends to exceed that of all others. With us how so very mechanically they go to the opera, to a drama, to an exhibition of pictures, they seek amusements or distractions, but no one almost relates seriously, reverently towards artistic creativity, as towards something of value absolute, liberating and salvific. For many years there has existed for us the first-class artistic journal, the "Mir Iskusstva" {"The World of Art"], which would be accorded honour and love by an European land, but the better part of our intelligentsia have never read it, have not even known about its existence, or at best were indifferent to such an unneeded luxury. And the "Mir Iskusstva" was not only an excellent artistic journal, with great boldness reproducing and defending the finest productions of modern art, but it was also the most literary of all the journals, which we have had up til now, the first European-cultural journal. In it were published very outstanding and remarkable works of Merezhkovsky, of Shestov, Minsky, very remarkable, with genius in places, the articles of Rozanov, verses of the most talented of our poets, brilliant, refreshing articles as regards the artistic critiquing of A[leksandr] Benua and others. In the journal has been nothing tactless or unslovenly in a political regard and as regards its spirit it, certainly, was revolutionary, but it pursued creative, cultural tasks, and for this there was no forgiveness for it from the intelligentsia old-believers, the bearers of the assigned arithmetical truths. They nihilistically and ascetically ignored it. Particularly telling was the castrate-like, nihilistic-ascetic spirit of our intelligentsia in this contempt and indifference, with which it regarded the creativity of beauty in its own life, such as would be an outward beauty of form and an inward beauty of outlook. All the efforts to embellish life, to struggle against ugliness and tastelessness are considered bourgeois, but they fail to take note of that vile philistinism, that slovenliness and vulgarity of taste, with which the life of our intelligentsia society is filled.

Shocking by its lack of culture and flippancy is the attitude, which among us exists towards the modern poetry, towards the so-called "decadents". The "decadents" indeed are the solely talented poets in contemporary Russian literature and together with this the most literate literarily, the most cultured of people. Despite their tendency towards innovation, the search for new forms and new outlooks, it is only they among us who esteem the history of literature, of the great writers of the past, Russian and worldwide, which is already proven by their elegant translations of many a classical writer. It is time already to finally and decisively admit, that we have a whole series of talented poets, who have produced a turnabout in the history of Russian poetry, who have created a completely new form, and have expressed completely new ideas and approaches. Suchlike first of all is Valery Briusov, a first-class, original, growing talent, who certainly ought to occupy a visible place in the history of Russian literature, and suchlike are K. Bal'mont, Z. Gippius, F. Sologub, V. Ivanov. It is necessary to actually read, and not merely beforehand to smirk, and it is time already to be done with the vile habit to term rubbish that, what one does not as yet understand, what one is not yet mature enough for. Our intelligentsia society and many of its literary representatives overstrain their lives with laughter, when there is something they do not understand, and there is still quite much they do not understand, they often do not understand the need itself to create culture.

But nothing already besides sneering and loathing is expressed in the finest part of our intelligentsia society towards mysticism, to any appeal for religious creativity. And this in the land of Dostoevsky, the prophet of the mystical future of Russia, in the land, in which Gogol' fell victim to his own religious thirstings, in which the healthy, the earthy, the mighty L. Tolstoy nearly went out of his mind with religious doubts, the land in which the finest Slavophils envisioned the religious vocation of their native-land. With us there has begun a profound religious tumult and in a certain, altogether unique part of our intelligentsia, and in the people, and in the awakened parts of the Church, but the officio-vanguard intelligentsia remains deaf and dumb, it does not want to and cannot see or hear. With us there has been the journal, "Novyi Put'", which modernly posited a whole series of religious problems, and in which were published the very interesting, the politically even interesting protocol-minutes of the "religio-philosophic" gatherings. Some of our perhaps most talented writers have written there. Few men have essentially an interest in this current, the rest however either have ignored it altogether, or have attempted to research something reactionary, so as yet again to yield an utilitarian judgement upon mysticism. Many were the insufficiencies and failings in "Novyi Put'", but in it was something truly revolutionary, a thirsting for religious creativity and a new, transfigurative culture. We stand too close to this tumult, too akin to it in spirit, if not in word, to speak about it merely from the sidelines. In any case, the hour has begun, when facts and actions compel finally the turning the attention of our radical, more accurately conservative, intelligentsia upon that which is now and eternal, what is to be created within the contemporary consciousness.

What however explains this engrained lack of culture within the Russian intelligentsia, having devoted its life to the struggle for freedom, the welfare of the people, its hopeless conservatism, its incapacity to love, to appreciate and understand the creative strivings of others, its emasculation as it were? The reader, surely, has a ready explanation and is indignant with me, how that I, knowing this explanation, have instead decided to write what I write. I have not for a minute forgotten the grievous, often martyr-like conditions, in which happened to live and struggle that select part of the Russian intelligentsia. The prevailing nihilism for a long time involved an organised mindset against the creative process of life and produced monstrous renunciations within intelligentsia souls, it tended to cripple and maim life. They are wont to say: for us it is not to grow fat, it should be to live. These people have saved their own soul, in having perished it, in having given it for their brother. Herein especially we come also to the very root, to the as such very deep religious cause of that strange phenomenon, which we have made the theme of this article. External political causes, certainly, play a great role and stand out before the eyes, but for us there is hid something immeasurably more important and noteworthy, a sort of primal-principle metaphysics, by which history tends to move.

Of what sort however is the subconscious metaphysics of the Russian intelligentsia? This metaphysics is purely ascetic, akin to the old, churchly Christian spirit. In it is alive furthermore, in the depths of its element, a sense of the sinfulness of the affirmation of the fullness of existence, the sinfulness of the flesh, the sinfulness of the creativity of culture. But with the intelligentsia, atheistic and materialistic at the surface of its consciousness, this asceticism is ordinarily expressed thus: the sin against the people, the sin against the working class, the sin against the progressive tasks of the times, the sin against progress, this ultimate idol. Art, literature, philosophy, the beauty of the flesh, love, the joyous feast of life, exuberance to the extreme, are likewise little revered by the Russian radical and atheistic intelligentsia, just also as by historical Christianity. This asceticism is one of the poles of the religious consciousness, the pull towards non-being, Buddhism, a penultimate nihilism. Our ascetic intelligentsia -- are fanatical lovers of mankind and morals, a vapid morals, suspended and hanging up in the air, desolate. The polar opposite to this pole of religious consciousness instead affirms the fullness of existence, has reverence for culture, and leads to a new, transfigured world, but the revealing of this opposite pole demands religious creativity.

Whilst abstemious and denying in the creativity of culture, the radical, the actually finest part of our intelligentsia affirms a truth within politics, and in this is its great mission. But in this politics always there has been moreso a self-renunciation, rather than self-affirmation, and therefore but little of a vital realism. Greater was the love for equality, for justice, for a sacred self-restriction, than for freedom, for rights, for expansion of its existence. As regards the more moderate strata of the intelligentsia and society, about them this is what was said: "I know thine works, thou art neither cold nor hot; O, if but that thou wert cold, or hot! But as thou art lukewarm, then shalt I spew thee forth from out of My mouth" [Apoc./Rev. 3: 15-16]. They likewise deal with useful and necessary matters, but in them the opposite poles of the religious consciousness has led to staleness. In recent times there has appeared already the altogether non-ascetic based upon wordings of the Marxist model, which exalt life and hint as its own the tendency towards earthly orgies, but these motifs sound operatic against the tone of that drama, which is playing out within Russian life, and is indeed too powerful in their bits of the old nihilism.

Two types of "positivism" can be posited: a positivism ascetic, practising abstemption in the name of its truth, subconsciously religious, though also only upon the one pole of religiosity, and another positivism self-sufficing and limited, hedonistic, bourgeois in the profound sense of this word, already totally irreligious and stale. And too often in recent times the self-sufficing and stale positivism tends to appear under the pretty mask of man-godhood. But all the views of positivism are fixed upon an ultimate non-being, and it leads to an unconquerable death.

The tragic rift between the political and the cultural, between the dealing with elementary matters of welfare and the creating of new values rests not only upon our grievous societal conditions, but also upon the ascetic positivism of one part of our intelligentsia, and the self-sufficing and limited positivism of its other part. And therefore the fate of the impending Russian rebirth will depend not only upon a liberation political and social, but also the still more radical liberation from beneathe the oppression of both forms of positivism.

But as yet the condition of our culture presents a pitiful spectacle. In our journals, the most popular, instructive, there is almost nothing of literature, to it is devoted all less and less space, and most of all what they call literateurs are mere social activists, writing articles on matters of the "evil of the day" questions. About the creativity of new ideas they are not given to ponder, and even with the old ideas they are interested all less and less. Literature, ideology have ultimately blended together and become identical with societal activism, at times very shallow, and having lost all unique significance. The greater part of our journals are published not for mature cultured people, in them can be found only an elementary level of teaching and in a majority of instances it is very much a matter of routine, reflecting in spirit a new sort of bureaucratism, apprehensive in regards to the new. These journals serve a noble, useful, necessary purpose, but let them not be called literature, let them straight out say, that they do not have a part within the creativity of culture. It is indeed impossible to meet with a single considered word in our journalism on new currents, about the creative efforts of people of a different spirit, and there is not the slightest attempt to investigate, to analyse, what is involved, in order to critique in an authentic manner. Our liberals know how to dispute with conservatives, the Marxists with the liberals and the populists, the populists with the liberals and Marxists, but none of them know how to dispute with the mystics, the idealists, the decadents, with the cultural and religious revolutionaries. Here however the planes of view are totally different, here the language is not in common, the experience is different, and therefore transpires the restriction whether by belittling, or by sneering, or just our customary manners of derision.

Soon indeed already will ensue the desired moment, when our elementary task will be decided, and the historical duty of the moment fulfilled. What then will be? Connected to what will be our glance forward, and not backwards, the concern about building for the future, and not only the destruction of the past? The joyful minute of liberation may prove fateful for many, since it will uncover all their piteous poverty, their total absence of creative ideas, and barbaric lack of culture. Up to the present much has been veiled over and obscured by that external oppression, which created an agitated and intense political effort. The values of people, their inner wealth has been determined by conditional and temporal criteria. Our radical intelligentsia has made for the heights, whilst yet the spirit of non-being stirring it has begotten with the times lofty images of existence. Their creative impotence and lack of culture of our journalistic literature has had this hint of justification, in that it has been dealing with the most necessary and urgent matters of the times. But soon, I believe, that soon already it will be different. There will occur a cultural differentiation, politics will be relegated to the practical life and to newspapers, and it will become impossible still to pass off the societal arithmetic as literature, as the creativity of culture. What then will happen with our journals? By what sort of uplifting trends will live our vanguard intelligentsia, if the external, the almost mechanical oppression not still face them? There would shew forth a field for the creativity of a self-smug, delimited bourgeois positivism, for indeed the bourgeois aspect is there also already within socialism and it is hopelessly bourgeois, insofar as socialism is rendered into a religion, ultimately.

But there is still hope, that the at present subconscious religiosity of the finest part of the Russian intelligentsia, and for us unknowable, the elementally enormous religiosity of the Russian people, that it not permit of this transformation into a philistine domain, of the average mean, in all its dullness, in which endlessly the human anthill would rearrange and enhance its prosperity. For this, one mustneeds first of all appreciate the creativity of culture, to know and to read one's national heroes and creators, just as all the cultured lands of the world have done, to discover one's historical flesh and blood, to perceive of one's own fore-ordained destiny. Then only will Russian culture not only be, but also will receive, an universal meaning and significance. Otherwise a terrible bankruptcy threatens us, since we lack the wherewithal to be all the equal of the fine bourgeois, positivist, American land, for not of such a material are we wrought. Perhaps it is not too late to turn our attention to the prophetic significance of Dostoevsky and render it a land, worthy of his verymost great genius. We are speaking not about arithmetical errors, which he often made in his "Diary of a Writer", but about his utmost mathematics which even Europe knows not of.

But here, what would result is something for us to deeply consider. Russia is experiencing an era of historical cataclysm, the dormant powers of a great land have been roused, a completely new era is perhaps opening, and we stand bereft of all pathos, all fervour. Both the moderate and the radical intelligentsia have lost heart to fulfill their historical duty and they do not realise, evidently, the immeasurable and direct metaphysical significance of these moments. The pathos of a liberal and liberating pathos of the year 89 [i.e. 1789 French Revolution] or that surrounding the year 48 [i.e. 1848 European revolts] we can no longer have, we are too belated, have gone along too far in awareness, this matter presents itself as too elementary, and indeed the experience of European liberalism weighs upon us like a nightmare. But we also cannot still have the classical socialistic pathos. Socialism for us is not a real historical task of the times, but rather like an idealistic outlook, like a religion, it is too primitive, it cannot yet prove satisfactory to the modern complex and elaborate consciousness, given to fatal doubtings.[1] The illusions of a revolutionary romanticism have long since already floundered in Western Europe, and in Russia they are only stealthily sustained by the oppression and lawlessness. It involves certain elements of a paradise upon earth, which would be constructed in place of the paradise heavenly, in a sometime when they have become religiously enraptured, but at present it still rings false, seems stale, comes nigh to the hedonistic. It is not the bourgeois, moderate,

[1] I entreat the roused and irate reader to remember, that from my side this is not an argument against socialism, the quality of which, as the boundary-limit in thought in social-economic organisation in our era, is for me indubitable.

middle-course critique that has demolished the romantic aspect of revolutionary socialism, the legend about a socialistic golden age, but the rather moreso military factours, before which become fruitless and powerless all the noble, the pure-hearted, the all quite too simplistic old-believers. Indeed in Europe there was Nietzsche, in Russia -- Dostoevsky, and we indeed have experienced a profound decadence, which always betokens a renaissance. It is not a political renaissance only being spoken of, but about a cultural, about a new culture, set upon mystical, religious principles.

And we await a great cultural renaissance for Russia, have wanted to be at work for it. But everyone says to us: later, not today, tomorrow, not yet is the time for it. But eternal matters have not a special time, and it is impossible to postpone, if the awareness is there manifest. Many a tomorrowed day has already passed within Europe and nothing has appeared, it has all gone the path of a stale, self-smug hedonistic positivism, gone down the path of non-being in a most profound and true sense of the word, if the tendencies of American civilisation hold sway. We love the cultural and liberating Europe, we are patriots of Western Europe, as was Dostoevsky in speaking of this, we are Westernisers, and not Easternisers, but for all this we ought to ponder upon two paths, which open afront a liberated Russia.

Usually they think, that Russia either will perish, will die, if there continues to hold sway our historical, our devilishly-dark reactionary nihilism, if it for long holds still its grip over the course of life, or otherwise there will win out the liberating forces and there will ensue a new life, bright, refreshing, and many, many a fine thing there will be. Certainly, the perspectives on the future differ whether it be amongst the moderate liberals, the radical democrats or the social democrats, and not for all does it stand as an outright dilemma: death or life. In actuality however our times are quite more complex, more dreadsome and in need of responsibility. For us, undoubtedly, death threatens, if the old nihilism should continue to prevail and extinguish souls, its dominion ought to have limits set to it, and there finally ought to be proclaimed freedom and the dignity of the human person. This concerns our looking at the past, but as regards looking at the future there appears a new dilemma, and we neither want nor have the right to refuse efforts to resolve it. Will Russia go along the oft-trodden path of a positivistic, philistine, irreligious culture, without any final affirmation of being, with an unvanquishable death? We desire not this path, to us it represents a new form of non-being and not in the name of it would we demolish the nightmarish phantom of our old non-being. Our hope is bound up with a new religious, tragic yet joyful culture, with an ultimate victory over death and an ultimate affirmation of the plenitude of being. We desire this path, and we are acutely aware, that the hour of a turnabout has begun, not only the turnabout of an outward, societal organisation of life, but also of an inner, metaphysical turnabout.

A great land cannot live without pathos, without creative inspiration, but a pathos purely political, a pathos of an earthly human saeity cannot yet however be for people of a new consciousness, and we can only trust upon a pathos religious. The realisation of our century-long political dream, ought to be bound up with a great cultural and religious renaissance of Russia. Then only would we know, in the name of what to act and to create. We set as our aim not only an elementary liberation, but also a renaissance cultural, the constructing of a culture upon the groundwerk of a renewed religious consciousness. Then not only the fanciful, but rather the concrete, endowed with flesh and blood aspect of our historical being will possess universal a significance, bound up with the meaning of worldwide history.

The Crisis of Rationalism within Contemporary Philosophy

(Windelband. Präludien)

(1905 - 119)[1]

There has appeared in fine Russian translation a book, admittedly almost a classic and very excellent exposition on a system of Critical Idealism. The "Präludien" of Windelband [Wilhelm, 1848-1915] occupies a visible place within modern Neo-Kantian literature, and it is impossible not to take this book into account. Windelband is one of the teachers of German philosophy, the creator of an original school of teleological criticism and moreover he is very characteristic for the modern consciousness. To reckon with Windelband and such talented spiritual offspring of his, as for example Rickert [Heinrich, 1863-1936], means to reckon with all the poles of thought, deriving from Kant. The "Präludien" -- is a modernised Kantianism; in Windelband there is reincarnated, if not the actual spirit of Kant, then in any case the most characteristic of his sides.

And indeed the significance of Kant is by far not only academic, and it lives on not only in the reasoning mind of those with a wont for philosophy. Kant -- is a mighty factour within European culture, and few are they that have escaped his influence, if not deliberately, then unconsciously so. With his theory of cognition, this mighty genius set an indelible imprint upon the whole scientific spirit of the XIX Century, upon all our cognitive knowledge; in effect he undergirded the fortress under everything, as such quite dear to the positivists, although only the most refined of them would admit to this. By his gnosseological turnabout Kant lives on up to the present among the "idealists" of every shade, and taking

[1] KRIZIS RATSIONALIZMA V SOVREMENNOI FILOSOFII. Article first published in monthly St Peterburg journal "Voprosy zhizni", № 6, June 1905, p. 168-184.

their inspiration from him are those, who present so enticing an argument as to the illusory aspect of being, which hints at and leads to an idealistic "nothing", non-being. On another side, by his "practical reason", Kant fortified the sovereign position of the good, he introduced into awareness the idea of a moral categorical imperative, as the singularly saving factour, -- a matter on which the bleak and bloodless asceticism of the people of our culture have much denounced Kant. In Kant, the asceticism of historical Christianity has become desiccated, has become bereft of flesh and blood and become transformed into a morbid beckoning, not in the name of utmost being, but rather in the name of a phantom, non-being, manifest as a formal moral law. The moral philosophy of Kant makes a singular of its sort attempt to extract from the human heart every hope for an utmost, a full and joyous mode of existence (good for the sake of the good, morality for the sake of morality). Kant was the creator of the cognitive and moral values, by which live a great many of the people of our cultural era, but he shrivelled up their souls, rendered them positivists, took away the hopes, the vital blood and affirmation of existent being. And often they tend to say, that Kant fought against rationalism, hemmed in its rights, but in essence he was himself a verymost refined rationalist, very strongly a rationalist. Characteristic to Kantianism moreover is this, that it serves as a surrogate for religion, a substitute. This is an arid, abstract-moralistic religion, having replaced the living Saviour with the deathly-cold categorical imperative, very characteristic to the entire era, in which religious hopes had tended to fade. Let us look at the legacy of the Kantian spirit.

Windelband makes an effort at an unique interpretation of Kant's system, he attempts to purge it of its most profound contradictions, from the antinomies, in which perhaps consists all the strength of Kant, and thus to convey Kantianism over towards a pure idealism, remote alike from both metaphysical realism, and also from positivist realism. "Philosophy ought not to be a copy of the world, its tasks -- is to introduce into the consciousness of people those norms, upon which depend the value and significance of all thinking".[1] "Kant in general destroyed the concept of "world-order" in the old sense; the duplicative copy of actuality for him became bereft of all meaning, and therefore he learned nothing from it, as how to "integrate" with each other such matters as knowledge, faith and

[1] "Präludien", p. 113.

feeling, in the construct of this picture of the world. Kant sees the task of philosophy to be in an "explication of the principles of reason", i.e. in absolute norms, and these latter henceforth derive not from the rules of thought, but the rather encompass also the rules of volitional life and feelings".[1]

Kant conceived of the essence of cognition and the task of philosophy, as a revealing of values, lodged within the nature of reason, the discerning of the transcendental principles, the significance of which are operative nowise by those, such as are grasped relative to the nature of the world. All knowledge, and philosophic knowledge also, is not a teaching about being, about the existent, about the objective actuality, about the real, but merely a teaching about reason itself, about the normative consciousness. In this splitting off from a realist understanding of cognition, the splitting off from an admitting of transcendent being, as an object of cognition, and off from all ontology, Windelband considers it to be the very core point, of the turnabout wrought by Kant. But what however has remained afterwards, wherein the real living world has vanished, wherein being was declared an area no longer under the jurisdiction of philosophy, whereby a great nothing has come to stand opposite to reason, the afterwards, wherein philosophy has ceased to be a world-conceptualising, a world-understanding and world-perception activity?

The old antinomic aspect in Kant was twofold, and from it was begotten all the further history of philosophy, which led to Fichte, Schelling and Hegel. But Kant, in the modernised and retrenched positivist sort of spirit of the XIX Century, Kant, having purged modern critical gnosseology from those problematic and vexing "things-in-themselves", would reply thus to the question posed by us: there have remained the norms, there have remained values, there has remained reason itself. Under philosophy, Windelband understands "only *the critical science concerning generally-binding values*. A science *concerning generally-binding values*: this defines the object of philosophy: *the critical science* -- this defines its method";[2] "philosophy is the science concerning the

---

[1] Ibid., p. 115.

[2] p. 23.

normative consciousness",[1] and "philosophy is the science concerning the principles of absolute a valuation".[2]

This is firstly a characteristic trait of Windelband's stance in modern Neo-Kantianism: philosophy wholly aligns towards the critical teaching about norms, about an imperative ought, but not about existent being, and it falls back onto logic, ethics and aesthetics in regards to three forms of valuation, as to the true and the false, the good and the bad, the beautiful and the ugly. Amidst this, the logical and ethical and aesthetic norms become united in a transcendental unity, within the normative consciousness, between the logical validity and the moral validity there obtains full an analogy. The normative ought to triumph within the empirical consciousness, and this would be a triumph of reason. But the significance of the universally-binding normative is not determinate upon this triumph, since the value remains absolute, even if it should never be realised, never come into realisation within the empirical world.

And Windelband with greater still a justification can be called a Neo-Fichtean, rather than Neo-Kantian. In following Fichte he cleanses Kant of the metaphysical realism, contained in the teaching about the "thing-in-itself", and thus shifts the centre of gravity from the existent to instead the imperative ought, although in the modern teleological idealism there is not the sweep, the soaring and enthusiasm of the old classical Fichte.

The modern system of idealism, advocated by Windelband in the "Präludien", comes across as very tempting and it has led and will lead many into temptation. And actually: the profound duality and contradictory aspect within Kant becomes as it were removed, and alike are dispersed the extremes of positivism and metaphysics, and theoretical philosophy comes to be likewise a teaching about the ideals of mankind. But how indeed does Windelband come to terms with all the teleological criticists, all the idealists, in his position dealing with the age-old and very fateful problem of the theory of cognition -- the problem of the relationship of thinking relative to being, of the cognitively knowing subject to the cognitively known object? His seeming resolution also leads him possibly into the most hopeless absurdities.

---

[1] p. 37.

[2] Ibid., p. 38.

The great difficulty issuing from the gnosseological problem of the relation of the thought process to being for Windelband, in following almost all idealists, is bypassed by this, that it abolishes being and seeks an antidote against subjectivism and solipcism within the normative aspect of thinking, of reason. The object of cognition is constructed by reason itself (transcendental, and not psychological) and the products of the normative cognition are rational, of reason, universally-binding. But Windelband namely and his most talented and like-minded colleague Rickert, moreso profound than other Neo-Kantians and criticists, have been conscious of the insufficiency of rationalism and have allowed for the irrationality of everything individual, of all the living actuality. And value is acknowledged not only for the rational norms, but also for the irrationally individual.[1] And in such manner through another door via the irrational appears the banished "being". But the "thinking" desires to know nothing about this "being", it remains as it were involved merely with its own normativeness. And herein the Kantian dualism has further intensified. "Being", the world, actuality -- are irrational and can never be fully grasped by reason, nor assimilated by cognition. "Thinking", reason, the subject, -- are capacities to rationally conceive of, to realise norms and to posit universally-binding values of knowledge, -- but all this has no sort of relationship to the real actuality, to "being". The initial gnosseological question about the relationship of thinking to being originated, in that thinking thirsted to grasp the mystery of being, and in the very setting of the question there was included healthy and eternal a realism. But here the subsequent say of European philosophy wants to persuade us, that thinking is independent of being, that there is no being at all, but rather only the imperative ought, and that the mystery of knowledge is not in a co-unity of thinking with being, but rather in an accordance of reason with itself, and that any sort of judgements about the world there neither are nor can be. In the gnosseological problem this would mean, that there are not two magnetic-sort poles, but rather the all itself alone reason, seeking out and realising its particular normativeness, creating all the objects of the cognitive knowledge. Rationalism has as it were thus won the ultimate victory, whereby the *ratio* abolishes the world and thereupon creates it

---

[1] Vide the curious book from the school of Windelband, -- by Emil Laska [alt. Lask, 1875-1915] -- "Fichtes Idealismus und die Geschichte", 1902.

anew in its own image and likeness; but it will not have succeeded in abolishing "being" by the gnosseological theories of the idealists. Yet it nonetheless breaks its way through and loudly declares its rights. Kant was beset by the antinomic, and the dark irrationality or supra-rationality of being gave him no rest. A thus delimited idealism and the exclusive triumph of reason led Hegel to an ontology crazy in its boldness. And Windelband and those like him from the rear doors bring in the irrational, and in it, only in it there stirs something alive and individual, of some whatever sort "being", with which again it is intended to co-unite our "thinking". The far-flung theories of cognitive knowledge -- the rationalistic, the critical and the empirical, get enmeshed in whatever the strange sort perplexities, which can open onto only new and evermore circular paths. It is clear, that the idealistic rationalism in all its variants and varieties detaches thinking from being, deadens being, and leads to illusionism and nihilism, and bears with it the spirit of non-being.

In what manner can reason (thinking) penetrate into the actual, i.e. into something foreign and of an other sort, and grasp it, assimilate it to itself? This -- wonder of wonders, is a verymost mystery, over which philosophic thought has struggled since ancient antiquity. There can be only two types of the theory of cognitive knowledge and two decidings of the gnosseological problem of the relationship to being: -- rationalism and supra-rationalism or mysticism. Such a sort of classification can prove paradoxical and completely unacceptable in the philosophic literature; it requires a special justification. It will be asked: whither then the very extensive gnosseological currents, and criticism and empiricism? They need to be wholly ceded over to the rationalistic type, -- in this is our unique point of view. Rationalism chops apart the living, unmediated and primal consciousness, and by way of an artificial conditional opposition between the subject and object, it creates a secondary rationalised consciousness, in the domain of which transpires our everyday life. Being falls into the clutches of this lesser reason and withers. It cannot live in that cage, which is created by the categories of reason; it is too tight in size and time; the alive cannot endure a logical despotism, created by the dictates of abstract reason. Rationalism takes pride in that it creates the object of cognition, but in this object nothing exists, all is deathly cold, in it are merely conditional signs. If the object be stipulated by the subject (reason), if within it reason recognises its own particular nature, then evidently, there is nothing unconditionally absolute in it, there is no being in it, nothing truly existent.

The empiricists swear by experience and even completely deny reason with its *a priori* categories, but they are likewise rationalists, only naively and unconsciously so. For indeed the "experience" of the empiricists is a rationalised experience, happening within delimited settings, within the confines of that conditional opposition of subject and object; in this sort of experience there cannot be anything miraculous, and herein we meet with a supreme faith in a conformity to law, the firmness of nature. And why can there not be the miraculous, with such a faith in "conformity to law"? Because that the empiricists are very naive people, that their god of all is this law-bestower named reason, providing a guarantee, that everything in experience will all be in accord with a law and that the miraculous and suchlike disruptions will not occur. Only through a philosophic confusion are they enabled to assert, that experience lacking a rudder and sails can be their last resort.

The criticists, variously in relation to Kant, most of all have thought over the gnosseological problem and have thought up much that is clever; they modernised and refined rationalism and took it to an extreme degree. Under consideration now is chiefly the criticistism, since the old rationalism and the new empiricism play almost no sort of role in contemporary philosophy.

The criticistism of all shades and views constructs all the given world for us from out of reason and sets us forever in a domain of ideas and concepts; it is thoroughly idealisticised. The criticistism persistently jumbles together consciousness with knowledge, with the subject (in gnosseological a sense), with reason, and instead of situating being in a consciousness that is primal, integral and boundless, being gets situated within a consciousness that is rationalised, fragmented, and conditionally delimited.

The rationalism of all shades (i.e. both empiricism and criticistism) cannot resolve the problem of the relationship of thinking to being, and as such is not in a condition to construct suchlike a gnosseological theory, midst which should open forth doors to a cognitive knowledge of being, of the real, of the existent. Rationalism either attempts to deduce it from the reason, from the conceptual teaching about being, whereby being is impermissibly relegated to logic, or else being becomes completely abolished and transitions towards illusionism, or else there is naively admitted as being something that merely seems so and is conditional. It becomes necessary to emerge from the stifling prison of rationalism out into the fresh air, onto the vista of living being. And this is possible only in that instance, if there is cognition without a splitting apart into subject and object, a cognitive act, not rendering its object conditional and moribund, literally a cognition, in which there obtains an absolute sort of identity of subject and object and in which, consequently, we come into contact with the actually existent being of the world.[1] As already accepted in philosophic terminology, such an act of cognition might be termed mystical as an opposite to the rationalistic, wherein gets preserved merely a relative scientific correctness. And it follows all the moreso to repeat, that not only reason is manifest as the source of metaphysics, but also sensation, or the sensory, with thus as it were a supra-rational reason.

This gnosseological mysticism is likewise an authentic realism, since it leads us to an unmediated direct contact with real being, at a point where rationalism irreparably has become idealised and leads us into a connection only with ideas. The theory of cognition advocated by us acknowledges the transcendence of all being over thinking, over the rationalising consciousness, and together with this also acknowledges the immanence of being by a consciousness that is primary, non-fragmented, living. Therefore, from our point of view becomes possible the transcendent, the metaphysical experience, in which should obtain a nowise limited richness of being. The concept of being is worked out from the materials, given within the unmediately living, non-rationalising consciousness, and every being proves individual and alive, i.e. a concrete, spirit-based existent. The manner in which every being appears is as with my "I", which as an "I" is what I mystically perceive of without a splitting into subject and object, since it is as an "I" which I do not posit myself in opposition to my "I", as subject and object, I do not transform this "I" into something merely conditional and moribund. The materials of a primary non-rationalised "mystical" experience can be worked at by the metaphysical reason, which this would do without the creating of the conditional object. And the metaphysical reason formulates a concept of being, as a substantia which is always individual, always alive, and concretely-spiritified.

---

[1] Closest to this is Schelling.

In such manner, there is acknowledged the primacy of being over thinking (i.e. realism, and not idealism) and reason does not construct experience (nor being), but proves rather only an instrument, by which is handled material of an experience set beyond it. This is one aspect of that, from which are opened doors for a mystico-metaphysical grasping of the essence of the world. And yet on the other hand, reason creates a world of rationalised experience, the spatial-temporal world, with which both science and 'practical" life tend to deal. But these two worlds then are not split apart, the transcendent in a certain sense is immanent and this connection lies within the depths of human experience, in which, as at the centre, are interwoven the nodes of two worlds: the true metaphysical and the apparent empirical. I am conscious of "I" myself both as an existent being in the spatial-temporal, relative regard, as a "son of he earth", and together with this as an existent being unconditional, an extra-temporal and extra-spatial spirit, a "son of heaven".

This -- is the twofold aspect of a consciousness that is primary, alive, non-fragmented, and also of a consciousness that is secondary, fragmented. And we desire to restore a living integral wholeness of the spiritual-fleshly essence of man, amidst which only becomes possible for him to be contiguous with the "other world". Only in this living integral wholeness does man encounter both himself and his fellow man and the living God. This is a transition from an abstract, rationalistic worldview to a worldview that is concrete, sensory-mystical, which returns us to faith in a spiritually-grounded world, the living soul of each blade of grass, growing forth in the world, in the reality of the religious life of former times. The meaning of world history and individual human life can be conceived of only mystically, only as a mystery, and not rationalistically, as the limited faith of people of our time tries to do. Windelband has wanted to see this meaning in a triumph of rational norms, the triumph of the transcendental reason, of the logical, the ethical and the aesthetic. But in his gravitating towards the irrational and the individual, which comprises the second half of his idealistic system, as developed by Rickert, Laska and others, there is sensed a yearning as regards mysticism, and there becomes revealed all the inconsistency of his gnosseology. The final fruits of the critical philosophy lead towards a crisis of rationalism, towards a crisis of the entirety of European philosophy. Idealism has not justified the hopes accorded it, it has not united us with the depths of being, but instead ultimately has disunited. And forward ahead is seen only one path -- from idealism to mysticism. Mysticism can and ought to have its own theory of cognitive knowledge and its own metaphysics, although the fullness of metaphysical experiences, given us in a primal and transcendent psychology, are attainable only in religion. Besides the scientific, the rational-conditional knowledge, which deals with a knowledge that is secondary and non-living, there is still another and higher knowledge, an insightful knowledge, a comprehending, in which we in feeling become united with being, and in which fall away the conditional distinctions "reason" and "experience", between the "*a priori*" and the "*a posteriori*", in which the alive object of cognitive knowledge is not subjected to logic, not rendered conditional nor moribund by the *ratio* (the criticists and idealists boasted these crimes as something creative). This is not a faith, this is knowledge, and it seems to us, that by this path it is possible to construct a metaphysical teaching about being, which comprises only one side of an ultimate religious knowing. This is thus a sketch of sorts by us for a turnabout in contemporary philosophy, a way out from the fraught crisis of idealism, the fruition as such of the entire rationalistic culture.

The dualism of the criticist and the genetic method leads to this, that not only is Windelband unable to resolve, but he is also unable to even pose the question concerning the roots, the groundings, from which can grow forth in the world the likes of truth, the good and beauty. The norms hang up there in the air with nothing of any sort to support them, no sort of basis. These norms are oriented towards the earth with a whole series of commands: thinking in universally-binding a form ought "to strive towards the attaining of its ends -- the holding of truth, of the will -- towards its end -- to be good, and the senses -- the gaining of beauty".[1]

The world however is non-normative, in it rules the lie, evil and ugliness, within it is there not a natural logic, a natural ethics, a natural aesthetics. But in the name of what living thought process, what living will, what living sensation will there be realised these norms, what sort of creative force will set it in motion for us? Evidently, in human nature and in the nature of the world there has to be a basis for the creative realisation of values, evidently, there becomes inevitable a transition towards metaphysics, towards ontology, in order to grasp and give meaning to the secret end-purpose of man and the world. And these abstract deathly-cold

---

[1] "Präludien", p. 234.

norms leave us strongly suspicious, that they reflect feudal-like tendencies, to advantageously hold fast the given world, to limit and not liberate it, not transform it. Psychology lacks the wherewithal to decide all these problems, and the teleological criticism has not an instance, to which it might appeal.

And there is likewise possibly much to object to regarding Windelband's normative understanding of logic, but this is a special question, beyond the extent of our theme. I stress only, that the purely normative interpretation of the laws of logic leads to great a difficulty, since the natural process of thinking proves to be non-logical or outside the logical, and indeed without logical groundings no sort of thinking is possible. In general, the entire normative theory of cognition by Windelband and other teleological criticists provides an illusion of orderliness and of veracity, whereas in actuality it is a distortion of the natural thinking process and runs alongside a very basic problem, it pushes everything over into another, a phantasmic plane, and human beings are left to the caprice of fate. Only an existential philosophy can satisfy us, oriented towards our own blood and flesh.

In the article on "The Principle of Morals", Windelband very consistently introduces the moral problem into the system of teleological idealism, and here already we want not merely to object against it, but to scream. All the signs of the old Kant have been inherited by his most recent disciple, but it is a Kant rendered trite, bereft of his mysterious wont for the antinomic. The despotic autocracy of the moral good, the lifeless law has neither been enlightened nor sanctified by any sort of other-worldly rays of light. The words of Windelband concerning morals are unworthy of a philosopher; in essence they align towards the teaching about dutiful obligation, from the formal side -- to duty, while from the material side -- to the morals of a given society. "Ethical terminology calls this a command, the fulfilling or non-fulfilling of which determines a value, by an imperative ought, and in such manner it is possible to assert, that the ethical valuation would have been impossible, if we had not had a conscious awareness of obligations, which ought to be fulfilled. This conscious awareness is a principle in the sense, that it is the utmost conditional possibility of moral life. The contents of this dutiful ought can be varied, depending upon circumstances, peoples and era; but the admitting of duty in general is itself in accord with reason, with every evident basic condition of the moral life. A man, not admitting to any sort of command, denying all duty, in effect for himself would have renounced all values; and from another side, we would have acknowledged such a fellow as absolutely immoral".[1] Windelband, however, in very positivist a manner, derives the content of the morals from the established morals of a given society and calls for an obedience to them.

True, it sometimes seems, that philosophers should stop talking about morality, -- since that they have uttered so much that is trivial. We shall not overly much criticise the morals of Windelband, since this is an everyday and bourgeois sort of morals, a morality comprising philistine morals, quite rather in bad taste also from a social-political point of view, since it serves conservative powers, hostile to freedom. But it is very interesting and important to consider his construct of moral norms analogous with logical norms. The attempt to establish the moral law, moral norms, as similar to logical norms, is based upon the premise, that it is possible to rationalise moral experiences, to logicise ethics, but against this also we quite protest. The depths of the so-called moral life, which often get little noticed by philosophers, are essentially irrational or outside the rational; a moral logic herein is not and cannot be possible, since everything here involves living experiences, the experiential, in heated passions and desires. And this leads us not to an empirical psychology, but instead to a psychology moreso profound, and transcendent. Windelband has as it were suggested as "absolutely immoral", as having spurned the "commands of imperative duty", of suchlike people as have undergone the most intense moral experience and moral sufferings. The Person of Christ teaches us a mystical trans-moralism, since the Saviour did not see salvation as consisting in mere morality, in a moral law-form, irregardless of how many modern positivistic moralists have attempted to render the religion of Christ with its sacramental mysticism into a teaching about moral virtues. In the deathly-cold schematics of the German professors of philosophy there is no place for all this, and in general they only little, very little can seem able...

And indeed the concepts of a "law", of a "norm" are thoroughly rational, logical, they are applied only towards rationalised objects, they have place only in that element, governed by reason. Kant and the Kantians want also to relegate moral life subordinate to reason, to its law. The practical reason, as reason nonetheless, is a moral law-giver, a norm-giver.

---

[1] Ibid., p. 254.

Irregardless of whatever the criticists will have said, but this is a very extreme expression of rationalism, amidst which is deadened the sensory moral life, casting aside all moral experience, whereby morality becomes transformed into a deciding of arithmetic sort tasks in accord with certain rules. But that, what they term as moral experience, has nothing in common with a rational deciding of assigned tasks, with logic, with lawfulness and normativeness, since herein everything instead consists in tragic an experience, in transcendent a sense. Kant in extreme measure recognised the "radical evil" of human nature, and this limited his moral rationalism, but Windelband hearkens back to Socrates, forgetting about its irrational aspect, which obviously, is impossible to align into whatever a connection with norms.

And here moreover the following should be noted. The word "ought" can be used in two different meanings: in the formal, the gnosseological, when one says, that something ought to be, in contrast to what is, and also in the psychological useage, when one talks about suchlike experiences, amidst which a man is guided by an awareness of an ought, a sense of duty, subjecting himself to a norm. But the teaching about a moral ought of duty, is something desiccated, bloodless, and is the product of a rationalistic culture. The imperative ought in the first sense (the gnosseological) is the product of the rationalisation of the moral problem, considered as a logical problem; the imperative ought in the second sense however (the psychological) is the product of a rationalisation of the entire human being, the deadening away of the experiential, a considering of the concretely existing being as but logical a machine. The sensory-religious eras do not know suchlike an imperative ought, and even the asceticism in these eras does not become so bloodless and gloomy, and it is perhaps merely another one of the forms of the orgiastic. The moral problem gets posed and decided in full-blooded human hearts, not simply heeding norms and laws, and not in the rational desolation, whither such convey Windelband. It is namely in this attempt to rationalise morality, to treat ethical norms as logical a matter, that the system of teleological idealism becomes particularly vulnerable; and here the fiction of a transcendental unity inevitably implodes, and the normative monism collapses.

Windelband seeks to consolidate the autonomy and sovereignty of morality, and through morality he seeks to justify all and everything, to consign us over into its grip, while at the same time, that morality itself stands in need of justification, where the very "norms" have an ought of rehabilitating their tattered reputation. And this will not be so easy to do. Morality overall is not so doubtful, as the critical idealists tend to think. We seek a sanctioned approval of something higher, than the moral, a religious sanction. The crisis of the contemporary consciousness ought to find expression in a transition from rational and normative a morality over into instead a supra-moral and supra-rational mysticism. Ahead upwards from morals there is only a path towards religion.

In the "Präludien" there is the sketching out of a philosophy of religion under the title, "Sanctities", and also with the article entitled, "Sub specie aeternitatis",[1] likewise concerning religious experiences. Windelband, certainly, acknowledges the necessity and importance of religion, and he, in all probability, is a very pious Lutheran -- as would befit a German professor and an idealist, of already suchlike a tradition, of already suchlike a semblance of orderliness. This latest idealist system encompasses everything within it, and where that religion has entered into it as though fully, but still as a chief aspect, as a singularly chief aspect, in it there is nothing. Windelband's attitude towards religion comes across as incomprehensible and repulsive for us in the land of Dostoevsky and Lev Tolstoy. People of the modern religious temperament always presuppose a rebellious atheistic sort of God-struggle, they see in this an incomparatively greater religious depth, than in the middle of the road approach, assimilating everything within it whilst having deadened everything.

Windelband writes beautifully, but his pathos seems to us contrived and cheap, as when he says: "This is something eternal, all-significant, in what I am grasping at, in order to secure for itself a firm support in the onrush of time -- let people call it, what they will! I am come nigh to it when in a serious pondering I subject my thoughts to a strict norm and try to comprehend the rhythm of what is transpiring, which, as that abiding within the changing, is itself a reflection of the grandeur of eternity; I experience it, when the utmost aspirations for mankind compel my heart to beat moreso the strongly, and when, having won a victory over my own impulses, there rises in control within me eternal the commandment; I am filled with delight, when in a dispassionate

[1] *trans. note*: perhaps this served as the inspiration for the title of Berdyaev's present book?

contemplation I imbibe within me the pure picture of things as it ought to appear to all. Everything always tends towards this, that for me the temporal gets transformed into the extra-temporal, the existent into the ought to be. In eternity we become convinced, when from the chaos of opinions we hearken to safety in the cold clarity of science, when the passionate intensity of our impulses is pacified by the might of consciousness of morality, when having foresworn impulses, in a blissful calm we incline the weary keenness of the head onto the bosom of art".[1] The religious pathos of Windelband -- is in a fondness for norms, for rules! On tastes, of course, there is no disputing, but all this still is too strange an object to be religiously fond of. Making a god out of the norms, the rules, is a vulgar surrogate for religion. The norms do not include within them religious hopes, their exclusive grip kills the hope to an absolute plenitude of eternal being. The transcendental illusory aspect leads to a religion of non-being. True, in the article on "Sanctity", Windelband speaks about the transcendent, brings it to attention amidst a consideration of the religious problem, but this involves some strange sort of misunderstanding. Windelband reckons it necessary to encompass everything, and indeed he is too afraid of a radical rejection of being, since after all he is a faithful Lutheran, and therefore, forgetting for the moment his gnosseology, he once again sneaks in an irrational sort of being through the back doors. The untended infirmity of European thought, the infirmity of rationalism, irregardless of how much it be doctored with "criticist" palliatives, is heading towards a final crisis. This crisis, which we see clearly also in the book by Windelband, is very instructive, but we cannot and ought not relate like schoolboy students to the German philosophy of this decadent era. The future belongs to a transcendent psychologism. We also are very much in need of a philosophic culture, for without philosophic knowledge we cannot resolve the fateful questions of the times, but within the modern Russian people there are indeed creative resources, rather than in the Windelbands, rather than in the German academic idealism, wherein rests our salvation.

---

[1] p. 310.

K. Leont'ev -- Philosopher of a Reactionary Romanticism

(1905 - #120)[1]

Is it not terrible and is it not an insult should one think, that Moses went upon Sinai, that the Hellenes built their elegant Acropoliseis, the Romans waged the Punic Wars, the handsome genius Alexander in a feathered-sort helmet crossed over the Granik and battled 'neathe Arbela, that the Apostles preached, the martyrs suffered, the poets sang, painters painted and knights gleamed at their tourneys for this only, that the French, the German or the Russian bourgeoise in their ugly and comic attire might be smugly "individual" or "collectivist" upon the ruins of all this past greatness?..

It is necessary *to freeze* Russia tho abit, that it not "become putrified"...

K. Leont'ev

I.

There exist writers with an inexpressibly sad destiny, not acknowledged, not understood, attracting no one, dying in spiritual solitude, though having been bestown of talents, in mind, in originality they stand many heads above the acknowledged great. Such an one was Konstantin Leont'ev, a very imposing, the sole imposing thinker from the conservative camp, and altogether indeed one of the most brilliant and original minds in Russian literature. Katkov was the foremost political publicist of conservatism, here he ruled, but never was he a thinker, a philosopher of conservatism. The foremost and sole philosopher of

---

[1] K. LEONT'EV -- PHILOSOPH REAKTSIONNOI ROMANTIKI. First published in monthly S.-Peterburg journal "Voprosy zhizni", №.7, 1905, p. 165-198.

conservatism, and more truly, not even conservatism, but rather reactionism, was K. Leont'ev.[1]

Poor Konstantin Leont'ev: he is worse off than they know, and very cultivated people even get him confused with the tedious classicist Leont'ev, co-editor with Katkov on the "Russian Messenger". Herein indeed the irony of fate! K. Leont'ev dreamt about having a political influence, he wanted to play a role in the capacity of a leading reactionary publicist, but in this even he did not recognise himself. The conductor of conservative politics would be Katkov, staid and positive, who had the feel of real ground under his feet, and not Leont'ev, the romantic and dreamer, a preacher of fanaticism in the name of mystical ends, of a foolish reactionism, bordering on a mysterious sort of revolutionism. K. Leont'ev did not leave behind a perceptible mark within the history of Russian thought and Russian spiritual cravings. For the progressive camp with all its factions he was absolutely unwelcome and could evoke only contempt and indignation, while the conservatives however saw only the surface of his ideas, in similitude of Katkov's, and they did not perceive his mystical depths, his illegitimate romanticism.

But people of our mindset ought to ponder over Leont'ev, over his sad fate. K. Leont'ev -- was a strange writer, strange also for the whole of historical Christianity, strange and seductive compared with many a romantic and mystic. This solitary, almost known to no one, Russian man in much anticipated Nietzsche. He already came nigh to the abyss of the apocalyptic mindsets, by which at present we have many an ill, and in Christianity he attempted to reveal the features of a dark satanism, akin to his sick spirit. Leont'ev was a very complex writer, deeply contradictory, and it is not wise to understand each word of his too simply and literally.

In the dark and aristocratic soul of Leont'ev burned an aesthetic hatred for democracy, for the bourgeois middle ground, for the ideals of world harmony. This was the strongest passion in his life, and it was not held in check by any sort of moral hindrances, since with disgust he denied anything moral and considered everything permissible in the name of the

---

[1] In the Slavophil camp there were outstanding thinkers, as for example Khomyakov, but the old Slavophils were only half-wise conservative and in any case not reactionary. The generations succeeding them in this were insignificant and pitiful.

highest mystical aims. With Leont'ev still there was a positive passion for the beauty of life, for its mysterious charm, and perhaps, there was the thirst for a full life. Beyond the unique, the bold and the harsh, feignedly-cold style of his writing is to be sensed a passionate and fiery nature, tragically-divided, having lived through the burdensome experience of the hypnotic might of ascetic Christianity. A man of strong fleshly passions and a thirst for a robust life is drawn sometimes incomprehensibly and mysteriously to the polar opposite, to the beauty of monasticism. The aesthetic hatred for democracy and bourgeois contentment, for hedonistic culture, and the mystical pull towards a dark monasticism led Leont'ev to the romantic fondness for past historical epochs, to a mystical reactionism. He was not given to moderation, the middle ground, and he arrived at a most extreme fanaticism, he became a preacher of compulsion, oppression, the knout and the gallows. But in the strange and repulsive words of Leont'ev is sensed not a real reactionary Katkov-politician, but rather an illogical dreamer, an unhappy romantic, lost and perishing in an epoch alien for him.

We do not propose the significance of Leont'ev to be with realistic convictions. This man deemed the meaning of world history to be in the capricious advance of a few chosen ones in the name of mysterious mystical goals. Only in this aristocratic blossoming did he see the beauty of life and he suffered unreasonably from the awareness, that "liberal-egalitarian progress" carries mankind off to the opposite side, to the reign of the petty bourgeoise, evoking within him the disgust and aversion of the aesthete and aristocrat, the romantic and mystic. He snatched as one might after a straw, as Russia, at Slavism, he saw herein his final hope, an almost dying hope to save the so dear to him meaning of world life. For Europe there was no hope, it should go on off to its ultimate extremes of socialism and anarchism (for Leont'ev this was even pleasing a prospect, as in everything extreme), but through Russia it was possible still to save the world, and for this it was necessary to freeze it, to put an halt to the liberal-egalitarian progress, though this be at the price of the greatest sacrifices, though this be by the quite darkest compulsion.

And K. Leont'ev seeks for salvation in Byzantium. "Byzantinism hath bestown us all our strength in the struggle with the Polish, with the Swedes, with France and with Turkey. Under its standard, if we be faithful, we certainly shall be able to hold back the onrush and aims of an international Europe, if it, having destroyed for itself everything noble, if it somehow also for us should dare prescribe the rot and stench of its new laws about a shallow happiness for all the whole world, about a radical all-triteness for the world".[1] "The idea of the welfare of all mankind, the religion of utility for the whole of society -- is very cold, prosaic and moreover incredible, unfounded from any of the religions".[2] I shall provide still more in a series of places for the general characteristics of Leont'ev.

"What does it matter for a venerable, an historical and real science, the extents of discontent, the extents demanded, the extents of despotism, the extents of the suffering? For what are these unscientific sentimentalities, so exhaustive in our time, so prosaic moreover, so ungifted? For me what does it matter in suchlike questions as far as the very groanings of mankind".[3] As far as sufferings, Leont'ev loved to wear a mask of harshness and trans-morality.

"And suffering? Sufferings accompany both together the process of growth and developement, and the process of decay... all is sick from the tree of human life"...[4] "This is all but the means of confusion, -- he says about the contemporary forefront culture, -- this is a gigantic surge, in all and everything jostled into a single lump of pseudo-human triteness and the prosaic; this is all a complex algebraic exercise, striving to bring all and everything to a common denominator. The exercises of egalitarian progress are composite, a coarse goal, simple as regards thought, ideals, influence, etc. The goal of it all -- is the mediocre man, bourgeois, content amidst millions of precisely indeed the same mediocre people, likewise contented".[5] "Progressive ideas are coarse, simple and capable for everyone. These ideas seem rational and profound, as though worthy of some few chosen minds. People of a lofty mindset have ennobled them by

---

[1] Vide: K. Leont'ev. "Vostok, Rossiya i Slavyanstvo" ("The East, Russia and Slavism"), t. I, p. 98.

[2] Ibid., p. 105.

[3] Ibid., p. 145.

[4] Ibid., p. 146.

[5] Ibid., p. 164.

their brilliant talent; the ideas themself, however, essentially are not only mistaken, they are, I would say, crude and contradictory. They are a felicitous earthly outlook and an impossibility; the realm of an equitable and universal human truth upon the earth -- is an outlook and furthermore an outrageous untruth, an insult to the best. The Divine truth of the Gospel did not promise an earthly truth, it did not preach a juridical freedom, but only rather a moral and spiritual freedom, accessible even in chains. Under the Turks there were martyrs for the faith; under the Belgian Constitution there can hardly be any saints".[1] There are few to have written in such an incisive, bold and extreme a style. Behind each word there boils up a sick hatred towards the present culture, a romantic passion for the past. "Having turned abruptly from the paths of the emancipation of society and its persons, we have entered upon the path of the emancipation of thought". "It is time to put a limit to the developement of bourgeois-liberal progress! Whoever is able to do this, will be right also afront the judgement of history".[2] "The mistakes, and defects, and stupidity, and ignorance -- in one word everything, that is considered bad, bears fruit and enables the unintended attaining of these or other mysterious ends not foreintended by us".[3] "It would be shameful for mankind, if this vile idea of an universally useful, paltry work and disgraceful prosaity should triumph forever!"...[4] "It is stupid to believe so blindly, as believes now the majority of mankind, with their European upbringing, in nothing that is not possible, in a final kingdom of truth and bliss upon earth, in a bourgeois and workers order and an impersonal earthly paradise, lighted by electric suns and conversing amidst telephones from Kamchatka to the Cape of Good Hope... It is stupid and shameful, furthermore for people esteeming realism, to believe in such an unreal thing, as the happiness of mankind, and furthermore as closely nigh... It is ludicrous, repudiating every positive, mystic orthodoxy as restrictive for us, reckoning every like faith the realm of the naive and the backward, to worship instead the orthodoxy

---

[1] K. Leont'ev. "Vostok, Rossiya i Slavyanstvo", t. I, p. 265.

[2] Ibid., p. 283.

[3] Ibid., p. 294.

[4] Ibid., p. 300.

of progress, the idol of the progressive movement"...[1] "An admixture of fear and love -- here is what human society ought to live by, if they want to live... An admixture of love and fear in their hearts... It is a sacred terror afront certain ideal limits; it is a loving of apprehension before certain persons; it is a sensation sincere and unpretentious, only for politicians; it is a reverencing, under the guise even solely, of some material objects"...[2] "How am I, a Russian man, to comprehend, tell me, that for a shoemaker it is easier to be obedient, than for a priest or a soldier, blest by a priest?"[3] And here are words of Leont'ev's kinship with Nietzsche, whom he knew not, but only anticipated: "For one, who does not reckon bliss and absolute truth as appointed for mankind upon the earth, there is nothing terrible in the thought, that millions of Russian people should dwell whole centuries under the pressure of three atmospheres -- the official, the estate and the churchly, though it be but for this, that Pushkin could write Onegin and Godunov, so that they might construct the Kremlin and its cathedrals, so that Suvorov and Kutuzov might seize their national victories... Since glory... since military glory,... yes, that military glory of the realm and nation, its art and poetry -- are facts; these are real manifestations of an actual nature; these are attainable goals, and together with this, they are lofty. But that godlessly-righteous and dully-blest mankind, for which gradually and with various contemporary gestures ye want to strive, such a mankind would be obnoxious, if it were to be possible"...[4] "For the aesthete particularly it is properly becoming during times of immobility to be for movement, during times of dissoluteness to be for strictness; for the artist it would be proper to be a liberal under a domain of slavery; it would become him to be an aristocrat amidst the tendencies towards demagoguery, a bit of the *libre penseur* amidst an hypocritical khanate, devout amidst the godless"...[5] This is awfully characteristic a recipe for Leont'ev, and here

---

[1] Vide: K. Leont'ev. "Vostok, Rossiya i Slavyantsvo", t. II, p. 38.

[2] Ibid., p. 39.

[3] Ibid., p. 39.

[4] Ibid., p. 50.

[5] Ibid., p. 56.

he gives himself away, but regretably, as we see below, he himself was not always consistent in following the aesthetic imperative. I shall present yet still some several characteristic places: "The culture *from the former evil* has given the world such an abundance of great minds... The new culture, *cleansed* -- in the area of thought provides us either the indisputably untalented [Georg] Buechners, or the [Eduard] Hartmans, talented, but denying any actual benefit of progress"...[1] "During the difficult and dangerous moments of historical life society always stretches out its hands not to the orators and not to the journalists, nor to the pedagogues and lawyers, but to people of ability, to people who command by know-how, to compel by boldness!"[2] With Leont'ev there was an aesthetic cult of force, and Christianity itself, as I have attempted to show, he contrived to explicate as a religion of dark coercion, of fear and not love. "European thought bows down in worship to man only because that he is man. It seeks to worship him not for this, that he is an hero or prophet, a tsar or genius. No, it worships him not for such a special and lofty attainment of person, but simply the individuality of every man, and every person it wants to render happy, enjoying equal rights, tranquil, arrogantly-pure and free in the area of certain morals. This very seeking after for all-mankind of equal rights and an all-human truth, issuing forth not from any positive faith-confession, but from this, what philosophers term a personal and autonomous moralness, this very thing also is an hades-hell, the most subtle and most powerful of all such related contagions, decaying by its gradual action the whole of European society".[3] This already is a total negation of morals, so characteristic of Leont'ev. "And here is the kingdom of this truth! And here it is the person, person, person!... And here freedom!... And here the European individualism, so deadly for genuine individualness, i.e. for the exceptional, the separate, strong and expressive developement of character! And here is the autonomous, the self-affirming morality, so proud and at the same time so shallow, a pharisaeic

---

[1] K. Leont'ev. "Vostok, Rossiya i Slavyantsvo", t. II, p. 70.

[2] Ibid., p. 81.

[3] Ibid., p. 93.

"respectability".[1] "For the understanding of poetry there is necessary a sort of idle time, not that which is cheery nor that which is melancholy, but we are now ashamed of everything such, and even of poetic idling itself".[2] "The great freedom against the former has led the person only to a great sterility and empty triumph... from which it emerges but in those moments, when life is as though somehow returned to the old".[3] "Socialists everywhere scorn your moderate liberalism... the French socialists and the altogether extreme radicals scorn all those Em[ile de] Girardins, Thiers and Jules Favre... And they are right in their contempt... and how should these people not be hostile against the present guardians or against the forms and manners of guarding, unfavourable to them, but all essential to the sides of the guarded teachings they themself need. For them there mustneeds be fear, there mustneeds be discipline; for them there must be submissiveness, the habit for obedience; there are people, successful in manipulations of their own economic life, but nonetheless upon earth there are malcontents, and they then flare up with a new blaze towards mystical teachings"...[4] "On the one side, I esteem, the baronry; on the other, I love the naivte and gruffness of the peasant. Graf Bronsky or Onegin, on the one side, and the soldier Karataev -- and who?... well, though be it a wolf of Turgenev, for me it is better than that "mediocre" bourgeois type, for which progress now reduces little by little both at above and at below, both the marquis and the shepherd".[5] "For the developement of great and strong characters there are needful great social injustices, i.e. class oppressions, despotism, danger, strong passions, prejudice, superstition, fanaticism, etc., or in a single word, everything against which the XIX Century struggles".[6]

---

[1] K. Leont'ev. "Vostok, Rossiya i Slavyantsvo", t. II, p. 95.

[2] Ibid., p. 144.

[3] Ibid., p. 154.

[4] Ibid., p. 157.

[5] Ibid., p. 213.

[6] Ibid., p. 215.

"All the true poets and artists in their soul have loved the nobility, the high brilliance of the court, military heroism, etc.".[1] "Everything elegant, profound, outstanding somehow, and naive, and refined, and primordial, or the capriciously unfolding and glittering, or wild, falls back, and retreats before the firm press of these grey-dull people. But what reason is there to discover a servile joy?"[2] "No, I am right to scorn so pallid and unworthy a mankind, -- without vices, true, but also without virtues, -- nor do I desire to take a step for suchlike a progress!... And moreover: if I had not the power to do so, I would still passionately dream about defiling the ideal of universal equality and the foolish all-social movement; I would destroy suchlike an arrangement, if I had the power, since I love mankind too much, to wish for it so tranquil, perhaps, but so trite and degraded a future".[3]

I have made so many a citation, since Leont'ev is rather unknown for us, and I wanted to provide some familiarity with him. Evidently, this was a gruff man and an outstanding writer, original, taking everything to its ultimate limit. His impassioned thoughts for us are full of deep significance, and his themes can also prove fateful for us. Beneathe the writings of Leont'ev there is a sense of profound torment and immeasurable anguish. He did not find happiness for himself, and his suffering blazed forth into a malevolent preaching of force and fanaticism. Strange and mysterious was his person. An aesthete, an immoralist, a revolutionary by temperament, a proud aristocratic spirit, captivated by the beauty of the forces of life, in much anticipating Nietzsche, romantically in love with the power of past historical epochs, under the burden of an as yet unrecognised and mysterious mysticism, while also -- the preacher of a monastic, strictly traditional Orthodox Christianity, and the defender of the despotism of a police state. Herein such the irony of fate! Leont'ev wanted to be saved from the triteness, the insipid, the mediocre, the narrow-minded bourgeoisness, the harsh odour of progress, and he fell into a place of intolerable stench, in which there is nothing creative or original

---

[1] K. Leont'ev. "Vostok, Rossiya i Slavyantsvo", t. II,, p. 216.

[2] Ibid., p. 219.

[3] Ibid., p. 382.

and beauty is defiled by each step. And he was harshly punished. No one wanted to hear a preacher of "autocracy, orthodoxy and nationality". Decent people held their noses, the nose even earlier than the ears. Reactionaries seemingly like-minded to Leont'ev were unable to understand, for them what was evident only the apparent side of his world-outlook, and they made use of it for their own dirty deeds. But Leont'ev is little useful for the real, the positive goals of reactionary politics. Here was profoundly individual a thinker, splintered off from the great historical path, with a presentiment of much too early, and his fateful connection with reactionary politics was in an ultimate sense for him a matter of chance, and deeply tragic. His thirst was for the eternal and together with this also for the new, within his consciousness blazed up something beautiful and ultimately righteous, and on the great historical path of his native-land he practically froze the rot, as he floundered about in the stinking fetid pit. We shall look closer, at what sort of theories Leont'ev constructed, in order to justify his hatred for liberal-egalitarian progress and to clear the path for his mystical sense of universal history, and to construct a temple both aristocratic and aesthetic.

Leont'ev, -- a romantic and mystic at his core, enters into the role of the defender of an unique sociological realism and even naturalism. He was an adherent of an organic theory of society and he sketched out an original theory of developement (not without the influence of the far less gifted Danilevsky). On the question concerning the organic developement of society we constantly meet in Leont'ev with ultra-realist and ultra-positivist arguments, a bit strange for a mystic, but customary for people of another tendency. This organic theory of developement reduces to the following: "A gradual ascent from the simplest to the most complex, a gradual individualisation, a separation, on the one side, from the surrounding world, and on the other side -- off from the similar and kindred organisms, off from all the similar and kindred manifestations. The gradual ascent is from the colourless, from simplicity, to originality and complexity. There is a gradual complexification of composite elements, an increase of inner richness and at the same time a gradual strengthening of unity. Thus that highest point of developement is not only in organic ends, but also in general in organic manifestations, in an utmost degree of complexity, united by a certain inner despotic unity".[1] State organisms passed through three periods: 1) an "initial simplicity; 2) a blossoming complexity, and 3) a secondary mixed-jumble of simplification".[2] All this necessitates the result that: "the egalitarian-liberal progress is the antithesis to the process of developement".[3] Contemporary European culture with the triumph of freedom and equality is, according to Leont'ev, that of "a secondary mixed-jumble of simplification", i.e. a disintegration, a decay, a decrepitness. According to the destined, non-vacillating organic laws, every nation, every state decomposes and dies. And the decay ensues then, when there begins "the mixed-jumble simplification", when the liberal-egalitarian process destroys inequality and diversity. "The "blossoming complexity" involves the greatest inequality of position, the greatest diversity of parts, held in check by despotic unity.

The theory of Leont'ev is a variant of the organic theory of society and together with this it is an historical fatalism. Like the positivists, he does not acknowledge progress, but rather only developement, evolution. He is proud of his objectivism, of his callous and harsh realism, and he speaks suspiciously much about his scientific attitude, about his naturalistic attitude towards human societies, and towards state organisms. With Leont'ev there is not even a shadow of scientific realism, and his passionate nature was least of all capable of objectivity, and indeed his undertaking were not suitable for scientific-sociological investigations. For him it was needful that there not be dismissed the hateful aspect of the idea of universal prosperity, of the triumph of truth and happiness upon the earth by way of a liberating and guiding progress. In the name of this subjective, passionate, altogether unrealistic and unscientific end he also grasped after a completely unsustainable organic theory of the developing and expiring of nations and states. Besides the naturalistic sociology of Leont'ev there was likewise his mystical philosophy of history; they both one and the other served the same end, but there was completely no connection between them.

---

[1] Ibid., p. 137.

[2] Ibid., p. 143.

[3] Ibid., p. 144.

Concerning this philosophy of history we shall speak in connection with his understanding of Christianity. To refute the organic-naturalistic understanding of societies, of nations and states is unsportive an hunt, since there already has been acknowledged the unsustainability of all those attempts within the contemporary sociological methodology.[1] It is first of all necessary to consider as firmly established, that the naturalistic method is unacceptable for the social sciences, and it leads but to fictitious analogies. The life of societies is not an organic life in the biological sense of the word, and the concept of death from old age can be applied to it only in a transposed and conditional sense. But what it shows is the total naiveté and critical lacking of Leont'ev, since this is his faith in organic laws of historical developement. The absurdity and contradiction of the very concept "historical law", of a "law of developement" has now been sufficiently disclosed by Rickert and a whole series of gnosseologists and methodologists of the social and historical sciences. The individual peculiarities of every developement, of each history, do not permit of an established set of laws for a concrete course of life. To insist upon an inflexible course as it were of an organic developement of societies would be more appropriate to the Darwinist or to the economic materialist, than to Leont'ev.[2] How did he manage to unite this historical fatalism, a conviction of the naturalistic inevitable ruin of national cultures in a certain year of their life, to unite this with Christian mysticism? Herein the passionate will blinded his reason. For Leont'ev there was a complete absence of the idea of *freedom*, to what it produces for us be it religion, or philosophy, or science. His hatred for democratic freedom reached such

---

[1] Within Chapter II, "Person and Society", of my book, "Subjectivism and Individualism in Societal Philosophy", I subject the organic theory of society to critique. I refer to it, since I reproduced therein quite fully cited sociological arguments.

[2] In defiance to the philanthropists Leont'ev says: "Ideas do not possess an human heart. Ideas are inexorable and harsh, since essentially they are nothing other, than clear or obscured conscious laws of nature and history". t. I, p. 25. Such confused assertions are possible only in the mouths of the most naive materialists and positivists.

an extent, that he combined dark apocalyptic predictions with purely naturalistic apologetics for the death of nations and states.

In that the real social science of our day is held in check by the philosophic and religious teaching about freedom, it tends to see the nature of society in the psychological interaction of individualities, and the intimate essence of the historical process to be in the free creativity of mankind. Science therefore disdains historical predictions, and the mystery of the future it consigns to the realm of religious freedom.

In close connection with the teaching of Leont'ev concerning organic developement stands his theory of national types and the national mission of Russia. All the nations of Europe, all the cultures of the West have reached a terrible point, they have entered upon the path of organic disintegration and death, the "blossoming complexity" for them is in the past, during the era of the Renaissance and suchlike. There, in Europe, the leveling and disorganising process of democracy has destroyed everything. In the Western culture of the XIX Century Leont'ev esteems only the pessimism, only Schopenhauer and Hartmann, who honestly rose up against the illusion of "progress", against the hedonist hopes. The flourishing of culture, the "blossoming complexity", is possible only for Russia, for Slavdom, united not by liberal-democratic dissipative principles, but by Byzantine organisative ones. In such manner upon Russia is entrusted a great mission to be the bulwark of world guardianship from terrible ruination, from universal disintegration, from the death of all the state organisms. But the mission will only then come to fruition, if Russia creates a completely original culture, distinct from the Western European. The foundations for suchlike an original culture Leont'ev considers to be not in the great traits of the Russian national spirit, but in the Byzantine autocracy and Byzantine Orthodoxy. Here indeed the mountain begets the molehill!

Leont'ev had a very complex and disjunctive soul, and between its parts there was as little a connection, as between the parts of his world-outlook. The "blossoming complexity", the diversity of culture, beauty, strength and individuality -- all these Leont'ev loved, like a pagan, like an Hellenic Greek, but the gloomy elements of his nature gravitated towards a dark Byzantinism, towards a monastic asceticism, towards autocracy and Orthodoxy. For Leont'ev why was this blossoming of culture necessary, for what was the beauteous complexity and diversity, in the name of what was this cult of strong individualities, which the contemporary "individualism" is destroying? The religion of Leont'ev provides no justification for this, it preaches personal salvation and the path to it is regarded to be in the ideal of monasticism, which in its essence is hostile to culture and to this pagan love for the beauty of life. Leont'ev became a novice on Athos and at the end of his life he was a monk, he saved himself from the Nietscheanism, which was in his blood quite independently of Nietzsche. Here was a tragic man, polarised at separate extremes, and in this he was both of interest and also close to us.

Leont'ev was not able to work out for himself an overview of world history, and actually, he had for it two visionary senses of meaning. At times he would understand the world process naturalistically, at other times mystically. He worshipped power, beauty, heroism, the individual flourishing of life, and alongside with this, he humbled himself before monastic Christianity. Terror of the end, the final boundary, frightened him, and he grasped at the Byzantine rubbish in a fit of despair, from frustration, from a spirit of contradiction of someone or something... In what however is the guarantee, that Russia will fulfill its mission, that it create an unique culture, that it not be subject to Europeanisation, to the "liberal-egalitarian" decay? An original creativity demands the freedom scorned by Leont'ev, but this hapless man went so far, that he placed his hope, the hope of desperation, upon a well-organised police, on physical coercion, towards which he cherished some sort of distorted passion.

That the meaning of progress, liberal and egalitarian, can be understood non-hedonistically, that the meaning of this can be seen in a metaphysical liberation, transcendental in its delimited perspectives, and not in a bourgeois prosperity and contentment, -- Leont'ev did not suspect that this could be so. His reactionary pessimism is but the obverse side of hedonism, of a progressive optimism, with its insipid faith in an ultimate triumph, without tragedy, of happiness and good upon the earth. But it is indeed possible to altogether exit from this cycle, to depart this side of an hedonistic optimism and pessimism, and above it, to comprehend the world and the historical process in its mystical ends. And thereupon this deduction will appear absurd, that it is necessary to halt progress, in that the happiness upon earth might not be all equal or that the prosperity might decline.

In his naturalistic zeal, in his pretensive and uncharming realism, Leont'ev denies all *values*, all teleology. The highest criterion for him appears as it were to be the developing diversity of the social organism, he values individuality only as some sort of fictitious end, and not as a living human individuality. This worship of Leviathan does not include within it anything of the mystical and is a very vulgar realist superstition, which we encounter in all the positivist statesmen and positivist adherents of the organic theory of society. What indeed was from the mystical, from the Christianity of Leont'ev, wherein he so unsuccessfully feigned realism and created for himself an idol from the state organism? It is interesting to make analysis of Leont'ev's explanation of Christianity and his attempts to connect the religion of Christ, all His mysticism, with the reactionary misanthropic politics. This is an absorbing and tremendous theme in its significance, and with its resolution is connected the fate of Christianity within the future human history.

For Leont'ev Christianity is not a religion of love and joyful tidings, but a dark religion of fear and coercion. He most of all esteemed within Christianity the pessimistic predictions about the future of the world, about the impossibility upon it of the Kingdom of God. Though it seem strange, but the Christianity of Leont'ev had its greatest attraction for him in its teaching about evil, about the godless Anti-Christ principle, hid within the religion of Christ. And Leont'ev I have decided to term a satanist, dressing himself up with Christian features. His religious pathos was directed towards apocalyptic predictions regarding the impoverishment of love, the death of the world and the Dread Last Judgement. This dark future gladdened him and did not evoke another, a positive side of the predictions: about the Resurrection, about the ultimate victory of Christ, about "a new heaven and a new earth". In the polarised and distorted nature of Leont'ev was lodged the dark pathos of evil, and coercion he esteemed most of all in the world. The malevolent side of the apocalyptic predictions provides the possibility to interpret Christianity as an aristocratic religion, and this gladdens Leont'ev: "It is eternal (the Church) -- in this sense, that if 30,000 or 300 men, or *all of three* men remain faithful to the Church to the day of the perishing of all mankind on this planet (or to the day of the destruction of the earthly sphere itself) -- then these 30,00, these 300, these three men *will be one in truth and the Lord wilt be with them, and all the remaining millions wilt be wrong*".[1] Leont'ev both desired, that there be "*all of three* men", and he rejoiced not so much over their salvation, as that "there perish the remaining millions". The aesthete and Russian precursor to Nietzsche exclaims: "I deal with only the *plastic* side of history and even in sickness and suffering I strive to view only suchlike, as in beauties *musical*, without which the picture of history would be incomplete and dead".[2] And this man, with yet another, a Byzantine-Orthodox voice cries out: "The idea of Christian pessimism, whereof all the essential, and it stands to reason, the never irremedial tragedy of our earthly life presents itself both justified and terrible... Sufferings, losses, disappointments, injustices -- there have to be: they are even useful to us for our repentance and the salvation of our souls beyond the grave".[3] The ancient pagan preached beauty and love for life, but the byzantinist -- a state-police force, into the power of which he completely gave over the universal fate of mankind. But this sinful man thirsted for individual salvation and he moulded his heart into attachment to asceticism and monasticism, in which he saw the chief point of the religion of Christ to consist. Leont'ev particularly disliked the "sentimental" or "rosy" Christianity, of which he accused two of the greatest of Russian geniuses: L. Tolstoy and Dostoevsky. Even Dostoevsky seemed "rosy" to his black soul! So hateful was everything to him, that it blew away the "moral" preaching of love. Fear, fear, and not love -- here is the cornerstone! "The highest fruits of faith, -- are for example, the constant, almost minute by minute disposition to the love of neighbour, -- either for someone inaccessible, or accessible very little; for some -- by an especial kind of grace of a fine nature, for others -- the consequence of a many-year prayerful struggle with difficult inclinations. Fear however is accessible to everyone: both to the strong, and to the weak, -- the fear of sin, the fear of chastisement both here, and there beyond the grave... and to feel ashamed at the fear of God is simply silly; whoso is admitted by God, that one ought to be afraid of Him, since the powers are too incommensurate. Whoso is afraid, humbles himself; whoso humbles

---

[1] Vide K. Leont'ev. "The East, Russia and Slavism", t. II, p. 180.

[2] Ibid., p. 215.

[3] Ibid., p. 224.

himself, that one seeks for a power over himself, a force visible and tangible"... Leont'ev did not love God and blasphemously he denied His goodness. God was for him a dark principle, and it is with fear and the gritting of teeth that he worshipped Him, as Creator of evil in the world, and he gave thanks to Him only for this, that he could in His Name appeal to force, to the torment of every living thing. All the attempts to realise the Kingdom of God, a kingdom of love upon earth, drove him to madness. "Love without the humility and fear in facing a positive faith-teaching, it is fervent, sincere but in the highest degree it is self-will, either it is quietly and hiddenly proud, or it is noisily boastful, and it issues not directly from the teaching of the Church; it has come to us not very long ago from the West; it is the self-will fruition of anthropolatreia [the worship of man], a new faith in earthly man and in earthly mankind, -- in the ideal, the independent, autonomous worth of the person and in the high practical significance of all "mankind" here upon the earth".[1] "Christ did not promise us in the future a reigning of love and truth upon the earth, no! He said, that "at the end love will slacken"... But we personally ought to do the deed of love, if we want for ourselves forgiveness and blessedness in the life beyond the grave -- and herein is everything".[2] In suchlike a manner, the religious meaning of universal history is completely negated. "Faith in the Divinity of the Nazarene Crucified under Pontius Pilate, Who taught, that on earth everything is transitory, but actuality and eternity will ensue after the destruction of the earth and everything living upon it, -- here is that tangibly mystical point of support, upon which has balanced and balances til now the gigantic lever of Christian preaching. Christ and His Apostles do not promise a full triumphing of love and universal truth upon this earth, but on the contrary rather this, something of a sort of seeming failure of the Gospel preaching upon the earthly sphere, since the closeness of the end ought to coincide with the final attempts to render all as fine Christians"...[3] Leont'ev very much holds dear, that "upon earth everything is false and everything is unimportant" and that at the end few

---

[1] K. Leont'ev. "The East, Russia and Slavism", t. II, p. 269.

[2] Ibid., p. 270.

[3] Ibid., p. 285.

will be "fine Christians"; this is pleasing to him aesthetically. "One thing only is certain, -- precisely, one thing, one thing only is undoubtable, -- this, that everything here now ought to perish! And therefore -- for what is this feverish concern about the earthly welfare of future generations? For what are these childishly-sick daydreams and raptures? The day -- is ours, the ages -- are ours!"[1] "Brotherhood such as is possible and humaneness actually are recommended by Holy Scripture, by the New Testament, for the salvation of the person's soul beyond the grave; but in the Holy Scripture nowhere is it said, that by means of this humaneness people would arrive at a world of prosperity. Christ did not promise us this... This is untrue: Christ commands, or advises everyone to love their neighbours in the Name of God, but on the other side, He prophesies, that many will not obey Him".[2] And Leont'ev did not obey, he obeyed only the prophecy about this, that the commandment of love would not be fulfilled, and upon this prophecy rather than the commandment itself, he based his religion and politics. He would have had to acknowledge, that the mysterious teaching of Christ concerning love was unacceptable and contrary. "As regards the Christian teaching, voluntary abasement around the Lord is better and truer for the salvation of soul, than this proud and impossible pretension of hourly lack of malice and minute by minute oiliness. Many of the righteous preferred a withdrawing into the wilderness over active love; there they prayed God *firstly* for their own soul, and then for other people; many of them did this because quite correctly they did not hope upon themself and they found, that repentance and prayer, i.e. *fear and their own manner of abasement* is truer, than the pretension *of worldly lack of malice*, or than the self-confidence *of active love* in the multitudinous society. Even in monastic common-life communities, experienced elders do not much allow themself to be transported away into an active and fervent love, but first of all they teach obedience, lowliness, the passive forgiveness of insults"...[3]

---

[1] K. Leont'ev. "The East, Russia and Slavism", t. II, p. 290.

[2] Ibid., p. 300.

[3] Ibid., p. 301.

Leont'ev elevated into a religious dogma his dark hatred for the world and for people, and although secretly he had no love for people, nor about anything of the sweetness of the world, he often naively displayed this half of his nature. He took to the ultimate extreme the ancient teaching about God as a ruler and master, gloomy and chastising, and he reduced the relationship between man and God exclusively to one of fear and of submission. This is not a Christian teaching, within it is forgotten the idea of God-manhood, of the intimate closeness and union of the Divine and the human. For the contemporary, for the new religious consciousness, both unacceptable and horribly remote and terrible is the God of Leont'ev, to which he proposes to serve a black mass with his fanatical politics.

It has always appeared to me as blasphemous, hateful and base, every teaching about God as a ruling power, and about the human relationship to Him -- as submission. Power and submission are very dirty, very vile words, as much as any that exist in human language. These words are taken from a very shameful area of human life, and they want to adapt them to the verymost sacred and unutterable. The new man, anguished over the religious meaning of life, would not ever accept a religion of might and fear, he finds accursed these dark signs from the past, which led him to the torments of God-struggling, he finds only attracting him a religion of freedom and yet inexplicable love. The new religious consciousness, the so tormentedly desired religious Renaissance ought to transform within itself all the precious for us experience of the new history: the already old Renaissance, in which was begotten the new man, and the rise of reason, and the declaration of the rights of man and citizen of the great revolution, and contemporary socialism and anarchism, and the revolt of Ivan Karamazov and of Nietzsche, and the falling into decadence, and the apparent God-struggling, and the thirst for boundless freedom. We cannot still be pagans or only Christians in the historically limited sense of this world, we ought to emerge forth from the contrary opposition of the religious thesis of paganism and the religious antithesis of Christianity, we want to love the world with a new love. We should *accommodate* the already great plenitude of revelation, that of the preceding religious epochs. It is impossible to think out and fabricate a religion, it can only be revealed, but the plenitude of religious revelation can be grasped only within the expanse of the whole historical process, the soil for which is created by the endless human experience, and therefore for religious creativity there is no limit. The new mankind struggles against authority in religion, against theological despotism and demonic darkness, the heroes of thought in this struggle went into the bonfires, and we ought reverently to accept the legacy of this struggle. We do not acknowledge any sort of authority, any sort of external givenness binding for us in religion, but only our inner mystical experience, by which we bind ourself with that, which was revealed in the past, and our metaphysical mental reason, by which the religious experience is transformed into religious teaching.

Leont'ev himself in much, in very much was the new man, but his distorted nature led to this, that in religion and politics he made a genuine sadist of himself, he confessed a cult of sensual torment and torture. The fanatical core and amidst this the romantic reactionism of Leont'ev I see to be in this, that he forgot and did not want to know the most undoubtable truths of religious revelation, even in the religion of Christ also, -- the immeasurable worth of the human person, of the image and likeness of God, of the potential absolute, which is impossible to transform into a mere means. He says much about the aesthetic love for individualness, but the trans-worldly significance of all living individualness was for him foreign and unacceptable. Therefore for the world and for people with Leont'ev there was only evil and gloom, coercion and fear. Leont'ev's philosophy of coercion and reaction ultimately reduces itself to the following monstrous sophism: *the Christian religion predicts the triumph of evil in the world, consequently evil mustneeds be done, so that the predictions be justified.*

The satanic shadowing of Christianity eternally enticed him, and he made use of the religion of love only to make legitimate the torments. Leont'ev was one of the most terrible cynics in the history of Christianity, but in this cynicism there is a temptation, which the Christians of our day ought to take account of, those who want to justify liberal-egalitarian progress. The problem of the relationship of the religion of Christ indeed towards progress, towards culture remains up to the present open and fateful, and painful for the new religious searchings. For the Christian it would not be so difficult to refute Leont'ev, it might be comparatively easy to show, that in him there reposed the spirit of Anti-Christ, a satanic spirit, but how to replace this reactionary lie, how if Christianity commands all to turn away from the world, how then is a Christian politics to be possible? Vl. Solov'ev not so much resolved this question, as that he blunted its alacrity, mechanistically somehow recognising liberal-egalitarian progress. Leont'ev was one of the most bold, most audacious and extreme of thinkers, and he was crude of grandeur. Gathering the drift of his shallowness as regards reactionary intents, a fastidious man cannot compel himself to descend down to these treacherous fellows.

It is possible to ignore the sophisms of Leont'ev, but it is undoubtable all the same, that Christianity is by far not a "rosy" religion, that there is in it much that is gloomy, almost a fierce turning away from the world. There is within the religion this book of a mysterious, enigmatic, fully symbolic beauty -- the "Revelation of St. John", which is joyful for a few, but terrible, hopeless, abysmally-deep for those, "whose names be not inscribed in the book of life of the Lamb, sacrificed from the creation of the world" [Rev. 13:8]. We declare, that the religion of Christ does not justify the reactionary fanaticism of Leont'ev, that he has too sacrilegiously and blasphemously arrogated to himself and to his beloved despotic state a mission of the judgement and wrath of God. But how are Christians to justify "liberal-egalitarian" progress, the joy of life and much that is dear for us? Why has historical Christianity so often seen a God-struggle in the liberation process? Perhaps, still something new has to be religiously revealed, perhaps, there is yet to reveal itself the beginning of a new history, in a metaphysical mental reason and in a new mystical experience, whereby the past that revealed itself would be acknowledged as only a partial, one-sided, incomplete history.

Leont'ev was a very extreme state proponent, and with him it was a genuine cult of despotic state power, a worship of state coercion. "We have powerful and mighty only three things: Byzantine Orthodoxy, our native and unlimited autocracy and, perhaps, our agrarian village world".[1] Russia for him shone only with the reflected light of Byzantium, its power and beauty he saw not in its own original creative sources, but in borrowed Byzantine principles. In Russia he did not believe, he laughed at the naiveté of the Slavophils, but he deeply believed in and he worshipped Russian statecraft, created under the influence of Byzantium and Tatarism.[2]

---

[1] Vide: K. Leont'ev. "The East, Russia and Slavism", t. I, p. 98.

[2] *"We have squandered much, we have wrought little in spirit and we stand at our sort of terrifying limit"...* p.188. *These are terrible words.*

And Leont'ev becomes intoxicated by the state immoralism. "Very fine people sometimes dreadfully harm the state, if their political upbringing be false, and the Chichikovs and police-inspectors of Gogol are sometimes incomparably more useful for their purpose".[1] "A certain degree of wickedness in politics is obligatory"...[2] "In state affairs everyone is obliged to be if not crudely false, then wise, like a serpent... It is impossible to build a political edifice either upon the flowing waters of material interests, or upon the shifting sands of any sort of sentimental and stupid liberalness"...[3] "True Christianity teaches, what sort of thing should not be, as regards one's personal defects, and the earthly hierarchy, it is a reflection of the heavenly".[4] "The state is obligated always to be dreadsome, sometimes harsh and merciless, since society always and everywhere is too mercurial, wont to be poor of thought and too emotional".[5] "It is necessary to temper our powers beforehand with endurance and love for the sovereign powers, for but this only reason, that *they are in authority*"...[6] "Without coercive force -- it is impossible. It is an untruth, that it be possible to live without coercion... Coercion not only conquers, it also persuades many, when beyond them, beyond this coercion, is the idea".[7] "If wherein poetry and Christian morality fully coincide, this is so in suchlike incidents of unselfish movements in the use of those at the top holding power".[8] "Parliamentarism does not create leaders, but rather does

---

[1] K. Leont'ev. "The East, Russia and Slavism", t. I, p. 103.

[2] Ibid., p. 244.

[3] Ibid., p. 257.

[4] K. Leont'ev. "The East, Russia and Slavism", t. II, p. 41.

[5] Ibid., p. 43.

[6] Ibid., p. 48.

[7] Ibid., p. 80.

[8] Ibid., p. 278.

a real freedom, i.e. a certain degree of arbitrary self-governance. It is necessary to know how to hold power shamelessly!"[1] Leont'ev confessed a mysticism of power, he apotheosised the state, while the mystical meaning of freedom was for him hidden, and in this was his disformity and distortion. He did not wind up confessing his own aesthetic commandment: "It is befitting the artist to be a liberal under a domain of slavery; it would become him to be a *libre penseur* under an hypocritical khanate". It is quite inconceivable, how this subtle aesthete Leont'ev did not sense the harsh stench not only of coercive a domain, but also of every state, always indeed monstrous, always besmeared with filth! And to say nothing about the empirical manifestations of our own Byzantine-Tatar domain, here for the delights of which one must be bereft of the organs of smell. But herein I present a citation from Leont'ev, in which is expressed his revolutionary nature. He suddenly makes of himself a defender of *mystical anarchism*,[2] and this is terribly important for us.

He relates about two matters, the affair of the rogue Kurtin, who offered up his own son by birth in sacrifice to God, and the cossack Kuvaitsev, who dug up the corpse of his beloved wife, cut off her fingers and hand and kept them with him under a mattress. A civil court judges both Kurtin and Kuvaitsev, it threatens them with grievous punishment, and in Leont'ev is awakened all his romanticism. "It was a regular court-trial, exactly so, just as also a proper police inquiry, essentially involving "external rules", but neither the civil court, nor the so-called court of public opinion, nor the police interrogation could exhaust *the infinite rights of the personal spirit*,[3] to the depths of which the general rules of law and the muddle of public opinion cannot always reach. The judge was obliged to punish the criminals who had transgressed the social order, but there the only strong and fruitful life, was where the soil was original and deep even in their illegal doings. Kurtin and Kurvaitsev could be heroes of a poem moreso, than the quite venerable and respectable judge, who with full

---

[1] K. Leont'ev. "The East, Russia and Slavism", t. II, p. 167.

[2] I utilise this expression not in that specialised meaning, which it now has received with the "mystical anarchists".

[3] Italics mine.

legality sentenced them".[1] *The infinite rights of the personal spirit* -- here is that sacred thing, which Leont'ev so often betrayed and which should be revered by every romantic and mystic. "Whither is the gaze of a man to be turned, who is filled with dislike towards the other soulless and arid sides of contemporary European "progress"?"[2] This is already a romantic anguish of the will, the anguish of the "personal spirit", "the infinite rights" which are abused by the state, by the positivist ordering of life.

Leont'ev was a man of extraordinary mind and talent, but in politics -- he was as a little child, he understood nothing in it, and beyond his preaching of real beastliness and brutality one senses the prattling of a romantic, lacerated from the terrors and deformities of a bourgeois culture, anguishing over "past grandeur", as regards Moses climbing atop Sinai, as regards the Hellenes building their elegant Acropoliseis, the Romans conducting their Punic wars, or the handsome genius of Alexander, or the Apostles, the martyrs, the poets and the knights. And this anguish is ours, this repugnance towards the intrusive kingdom of philistinism, and we sense, that there was some sort of crude truth in the senseless romanticism of Leont'ev. Let us see, could it be that the romantic was not a reactionary, could it be mysticism and not a justifying of the old power, and rather an hurling it a challenge in the name of freedom and the infinite rights of the personal spirit? Might it not appertain in future to mystical anarchism[3] and the metahistorical, towards an orientation forwards towards aristocratism?

II.

Is mysticism compatible with the cult of a positivist state? Or otherwise: how to reconcile theo-cracy with any other, any non-godly *cracy*, how religiously to justify the rule of power, the sovereignty of the state? I think, that state positivism in all its appearances and diverse forms is at its core contrary to every mysticism, to every idealism to every romanticism of construct. I know, that history has created very clear forms

---

[1] Vide K. Leont'ev. "The East, Russia and Slavism", t. II, p. 17.

[2] Ibid., p. 18.

[3] i.e. anarchism upon a religious, and not a positivist ground.

of the mystique of power, and an example of this is our Leont'ev, that the state too often has made bad use of religious sanction, but references to the empirical examples prove nothing is impossible, since it is possible to prove anything.

As state positivism I term the theory, which sees the source of the person's rights, "the boundless rights of the personal spirit" to reside within the state, in a certain sovereignty of power, bestowing and distributing these rights. The source however of state power therein might be variously understood: one might see it in the sovereign, unlimited will of the monarch, just as another might in the sovereign and unlimited will of the people; for others the form of state power might be explained by religious authority, while for others by production and economic relationships. To the state positivism type it is possible to impute quite contrary the teachings, -- the theory of the despotic and monarchical state and the polar opposite theory of the democratic and socialistic state. The common sign of state positivism is the subjection of the "boundless rights of the personal spirit" to the state power, which grants value to everything and allocates everything: in despotism ultimately it kills not only the "boundless-infinite rights", but also those that are quite finite and elementary, in democracy the "finite" rights are allowed and justly granted amongst the people, but with the "boundless rights" it, this power, cannot become reconciled through the limitedness and shallowness of its nature. In positivo-state despotism they do not at all permit people to shift about, while in positivo-state democracy they freely permit people to go about on the horizontal, but to ascend to lofty heights they do not allow, either there or here. And to ascend the lofty heights is "the boundless right of the personal spirit".

To state positivism are opposed the teachings, which see the source, sanctioning state power, as in the rights of the person, in the "boundless rights of the personal spirit", while the source however of the inalienable rights which are not subject to assessment, they consider to be the inner nature of the personal spirit. The essential-rights theory regarding the state ought to acknowledge the rights of the personal spirit as boundless and absolute as regards its source, whereas the power of the state is limited and derivative. Limitative idealism of the human societal type, contrary to statist positivism, ought to acknowledge an ultimate anarchy, non-power, as a substitute for the state union which is always coercive by an union which is free and of mystical-love. The cult of power, by which are infected not only the reactionaries and conservatives, but likewise also the progressives and revolutionaries, ought to be replaced by a cult of freedom, and the human will ought to be educated in reverent respect not only for statism, though it be quite democratic, but for "the boundless rights of the personal spirit". But positivism does not acknowledge either "the personal spirit", nor its "boundless rights", nor that there be any sort of inalienable, unconditionally valued rights. Only mysticism can acknowledge and make sacred these boundless rights. But first there faces us the eternally fateful question: what is mystically, what is the closer to God -- the personal spirit or the state? the infinite rights of the first or the power of the second? What religiously does the mysticism bless: freedom or power? So as to anticipate an answer, we ask further: what is the more mystical, what is the more religious -- love or coercion? -- a live "image and likeness of God" or a positivist state, Leviathan?

The theocratic variety of state positivism fell into being a sacrilegious sophism, into so coarse a lie, that one is struck straight off, how could they endure it. Reactionary theocrats applied to the teaching about the state that, which was applicable only to the teaching about the Church, and by this they diminished the sanctity of the Church, they sought to seduce it with one of the temptations from the devil in the wilderness, to which Christ answered: "Depart from Me, Satan, since it is written: thou shalt worship the Lord thy God and He alone shalt thou serve". The theocrats ought to have taught, that the Spirit of God has resided in the Church, in a mystical union of love, and to see in it only the soborno-catholic principle, ascendant over the personal spirit, and in it only to worship the Lord its God, but it is instead wrought appertaining to the state and there it is worshipped as something in a positivist union of coercion, and is yet otherwise, it is already not God that is worshipped, but rather the kingdom of this world and its prince. True theocracy can preach only the replacement of the state by the Church, a casting down of the union of coercion, of the kingdom of the prince of this world and the establishment instead of an union of love, it can justify only the mystical ordering of life, and not the positivist. And it is only this that we stand to hear, whoso admits of the religious sanctity of "the boundless rights of the personal spirit". The state cannot become the intermediary betwixt the personal spirit and God. The personal spirit is infinite and holy as regards its nature, -- whereas the state is limited and positivist. The Spirit of God has reposed, has mirrored its infiniteness not upon the collective unity of the state -- unliving and unreal, but upon rather the personal human spirit, this second having been wrought absolute. The mystical and the godly we see only in the personal spirit, and only through it can the state become consecrated, insofar as it humbles its power in the face of its "boundless rights". Every coercive state power is from evil, it is a child-offspring of the evil principle in the world, of that metaphysical principle of constrictiveness, in the liberation from which it is necessary to see the meaning of the world process. We do not believe the positivist dictates regarding, that the mission of the coercive state should be a struggle against evil, against the imperfections of human nature. It itself in evil was begotten and evil it hath served. In the remote past this coercion was rooted in the metaphysical primordial-origin of evil within the world, and subsequently it takes captive those, which barter off the boundlessness of their rights, of their first-bornedness for an earthly contentment, they exchange the eternal for the limitative kingdom of this world. We have already seen, that Leont'ev made of himself a genuine satanist, when he worships not the Lord his God, but instead coercive statism. He perished, since he was not able to unwravel this mystery, that the beautiful and the romantic is only of freedom, that the mystical is only of the infinite nature of the personal spirit, that the coercive state is always positivist, utilitarian, and deformative in its limitedness. How Leont'ev did not understand and did not see this, that his hateful distaste for the smug earthly contentment of people, of earthly comfort is wrought particularly by the coercive state, but freedom, tragic in its own nature, leads us beyond the bounds of the given world! Only love can place a limit to the freedom of the personal spirit, but all however is a free love, all however is a liberative spirit ultimately. God -- is absolutely existing freedom and love. Power however is fear derived from evil.

That which we have said about the state, ought to be applied also to the family, and to the other little leviathans. The personal spirit with infinite rights (the concrete, the living manifold of being), the Absolute Spirit, the free and loving mystical union of the multiplicity of individual spirits in the One Spirit[1] (in this unity is attained the absolute plenitude of being) -- only these three elements are justified by a true mysticism, and

---

[1] i.e. the Church, and not the state.

for power and coercion here there is no place.[1] The old understanding of heaven, as authority and power, led to the justifying of earthly coercive power; however, a new and free understanding of heaven would sanctify and strengthen earthly freedom and non-force anarchy.

Lev Tolstoy caught sight of a sort of tremendous truth in his teaching about idealistic non-force anarchism, and it should gain strength in the consciousness in future. But he was mistaken in the ways of its realisation, repudiating all real politics, every struggle of powers. Bakunin and his disciples also grasped it somewhat, but they fell into another fatal misunderstanding. They hoped to destroy coercion in the world and to strengthen freedom in the world -- on the soil of materialism and positivism. But what can materialism and positivism oppose to the external coercion, while also denying the deep inner nature of the personal spirit and its boundless rights? Either nothing, or else again a new form of external coercion, allowable merely as a temporal means, but not as a source and end. With the materialists and positivists there are no inner creative sources for the kingdom of freedom, and therefore ultimately and fatally they fall into the cultivation of coercive statism.

Every romantic, hostile to culture, has to be termed a reactionary in a very strict sense of the word. And customarily on the one side the romantic denies culture, rejecting its as bourgeois, while on another side -- he serves to the transformation of culture. The romantic is fond of the primal elements of the earth. Leont'ev was an enemy of culture and bourgeois progress, but together with this he thirsts for a new culture, original and beautiful. In his dreamings he looked backwards, to primordial nature, to the beauty of the past, but here he just stumbles about...

---

[1] To avoid misunderstanding it ought to be said, that I use here the word "spirit" not in its opposition to "flesh", but as an acceptable signification of metaphysical concrete being, which in full I acknowledge as spiritu-fleshly. In philosophic terminology the concept of "spiritualism" possesses a completely different significance, than it has in the religio-cultural and moral problematics of asceticism. I am a resolute adherent of philosophic spiritualism or pan-psychism, and together with this also at enmity with religious and moral spiritualism, i.e. asceticism.

A restoration, a return there is not and cannot be, there can only be a rebirth, which is always a new creativity, a begetting of the future from the seeds of the past. Yes, much in the past was beautiful, and we constantly ought to turn ourselves towards it, but a return backwards is death, a free return -- is a death sometimes colourful, sometimes forceful -- but death is always deformative. Under the fear of death and from the thirst for being we ought and we desire to create culture, and not only a culture spiritual, but also material. The metaphysical and religious significance of cultural progress is in this, that only by its path can there be attained the ultimate freedom and plenitude of universal being, in which each "personal spirit" possesses an "endless right". In the name of this mystical and romantic, mysteried end we cannot nor do we wish to repudiate culture and progress.

"Liberal-egalitarian" progress can and ought to be affirmed and accepted mystically and romantically, since its purpose is not in this, "that the French, the German or the Russian bourgeoise in their ugly and comic attire might be smugly an "individual" or a "collectivist" upon the ruins of past grandeur"... Leont'ev did not understand the religio-metaphysical significance of the world-historical process, since his religiosity was individual-ascetic. Regarding the historical process, ultimately, he held positivist views, and in him these views evoked a just loathing, the romantic's loathing, of the positivist aims and results of progress.

If a realm of democracy and socialism is the sole aim of progress, and not its temporal means, if the limiting happiness, prosperity and well-being, which impel them to forget about "the boundless rights of the personal spirit", if they will be the sole results of progress, then we shall fall into embracing the reactionary romantic. But this is not so.

In the aesthetic and mystical hatred of Leont'ev towards democracy and towards plebian culture there is some sort of truth, but there is also a crude falsehood, a crude misunderstanding, which we ought to examine. I would propose suchlike a formula paradoxical only in the externals: the triumph of democracy and socialism in the name of the ultimate triumph of aristocracy. Democratism and socialism are however capable of manifesting a true, meta-historical, mystical aristocracy, since by this capability there is eradicated the false, the chance-historical, the positivist aristocracy. As a romantic Leont'ev did not understand, how it might be possible to prefer the shoemaker over the priest or the soldier, but indeed the deficiency in this also consisted in, that historically the priest or the soldier too often was a shoemaker in the most authentic sense of this word, while historically with the shoemaker there may have been the soul of a knight. Political and social democratism is capable to set aright these positivist, political and economic impediments, which they consolidate, and by no means do they mystically consolidate, for shoemakers the position of soldiers or priests, or for true soldiers and priests -- the position of shoemakers. Together with this, political and social democratism is a way, only a way, towards the recognition of the "infinite rights of the personal spirit", i.e. towards transcendent ends. It is too elementary a thing to insist upon this truth, that the knights by spirit be recognised not through political and economic prerogatives, created by the positivist ordering of life, that aristocracy can be discovered only then, when the human countenance is defined by the depths of the "personal spirit", when that aberration collapses, which was evoked by the material historical means.

In historical aristocracy there were noble features of the highest human type for those times, for which, we confess, we foster a romantic weakness, but these features have been deformed too much, and in the bourgeoise they have ultimately vanished. Terrible and tragic be this -- that the democratic progress as it were lowers the human type, leads to a crumbling, a weakening of cultural creativity. This is the obverse side of democratic fairness, in view of which it is impossible to look upon democratic culture as a goal or end. Progress and culture are antinomic, here is the tragic contradiction, from which there is no empirical egress. But in any case one might think, that after the epoch of democratic fairness, after the socialist epoch of the organisation of human sustainance there ought to ensue a new, a free aristocratic epoch, which it is necessary to prepare for already now, not in counter-action to democracy and socialism, but in the fulfilling of their destiny.

We are not adherents of individualistic asceticism, because we cannot be indifferent to the organisation of the material culture of mankind. Real science and experience indeed do not prompt us for the ensuing historical period with other ways of the organisation of material life, other than the collectivisation of production and the corresponding change of the forms of ownership. Marxism has said much that is correct about the capabilities of the struggle of mankind with "nature" and about the reflection of this struggle in the material order of life. And we ought to accept the truth of socialism, so as by this itself to contend against the pseudo-religious pathos of socialism, against the cult of social democratism as ends, and not for a time mere means. The collective material and corporeal life of mankind will cease to be petty and drab only then, when it is rendered religio-aesthetic, when there is brought back into our new culture a collective mystical sense of past religious epochs and conjoined with *a free individualness* of religious mindset.

Is there possible a mystical anarchism and a mystical aristocracy, receptive to socialism and proceeding on through it? Here is the problem, to which Leont'ev leads us, as well as the whole of contemporary culture. Mysticism and the romantic aristocratism of Leont'ev are profoundly an individual thing, situated off from the great pathways of Russian history. He himself did not understand this, but for us there is value in this strange, this solitary writer, full of contradictions and frightening extremes, outside of that historical falsehood and historical evil, in which his tragic fate plunged him. Perhaps now, at a time when the truth is laid bare, Konstantin Leont'ev might be accorded the honour of a romantic and might pronounce a mystical judgement over the historical evil of Russia. Or would his fanaticism be rendered yet more dark, but altogether yet unreal?

In Defense of the Word

(1905 - 121)[1]

"The necessity and benefit of freedom of the press is for me as much an axiom, as is that twice two -- is four. And to prove it, I do not have to". With these words of N. K. Mikhailovsky begins the anthology, "In Defense of the Word", a work undertaken during the most gloomy of times for the Russian press during the Pleve period. P. N. Miliukov in his contributed article, "The Subjective and Sociological Groundings for Freedom of the Press", the most theoretical and principle-based in all the collection, says: "If you were to ask the everyday average Englishman, what he thinks about freedom of the press, he would actually be very amazed and would be put in a quandary: it is a long time already that he has even been given to think about the subject. And if nevertheless you were still to insist that he, perchance, should tell you what sort of judgement to have on freedom of the press -- this would be on the selfsame order of opinions, as explaining about the importance of health, about the usefulness of fork and knife at table, about the irreplaceable utility of the railroad for civilisation or about the usefulness of glass: and that best of all, all these themes are on the level for discussion in mid-level gymnasium school classes".[2]

By the will of the fates our woesome Russian history has been such a complicated mess, that "themes for gymnasium middle classes" are rendered predominant, and that our pathos goes almost entirely to the demonstration to the benefit and "usefulness of fork and knife at table". And this is profoundly tragic for those, who cannot live by an arithmetic sort love for mankind, who thirst to create utmost values. What is a man to do in our day, who loves creativity more than pedagoguery, its "phantasms" more than "people"?

---

[1] "V ZASCHITU SLOVA". Article first published in the monthly St Peterburg journal "Voprosy zhizni", № 8, August 1905, p. 165-168.

[2] "In Defense of the Word", p. 10. [Published 1905].

We likewise do not have to prove the necessity and benefit of freedom of the press, since these are truths that obtain for us as absolute and elementary. It is impossible to be a writer, worthy of the name, whilst denying freedom of the word. The demand for freedom of the word and a reverent respect for it -- this is an *a priori* to all creativity. In the "In Defense of the Word" anthology, a group of noted literateurs with a delimited and not so much literary, as rather societal physiognomy of outlook, expressed certain elementary, clear, needful truths, crudely scorned by our governing actuality. In this collection of articles, it would seem, there is no sort of "guidance" besides that of a societal propriety, love of freedom, progressiveness, disdain for violence and murkiness, just as, it would seem, the collection tends to include no sort of philosophic "presuppositions", no sort of world-concept or world-order. This noted and well-intentioned anthology needs to be acknowledged, since it is against undoubtable evil and for the undoubtable good just the same. But does it thus assert this, and in the name of what does it assert it?

With grief we have perused this collection, and for us terrible would be the future of freedom and the future of the word. There is not to be sensed in this anthology a genuine love for freedom, nor does it give the feel of the sanctity of freedom. At a very elemental level they demonstrate the advantage and need of freedom of the word and the press for the societal-political ordering of life. But we well know: when freedom and the word are acknowledged as a means, when this gets defended in the name of an utilitarian god, then in the name of this utilitarian monstrosity -- freedom very quickly will have limits put on it, and as regards the word they will have no desire to hear it, instead they will instigate persecution against the free word as comprising something disadvantageous and unnecessary, considering the harm it will bring to every arrangement, to every aspect of calm and of stability. The heroes of the free word suffer not only from utilitarian reactionaries and conservatives, but also from utilitarian liberals and radicals. Little grand inquisitors appear beneathe their various masks, some reactionaries, others progressives, and they spout freedom, a good supra-human, in the name of a good that is human, of the people's tranquility and the welfare of the state (either conservative or radical). And it is clear, that the word for them was never something sacred, emanating from the *Divine Logos*, that within it they have not detected the reflection of our infinite nature; for them rather freedom of the word involves but utilitarian means for various ends, some bad, some good, indicative of the contributors to this aforementioned anthology.

The demand for freedom of the word and of the press comprises an elementary paragraph of every liberal or radical sort societal-political programme, -- this is one of the absolute "Rights of Man and Citizen". And as a political sort of right, freedom of the word is defended and utilised in the political struggle and together with this is manifest as a weapon of every political activity, a necessary preliminary condition of every societal self-definition. S. N. Prokopovich writes in the anthology: "The defense of freedom of the press, from the perspective of the free developement of artistic and scientific literature, from our end would be an inexcusable and irreparable mistake. We ought outright to declare, that freedom of the press is needful for us for the realisation of the societal-political tasks accorded the printed word".[1] As a societal activist, Prokopovich speaks accurately, and reflects a societal moment experienced by us. But how can a literateur say only this, can he be so indifferent to the fate of literature, to the fate of the word itself.

And here is this anthology, as a literary phenomenon, as characteristic to our culture, and it quite saddens us, it is imbued with a "guidance" profoundly foreign and contrary for us. We find it hard to endure this indifference towards the word, and we should want to see in a literary collection a greater love for literature, a greater taste for literature. The necessity of freedom of the word and the press seems a truth axiomatically-clear, not subsumable to some proof, but rather so elementary as to whether this problem should even be posited. The indeed genuine, as desirable by us, freedom of the word is not there even in some other yet land of Western Europe: far too much is the hypocrisy and cant there, too much still the innate conservatism and attachment to an imposed arrangement of life. Oh, certainly, freedom of the word is urgently needed for us for the realisation of societal-political tasks, but is it indeed possible for us not to need freedom of the word for religious thought and religious life, possible not to need it for a revolution of morals, for the radical positing and radical resolution of the most fateful, the mysterious problems of human life, remote it would seem, from the superficial aspects of societal life, but at its root very immediate. Moral censorship all still but yields a philistine European society, and still does not permit of an open

[1] "In Defense of the Word", p. 181.

radicalism as to questions about sex, about the family, about morals, about the new in religion, though there be preached superficial and shallow materialistic theories, radical only outwardly, but in spirit hopelessly quite middle of the road.

And the contributors to our anthology are too conservative in spirit, to desire this immeasurable freedom of the word, they too little believe in new revelations through the word and they do not anticipate any sort of turnabouts, besides the realisation of elementary societal-political ideals (liberal or socialistic). And too radical a spirit, too powerful a faith in the catastrophic revelations of the word would seem to these people just as incomprehensible, as the long ago written: "In the beginning was the Word, and the Word was of God, and the Word was God" [Jn. 1: 1]. Often through an historical aberration, for people of too conservative and too moderate a spirit, words truly radical would tend to seem almost reactionary.

No, we do not desire freedom of the word in the name of deciding of societal-political tasks, we desire the deciding of societal-political tasks in the name of the freedom of the word, in the name of the Word, such as is the fulfillment of the meaning of the history of all the world. To struggle for freedom of the word is necessary not only for the ordering of our state affairs, but also as a counterbalance to all positivist statecraft, to all established societal opinion and societal morals, always conservative, even though it be hid beneathe the mask of a social and political radicalism. And the struggle also is in the name of the transcendent aspect of the uniqueness of the person, such as is reconcilable only with the universality of the Divine Logos.

Concerning the New Religious Consciousness

(1905 - 122)[1]

Heaven -- above, heaven -- below,
The stars above, the stars -- below,
All, that is above -- all is also below;
If thou doth grasp, -- good for thee.
I and the Father -- be One.

Cf. Jn. 10: 30.

In his article about D. S. Merezhkovsky, so very characteristically entitled -- "Amidst the Foreign-Speaking", V. V. Rozanov dwells upon the sad fate of this remarkable writer. Something not quite Russian and distant strikes Rozanov about Merezhkovsky, something in the spirit of the "eternal fellow-travellers" of the great European and ancient traditions. Rozanov laments the fate of his literary friend, but he is not surprised at this, that this European sort remarkable writer is so little esteemed and understood among us, that our poorly cultured intelligentsia have no desire to hear him, that in his own land he is like "amidst the foreign-speaking". Merezhkovsky at one time was close to a Slavophil faith in the religious vocation of the Russian people, and he more deeply than others understood Pushkin and Dostoevsky.[2] And yet all the same he has remained a foreign "Westerniser" for the Russian intelligentsia community. They read him, and to him more or less is accorded one of the foremost places of contemporary Russian literature, but his calling is not heard, his themes remain worthy of only but few. In what indeed is this secret?

---

[1] O NOVOM RELIGIOZNOM SOZNANII. Article first published in the monthly St Peterburg journal "Voprosy zhizni", № 9, sept. 1905, p. 147-188.

[2] To Merezhkovsky belongs the finest article in Russian literature concerning Pushkin, apart from Dostoevsky's speech of genius. In general, he is the most remarkable literary critic among us.

Rozanov has a remarkable aphorism: "Myself I am ungifted, it is my theme that is talented". The author of this aphorism is extraordinarily talented, and Merezhkovsky is very talented, but their themes are even more talented. And this very talentedness, this genius of the themes of Merezhkovsky cannot be digested by people capable only of ungifted themes. And indeed the greater part of our intelligentsia community, confessing a positivistic faith, lives on ungifted themes, carries out its work on themes very banal, humdrum, tedious, and is proud of this most of all. Not only do they not understand themes that are talented, new, and great, but they also do not accomplish those, put to them, to what it calls for. There becomes apparent a sort of slave-like malice against noble themes, those of genius, freeing one to the very depths of one's being. And Merezhkovsky undoubtedly has suffered for the talent and universality of his themes. The Russian democratic intelligentsia, Western in its superficial beliefs, is still too reminiscent of a poorly attired provincial, there is still too little in it of the great universal traditions, of the universal spirit, and it still only with difficulty perceives anything too cultural and complex. But here the shortcoming rests not alone upon the hapless Russian intelligentsia, which all the same still is higher than the European cultural philistines, here the shortcoming involves all the entirety of our historical epoch -- the degenerative shallowing out of culture, the betrayal of truly universal traditions, the spirit of positivism, that of the paltry devil of the earth, of the middle course and the triteness of the bourgeois age. Even in Western Europe Merezhkovsky would sense himself "amidst the foreign-speaking", though there they know and appreciate him, since his books have been rendered into various languages. Even there, in cultural Europe, full of great memorials of the past, the themes of Merezhkovsky are ill-suited and contrary to the spirit of the times, in its betrayal of the great universal testaments. There he would not have even those few friends, suffering a thirst in common with him, which he has in his own native land, in the land of Dostoevsky.

The misfortune is not in this, that Merezhkovsky is insufficiently Russian, and too cultured a man, for in a certain sense he is even very Russian: the misfortune for him rather derives of his enormous themes, it has estranged him from the times and from timely people regarding that universal spiritual native realm, from which he conveyed these themes. The spiritual stature of Merezhkovsky has transpired within a totally unique atmosphere, remote from the interests of the moment, from the trifling

debates of the decades, his attention has been riveted upon pr millennium and he, perhaps, insufficiently has caught sight been happening around him, where his words have sounded t The disputes of the Marxists and the Populists, the factional d political malice of the day, the rapid change of sociological tren what the enormous part of the Russian intelligentsia sees as "lif which it so busies itself, all this has been foreign to a man, torn the thousand year universal theme concerning the relatior Christianity and paganism, which has seen "life" and sensed i Greek tragedy, in the death of the pagan gods and in the birth Christian God, in the era of the Renaissance with its great art, resurrection of the old gods, in the mysterious individualities of Juli Apostate and Leonardo da Vinci, and in Peter the Great, in Pu L. Tolstoy and Dostoevsky. This romantic trait in Merezhkovsky -- re an aversion to the trifling scale of modernity and a reverential respec the grand magnitude of the worldly past. Merezhkovsky has underg experiences of the past, of great times, he has sought to penetrate mystery, lodged with the soul of such tremendous people, as Julian, Leonardo and Peter, because their secrets seemed to him to be univers In the philistine and godless European culture, oblivious to universal ide and living by partial, petty, provincial interests, Nietzsche alone impresse him, going insane through religious torments; akin to Nietzsche seem only the "decadents", forerunners to an advent of rebirth.

It is indeed impossible to deny this evident truth, that modern culture is insignificant and petty in comparison, for example, with the era of the Renaissance or the flourishing period in Greece, that the prevailing spiritual life no longer still concerns itself over the resolving of world questions, that geniuses and heroes are died out, that the meaning of life has been lost in the successes in life. We have to have the courage to say, that the realm of democracy, on its one side affirming an indisputable justice, yet on the other side infringes upon noble values, and the heights it transforms into level flats and has no sort of anything "in its name". It is possible to consider social democracy, this axis around which the history of modern days revolves, as a matter just and fine, useful and necessary, but within it there is not a truly universal spirit, there is instead sensed

---

[1] Merezhkovsky is quite the literateur and what he writes, tends not to resound as a vital religious preaching.

ɔrt of provincialism in all these disputes between the orthodox sort ırxists and the Bernsteinists etc, obscuring the solely important question: the name of what sort of God does it stand for and live. All -- are a nch of Marthas, worried over many a thing, and Mary is nowhere to be en [cf. Lk. 10: 39 ff.]. Godless eras, living without God, setting about e ordering of life, independent of its meaning -- very dreary, boring, drab ıd stale eras; within them even there cannot be even God-struggling in the rofound and terrible meaning of this word, and atheism then bears the atent imprint of lackeyism, in them all is most bereft its value, and liminished. The decadent ones, the "decadents", so despised by the philistine society, -- are the great offspring of a great universal culture, torn off from what at the present time is customary to term as "life", in their anguish for a new and mighty culture. Within the soul of the new man there intersect layers of various great epochs: paganism and Christianity, the ancient god Pan and the new God dying on the Cross, the Greek beauty and medieval romanticism, Dionysos, in whom the image of the pagan god conjoins with the Christian God, and rebirth -- the birth of the man of modern history and the thirst for a new, a coming rebirth. The new soul is divided, complex to the ultimate limit, and it heads towards some sort of crisis, both desired and terrible.

The decadents have been transformed into symbolists and mystics. In us, the gods and God are resurrected, again the universal themes enter into their own eternal rightful claims, and are rendered very important. And we live not only in an era of decline and the lowering of culture, in a godless era of small deeds upon the level flats, but also in an ensuing era grasping its own world significance and interests, that of a new religious rebirth, the igniting of a new religious consciousness.

The characteristic, the essential uniqueness of this our new rebirth, is that it is dual, twofold: reborn, the Christian God resurrects, and the pagan gods are reborn, they resurrect. We experience not only a Christian renaissance, but also a renaissance pagan. The appearances of Nietzsche in the West and with us of Rozanov, the rebirth of Dionysos in contemporary art, our tormentive interest towards the problem of sexuality, our striving towards a sanctification of the flesh -- all this points to the duality of our renaissance. We are fascinated not only by Golgotha, but also by Olympos, we feel the call and attraction of God suffering, dying on the Cross, but also the god Pan, the god of the earthly element, the god of sensual life, and the ancient goddess Aphrodite, the goddess of the plasticity of beauty

and earthly love. In our golden dreams we muse about not only Heaven, the dwelling place of bodiless spirits, but also of a transfigured earth, spiritualised flesh, and there is the musing on nature, enlivened with fauns and nymphs, and we reverently bow not only before the Cross, but also before the divinely-beautiful aspect of Venus. This golden age usually is dreamt of by people as either in the past or in the future, within time, within the empirical existence; but also in eternity, in extra-temporal existence, it is possible to anticipate a resuscitated earth, a sacred flesh and see a sacred path towards it not only upwards, but also downwards. This up to the present has not been comprehended, but we already begin to perceive something.

The man of the new religious consciousness can abjure neither paganism, nor Christianity, both there and here he sees a divine revealing: in his veins flow the streams of blood and they produce a tumult, and in his head the thoughts are twofold. There is no return to paganism, posited as a sort of thesis, and to Christianity, as a sort of antithesis, the very contrast is too old. The new religious consciousness thirsts for a synthesis, a surmounting of the duality, an higher fulfillment, there has to meet together something such, that earlier was not conjoined, to unite the two poles, the two contrary depths. Within historical Christianity it is impossible already to find antidotes against the new allures of a resurgent paganism, just as in the old paganism it is to find antidotes against the failings of historical Christianity. When we speak about a new religious consciousness, then least of all do we intend to say, that all the former religions were mistaken and that it is necessary to discover a new religion. If religion in general is both possible and necessary, then upon the entire worldly and historical process it is needful to look, as upon a Divine revealing, as upon an intimate interacting between man and God. The new religious consciousness represents a continued revealing, encompassing a greater fullness of religious truth, since upon the former stages of a religious revealing was disclosed merely a partial, non-total truth. Counter-productive and godless is that assertion of the parochial representatives of historical Christianity, that within paganism God did not reveal Himself. Christian theologians look upon the pagan gods the same, as the positivists and rationalists look upon the Christian God; they are insufficiently mystical, their religious consciousness is insufficiently broad, in order to glimpse in the pagan gods under various masks a revealing of the Great Visage of God the Father, of God the Creator, no less perfect a revealing of Him, than in the Old Testament Jehovah. And historically the fatal opposition between paganism and Christianity, their irreconcilable hostility, dividing our modern soul, -- is it not the apparent result of the incompleteness of what has been revealed to us, is it not a matter of our limitedness, transforming the historical relativity into an eternal divide between God the Father and God the Son? Would not a new religious synthesis encompass such a fullness of revelation, in which the opposition between the pagan thesis and the Christian antithesis would vanish, like a miracle? This is our religious dream.

If the revelation of the Divinity up to the present had not occurred in the world and the history of mankind, then also it would never be, then the rationalists and the banal Deists would be right, considering God as unnecessary and remote; if however there has been a revelation, then it ought to continue and would be continued, since the fullness of religious truth is attainable only across the extent of all the historical process, and this process ought to be Divine-human. The question about the connection between the relative temporal historical revelation, and the eternal and absolute mystical revelation, ought to be looked into and worked through by a new sort philosophy, mystical and together with this a critical philosophy of the future, which would act to serve the new religious awareness. Only from the uniting of religious experience with an higher philosophic knowledge can there be engendered a true gnosis. Only then would be breached the historical limitedness of the theological schools, and external authority would be replaced by an inner freedom and there would be continued the path towards a plenitude of a mystical God-cognition.[1]

* * *

---

[1] This signification of philosophy is finely understood and expounded upon by N. Minsky in a recently appeared [1905] interesting book, "The Religion of the Future". Vl. Solov'ev did much for the philosophy of religion, and it is inconceivable, how amidst such a sharp philosophic awareness that he could subordinate himself to an historically-limited external authority.

I know of no other man in Russian and European literature, who would have sensed the dual religious rebirth, would have so penetrated into its mystery, would have been so aware of the inevitability of the overcoming of religious duality in the plenitude of a new religious synthesis, as has D. S. Merezhkovsky. The basic and invariable theme of all the writings of Merezhkovsky, of all his ponderings and experiences, the most important and necessary, universal theme -- is that of the two poles of religious consciousness, the two contrary deeps: of Christianity and paganism, spirit and flesh, heaven and earth, God-man and man-god, Christ and the Anti-Christ. For the resolving of this theme concerning the duality, passed down to us by universal culture, of all the religious history of mankind, Merezhkovsky also had the intent to deal with this in his trilogy, albeit not totally successful in artistry of fulfillment, but remarkable in its plan. The selfsame theme concerning duality, demanding of resolution, fills the most remarkable work by Merezhkovsky, upon which would be established his reknown, his two-tome collection entitled: "L. Tolstoy and Dostoevsky". In this book he marks out a path to a resolution of the problem, but he does not yet ultimately pass over from the Two-divided into the Three-united. On the surface level, the views of Merezhkovsky tend to shift, and this particularly catches the eye, when one reads one's way through all the parts of his historical trilogy, but essentially it remains all the same, the same twofold aspect of thought, the same presentiment of *the third*, reconciling the two abysses, the anguish for an heavenly earth and an earthly heaven. Merezhkovsky at the very beginning of his path sensed, mystically felt, that salvation is not in this, that one accept the one abyss whilst renouncing the other, and that sanctity is not at one only pole, and that a returning back, to an one only pagan earth or an one only Christian heaven, is not viable.[1] In this is his tremendous merit, his tremendous significance for the contemporary religious movement. His torment, a torment innate for us, lies in the eternal danger of a confusion, a substitution into a dualised Visage of Christ with that of the Anti-Christ, in an eternal terror, that one be not worshipping the True God, that one

---

[1] Merezhkovsky perceived, than an egress from the religious dualism, from the opposition between the two abysses -- heaven and earth, spirit and flesh, the pagan delight in the world and the Christian renunciation of the world, that this exiting out is not by way of immersion into one of the Two, but in the Third: in Three.

perchance be renouncing one of the Visages of the Divinity, one of the deeps, not contrary to God, but merely the contrary and yet same Divine pole of religious consciousness. This -- is the tempting torment of an ultimate religious freedom.

Merezhkovsky is not an artist purely and not a thinker purely, and with him often is no grasp of an artistic gift for creativity of images nor the thinker's gift for creativity of philosophic conceptions, but he is peculiarly an artist-thinker, he has the gift to create an artistic conception of thoughts, with the capacity for an intimate knowledge and insight. This is an unique type of gnostic of our times, amazingly interpreting texts of the Gospel, penetrating into certain details. He sets himself impossible and too enormous tasks, with which he cannot always cope, but all the same he paves a new path. Merezhkovsky has learned much from Nietzsche, from Dostoevsky and in part from Rozanov, but it is impossible to deny his originality of religio-artistic concept, in an enormous ability of insights into new mystical paths. He is a radical, a revolutionary by temperament, by turn of thought and strivings, eternally inclined to extremes, and he cannot reconcile himself with all the middle of the road, moderate, merely reform type trends. To him is necessary not reform, but rather a turnabout, not a reformation, but rather transformation, and in his religious consciousness he goes a path revolutionary. He is far bolder, more radical than was Vl. Solov'ev, who aspired moreso to justify the faith of the fathers, and in quite much Vl. Solov'ev was conservative, he feared new currents, he got caught up with certain direly fatal themes and in regards to many questions he resorted to compromised views, all over the place.

What does the new religious consciousness want, what is its ultimate desire, what distinguishes it from the old awareness? Our ultimate desire, attracting us to religion -- is the thirst for eternity and for the fullness of being, the ultimate victory over death and the constraints of life. Each human being ends by death and all mankind ends by death and all our life is filled in part by death, -- this pervasive terror of a finalative non-being we cannot, want not and ought not to tolerate. And, in the final end, there are only two religions -- a religion of being, of the affirmation of the eternal and immeasurable fullness of life, in contrast to a religion of non-being, of final death. The world knows indeed one great religion of non-being -- Buddhism. This is a very profound and accomplished attempt to defeat the terror of death and suffering by an ultimate universal death, by a mysterious abyss of non-being. But what about the XIX Century positivism so external to religion, which so avidly sets about the ordering of life? Positivism has despaired of grasping for the meaning of life and defeating death, positivism knows, that death is the allotted portion of each, of every and all, it reconciles itself with this, that non-being is the ultimate limit, having its final word. Yet over atop this in-common abyss and ultimate non-being the positivists want to construct life, to alleviate existence, to ease the suffering of this small, brief, constrained and illusory in its meaninglessness type of being. The merry positivists, singing the praises of life, have to understand life, as a "feasting during a time of pestilence", since an eternal, unhealable "pestilence" accompanies human history. Only desolated, stale, lackeyist and self-smug souls do not sense the terror at this "pestilence" and the impossibility of this "feasting". And the hapless positivism in its subconscious religious aspect aligns with the religion of non-being, with a tendency towards asceticism, and with but a weak voice seeks to defend the constraints upon being.

What leads us to religion is the thirst for an eternal "feasting", but not "during a time of pestilence", not set over the abyss of non-being, but rather after a final victory over every "pestilence" and over all non-being. *Religion teaches of an universal struggle against death, against the spirit of non-being in the name of absolute and eternal being.* It is rooted in that most profound and ultimate awareness, that the victory over death in the world and the winning of life absolutely full and eternal can be attained by man and mankind only in union with God, the source of all being. And therefore the meaning of life can be realised, death defeated, eternity and the fullness of being won, the person affirmed not in a merely human process external to religion, but rather only in a process Divine-human, in a religious unification with God. A path only human and godless is the path of non-being. *Religion teaches likewise an ultimate universal liberation, a struggle against necessity, against restrainedness and limitedness, in the name of an absolutely free and unlimited being.* By a path only human and irreligious freedom cannot be attained, the spectres of the limits and boundaries of necessity rise up everywhere, and such a path is the path of slavery.

If there be an ultimate victory over death, an ultimate affirmation of an eternal and full life and boundless freedom only upon a path that is Divine-human, only in an intimate union of man with God, then within the world God has to be to be incarnated, and thus there then had to appear the God-Man. Within the history of the world there was a singular, an unrepeatable point of conjunction of the human and the Divine, within it was given an unseen and victory-bearing Divine-human battling against death, against the spirit of non-being -- for life, for joy, for freedom, for eternity and the fullness of being. In Christ human freedom, the freedom of choice was delimited by Divine love, but from this it, this freedom, so dear to us, was not limited (this word reflects only the imperfection of our language), it was rendered still greater, it desired the salvation of man and the world within the Kingdom of God, since within it only would there be the salvation from slavery and non-being; mystically there was reconciled human freedom with Divine necessity or, what is virtually the same, with Divine freedom. God [the Son] Himself died upon the Cross and was resurrected, in order to reveal to the world the truth concerning the universal resurrection, concerning the ultimate victory over death, concerning the eternal joyous and free life.

And from that time the world began to be crucified with Christ, Golgotha cast a dark shadow upon human history, the death of Christ fascinated mankind, and His resurrection was not understood or was understood incompletely. Historical Christianity encompassed only the negative, the ascetic half of the religion of Christ, it conceived of heaven, as the denial of the earth, and of spirit, as the denial of the flesh, and the deeps of the pole opposite was spurned, as a diabolical temptation. The dualism of heaven and earth, of spirit and flesh tended to poison life, it plunged the world into a constant sinfulness. And the life of the world went its own usual path, justifying itself with a sanctity not Christian. The sexual life, the social life, all the allurement of world culture, of art and science tended to seem at the pole opposite to the religious consciousness of historical Christianity. Yet here there ignites a new religious consciousness, which cannot still endure this rift, this dualism, it thirsts for the religious sanctification of life, the sanctification of world culture, for a new holy love, an holy societal aspect, an holy "flesh", a transfigured "earth". The new religious consciousness orients itself towards the profound wellsprings of all religion, to the surmounting of death in the eternal, the full and free existence of the person and the overcoming of Golgotha within the Resurrection. The Christian renaissance will ensue, when "there is an end to the negation, the resignation, the dying away, when instead there begins affirmation, expectation, resuscitation. From the first -- from the sorrowful, the grim, the mysterious Visage of the Lord Christianity then would orient itself towards the second -- to the joyful, the radiant, the glorious. This verymost great cosmic turnabout also now would happen almost intangibly, imperceptibly, as also always happen suchlike cosmic turnabouts".[1]

Here with the following words of Merezhkovsky is how he characterises the new religious consciousness, and foresees in it a new, or more accurately the eternal and sole religion, but encompassing a greater fullness, than the historical religions: -- "For up to the present, it seems to us, that to be a Christian means to love heaven, only heaven, having cut oneself off from the earth, hating the earth. But here is Christianity -- not as a renunciation of the earth, not as a betrayal of the earth, but rather as a new, a still unprecedented "fidelity to the earth", a new love for the earth, a new "embracing of the earth". It would seem, that not only can one love the heaven and earth together, but that otherwise also it is impossible not to love them as together, while too it is impossible to love them separately as regards the teaching of Christ. Although we love heaven or earth not to the end point, not to the final limit of heaven and earth, it seems to us thus, as it did to L. Tolstoy and Nietzsche, that the one love negates the other. It is necessary to be in love with the earth to the very end, to the final boundary of the earth -- to its extenting to heaven, it is necessary to be in love with heaven to the very end, to the utmost boundary of heaven -- to its extenting to the earth, and then we shall perceive, that this not two, but the rather one love, that heaven descends to earth, embraces the earth, as the lover embraces the beloved (the two halves, as it were the two sexes of the world) and the earth yields to heaven, opens to heaven: and the earthly mystery, in the expression of Dostoevsky, "becomes contiguous with the starry mystery"; in this "contiguity", in this uniting is also comprised the essence, if not of historical Christianity, then at least of the teaching itself of Christ. The tree of life extends not only into the innocent blue sky with merrily attached leaves, but also into the dark, the eternally-begetting, eternally pleasurable "womb" of its mother the moist earth with its roots. Although the earth is not heavenly -- it is all still the old, the pagan earth; although heaven is not earthly -- it is all still the old, the non-Christian, the only seemingly "Christian" heaven. Thereof will not be "a new earth and a new heaven", this means rather that there will be an earth heavenly and an heaven earthly. "Thy Kingdom come. Thy Will be done, on earth, as it

---

[1] Vide the Preface of Merezhkovsky to Tome II of "Lev Tolstoy and Dostoevsky".

is in heaven". Not only in heaven, but also upon the earth. Let Thine Will unite earth and heaven, let earth and heaven not be two, but rather one, just as *I and the Father be One*. Here is the salt of the salt in the teachings of Christ; here already it is not the water, but rather the "fire" of Baptism. Baptised only by water, we have not understood this, and now only do we begin to understand, that in not having understood this, we have basically understood nothing in Christianity".

Merezhkovsky with an especial acuteness has posited the problem of the relationship between spirit and flesh, he resolves it with brilliant an interpretation from the Gospel texts, with artistic an intuition and a mystical presentiment of the future religious culture. The fate of the new religious movement is bound up with a radical resolution of the fundamental, yet new theme concerning the relationship of religion towards the "flesh", towards the "earth", the religious sanctification of culture, of the societal aspect, of sexual love, of the joy of life. -- "The knighthood chivalrant has not fulfilled its task, since it strove towards it too early and too unconsciously, -- but the task was true; this all still to a remarkable degree is also our task: to sanctify the unsanctified or insufficiently sanctified by the Church, from the churchly point of view, all still too mundane, pagan; to sanctify not merely one part, but rather the whole of life, not one pole, but both, not only the *not-I*, with its renunciation of person, but also the I, with its affirmation of person in the consciousness of personal dignity, honour, in the old heroic, valiant love for native-land, for the earth, for the people, for all the Christian world, and in a new extra-marital, extra-familial love for womankind". -- The duality ought to be surmounted within an higher affirmation, and not negation, our pagan rebirth, the rehabilitation of the flesh and joy earthly, ought to be acknowledged as equal in sanctity and godliness with the Christian rebirth, with the yearning for heaven and grieving of spirit. God is One within the depths of the two opposite abysses, only but two poles of a single religious awareness, co-united in the fullness of revelation. The blunting and belittling of this theme leads to a withering and religious sterility. But the problem of spirit and flesh can be posited still otherwise, purely philosophically, as an ontological problem, as concerning this, as concerning what is being, of what is being comprised, its essence. The totality of religion cannot but have its own ontology, its own understanding of the existing composition of the world and therefore cannot manage without metaphysics. Merezhkovsky constantly speaks about the ascetic metaphysics of historical Christianity, about the opposite metaphysics of paganism, but he never does attempt philosophically to posit and resolve the problem of spirit and flesh. This is his weakness. In philosophy, judging from certain places, he follows Kant, yet without having given an accounting, on how a philosophic surmounting of Kant is needful for the religious consciousness, and furthermore on how it is impossible for a mystic to be a Kantian.

* * *

Merezhkovsky is a decided antagonist to spiritualistic metaphysics, the struggle against the spiritualism of historical Christianity -- is his fundamental motif. Yet in this the tremendous merit of Merezhkovsky can readily get entangled with an enormous error, if one fails to subject this problem to philosophic an investigation. The issue consists in this, that the religious problem of the relationship of "spirit" and of "flesh" does not completely coincide with the philosophic problem of spirit and matter, of soul and body, of the psychical and the physical, though it touches alongside it. The "flesh", about which Merezhkovsky speaks, is a symbolic concept, it personifies itself and the earth in general, and the entirety of culture and the societal aspect (the "body" of mankind), and the entirety of sensuality, and sensual love. In this "flesh" there is too little of what we in philosophy term as "matter", as a manifestation physical in contrast to the psychical, while in it there is too much of what we in philosophy term as "spirit", as a manifestation psychical in contrast to the physical. This "flesh" is not definable by physical properties and chemical composition, and this "earth" does not consist of geological strata. The spatial extension and temporal aspect of the empirical world is not a binding condition of the being of this sort of "flesh", and impermeability is not the same unique property, as obtains for us with "matter". "Flesh" moreover is not phenomenal, manifest in opposition to "spirit" -- the noumenon, the essence, in it there is that which is noumenal, metaphysically initial. But how is there to be connected the religious and culturo-historical problem of "flesh" (the affirmation of culture, of the societal aspect, of sensuality, sexuality, literally, of embodied spirit) -- with the ontological problem, of what is being, of what is it comprised, and also with the gnosseological problem, of what is noumenon, and what is phenomenon, of what are the conditions of the forms of the empirical world?

The theory of cognition, in what seems for me the solely possible, the solely true and for the future fruitful, tends to see in the empirical, the space-time world comprising the merely conditional and relative, as has seemed, and not the true being, merely for us a substitute noumenal essence. In this "world", which knows science and which to the positivists seems as the sole and comprehensibly explicable one, in this "experience", which we term secondary and rationalised, it is impossible for the composition of being to be revealed, within its noumenal essence, and hence not in the manifestations "physical", nor in the manifestations "psychical", not in "body" nor in "*soul*".[1] Only within experience that is primary, non-rationalised, there is mystically revealed to us true being, the really existent, the metaphysical "spirit" and the metaphysical "flesh" of the world, not only our mystical "soul", but also our mystical "body". Philosophico-critical mysticism teaches, that the most mystical is the most real, actualising, the most incarnate though also not by laws rational, and which gives justification to the "experience" of Dostoevsky. And all those positivist "realists", in being tied down to the empirical actuality, tend to live in a world illusory, since the world of noumenal essences are not incarnated for them nor within them.

That from baseness with the soul
Might man be lifted,
With ancient mother earth
Enter he in union e'er.
(*from F. Schiller's "Hymn to Joy"*)

About this union, this coalescing "with ancient mother earth", all the great religions tend to speak, the great poets of the past, they anguish over the moist mother earth, they see in the uniting with it very great a religious experience. This "earth", our Primagenitress, the divine and noumenal element of the earth which the positivists and rationalists do not know of, or they have forgotten about it, -- is not encompassed, not embodied within their rationally-limited experience. They live as it were upon a different earth, a different planet, defined of a chemical composite,

---

[1] Vide my articles -- "Concerning the New Russian Idealism" and the "Crisis of Rationalism within Contemporary Philosophy", in which there is noted the possibility of suchlike a new gnosseology.

formed of theoretical layers, and only it, a dead and dessicated figment of an earth do they admit of. The "earth", which Merezhkovsky wants to unite with "heaven", is an abyss from below -- noumenal, a metaphysical "earth", a "flesh" transcendental. The spiritualism of historical Christianity is a fidelity to heaven, to spirit, but also a betrayal of divine earth, of mystical flesh. The irreligious positivism of the XIX Century is a betrayal both of the mystical "heaven" and the mystical "earth". The rationalistic positivists are likewise as remote from the abyss of "flesh" as they are from the abyss of "spirit", they are somewhere in the middle, upon the flats, bereft of a mystical sensitivity for "earth" and of the yearning for "heaven". All this mid-level rationalistic culture is soulless and sterile, it lives at the surface level of physical and psychical appearances, but it does not plunge itself down into the depths of noumenal "spirit" and noumenal "flesh". And only at these depths also is posited the problem of Merezhkovsky. If the spiritualism of historical Christianity has deadened the "flesh" and by this infringed upon the foundational, the Divine element, if it has inclined itself towards Buddhism, then also the materialism of the irreligious era has deadened the "spirit", likewise not having returned to the depths of the "flesh", and therefore it has proceeded towards an ultimate non-being, towards an illusory existence upon the superficiality of the flat-surface plane. Those who rehabilitate the "flesh", who return to the "ancient mother earth" are not the materialists, knowing only the phenomena of matter, but rather such mystics as Rozanov, in perceiving the ancient secrets of the "flesh" of the earth. Only for genuine mystics, having sensed within themself the ancient chaos, of the earth full of great secrets, only they can reveal in its depth the treasures, and make the earthly mysteries, returning us to the Eleusinian mysteries and to the festivals of Dionysos.

And thus, "spirit" and "flesh" for Merezhkovsky and for the neo-mystics, people of the new religious consciousness, this becomes not a matter of noumenon and phenomenon, of soul -- the psychical, and of body -- the physical, nor moreover certainly, of good and evil. Merezhkovsky sometimes gets himself entangled as a consequence of the absence in him of a philosophic critical ability, but at the basis of his world-perception lies a very profound idea of noumenality, of a metaphysical primordialness not only of "spirit", but also of "flesh", not only of "heaven" but also of "earth" and of their religious equality of worth. The "flesh" of the world, of sensuality, its embodiment within the societal aspect and earthly culture, in the love between the sexes, in the orgiastic, likewise is noumenal, metaphysically primordial, divinely-mystical, as is "spirit", as is "heaven". This is fully conjoinable with the spiritualism or panpsychism in ontology, which teaches, that being is comprised of complex, interactive an hierarchy of concrete spiritual beings, spiritualised monads, united in an universal unity of the Primal Divine Monad, containing within it the absolute plenitude of being and by way of emanation praeternally creating the manifold of being. One can dispute the quality of the old traditional term of spiritualism, but suchlike a sort of ontology has to be admitted by the trans-historical new Christianity.

The failure of historical Christianity was not so much in its spiritualistic ontology, not in its competency to resolve our problem of "spirit" and "flesh", as rather in its dualism, by which "spirit" was admitted as Divine and good, whereas "flesh" was seen as godless and evil. But indeed there can exist a philosophic ontology, which altogether would deny the existence of matter, would admit of the physical world on a fictitious conditional basis and such a sort of panpsychism would be conducive only to the rehabilitation of the "flesh". The roots of sensuality, of the orgiastic "flesh" are lodged not within the empirical, the material world, these roots rather are transcendental, within unfathomable depths, upon one of the poles of "spirit", if the world be spirit.

Metaphysics can teach us this awareness, that worldly being ought to become freed from the bonds of "matter", from the laws of "nature" weighing us down, that space and time ought to vanish, like a nightmare. And this fully coincides with the most ultimate, the most important and the most mysterious idea of the religious consciousness about a transfiguration of the "earth", a transfiguration of the "flesh". There occurs the age-old battle against the primal enslavement, the slavery, termed "matter" by us, against the limitations of all space and time, but not against the "earth", not against the "flesh". There will be an "earth" transfigured, not tied down by material laws, but instead free, extra-temporal and extra-spatial; there will be the "flesh" transfigured, non-physical, but instead vigourous, sensual, mystically-delighting and eternal, freed of all material bounds. This mystical presentiment can be justified by metaphysics, but only in religion can this mystery be grasped. For man himself, sundered off from the Absolute Source of being, it is impossible to attain to the transfiguration of the "earth", its liberation from space and time, from the congealing and necessity, and likewise not to the transfiguration of the "flesh", the affirmation of its eternal, its undecaying individual being. But for God everything is possible and in the union with God, in the Divine-human process, there will be a true transformation. *The religious problem of spirit and flesh, of the polarity of abysses, of duality, is not engendered from an ontological duality of human nature, but rather for us the greatest mystery of the duality of God in two Visages and the relationship of this duality for the manifold world issuing from God; and religiously this problem is resolved, the duality is resolved within the third Visage of God.* In accord with the Christian teaching, here is the mysterious and seemingly to the world polarity of God the Father and God the Son, which -- are One, and the resolution of all the oppositions are in God the Holy Spirit. More about this later.

But our flesh, the flesh of our world is corrupt, defective, abnormal; not because, that the flesh is sinful in its essence, manifesting an evil principle and having to be deadened, but because, that it dies, it decays, sickens and suffers, it is not eternal and not free and has to be transfigured, resurrected. On this, it is needful to get beyond the issue of the old and eternally new question concerning asceticism. Not in the flesh is the curse of mankind, its ancient source of corruption, but rather in death, not in the free life is its sinfulness, but rather in servile constraint and limitation. The abnormality of the flesh is not in the orgy-like richness of life, but rather in the misery, the constrainedness and finiteness of the life of the flesh. And religion, conscious of the tragedy of worldly flesh, contends not against the flesh, but rather against the corruption of the flesh, not against the orgy-like fullness of life, but against death, its bonds, substituting a part for the whole. It is necessary to conquer in the flesh not that, which is in it -- being, but rather that which in it -- is non-being, not the living, but rather the dying, not to conquer in it the affirmation, but rather the negation. Asceticism can be one moment, one of the means, but never the entirety, never the sole means.

Ascetic religion, Buddhism, either the ancient or the most recent, in the tendency of historical Christianity towards a black monasticism, religion, caught up in warring against life instead of death, against being instead of against non-being, -- is not our religion; the spirit, in which every "yes" gets swallowed up by an enormous "no", tends to drown in the great "nothingness" contrary to the new religious consciousness. Orgiasm -- the tragic source of life, so little noticed by our drab and dull rationalistic culture, ascetic and corrupt as it is (this is always together), there gets so forgotten by us of the tragic orgiasm of the transcendental threads connected with our finalative religious entirety -- the affirmation of the fullness of being, conjoined with the Primal Source of all life. Not every orgiasm is a path, but is not religious an orgiasm a path to the victory over death, to the eternal entry into the Kingdom of God?

Merezhkovsky senses and understands all this. He sees the mystery of the religion of Christ, all its meaning in the most enigmatic, the most inconceivable words, which ever were pronounced: "And Jesus took bread, and having blessed it, and broken it, and distributing it to the disciples, said: Take ye, and eat, this is My Body. And having taken the cup, gave it to them, and said: Drink of this all of ye, for this is My Blood of the New Covenant, shed for many, unto the remission of sins". After this can the *New Covenant* be understood as a religion fleshless and bloodless? Merezhkovsky justly speaks about "the ulcer and misdeed of the whole of historical Christianity, the spirit of which all still up to the present is primarily monastic, bloodless and fleshless, disembodied, "abstract spirit", -- which all still has not given answer to the calling voice of Pan, has not joined in with the great feast of Dionysos, not "transgressed" beyond that final line, where heaven aligns with earth, a spirit -- with flesh and blood? "What is there behind this feast, in which participates each "charming insect", each "gummy leaflet"? Is it not the call of the "resurrected Pan"? Is it not a feast of flesh and blood, a mysterious vespers of a new Dionysos, saying of Himself: I am the true vine, and My Father is the vine-dresser"; a great feast, in which wine is transformed into blood and blood into wine?" The words here are of tremendous importance for the new religious consciousness. We call to mind the remarkable work of Vyacheslav Ivanov concerning the religion of Dionysos, the Hellenic religion of the suffering god. The strivings of Vyacheslav Ivanov are so characteristic of the new religious movement, and his efforts have to be admitted as a remarkable contribution into our Christian-pagan renaissance. The understanding of Dionysos, as a mystical presentiment of the appearance of Christ in the world -- here already is a path towards the so desired synthesis of Christianity and paganism. The orgy-like festivities of Dionysos shatter the bounds, they set free, the manifest the religious medium, in which will be incarnated the suffering god -- God the Son. The god Pan is still an aspect of the divine creative power, he lies within the religious atmosphere of father-godism, but Dionysos with his suffering-god festivities, is he not already reborn in the world in a religious atmosphere of son-godism?[1]

The *flesh* of the world indeed is sacred, divine not only because it is the creation of God the Father, that within it is reflected its eternal nature, but also because that in it God the Son is crucified and suffers and in Him the flesh resurrects, is saved from corruption and death. Both the complete presentiment, the still pagan religion of Dionysos, and the surmounting paganism, fulfilling the greatest prophecies of the religion of Christ -- is the religion of the *divinely-suffering earth.*[2] In the suffering of God, having been crucified for the earth, incarnated, -- the earth is resurrected and enlivened, the flesh of the world conquers death, and heads towards the eternal feast of life. But the black monastic, the fleshless and bloodless asceticism, is it not a fleeing from the world tragedy, a betraying of the earth, in which is incarnated and suffers God Himself, is this not an allurement by the spirit of non-being?

---

[1] *trans. comment*: What Berdyaev here is describing is a sort of decadentist-cultural psychological equivalent to Khlystyism (within its dynamics similar in ways to "holy roller" Pentecostalism). Berdyaev of course soon after this "outgrows Merezhkovsky" on his religious path to the Orthodox Church. Is the reader equally adept at surmounting the quandaries presented by Merezhkovsky here? Merezhkovsky in ways is similar to Lev Tolstoy, each with a mix of ideas creating his own "improved Christianity", in pseudo-gnostic fashion akin to the New Age era of our 1970's culture. Yes, in the wake of this "new religious consciousness", within Orthodoxy itself has become deeper a focus upon the signification of the Theophany, the Transfiguration, the Resurrection. Throughout Berdyaev's present book ,"Sub specie aeternitatis", Berdyaev is on a path battling his way, on one step-article at a time, through a thicket, a spider's web, of the rationalism he so decries; it is an omnipresent and ghostly-phantasm hounding him, which renders the real into the unreal, with the typical over-simplification (abetted by intellectual pride) characteristic to rationalism. True mystery is not subsumable to reason...

[2] Vide principally the important and remarkable article of V. Ivanov, "Concerning the Religion of Dionysos", in the July edition of "Voprosy zhizni". For Minsky likewise the earth is sanctified by a divine sacrifice, with God suffering in it. Vide his "The Religion of the Future".

Yet it is not spirit nor flesh that needs to be affirmed, but rather the person in the fullness of its own unique being, its transcendent individualness, which is "incarnate spirit" and "spiritual flesh". The idea of the person, of individuality ought to occupy a central place within the new religious consciousness, for only in connection with this idea can much be resolved. Merezhkovsky ought to have sensed the tremendous significance of the religious understanding of the person, but he insufficiently discerns this side of the religious consciousness.[1] God Himself indeed was incarnated in the form of [Divine] Person, and in this is latent the command of affirmation of person in eternity, the acknowledgement of the immeasurable worth of the individuality [unique to person].

The problem of the flesh[2] in its religious setting is inseparably connected with the problem of *sexuality*, and Merezhkovsky rightly considers this our ultimate problem primarily and with its resolution is bound up the fate of religion. It has befallen our lot, apparently, to posit this problem in all its acuteness, to lay it bare, to cast a challenge against the growth of its age-old hypocrisy. It is difficult to speak calmly upon this theme, it arouses enormous indignation not only against the philistinism and cant in modern society, but also against the horrid distortion of the thousands of years connected with it. If we speak about sex too much and too openly, if we too much rehabilitate its rights, bending the bow to the opposite side, as Rozanov has done, then this not only is excusable before an higher tribunal, but also provides a religious service. The indeed most philistine and dull souls have to perceive and sense in their intimate depths, that *sexuality* is the source of world history, that with it is connected the

---

[1] I see the weakness of Merezhkovsky to be in this, that he almost nowise discerns the religious idea concerning the unconditional significance of the human person, he but poorly understands the person, and mystically he is insufficiently sensitive to it.

[2] *trans. comment*: The entirety of Merezhkovsky's "flesh" motif seems to derive from a perception of the "*spiritual flesh*" in which Christ appeared *after* His Resurrection firstly to St Mary Magdalene and later the Apostles, -- all who failed to recognise Him initially. (Cf. Jn 20: 15ff). Merezhkovsky's schema is too superficially rationalised, too neatly facile, failing to go at depth into the significance of the Incarnation of Christ, too readily equivocating it to parallels in pagan mythology...

intensity and richness of being, that half of the life of the world is filled by it and upon it depends the second half, that within it is rooted the tragic aspect of life. With sexuality is connected the most secret and enigmatic depths of human existence, and all the greatest artists of the world have known this. But the most important and terrible problem of life has proven to be the least resolved and least posited, since this most intimate aspect has not been admitted as necessary for the course of history. This problem is all still under a thousand years stigma, considered shameful, indecent, improper and even immoral, not subject to discussion. And each one has put before him for resolution one of the most universal of questions, each has to hide within him a torment, nigh close for everyone, but forbidden to be open about it.

Can much be found in world literature and philosophy on the question of sexuality and sexual love? There is the "Symposium" feast of Plato, the most genius-inspired and eternal of everything written in this area, there are the Buddhist-like judgements of Schopenhauer, the insights of certain immense artists, the amazing article by Vl. Solov'ev entitled: "On the Meaning of Love", and works by Rozanov, and that is about it. And over all this are set the enigmatic, incomprehensible, immeasurable words of Christ. Within history -- there has been both the wildly fanatical and scoffing asceticism of the servitors of historical Christianity as well as the eternal temptations of Venus, undying, ever anew reborn from the foam of the sea. Over sexuality have been committed historical transgressions for thousands of years. Accursed by the religious consciousness prevailing within history, sex has been driven into the underground realm an there it makes for earthquakes and upheavals. The ancient goddess Aphrodite takes her revenge upon her persecutors, she brings ruination upon those historical religions, which fail to reckon with her divine will. The pseudo-Christian asceticism and spiritualism have poisoned the human soul and body, have corrupted with the consciousness of sinfulness, have transformed the sexual life into something abhorrent, dirty and shameful, have deadened the great religious dream of the sanctity of sex, the sanctity of love, the sanctity of the loving feast of life. Sex and the divine Eros connected with it was driven into the confines of the bourgeois family and only there was it tolerated, though the family finds justification not by a single word of Christ; it leads an irreligious existence in the coffee-lounges and public houses, this comprising the inevitable corrective of every familial order. Sexual love tends to exist outside of religion, unsanctified, left to the caprice of fate. The religious man of old inevitably defiles his beloved wife and is himself defiled, since every pleasure is reckoned fallen, of weakness, accursed of by mankind. Religious preachers, philosophers, the learned, the publicists, the societal activists consider it worthwhile and proper to speak and write about everything, about the most insignificant things, but not about sex, the source of torment and sufferings. For the positivists the problem of sex simply does not exist, for them it is only a question about emancipation in the family, the question of civil rights and the political economy, very respectable, certainly, on the question of medicine and hygiene, very likewise useful, but not the religious problem of sex. Among the larger number of the most avant-garde positivists it is possible to meet with the old religious ascetic spirit, although God in them is long since dead and replaced by morality. This morality, needful for successes in life, but not for its religious meaning, has cost too dearly and ought to be toppled by a new religious renaissance, in its essence trans-moral.[1] It is impossible to adequately appreciate the service of Rozanov given all his extremes, yet who so boldly and so radically has posited the religious problem concerning sex, and who in so revolutionary a manner has broken through the irrelevant moral pretensions. I do not share Rozanov's resolution of the question, profoundly foreign to me is this ancient Jewish apotheosis of the natal principle, holding sacred the pleasure of begetting, but I admire his mighty effort to expel from our blood the ascetic venom, and to restore sexuality to its paradise-like sanctity and sinlessness.

Rozanov undoubtedly has had an influence upon all the conceptualisation of the supra-historical Christianity of Merezhkovsky. Merezhkovsky acknowledged the challenges of Rozanov, stood at his side, but this challenge was addressed not to the religion of Christ, but rather to "historical" Christianity. Historical Christianity, in his opinion, has failed to encompass sexuality, has considered it accursed, but the religion of Christ is inclusive of sexuality, and the new, the supra-historical Christianity ought to disclose itself to us in connection with a resolution to this problem, since upon sexuality is dependent all the flesh of the world, the religious truth about the earth. Merezhkovsky all his life has been tormented by Aphrodite, the "white feminine devil" tempted him, and not in vain does she play such a role in his historical novels. And he strives to

[1] But not immoral.

discern in the statue of Venus the features of an ideal Madonna. Despite his seeming closeness to Rozanov, Merezhkovsky stands essentially at diametrically the opposite end: Rozanov discloses the sanctity and divineness of sexuality and amourous delight as it were prior to the beginning of the world, he wants to return us back to the condition of paradise prior to the sin-fall; Merezhkovsky in contrast discloses the same but after the end of the world, he calls for a pleasurable and sacred festivity of the flesh in a world-transfigured, redeemed and resurrected. Merezhkovsky is correct, since he gazes forward, and not backwards, but of what sort ought to be the path from the beginning to the end, and what ought to be affirmed along this path?

Sexuality is not only a biological concept, not only an empirical phenomenon, which as such could be abolished in the affirming of the realm of spirit, as having no place in heaven. Sexuality -- is transcendent, love possesses a meaning metaphysical, and with the love between the sexes, with the confluence of polarly opposite beings is closely connected the striving towards eternity, towards the affirmation of the wholeness of the individuality. But the sexuality is abnormalised, as it were corrupted, and love is rendered tragic. The frightful aspect is not in this, that sexual passion is sinful, but rather in this, that the wholeness and eternal aspect of the individuality within the empirical world is not attained by it, individuality remains fragmented, the life of sexuality leads to deterioration, and my unattained striving for perfection is passed on to offspring, doomed to suffer the same torment. On the other hand, sexual love itself constantly is fragmentive, serves the aspect of multiplicity and not the singular, and therefore attains not to eternity. This is the tragic aspect of sexuality, this its tendency towards decay is something that Christianity has not invented, and Rozanov is totally powerless in the face of this tragedy, just as in general he is afront the tragedy of death. Herein indeed is the fundamental antinomy of world history: the continuance of the human race is the result of imperfection, of mortality, of fragmentation of the individuality, and yet it is needful for the universal victory over death, for the ultimate affirmation of eternity and the perfecting of the individuality. The metaphysical meaning of love, of sexual love, is in this, that through it is affirmed the metaphysical person, the eternal individuality, and the decay-tending flesh of the world is suchlike, that sex also is subject to decay, to wither: there is attained not the eternity of one individuality into immortality, but rather a multiplicity of mortal individualities in deterioration, not a single eternal love, but rather a multiplicity of the decayed. The impersonal natal instinct is bound up with death, but in the eternal and perfective life of individualities there is neither death, nor birth. Can there be affirmed a sexuality that is not only of the pleasurable natal sort, but also individual and eternal? And here, just like everywhere, the aim cannot be achieved by merely the human path alone, rather only by a path divine-human, only in union with God.

The metaphysical purposiveness of sexuality is realised fully only within religion. If the wholeness of love and its ultimate purposiveness is to be realised by an union mystical, then the path to it, as also everywhere regarding multiplicities and individualities, -- least of all also does this path lead through a deadening of sexuality. There is a great danger of entering into a new form of asceticism, towards a negation alone without any affirmation, if there be not admitted the sanctity of the basis of sexual love, manifest not only within the confines of a churchly union. There is necessary a revolt not only against pseudo-Christian asceticism, but also against the familial union, such as is subject to coercion, always irreligious and contrary to the eternal aims of love. The family indeed -- is an union serving the earthly good-arrangement, an union involving the natal moreso than the individual. Christ taught not an endless reproduction unto a continuance of imperfection and death, but rather eternal life and the perfection of the person, of the individuality. Nowhere do we meet with such an insurmountable conservatism, as here, nowhere else do the old feelings and the old morality prevail so despotically. Even Merezhkovsky speaks with too weak a voice, he insufficiently reacts, he wants to find a common ground for reconciliation with the old Christian teaching on marriage. The sexual marital love ought to be a sacramental mystery, ought to be sanctified in a religious uniting, so that its meaning and purpose should be eternal, and this is undoubtedly so, but there ought namely to be declared war against any idea of a marriage merely familial, against any coercive force either external or internal, against any rule of authority over the orgiasm of sexuality. The very concept of a corrupt perversity -- is an old and bourgeois concept, the product of an abstract moralism, and ought to be subjected to a judgement aesthetic and ultimately religious.

Through sexuality there ought to be accomplished not only the uniting of two into an eternal wholeness of individuality, but also the uniting of all within the societal aspect since, perhaps, the enigmatic mystery of Christian love consists also in this, that the love which unites people is not only brotherly, but also marital, a mystical sort being in love, and not merely pity and altruism. Close also to this is Merezhkovsky. In sexuality, in love is included both a mystery of individuality, of the person, and a mystery of universality, of Sobornost'-communality. Rozanov in general poorly understands individuality and therefore for him is hidden the true meaning of love, his sexual sort orgiasm is impersonal, but that through sexuality lies the path to the communal religious life, this he does have a sense of, like no one else. Vl. Solov'ev tends to speak on the mystical aspect of being in love, and with it he connects much.[1] It is namely in regards to the question concerning sexuality and love that most of all distinguishes the attitude of people of the old religious consciousness and the old irreligious consciousness, from that of people of the new religious consciousness. The new religious people, people of the future religion of freedom, ought to have done with hypocritical moralism, to hurl a challenge to the civil-familial unions based upon good-order, and instead become devoted to revolutionally mystical outlooks, in which, the problem of sexuality and love will be posited and decided religiously, and not positivistically, nor socially, nor morally.[2] But timidity in facing the old powers all still restrains too many.[3]

With Merezhkovsky there is a very radical temperament of idea, he thirsts for great and worldwide turnabouts, but sometimes he speaks falsely, as though not with his own voice; with him there are two voices and only one of them is genuine, authentic. It seems to me, that his voice

---

[1] The extraordinary and genuinely mystical ideas of Vl. Solov'ev concerning the meaning of love, concerning the eternal feminine, concerning the mystical aspect of love is sharply contrary to the banal and old morality, such as was developed in the weakest of his works, -- the "Justification of the Good", in which he strays off into "moralism", as an "abstract" principle.

[2] Much of value in this regard can be found in the articles penned by Anton the Extreme [pseudonym of Zinaida Gippius] in "Novyi Put'".

[3] Even Rozanov is not free from fear, he is afraid, that they will cease admitting him into the "respectable homes", and hence he does not express himself totally. Vexing for us is this censuring by society, this coercion under a false conscience and philistinism.

betrays Merezhkovsky every time, when he attempts to go for a compromise, to find grounds for agreement with the old, with the old statecraft, with the old churchliness, every time when he gropes for a firm grounding in common with other people, when he is afraid to follow through on his excessive radicalism. With Merezhkovsky there is a sincere, his own particular, new, free religious outlook, there are prayerful words, innate to people of the new religious consciousness, but sometimes there occurs a sort of tendency, there appear falsely sounding words, the old-churchly, old-stately, old and not ours; as though he suddenly becomes frightened of his own "decadence", grasping for the old stability. And with such a false tone, grating unacceptably upon the ear, is written everything, that Merezhkovsky says about the excommunication of Lev Tolstoy from the Church;[1] and it is not with his own voice, not with his own words that he craftily attempts to connect himself with the historical church, with the state body of Russia, suddenly he becomes frightened of heresy, although this fear is not there in his face. It makes me sick to read those places in the writings of Merezhkovsky, in which he strays from his path, and hits false notes, betrays his natural radicalism, for his investigations are too dear to me and I too much desire, that these searchings not prove patently suspicious and subject to reproach. Nothing has been so injurious to Merezhkovsky himself and the great deed of the religious rebirth of Russia, as the false notes in regard to the question concerning the state and the societal aspect. He clearly strayed from the path, when one time he began resetting the old Slavophil teaching about the state, when with a strange voice he attempted to speak about the mystical power of authority, when he attempted to bring alive an historical corpse. It is striking, how this Merezhkovsky, quite so radical, so full of revolt, so free and new in his thirstings, how yet Merezhkovsky has failed straight off to realise, what now apparently is beginning to be realised, -- that the state, that this sort of kingdom is one of the devil's temptations, and that every rule of power earthly, that every prince of this world is not of God, but from the evil one, that a new societal approach ought to be affirmed not upon a coercive state

---

[1] Merezhkovsky has said much that was accurate and profound concerning Lev Tolstoy, about "Uncle Eroshka" [Cf. "The Cossacks"] and the weakness of Tolstoy's awareness, but he completely failed to appreciate the religious significance of Tolstoy's repudiation of power, of Tolstoy's protest against the official deceit and falsehood.

union, but rather upon a free religious uniting, that there is no place for coercive force, where is proclaimed the realm of love. The awareness of the person, so important for the new religious consciousness, is something he has not attempted to transfer over into politics. Merezhkovsky often comes nigh close to the true teaching about powerlessness, about the mystical non-stateness, and then his voice sounds so sincere, so in harmony with the new religious consciousness, but alas had he not strayed! With him is repeated the selfsame history, which there was in Dostoevsky, which obtained within the "Grand Inquisitor", very profound and passionate, unique within world literature, and a basis for anarchism upon a religious grounding, the immeasurable freedom in Christ, but alongside this he defended the very old and banal state ideas. And Vl. Solov'ev thus nearly to the end also did not realise, that the idea of an universal theocracy, the Kingdom of God not only in heaven but also on earth, is incommensurable with the admitting of an earthly power of authority, incommensurable with the coercive-force state. One mustneeds choose: either to follow Christ, spurning the temptations for earthly kingdoms in the name rather of boundless freedom and free love, or to follow that one, who tempted Him in the wilderness. Merezhkovsky however has long been tempted by the *imperium romanum*, the idea of a mystical monarchy and the grandeur of Caesar, to whom he is prepared to cede over the portion, which is God's, though this Caesar was never empirical, but merely a romantic fancy. He worships Napoleon, a super-man, a man-god, which indicates, that the influence of Nietzsche has not vanished for him. In Peter, the greatest of the tsars, he sees an example of the mystical monarch, fulfilling a religious destiny, instead of seeing in him simply a genius, with forward a vision for setting the course of history.[1]

All this old romanticism in Merezhkovsky also stirs him with repulsion towards philistine democracy, towards the irreligious politics of our intelligentsia, forgetful of great ideas. In the modern liberal, democratic, socialistic, positivist-state ideas there is little of the great, these are not universal ideas, nor connected with the religious meaning of life, these are but "bourgeois" ideas. But of what sort at present can there

---

[1] The views of Merezhkovsky on Peter the Great are striking by their lack of clarity, a twofold aspect, and this connected, apparently, with the lack of clarity and a twofold aspect also in all his thoughts concerning the Anti-Christ.

be of a great, universal, religious state idea? Already, certainly, it is not the old, the dead idea of earthly power, which not only was repudiated by the modern political, moral, non-religious consciousness, but which all the more radically ought to be repudiated by the new religious consciousness, concerning whatever the path of the spirit of non-being, such as tempted Christ-God in the wilderness.

The societal approach can be affirmed not upon state principles, upon the relationships of the holding of power, but rather upon new and eternal mystically-free principles, similar to how it is possible for an affirmation of love not within the familial union, but beyond it, in a mystically free union. Ought free love not to be of the boundless freedom in God, the sole basis of the new societal and sexual union? The great, the religious "state" idea, which upon a time Merezhkovsky sought after, already cannot be, the times for suchlike illusions and temptations have already elapsed, but there is possible still another great and religious idea of non-power, of statelessness, of a new theocratic and churchly union, freely of love, subjecting the person only to the will of God also upon the earth, in a denying of all the old, the coercive-state union, in a denying of subjecting the person to the godless mundane will. The positivists, howsoever radical the anarchists they may pretend to be, never, never are they free from the allure of the state, from the temptation of earthly kingdoms, since they passionately want to arrange life upon the earth, they are madly afraid of chaos and yet they know not in the name of what to repudiate the temptation of earthly power.

But how is one to regard the struggle for liberation, which fills modern history, with the proud vindication of the person, with the declaration of its rights? Social liberation has taken its course outside the religious consciousness, has remained unsanctified just the same, as is love, as is sexual life, yet we cannot but admit the subconscious religious sanctity of this great movement, for otherwise we should have to disdain the "earth". People of the new religious consciousness have to admit and hold sacred the struggle for freedom, the elimination of coercive force, oppression and the holding of power, although they can relate with repugnance towards the positivist arrangement of life, towards the cultivation of instincts seeking political power, which is characteristic of all the currents and parties, in setting themself the goal of holding the state. When within the political ideologies the idea of the power of authority, of every power of authority, be it monarchist or populist, or totally of the will of the people, -- when these begin to get replaced by ideas of absolute rights, the eternal values of all the freedoms, the dominance of the supra-human good, standing above the capricious human will, then by this itself is cleared the soil for the idea of an universal theocracy, for mystical the non-power. When the fate of human life is put dependent upon the supra-human good of freedom, then it is entrusted to the will of God, and that they have so desired, it means, the Kingdom of God also upon the earth. This trust has to be discerned, it has to be enlightened by the light of the religious consciousness. There has to be revealed the subconscious awareness of holiness amongst the lovers of freedom, the warriors for the image of God within man and the godlessness in contrast of the hypocritical official servants of religion.

Merezhkovsky has not up til now resolved the problem of the societal approach within its religious setting, has not found his politics, and often he has strayed into an admiration of statecraft, but this question is quite important for whomever dreams about "the heavenly kingdom". How fine it would be, if he were ultimately to speak out upon all these great themes, and went the right path, since there is the desire to accompany him towards a common goal. The name of Merezhkovsky would indeed be reckoned amongst the ranks of the vanguard alert predecessors of the freedom loving societal approach in an union theocratic,[1] which cannot be a state sort of matter, just as it cannot be familial, but providentially connected with non-power.

Historical Christianity, the ascetic, preaching individual salvation by way of forsaking the world, cursing the earth, in essence denies not only the religious, but also all the meaning of the historical process, worldly developement simply falls away from the religious consciousness, and universal culture is reckoned external to religion, or even anti-religious. But the pure, the medieval Christian spiritualism long ago already has died out and at the present time there is practised a sort of compromise, a deal with the earth, evoking horrid an hypocrisy. Religion is as it were occupied with being tolerable, peeks through its fingers at the course of history, is permissive of the growth of culture, but nothing does it sanctify, it fails to enter into the life of the world with transfigurative a power. They are saved outside the Church, the apostates of Christianity are saved,

---

[1] Vl. Solov'ev appears to be the predecessor of Merezhkovsky in quite much.

the God-strugglers and indeed, certainly, Leonardo da Vinci. And yet Goethe or Nietzsche are more fond of the children of God, than are a great numbers of the servants of historical Christianity. "If anyone speak a word against the Son of Man, it shalt be forgiven him; if however anyone speak against the Holy Spirit, it wilt not be forgiven him neither in this age, nor in the future" [Mt. 12: 32]. And the historical process, world culture, the greatest of its heroes are sanctified and saved by these words of Christ, since they have not committed blasphemy against the Holy Spirit. The magic-like circle of the mystical church coincides neither with suchlike an historical church, nor with suchlike the relative settings.

Merezhkovsky and people of the new religious consciousness cannot endure this duplicity, they want to sanctify their religion with meaning significant to world history, they want religiously to sanctify world culture, they desire the Church, which should encompass within it all the plenitude of being, in which be made all the sacramental mysteries of life. But to admit the meaning of world history, means to admit for it a final purpose, means to affirm the ending of world history and to evaluate everything in it in regard to this end, to sanctify everything, as the path to the completion of all. From a purely philosophic point of view, the idea of the end of the world can be justified, although it rationalistically is just as unthinkable, as is the absence of the end within time, as thus an infinite world process, and this is a bad infinity, in the expression of Hegel.[1] The good infinity, eternity, -- is not in the absence of an end within time, but rather in the surmounting of any sort of end, in the abolition of time, of extra-temporality. The idea of an infinite process, which the positivists of the XIX Century so revelled in, is very gloomy, insipid, shallow and contradictory an idea. How grey an anguish takes hold amidst every attempt to bring real this idea in thought and outlook. The endless increase of imperfection and again death, and no sort of dreams of life eternal, full and whole in its perfectness. And indeed the denying of an end is undoubtably a denial of the meaning of world history, a denial of progress, since meaning demands an end-point completion and the world tragedy has to have, just like the first, so also a final act. Psychologically however the idea of an end is so deeply innate to human nature, that it constantly

[1] Kant regarded this as one of the antinomies and did not admit of a rationalistic resolution of the problem of the final end or of the infinity of the world process.

appears in a masked form, gets reborn in the form of an idea from all one *Zukunftsstaat* [future-settings], of a perfect society, a golden age, the natural condition, the term of a "thousand-year reign", and of others in the form of a gloomy collapse, pessimistic non-being, full decay etc. But only mystics consciously and joyfully admit of the idea of the end and but few thinkers find justification for it.

The positivist and socialist would-be saviours of mankind want to transform, to reform the world, all want to better it, and thus so without an end-point, without its radical turnabout. But it is indeed possible to desire a greater, it is possible to desire the transfiguration of the world, the end of the given world, limited as it is, corruptive, mortal, with its replacement by another world, "a new heaven and a new earth". The idea of the end is a theme alluring, and a theme beautiful, in that together with this it is the idea of a beginning, not of death, but of eternal life, and it ought not to extinguish creative work, but rather intensify it. If tomorrow there were to be the end to time and the beginning of being eternal, then on this final day I would make still greater an effort, since for eternity I would want to do moreso, than for temporality. All the theories of progress, those most positivist, have their own naive eschatology, they lead with a fatal inevitability to the setting of the problem of the end, of the completion of the meaning of the history of the world. Especially within Marxism, as a religious system, there glistens this primitive eschatology, the involuntary understanding of the coming socialist society, as the end of history, as the beginning of another, a supra-historical process. And the new religious consciousness, connecting itself with the meaning of world history, inevitably should have to recourse to the Christian book, in which is hidden the mysterious prophecies about the end of the world, about the meaning of the completion of world history, about the final act of the tragedy, the "Revelation of St. John".

The idea of the end has become a basic religious idea of Merezhkovsky, and his conception of Christianity he terms apocalyptic, in contrasting it to historical Christianity. Apocalyptic Christianity signifies a breaking-point in world history, the end of history and the beginning of a process supra-historical. Up to the present the religious light derived from Christ having died on the Cross, from the past, in which was not still revealed the full truth, and the light since ever weakens and weakens, but here blazes forth a new religious light and it derives from the Christ to Come, it begins as it were a reverse movement of time. In apocalyptic

Christianity is revealed the nature of the Holy Spirit, the Comforter, promised by Christ, to encompass that, which was not encompassed by Christian history. There will be a new, an eternal church, the church of St. John, and a new, an eternal religion, the religion of the Holy Trinity, the fullness of the revelation of all the Divine Hypostaseis, in which will be overcome every duality, whilst embracing all the values of world culture. In the church of St. John, in the universal theocracy, from the formational outlook of which begins an apocalyptic process, there would be revealed the truth about "the earth", there would be decided the questions about sexuality, about bread, about the societal approach, all, that was impossible for the human historical process. Very close to such a sort of religious conception was also the great mystic-philosopher Schelling, but in this Merezhkovsky arrived at quite independently of Schelling, less so philosophically, and moreso upon artistically-vital a path.[1]

In such manner, the centre of the religious consciousness is transferred over into the prophetic sphere, and the congealed dogmatism, the historical limitedness is surmounted. But there is the danger, wherein the propheticism should prove dogmatically fettered, that upon it also should lay the seal of historical limitedness. Does Merezhkovsky admit of the freedom of propheticism and a new religious creativity? On the one hand, he calls for this, but on the other hand, it seems not. Howsoever he may tend to emerge beyond the apocalyptic aspect, yet indeed this Divinely-inspired symbolic book [the Apocalypse/Revelation of St John] is subject to varied interpretations and its eternal meaning is revealed only within our inner mystical experience. Merezhkovsky prophesies about the

---

[1] Schelling speaks about a religion of the Holy Trinity, about a new revelation of the Holy Spirit, about a church of St. John [the Evangelist, whose Orthodox churchly appellation is "the Theologian"]. And it is amazing, that the dry and rationalistic Chicherin in his chief work, "Science and Religion", likewise speaks about a new revelation of the Spirit within the future historical process, about a religion of the Trinity, about a church of St. John. In the Middle Ages there was the heresy of the Brethren of the Holy Spirit. The establisher of this heresy, a certain John, taught that the world process passes through three periods, in accord with the Three Persons of the Holy Trinity. The third epoch will be the epoch of the Holy Spirit and its forerunner was considered to be St. Francis of Assisi.

New Jerusalem with great joy and happiness of heart, his apocalyptic Christianity -- is white, yet for many others it -- is black, and the awareness of the end is first of all an awareness of the coming Dread Last Judgement, evoking terror and anguish within the heart.

The prophecy of freedom is revealed within the new mystical experience, within this is a great joy, but also a great torment. A very religious dogmatics ought to develope in growth under the influence of new prophecies and a free inner revelation, and not smother them. This finds a brilliant justification on the example of Merezhkovsky himself, the dogmatics of whom they might readily term heretical. But for Merezhkovsky there threatens the danger of falling into a certain schematism,[1] whereof then may fade the blossomings of the new and supra-historical Christianity. To grant the religious meaning of world history and the inevitability of its end does not mean however having to cram it into stifling schemata, in which gets swallowed up the greatest religious truth, the truth concerning freedom. Sometimes it seems, that for Merezhkovsky the fate of the world is decided entirely by the struggle of the Lamb against the Beast, having emerged from the abyss, the struggle of Christ against the Anti-Christ, while man himself, his creative freedom, here will be all for naught, to no purpose. Then the salvation of the world will have been a process not of God-manhood, but already altogether outside of man, altogether thus as non-tragic, since the tragedy -- consists only in the final, the human religious freedom. Here is this fatalistic schematism, this degeneration of the new propheticism back into the old dogmatism and I fear it most of all. And indeed is it not too early that Merezhkovsky has sensed the closeness of the end, is there not yet too much that still needs to be accomplished, the world having sufficient a freedom for the final act? Merezhkovsky has openly slightly into something new, terribly free, and suddenly again he slams it shut for himself and for others, and there thus disappears the perspective of an eternal religious movement, while he sets off again upon the path of the fancies of a dogmatic morbidity. The formative learning of the church is a process organic, and not mechanically-artificial: the church is not some sort of ramshackle lean-to, which makes holy whatever the place it is put; the church developes in growth from the sacred places of universal culture,

---

[1] With Merezhkovsky generally there is the tendency towards a contrived schematism, in which there are little of individual nuances.

its walls are raised up there, where the Divine is, in its fundamental significance, in art, in love and freedom. But the church invisible ought to be transformed into the visible, when the new religious consciousness is intensified. And every church ought to encompass within it free religious perspectives. So does Merezhkovsky indeed understand the historical embodiment, the realisation within time of the eternal Mystical Church?

When the sole source of religious light which is acknowledged is the historical embodiment of the Divine principle, as given in the past, this is completely other a position, than when the chief source of light is transferred into the future and not yet embodied in any sort of an historical given. And in the first instance our religious freedom is enormous, since religious truth is posited within the setting of an inner religious experience and then only the external empirical givenness with all its chance aspects finds meaning, but in the second instance this freedom is rendered boundless and tragic.

The revealing of the Spirit within the Divine-human process, to which each is called to participate in, is an invisible summoning of human freedom and together with this a principle of the utmost tragedy for mankind. Are not such principles revealing the Spirit already within modern history, in the modern experience, in philosophy, in art, in the liberation of the earth? Merezhkovsky as it were better than others understands that the religion of Christ is a religion of freedom, that in Christ -- everything in a certain sense is permissible, and thus dreadsome, so that he should not betray this understanding. Our religious tragedy is not the old tragedy of conscience, but rather a new tragedy of freedom, not "moral", but rather a religious tragedy of a finalative sundering apart and a finalative freedom of choice. Merezhkovsky followed out the tragedy within the heroes of Dostoevsky and we are very much appreciative of this.

For the bringing to a finish the meaning of world history, for its end there mustneeds be a liberation, the emancipation of the world and a dreadsome intensification of consciousness; the human person has to rise up in all its stature. Then only can there obtain the finalative battle of the two contrary principles of world life. Merezhkovsky has prematurely declared the end of Russian literature; yet there is still necessary literature, and philosophy, and the rebirth of culture, and political liberation, since for the end there mustneeds be an unprecedented freedom and an unprecedented consciousness. The positivists, the socialists and suchlike think, that people will be happier, calmer, more content, better off, when there no longer exist such hindrances to freedom, as famines and disorders. And yet this involves a very deep-rooted falsehood. People will be a thousand times unhappier, when their consciousness does not get distracted by external oppression and disorder, distracted from the most terrible questions of existence. Then their lives will become intolerably tragic and their boundless freedom will thirst for God, will pine for love of God. In this and only in this is the metaphysical and religious significance of the social liberation of mankind. Let freedom triumph along all the lines of life, let the social reforms feed and clothe man, so that there blaze up within him an ultimate awareness of his wanton poverty and servile incapacity, his inability further to live without God, fearing a finality of non-being after a moment of satiety and good order. Many are called to the feast of eternal life, all are called to participation in the realisation of the ends of world history, all are of equal worth before God. In this is the truth of democratism. But few are the chosen, not all freely have love for God, wherefore the realisation of the meaning of world history is perhaps the deed of not many. In this is the truth of aristocratism. The religious aristocratism, to which Merezhkovsky is inclined, is fully reconcilable with social democratism and ought to have nothing in common with the historical nobility.

And here we come nigh to a very dreadsome question and one that is very important. The history of world culture has led the consciousness of man to two very immense ideas -- the ideas of the God-Man and that of the man-god. The idea of the man-god tormented Dostoevsky and this torment found expression in the prophetic image of Kirillov. Nietzsche went mad over the man-god, and many positivists become delirious with delight over the man-god, although his image is diminished in their impoverished fancies. With the idea of the man-god, taken in its opposition to the idea of the God-Man, Merezhkovsky connects this directly with the idea of the Anti-Christ, as predicted in the Apocalypse. But in everything, that Merezhkovsky has written upon this theme, there is a sort of a fatal lack of clearness, a lack of clarity nigh close for us, our general lack of clarity. And is this not bound up closely with our tragedy of freedom? In his book, "L. Tolstoy and Dostoevsky", Merezhkovsky evidently tends to the view, that "the God-man and the Man-god -- are one and the same", just as one and the same -- are the two religious abysses, above and below, heaven and earth, spirit and flesh. Indeed, the new religious consciousness gravitates towards this, so as to admit finally than man-godism, God-struggling, demonism -- is a divine principle the same, as is the opposite abyss, to admit it only as a seeming evil; the devil however, the noumenal evil, it discerns to be in mediocrity, superficiality, triteness, in the spirit of non-being. He says" "as yet there has not been the awareness *to the very end* of the mystery of the finalative uniting: *I and the Father -- are one*, -- regarding the filial Hypostasis, the "I" would it not seem "demonic" in regard to the Hypostatis of the Father, to the "not-I", and on the contrary, of the Father -- in relation to the Son". Does Merezhkovsky now also intend to restate these mysterious and profound words? And further on still: "Perfect love, love to the end, to the extent of God and likewise a perfect freedom -- is not two, but rather one, and thus consequently, it is impossible to contrast in opposition a love without freedom, and a freedom without love... But in this is the "whole secret" of the Devil, that he does not desire for it to be taken to the very end; he does not desire, that the two should be one, and desires instead, that the two should always be two, and for this he himself makes pretense to be one of the two, now with the Father against the Son, then with the Son against the Father, not being either the one or the other, but rather a negation towards both; there is thus feigned a pretense to be one of the two polarities, equally in opposition to the other, wherein as both polarities are forever already comprised within the two-oneness of the Divine Persons, of the Father and of the Son; and the Spirit of the eternal Middle is only a negation of this mystical polarity, only a "mimicking", which with a mimicry of the two-oneness of the Divine Hypostaseis, distorts both Persons, jumbles and confuses them". "Another devil in general there is not, ...this is the genuine, singular Satan and.. and in it is to be posited the ultimate essence of the noumenal "evil". Merezhkovsky makes an attempt to avoid the temptings of demonism, in having posited Satan, in having understood the devil, as a total baseness and lackeyism. In his noteworthy article, "The Fate of Gogol", he further developes this point of view and in the images of Khlestakov and Chichikov he sees the noumenal devil, and it is towards the average, the state and trite, that for him the spirit of evil, the spirit of non-being, tends thus to be. But where then is the Anti-Christ, terrifying yet tempting him? The question concerning the origin and significance of evil in the world is a most difficult, indeed frightful and fatal question, for the future of every religion, with two possible recourses, the monistic or the dualistic. Either the devil is a wanton creature, having sown mischief between God and the world in the name of non-being, since he is unable to affirm any sort of being, and then within him there is no sort of abyss, but merely a middle-ground mediocrity, and hence in demonism is nothing tempting. Or the devil -- is a primordial, pre-world, uncreated principle, and then we approach the dualistic teaching about two eternal realms, facing us with a choice. Sometimes it would tend to seem, that the frightening words about a "fiery Gehenna" as it were confirm this tempting dualistic teaching.[1] Merezhkovsky has not yet resolved this problem. Freedom is a divine gift, but for a justification of the meaning of freedom, evil is necessary. Oh, certainly, in the mediocre average, in superficiality, the philistine triteness, the positivistic non-being -- there is the Devil, certainly, and in the great God-strugglers, in a profound demonism, is an honouring of the Holy Spirit rather than of the diabolical, but is there here not still some sort of a mystery?

The proud idea about the man-god and everything, that lies concealed behind it, for a devil-Khlestakov, for a devil-Smerdyakov, as mere mediocrity and triteness, is nowise settled. The affirmation of the person in its absolute significance is a matter divine, and not godless. Merezhkovsky senses this and says: "Kirillov takes to its end the chief religious thought of Nietzsche -- and here the kingdom of the "supra-man", foretold by Zarathustra, proves to be an "here and now eternal life", i.e. "the Jerusalem to Come", the realm of Resurrected Flesh, foretold within the Apocalypse: "*We shall hold dominion upon the earth*". One of the two equal triangle-corners is given a reverse position -- and both coincide. Thus, at their two extreme points, in the first -- in the idea concerning a beginning, about a divine necessity and in the last -- in the idea about the end of the world, about a divine purposiveness, the seemingly anti-Christian teaching of Kirillov and Nietzsche coincide with the teaching of Christ: and if two points intersect with two direct lines, then the lines themself ought to conjoin: this -- is an axiom of geometry". These words are very important for the characteristics of the new religious consciousness.

There is a superficial man-godism, leading along the path towards non-being, the positivists preach it, and this is when a man with a lackeyist

---

[1] I do not hold with the dualistic resolution and I point only to the enormous difficulty of this problem, which surrounds Merezhkovsky. The diabolical element is not only in staleness and triteness, but quite the more in malice and self-love.

smugness posits himself in place of God, has respect for nothing, and when everything supra-human is denied. "Man" for Gor'ky is suchlike. Here there is not a polarity of abyss, but rather a median mediocrity. But God has love for such noble God-strugglers as Aeschylos' Prometheus. As the Byronic Cain, as Nietzsche, Ivan Karamazov and Kirillov. Here there does exist the abyss, but perchance -- one of the Persons of God Himself.

Duality, two-polarly opposite abysses, about which Merezhkovsky speaks, -- this is not God and the devil, not a good and evil principle, but two equally-sacred, equally-divine principles, reconciled in trinity. Outside of Trinity, as encompassing the immeasurable plenitude, there remains the spirit of non-being, of the median mediocrity and triteness. The teaching about the Trinitarian aspect of the Divinity -- is one of the most profound religio-metaphysical teachings, which also the greatest philosophers have defended. To Schelling and Hegel the dogma of the Holy Trinity has not seemed confused and absurd, as it has to the superficial rationalists, but rather with this aspect of the Trinity they [Schelling and Hegel] have connected their systems. I note here only the following: in the egress from the Twofoldness by way of Triadity, in the teaching about the Trinity there is a Divine dialectic, admissible only amidst an admitting also of the teaching concerning the Logos, only amidst the metaphysics of the Divine Logos, since the category of enumeration (1,2,3) is a category of reason and is applicable only towards the Existent -- the Logos, and the dialectics of division and reconciliation (thesis, antithesis, synthesis) likewise is reconcilable only for an utmost of reason nature -- the Logos. Merezhkovsky is insufficiently conscious of this,[1] since he proceeds not by way of philosophy, but the quite more philosophical Vl. Solov'ev well understood this. In any case, great is the merit of Merezhkovsky, in having addressed an incomprehensibly-slumbering aspect within history, an awareness of the Three Persons of the Trinity, about the Spirit, and having connected this with our religious dissonance. And its religion is not historical Christianity and not Christianity, since this wording was formed only but from one of the Hypostaseis, and the religion -- of the Trinity, up til now is still not revealed. They tend to say: the Symbol/Creed of the Christian faith begins with a confessing of the dogma of the Trinity! But more amazing than this, is that the Trinitarian aspect has not been

[1] Merezhkovsky says nothing about the Logos.

encompassed by the Christian religion, has not been understood, has been forgotten.

There is a sort of mystery, which Merezhkovsky has not had the wherewithal to express, though tormentingly he attempts to do this. Does he not recourse upon the inexpressible, graspable only within the activity, in the mystery itself? Often I tend to think, that the whole of human creativity, all the human efforts are explicable by an anguishing over something, which is not. There is only one sort of secret needful for man to know and then all will be his, he will be terribly rich and joyful, then will cease all his efforts, and it will be unnecessary for him to create in philosophy, literature, art, politics -- all surrogates, substitutes for true life. Why then is there philosophy, the love for wisdom, if there is wisdom itself, when then is there music, poetry, sculpture, when there is the existent being itself -- of music, poetry, sculpture? In my writings I express only my own yearning as regards true, total, eternal, free and joyful existent being and the immeasurable desire to know its secret -- a singular secret. All that we write concerning this, which is not and for which we so thirst, such that in music we create sounds of an higher harmony, which we possess not, and in images of artistic beauty, which is not. The torment of all genuine creativity is a torment religious and is born whereof we have not the key to the mystery of being, from amidst the anguished searching for the key. We go the path of an universal culture, but when the solely important secret will be unriddled, then will begin an end to everything finite, a beginning -- to the eternal. Merezhkovsky as it were comes nigh to the riddle of whatever the secret, walks around it, but does he already know it or only know about it? Our wishes are quite similar to his, we want to unriddle this selfsame secret and therefore our path ought to be our own.

Revolution and Culture

(1905 - 123)[1]

More than once already there has been demonstrated the twofold character of the advent of revolutionary democracy in the world: it bears with it an undoubtable truth of social justice, but certain of its aspects -- are just as undoubtable an untruth involving negation and hostility towards values that are noble. Herein lies a tragic contradiction, which is just as insurmountable empirically, as is the conflict between the person and society, between freedom and necessity. The waves of the revolutionary movement in Western Europe smashed up against the craggy cliffs of a great culture, they purged it and were themself purged, having come up against great cultural traditions, with noble memorials. Books, in which was esteemed the spirit of eternity, had entered into the flesh and blood of the European peoples, beautiful temples, with which was connected the feel of a thousand year duration, had stood as it were sturdily resilient upon a soil trans-temporal. And the revolutions transformed within themself a great culture, transported it into their own future the precious and the eternal, which had been created in the past. European social democracy in its spirit had wanted as though to diminish cultural values, in its hostility towards everything too lofty, but it had to be cultural under a fear of spiritual death, had to stand guard over its Alexandrian library, whilst regarding it as superfluous and harmful. And the outward cultural aura all more and more defeats the vandalism of its inner indifference towards the creativity of culture.

In the Russian revolution much however is unique. This is a great revolution in terms of the power of evil and the untruths, which it was called forth by history to abolish and it has been filled with lofty meaning and worldwide significance. But with the Russian revolution in certain of its aspects it can seem the most uncultural of all the revolutions in the world, in it readily combine great truth and yet also effects of untruth and vileness. And this must be spoken about openly, sincerely and truthfully,

---

[1] REVOLIUTSIYA I KULTURA. Article first published in the St. Peterburg weekly "Polarnaya zvezda", № 2, 1905, p. 146-155.

since there cannot be and ought not to be any such temporalising tactics, as would justify the sacrificing away anything inherent to its values. The manifestations of the Russian revolution will prove uncultural and on certain of its sides vile, because that in the woeful past of Russia there was so little of culture and of anything noble. And it is not the official rotting Russia that can cast this reproach upon the revolution, for the government lacks the ability to speak let alone have any idea upon such things. With us was there not only an absence of that great culture, which adorned old Europe, but there was also no sort of cultural atmosphere, no sort of cultural traditions. Within the historical past of Russia there are of course to be met individual creators, there was Peter the Great, there was a great literature, there were the Decembrists, and also the intelligentsia, bold, original, scaling the very heights of European thought, but all these noble values -- are but flashes, extinguished in an ocean of barbarity and wildness. A truly universal culture beyond the national aspect we still have not; an universal culture would take a real effort, and even a luminous hundred with refined impulses towards cultural creativity and with a thirst for freedom, greater than that in the West, would dwell still in the midst of dark millions. And yet up til the present the Russian people remains a sphinx, the riddle of which is not as easy to solve, as would seem to our Social Democrats. It is not by the German, the half-obsolete books that this riddle is to be solved.

And perhaps there is playing out a terrible historical tragedy. The shackles of autocracy, the shackles of an unexampled within history oppression, having been lethal for life, creativity and culture, are being snatched off from the much-suffering body of Russia, and Russian culture is being set free, but of culture itself there still is not. With open wounds the body of the sufferer but barely breathes. Individual flashes flare up and it is necessary to safeguard them from the tumultuous ocean, dark and sterile. The nihilistic aspect within the Russian revolution is an offspring of the nihilism of our historical past, the nihilism of the Russian autocracy, and the unculturalness of the radicalism -- is a reflection of the unculturalness of the conservatism, of the vandalism by the old official Russia. In the revolutionary Jacobinism always indeed is recognised the mirrored spirit of a political autocracy and despotism. A revolution too often is infected by that very spirit, against which it fights: one despotism begets another despotism, one police state -- yet another, the vandalism of reaction begets the vandalism of revolution. This is but an old aspect of history.

And we -- seers and poets,
Guardians of mystery and faith,
Bear blazing lights
In the catacombs, in the wilderness, in the caves.[1]

Will the Russian revolution open up a broad and free path for a great and universal Russian culture, or will all the noble values remain only to be borne about "in the catacombs, in the wilderness, in the caves"? All these thoughts come to mind, when one reads within "Novaya Zhizn" ("New Life") the pronouncements of Maksim Gor'ky concerning "Philistinism". The judgements of M. Gor'ky are very flabby, politically boorish and simply mindless, foremost of all mindless, but they have a symptomatic significance. Gor'ky himself is interesting. In the immense all indeed individuality of Gor'ky there is personified everything, which is anti-cultural within the Russian revolution. Here already is to be sensed not only a righteous uprising against social injustice, but also an unrighteous malice against culture, against everything noble and eternally of value, and here the churlish feelings become intertwined into the social revolt. I cannot but term this article of Gor'ky otherwise, than as hooliganism in the most genuine and deep meaning of this word. This is not some Tolstoyan rejection of culture, while yet so fruitful for it, in demanding a revaluation of values, this instead -- is a display of an extensive churlishness, an insult to the eternal in aesthetics and the eternal in ethics.

Gor'ky came onto the literary scene with his refreshing words and in his first tales he was potent, original and talented. The world needed a telling about the vagabond tramps and their revolt. This new view into vagabondism acted with a dazzling effect upon contemporary society and had successes in the most bourgeois of levels, evidently in the contrast, of being tied down by nothing. Everyone acknowledged, that the tramps of Gor'ky -- represented a power insurrectional and revolutionary, some with rapture, while others with censure. The fame of Gor'ky all grew and grew, and he wrote all worse and worse: his novels were weaker than his first

---

[1] *redactor's note*: citation from 1905 verse of V. Ya. Briusov [1873-1924] entitled, "Грядущие гунны" ("The Coming Huns").

tales, the dramas weaker than the novels, and his articles already downright poor. In his gymnasium-school sort of exercise entitled "Man", the acclaimed writer expounded upon his symbol of faith, and even his worshippers were struck by the squalidness of this thing. Reading the article of Gor'ky on "Philistinism" one senses the pressing need to raise frequently the question, of what sort is the spirit of Gor'ky, that conveys into the world this vagabondism, not knowing kinship and furthermore, in the name of what is this display of revolt.

Now moreso than before, there is growing a cult of bombastic words, and what indeed a lackeyism there is involving such words as "proletariat", "the people", "revolution", "uprising" etc. And to quite pathological an extent is reached the demand to get down on one's belly before the idolised and all suchlike upon the earth. They are not accustomed to freedom, they cannot live without authority, without toadyism. Is the Gorkyite vagabondism indeed revolutionary, are there not here indeed contiguous points between revolutionary hooliganism and reactionary hooliganism, is this not indeed essentially the black violence of outrage, of abhorrence for the freedom of the person? Indeed the vagabonds -- of the Gorkyite type too often now prove to be the selfsame sort hooligans of the Black Hundreds type, and their revolt spews forth in the form of the most reactionary types of beastliness. Oh, certainly, Gor'ky has nothing consciously in common with the Black Hundreds, he does not recognise their heroes and he disdains their black deeds, but this is something also instructive. There is an hooliganism, hostile to culture, to ideas and eternal values, which can spew forth the same in a revolutionary, just like also in a reactionary form, and it is this spirit that Gor'ky would engraft onto the liberation movement. In the most recent article of his, "As Regards", the letters received by him, Gor'ky attempts to justify all the violence and cruelty, wrought by man, and he puts the canary higher than man, and admits a greater inherent worth for it. "Man" comprises a delimited idea for Gor'ky, his utmost dream and love, and in the name of this sort of man is allowable everything inhuman, every sort of viciousness both spiritual and physical, every manner of outrage against cultural values, against things great, against noble names and ideas. The religion of the human, only of the human, spurning values absolute and eternal, always leads to this, that man is looked upon only as a means [to be used/abused]. The absolute value of the human person can be acknowledged only by a religion of supra-human values. Godlessness grants more to the canary, than to man.

What does Gor'ky say in his articles concerning philistinism? It involves those, who hide themself away "in the dark corners of mysticism, in nicely pretty discourses on aesthetics... woefully and hopelessly they wander about the labyrinths of metaphysics and anew they return in knots, besmirched by the rubbish of the age-old lie of the footpaths of religion". "The philistine loves to philosophise, just like an idler -- goes off to fish, he loves to chat and to write abit about the fundamental problems of being, -- a concern, clearly nowise connected to the people"... The philistine -- is an "individualist, which is as true, as that there is no billy-goat without the smell of it". The philistine -- is L. Tolstoy and Dostoevsky. The philistine -- is the Russian intelligentsia. Philistinism -- is religion, philosophy, aesthetics, and yes in essence even science, philistinism -- is humanism, philistinism -- is the command "to love one's neighbour, as oneself", and philistinism -- is everything individual and free, everything cultural and refined. What then is not philistinism, what then is there that can be set in contrast to it? The cult of power, the worship of the working people, as a fact, as a victorious element, with malice against individual creativity, the denial of cultural values, and a view of the human person to serve but as a means and tool.

"The philistine loves to have comfortable a setting in his quarters and in his soul. When everything in his soul has been resolved, properly -- the soul of the philistine then is calm". This is well said, but is Gor'ky already so sacredly convinced, that he does not love this "comfortable setting"? Who indeed is it that so thirsts to arrange "a comfortable setting in his quarters and his soul", who is it that wants to rationalise the whole of life, to kill the inner agitation of spirit, the search for the meaning of life, who is it that smugly denies the eternal tragic aspect, guarding against any ultimate "comfort"? Certainly already not the mystics, nor the metaphysicians and aestheticians, nor Tolstoy and Dostoevsky, not the impassioned intelligentsia and not the idealistic liberals, but rather the positivists, the social democrats, the proponents of a rationalistic religion of human arrangements. Revolutionism of the hooligan type, so dear to the uncultured and crude soul of Gor'ky -- this indeed is very superficial, purely but an external rebelliousness; he allows for every outward manifestation of force, of every manner of boorishness towards human thought and life, every denial of the inalienable rights of the human person, and all this in the name of an ultimate tranquility upon the earth, in the name of "a comfortable setting in their quarters" for future generations, for whom are to be offered up in sacrifice the generations of the present. True indeed, with Gor'ky and his beloved Social Democrat positivists there is more of the "comfortable setting in soul", than with Dostoevsky, than with us, who nowise believe in the possibility of an ultimate rationalisation of life, the conquering by external means of the irrational tragedy of the world, to forcibly compel human society towards all that indeed "comfortable setting".

And there mustneeds be restored the true significance to words. Philistines are those, who by their spiritual poverty set matters temporal higher than the eternal, while absolute values they betray for the well-ordered and comfortable kingdom of this world, and they bear malice against a noble and great culture, against geniuses and creators, against religion, philosophy and aesthetics, against the absolute rights of the person and its restlessness, hindering them from ultimately being set into orderly an arrangement. Philistines are those, who construct a Babylonian tower, in which there remains not a place for religious life, such as always mirrors the antinomic and mysteried aspects of being. In the world there are sacred things and only philistinism -- in its impudence would put its hand over them. This incipient philistinism, hostile to everything truly noble, individual, creative and inwardly restless, ought to be amputated off from the cleansing truth of a democratic revolution, and we ought to raise our voices against it in the name of freedom and of values beyond those merely human.

How unaesthetic and unreligious the grovelling before the proletariat is, only because that it is the proletariat, that with it comes power, as decided by the workers, who themself are in need of light and awareness. The people, however, unenlightened by ideas, unillumined by the light of consciousness, can be rendered into the Black Hundreds sort, thousands, millions, and despicable is this idolatry, this thirst to possess a new sort domination. And who is it that brings the awareness to the working masses, with great exertion and self-denial? That selfsame intelligentsia, which Gor'ky maligns. The merits of the Russian intelligentsia regarding the liberation movement have been immeasurably great, since it was the bearer of the creativity of person and ideas of awareness. It is shameful to forget this in the lackey's fervour on whatever, such as obtains at the given moment. The Marxists are in denial over this since the rational theory, badly read out of German books by them, renders them in the grip of an irrational passion, but Gor'ky is no Marxist at his core, he is even for such insufficiently cultured, with him there are no sort of theories, and in him rather there is a contra-cultural element -- hooliganism. Sterile and desolate would be that revolution, which would look upon the cultural past only as upon a *tabula rasa* and set in opposition to eternal values merely a new arrangement for feeding. Upon this desolate soil cannot appear any sort of flora or fauna, cannot blossom any sort of flowers, since they grow only from eternity. The spirit of non-being is to be sensed within the articles of Gor'ky, in his incipient philistinism. "Man", in the name of which is aborted everything of value, everything eternally essential, the rejecting of world culture because of the aristocratism of its origin, -- is but an emptiness and non-being. Man -- is of the plenitude of being -- is the vessel of Divine values.

And it takes an enormous courage and requires an enormous energy to get it gathered, in order to contend against the cultural and political hooliganism, against the incipient philistinism, expressed already in Western Europe with its diminished values, against this churlishness towards man in the name of "man", this mockery of freedom in the name of "freedom". And in this regard we ought to be consistently incorrigible: absolute principles ought to be set higher than any tactics, that rely on fighting by insinuation and slander. It is terrible to see in the great, as regards its mission, Russian revolution the reflection of the hideous face of the old and police-autocratic Russia, with its violence and vileness towards free thought and conscience, amidst contempt for cultural values. And all this "Novaya Zhizn'" newspaper, and Gor'ky himself, and the project of a policing organisation for literature, suggested by the verymost modern inquisitor type Mr Lenin, and the toadyism towards the new power for former dreamers, and the cravenness of thought, the fearing of thought within the radical element, the fanatical intolerance -- all this is an indicator of the dearth of ideas and spiritual deadening, as with the extent reached by the autocracy of hapless Russia. The great revolution has to happen, in order to overcome the reactionary spirit, and there is no turning back. Ultimately there will be overcome this onerous nightmare of the past, and the chains of every sort of coercion be shaken off, even though it derive from Mr Lenin. To free the creativity of culture is possible only upon that path, which admits of freedom and the rights of man as absolute values, and upon which man with the noble content of his spirit cannot be rendered into a simple means. For this, there has to be not a new sort coercive violence, not hypnotic words and the elemental passions of the moment, but rather the might of eternal ideas and a new consciousness. Regarding all the lackeyism, I remember the words of one of the most consequential of Russian democrats -- N. K. Mikhailovsky: "On my table stands a bust of Belinsky, which to me is very dear, and here a bookcase with books, at which I have spent many a night. If Russian life were to burst into my room with all its wonted peculiarities and smash the bust of Belinsky and burn my books, I would not yield to the people and sit idly by: I would fight back, if understandably my hands were not tied down. And even if furthermore I were overshadowed by the spirit of the greatest meekness and self-abnegation, I would still all the same say, by and by: forgive them, O God of truth and justice, they know not, what they do! Indeed I all the same, it means, would protest. And I myself might happen to smash the bust of Belinsky and burn the books, if somehow an extremity of thought obtained, that it was needful to smash and burn them, but in the meantime they are dear to me, and not for anyone would I surrender them. And not only would I not surrender them, but with all my soul I consider that what is dear for me should become dear for others also, irregardless, whether it serve their wonted particularities". The elements of revolution need to be under control, be subject to ideas, to separate apart within it the right hand from the left hand by the criteria threaded to truth and beauty, and not cravenly cave in. There is need to safeguard the revolution against the black forces of reaction, rending its inner essence, in order that the truth of the revolution should prevail in its purpose.

Towards an History and Psychology of Russian Marxism

(1906 - #126)[1]

It is interesting for us to trace the fate of the idea of Russian Marxism, a fate woeful and strange, since these ideas with their seeming triumph ultimately have gotten lost. Our Marxism not so long ago was a trend in ideas, full of vigour and youth, it gave an upsurge to mental inquiries, it prompted a respect for knowledge, summoned forth a social science for deciding the fate of Russia, and seemingly introduced a certain cultural aspect into the barbaric norm of our intelligentsia, it fought against the old stereotypes, all the being stuck in a rut. Back then it was a struggle of ideas. But the god of historical irony transformed Marxism into a struggle of powers, gave it a grip on life, when the ideas of Marxism began to decay and fade, when the two souls, alive within classical Marxism -- the scientifico-realist and the religio-utopian -- separated and rose up in revolt each against the other. In the separating off of scientific realism from the religious utopianism there must be seen the essence of the crisis of Marxism, with its inner decay, and Russian social democracy, as a mighty struggle of powers, attempts to preserve within it the two souls, an inner peace, completely bereft of the idea of Marxism, and forgetful of its cultural conquests.

In the year 1899 K. Kautsky wrote me: "The Russians are called to further develope the theoretical Marxism. Thanks to the absolutism, the Russians have time for this. In Russia the social movement is still all a struggle for cognition, and not for power.[2] These were welcome words for

---

[1] K ISTORII I PSIKHOLOGII RUSSKOGO MARKSIZMA. First published in the weekly S. Peterburg socio-political culturo-philosophic journal, "Polyarnaya zvezda", P. Struve editor, 1906, № 10, p. 678-686.

[2] The correspondence with Kautsky transpired as regards my articles, published in the "Neue Zeit". [*trans. note*: article was entitled "F. A. LANGE UND DIE KRITISCHE PHILOSOPHIE in ihren

us, being then Russian Marxists, and they received unique a commentary in the furthermost developement of Russian thought and the societal aspect. In Russia attempts were made at the utmost theoretical developement of Marxism, and without boasting it can be said, that the Russian critical Marxists displayed great strength of thought and greater an audacity, than the German Bernsteinists [vide Eduard Bernstein, 1850-1932], but the result obtained for Kautsky's expectations and for Marxism was ruinous. It showed, that there could not be a furthermost theoretical developement of Marxism, that every effort of free thought leads to a decisive crisis and dissolution of doctrine. Critical Marxism was soon transformed into a totally already non-Marxism and even into an anti-Marxism as regards an insurmountable inner logic and psychology.

The furthermost searchings and creative attempts went along two distinct paths -- the scientific and realistic, and the religious and idealistic, since the system of classical Marxism was simultaneously both a system scientific and a system religious, was both a real politics and an eschatological vision.

Thus it was in the realm of ideas, but in life there was produced a grievous struggle with that selfsame absolutism which, according to the paradoxical opinion of Kautsky, gave us time to develope further the ideas of Marxism. The intelligentsia began a struggle for power with the ideational capital of the old Marxist apperception. And within social democracy in fatal a manner there ceased all mental life, any sort of critique. The sacredness of dogma was safeguarded, since with it easily and sweetly one could struggle for power, since with it the realism of life as it were could be blended with religion, and in the irrational mystique of revolution it is not easy to distinguish the real evil of the day from the eschatological expectations. The social democratic ideas began to reign, they took hold in the hearts of the masses, although obscured by the trappings of the widescale revolution happening in Russia. Social democracy became as it were the expresser of the Russian [1905] revolution, and the tragedy of the position here is in this, that from its realistic point of view however, what is happening in Russia is not a socialistic revolution, but rather a political liberation of the people, in which the working class plays a visible, but subordinate role.

Beziehungen zum Sozialismus", Neue Zeit, Stuttgart, 1899-1900, № 32-34; Klepinina № 104a].

And here the realistic and scientific ideas of Marxism are consigned to oblivion, and there instead triumphs only the mystique of "the class point of view" and social revolutionism. In former times the Marxists heatedly and brusquely came out against populism and the old revolutionary utopianism, they pointed out the truth, that in Russia is developing and would further develope a capitalistic production, that there is no overleaping and skipping the "bourgeois" order, that the most immediate of political tasks can only be a "bourgeois" revolution, guaranteeing rights and freedom for the ultimate struggle. In contrast to the populists and the old "insurgents" the Marxists were constitutionalists and social evolutionists. The basic scientific-realist idea of Marxism was the principle of the developement of the "material forces of production", this was the basis of all social developement and all social arrangement, and from hence was deduced the class struggle and class perspective. For scientific Marxism absurd and utopian would be the thought, that amidst whatever the condition of the productive forces of a land still an 8 hour working day is possible, that the social power of the working class can grow in nonconformity with the economic position of a land, rather merely as the result of the political efforts of the social democrats. The realist spirit of Marxism -- is in the idea of productivity, an incessant victory over nature, and thereof thus is to be deduced a distributive justice. But in Russian Marxism imperceptibly there has occurred a populist-utopian revival, the realist ideas got choked out under the onrush of revolutionary emotions. There appeared the inclination to overleap and skip the "capitalist" order with its social-political forms, to disdain political freedom, as a good merely "bourgeois", and imperceptibly to substitute in place of a revolution "bourgeois" a revolution "social", to which at present they consider it possible to enter upon. The subjective class psychology won out over the objective idea of social evolution. In the "bourgeois" revolution exclusive dominance would have to belong to the socialistic proletariat, and the "bourgeoise", to which is consigned everything not social democratic, then ought not to play any sort of role -- here is the paradoxical deduction from this "class psychology". Only Plekhanov, the most intelligent and cultured of the Russian social democrats, did not ultimately lose his Marxist head and he appealed to the Marxist conscience. All the victory-telling arguments of Marxism against "insurrectionism", against the old revolutionism, against the ignorance of governing the material culture, were forgotten. There remained only the eschatology of Marxism, the faith in a nigh-impending kingdom of truth upon earth, in the proletarian-socialistic righteous judgement, a faith, sundered off from its material basis within social developement. Who however is the culprit of the mental decadence of Russian social democracy, the forgetting of Marxist ideas within the struggle of revolutionary forces? This culprit is obvious -- the autocracy and its fanaticism, defining the character of the Russian revolution. The reactionary outrages by the government systematically have cultivated the idea of a social revolution and have fed that psychology, in which passions political pass over into passions religious, and politicians are transformed into fanatics. Amidst such tension, amidst such obfuscation it is impossible to have a grip upon human souls without requital. The idea of a social revolution is included within the system of Marxism. But within the Russian actuality it has ultimately become distorted, and the social democrats blindly hold dear this distraction.

In that history is full of every sort of "revolution", this -- is a fact, and it would be absurd to speak about the possibility or impossibility of suchlike a fact. The textbooks of history tell of these "revolutions", and suchlike a sort of "revolution" tends to happen even before our very eyes. This -- is the traditional understanding of the word revolution, nowise containing within it any sort of sociological worldview, nor presupposing any sort of theory of social developement.

Altogether different is the matter of a social revolution within the understanding of Marxism. The social revolution, which the social democrats await, rests upon a definite sociological theory of social developement and outside of this theory it possesses no sort of meaning. This Marxist social revolution is not a fact, such as can be wished for or not wished, assumed or not assumed, this -- is a false theory, an optical illusion. A "social revolution" there never was and never will be, although every revolution has its social side. The system of Marxism is to the highest degree a fanciful and uncritical intertwining of the sociological understanding of the word revolution together with a police mentality understanding, and this is rooted down into the basic twofold aspect of Marxism. This was evident in the well-known dispute of Bernstein and Kautsky. And P. B. Struve well wrote about this in the "Braun Archive". But in the social democrat consciousness this problem has remained obscured.

It is not difficult to define the outward signs of revolution in the traditional sense of this word, and they are purely negative. When the prisons get filled up, when there are demonstrations on the streets, when one part of the populace is battling against soldiers and the other part, when there happen various excited occurrences, prompting government repression, then ordinarily they tend to say, that there is a revolutionary movement in the land. What is revolution, and what is not revolution, is set by the state's police, as the gauge for determining revolutionism.

And it has become an indubitable historical truth, that revolutions are created by reaction, and independent of reaction they possess no sort of content, as such, i.e. as revolutions. Revolutions are characterised not by a radical end, not by a profound regeneration of societal existence and the nature of man, but rather by a passion of reaction against the evil of the past, against oppression, against reaction. The content of revolution therefore is very difficult to characterise in creative definitions, of forward orientation. The revolutionary, as a psychological type, is always oriented backwards, has only his negative attachment rooted in the past, from which his consciousness cannot tear itself away, has only the sense of the oppression, stirred up in him by forces of the past, the old, and they render him a revolutionary.

In its essence, the psychology of revolutionism is negative, oriented backwards, without upsurge, its paths fed by the hypnotic grip of the evil in the past, and any creative taking of wing is impeded by whatever the beloved hatred towards the past.

The revolutionary indeed cannot live without the reactionary, without oppression, without prisons and police, his life is not enriched, but the rather impoverished by the vanishing of these detested phantoms, deprived of its pathos. In this -- is the limitedness and conditional aspect of that, what we term revolution, in this -- is the moderateness and insufficient radicalness of all revolutionism. Turn the glance forwards, to be freed from the nightmare, and the pathos of revolution vanishes. It becomes evident, that the oppression by the gendarmes and police has painted into the revolutionaries a definite hue of colour, that the red colour was merely the mirroring of the blue uniforms, that the revolutionary nature was created by coercive rule. Revolutionism never glances down into the depths of things, it always remains at the surface, it is always conditional, relative and "in reaction",[1] in it there are embodied no sort of radical affirmations. The psychology of revolutionism, always crippling for the human person and darkening its awareness, the awareness of *the radical, the finalitive ends of life,* is an historical tragedy, begotten in fatal manner of the historical power of gloom and oppression. And the revolutionism is inescapable in the world, while there is repression, reaction, treachery, while the state's police, created by every earthly power, brandishes its imprint upon life. A similar-like revolutionism plays no small role in the psychology of Marxism, wrought in the revolutionary atmosphere of the year 1848 and sustained by the political reaction in Germany, a land all still of the police, run by a bureaucracy, from which always one can expect plottings against society and the people. But what is however such a "social revolution", a revolution in the sociological, and not police meaning of the word, a revolution, which the social democrats reckon as their specialty?

"Social revolution" is the Marxist understanding of social evolution. Marxism most of all has insisted upon the evolutionary character of the social process, for Marxism every societal turnabout can only be the product of socio-economic evolution, where every shift in the distribution of goods is dependent upon their production, upon a constructing social process. The one half of Marxism, the scientific-real, is a denial of social revolution, the denial of a social turnabout, since it sees the essence of the social process in an incessant affirmation, in a social enrichment, in economic creativity. That which are called political revolutions, can be thought of in negative terms, can abolish the autocracy, can topple the monarchy, can change the form of governance and even remove every power, but the fate of the socio-economic developement is wholly dependent upon the positive, upon productivity, and here by negation alone nothing is to be attained except impoverishment, i.e. a social regression. Marxism calls for an increase of productivity and enrichment, for a victory over nature by economic accomplishment. Marxism makes pretense to the organising of human sustenance, to resolving the problem of daily bread, and it would seem not its affair to disorganise the economy, to deny the indigent under the trappings of a social revolution. The epochs and types of the economic developement of mankind get measured by enormous spans of time, and here there are no sorts of abrupt breakthroughs.

---

[1] In the psychological sense.

It is scientifically established, that the transition from a natural economy to a capitalistic one is a process multi-centuried, not completed even at present, and the socialisation of production, from which perchance can be expected a better organisation of sustenance and a greater distributive justice, in a scientific-realistic sense is conceivable only as multi-centuried, a complex and manifold process, indistinct within the enigmatic mystery of the future. And for a realistic science, of which the Marxists are so fond of, there is permissible only an evolutionary and reformatory socialism, by which construct a social crash can be averted. But the social democratic faith in a social revolution is an anti-scientific and even anti-Marxist utopia, it is a religious thirsting and eschatological hoping. With the social turnabout for the social democrats there is connected a faith in the onset of a kingdom of God upon earth, with as it were the end of history amidst a struggle of contraries, as it were the principle of some supra-historical process.

In Germany the faith in a social Zusammenbruch [crash] underlies the reactionary politics of the government and the reactionary outlook of the bourgeois classes. Social democracy indeed -- is the sole liberal party in Germany, and it happens to wage the struggle for freedom and rights, for which all liberals ought to be struggling. In this tense, oppressive political atmosphere grow the intimations of possible political revolutions, and with them in fated manner gets blended in an enormous social cataclysm. There could occur still ten revolutions, but with this ultimate social revolution, which the believers await, these other revolutions will have nothing in common with it. And still to a greater degree this can be said for Russia. With us the hopes for a social revolution are fed by a reactionary regime, an unbridled despotism, by a constant awaiting of a clash with those holding power, of that feverish atmosphere, by that vexation, which is created by searches, arrests, banishments, executions, by the inexcusable economic oppression of the people. The course of Russian history, characterised by the progressive aspirations of society and by the stubborn reactionism of the authorities, has raised us in a spirit of extremes. For us everything seems, that it is either sink or swim, either all or nothing, either autocracy and an utmost degree of economic oppression, or a republic and socialism.

In the elements of revolution the whole historical perspective gets lost sight of. The taste for rights, for the benefits of freedom, has not been worked out with us. The accustomedness to oppression was so great, that the foundation, the social creativity tended to get left out of the building plan, and it seemed sufficient but to abolish the exploiters, in order to become rich and in order for social justice to obtain. They thought to attain rather moreso, than what there is in Western Europe, and everything because that we had so little, we were so miserable and downcast, so that out of gloom and terror the dreams blazed up. Here is why the dreamy side of Marxism won out among us, and its realistic ideas were forgotten.

The chief service of Russian social democracy has been primarily the cultural-enlightening. This was in the developing of awareness in the working masses, enlightening them, with the implanting of socio-evolutionary ideas. Marxism has been quite insistent upon this, that the fundamental regeneration of the societal fabric is dependent upon the developing of the productive powers of the land and of the awareness of the masses. But then the brutal tactics of Pleve [alt. (von) Plehve, Vyacheslav Konstantinovich, 1846-1904] and the Jacobinism of the bureaucracy inspired in our intelligentsia a Jacobin mindset of societal change. The enlightening of awareness was substituted for by agitation alone, which never indeed gets down to the depth of things.

Against the idea of social revolution can be advanced two sorts of objections, with various ends. First of all, social revolution is contradictory to the evolutionary understanding of social developement, is contradictory to the very nature of the economic process.

This is a purely scientific, realist argument, which is included also within Marxism itself. But social revolution is contradictory also to the idea of a constructive societal creativity. Faith in creative freedom, in the constructive efforts of people, is incompatible with an elemental sort of constructing a new societal aspect by way of externalistic and fatal catastrophes, by way of the accretal of evil, somehow passing over into its opposite; this faith desires to regenerate society by a changing of the consciousness of people, it wants incessantly to renew the societal fabric and by this as such to render unnecessary a fatal cataclysm. Within indeed Marxism also there is a large anti-Jacobin part, there is the teaching about change of consciousness of societal classes, as the sole path towards freedom. It should not be a bother for us now to remember both truths: either the realist thought concerning societal evolution, in which it is impossible to simply overleap entire periods and impossible also to transform social poverty into social wealth, or the idealistic thought concerning the changing of the consciousness of people, concerning the regeneration of society by efforts of the free spirit. I am somewhat apart from the ideas of Marxism, but a certain dose of Marxism I would consider useful to prescribe for our social movement. All this they will grasp, when the socio-economic problems are consciously posited in all their alacrity, forcing back onto a second-level plane the problems political, and this will quickly happen, since it is needful for us to eat.

But by my critique of "social revolution" I have not the intent of saying, that not in any instance and not in any sense is it impossible. A totally non-constructive, a purely destructive "social revolution" is possible, to it people can be led, but this would happen already on a religio-mystical, and not socio-positivist, plane. I know only, that a new societal aspect is never created by a social revolution, but the mystical side of social democracy inclines it towards a social revolution, and herein begins a chiliasm, opposite that of the Christian, an illusory dream about a thousand-year kingdom upon earth, but already not of Christ, but with another god. Against this are possible neither any scientific, nor political arguments, this is of an altogether different plane, and to converse here necessitates different a language.

We desire a neutral social developement, a neutral social medium,[1] the feeding of mankind and leading it out of a beastly condition, but not the rendering of social passions and illusory dreams into a religion, since only with a neutral human medium can we be in agreement with our own religion.

---

[1] With the concept of a neutral social medium is connected for me an entire socio-religious system. Against purely an human medium, and human powers, the transition from a natural and beastly condition, I contrast with the shewing-forth of supra-human religious principles. Within social democracy there are elements human, with which I am in sympathy, but there is also the framework of a supra-human religion, with which I cannot sympathise.

The Russian Gironde

(1906 - 125)[1]

The (C-D) Constitutional Democratic Party, evidently, is fated to play the role of the Girondists within the Russian revolution.[2] The French Girondists were very fine people, very intelligent people, and it would have been good, had they prevailed in guiding the fate of the French Great Revolution. Then France would have avoided the Jacobin terror and the military dictatorship, the constant back and forth of revolutionary violence with reactionary violence, and a true freedom would have reigned in it. But a true freedom up to the present in France there is not. The Girondists were swept away by elements of the revolution, their characters and all their worldviews were reckoned upon completely different a plane of developement, which history had not the wish to choose. The history of France got caught up into a sort of magic circle, from which through the present it has been unable to escape from. Already for more than a century the devil has been playing a bad joke upon freedom-loving France, making a mockery of the noble sentiments of the Girondists and of the well-heeled people like them.

I am afraid, that the same fate awaits also our Constitutional Democrats, i.e. the finest, the most idealistically disposed amongst them. The Russian revolution stubbornly resists going the path sketched out by

---

[1] RUSSKAYA ZHIRONDA. Article first published in St Peterburg daily, "Nasha zhizn'", № 362, 1906.

[2] The brilliant and comforting victory of the People's Freedom Party [official name of the Cadet or C-D Party] at the elections and its enormous role in the Duma has not dissuaded me from my views on this party. At the elections won not the C-D Party, but rather the liberation idea, and the enmity towards the reactionary governance, which is admitted even by the C-D's themself. Yet the opportunism with idea and politicisation of the party at the Duma and its lamentable "electoral appeal" demonstrate it as non-organic, lacking in idea and of non-populist a character. The party in better a sense -- is a liberation bloc, an "Union of Liberation".

them, it has overstepped already the fateful line, beyond which the plan, inspired by the Constitutional Democrats, has no strength.

The liberation of Russia could go suchlike a path or it could go a different path. If it were to go by this their different path, the Russian Girondist Constitutional Democrats would have decided the fate of the Russian revolution, leading the land out of crisis, and everything would be fine. But the revolution has gone by the same, not their different path, and this of course is very sad, but it is connected with the construct of quite different a plan for the salvation of our native land.

I -- am not a proponent of historical fatalism and I believe in the creative freedom of man, but it is impossible to deny the inner logic obtaining in a revolutionary epoch, a logic of madness, and it is especially impossible to deny the fatal psychology of such epochs. Indeed, "intelligent" and rational revolutions there have never been. I share in much the same a critique of revolution, to which with such self-restraint P. B. Struve holds to, but I do not see his antidotes of saving things from the hell of revolution; he is insufficiently equipped spiritually for the struggle with the elements, he is too rationalistic.

P. B. Struve -- is the most outstanding man of the Constitutional Democratic Party. His is perhaps the sole creative political mind within Russia. His moral courage is worthy of astonishment and of great respect. But the position of this man is very dramatic and constant. Struve wants the restoration of an idealistic liberalism in its supra-historical purity and absolute value. Theoretically, this is completely just: the principles of liberalism contain nothing of the bourgeois as such and they can only be posited upon the basis of socialism, the realisation of freedom and not trampling underfoot the person. But on the practical level idealistic liberalism can scarcely ignite in our hearts a sacred fire: it needs something greater. The pathos of the "Declaration of Rights" is artfully a stimulating inspiration, but its like sort is not there in the Russian revolution. I say this, although I think, that the "Declaration of Rights" is very sacred in the final reckoning of the religious side of the revolution.

The practical political task for Struve consists however in the forming of an "all the people" democratic party, in which would be united all the elements of a national renewal of the Russian people, in which all the new, the free, the people's Russia would rise up against the old, the autocratic-bureaucratic dominating Russia. This is a broad political plan, truly democratic and in the best sense of the word national. Struve is first of all a democrat, even his notorious "opportunism" rests upon various moral-democratic principles, the inadmissibility to perpetuate violence against society and the people, the inadmissibility of use of coercive force into the abstract ideals of the mass of the intelligentsia. They fail shabbily to understand this. Struve fosters the idea of a great "all the people" politics, with a broad historical scope and therefore he relates with hostility and annoyance towards the small circle coteries, towards the intelligentsia tendencies, towards the factional discords, towards the small-time politics, nowise of the people nor of history. In Struve is lodged the potential of a sort of great idea, standing infinitely higher than our intelligentsia sort word-hagglings, than all the radical words and bookish political theories. Struve is not a pedant, nor someone in a rut, he is not afraid of the grip that words hold, he is a free man in politics, and he sees true politics in constant a creativity, and not in some mechanical squeezing of all the wealth of life into prepared schemae and stereotypes. And for this let him be praised.

It is time already to be done with these old, weather-beaten, as though laid out in a market bazaar selection, of criteria of the radical and the moderate, of left and right. They are wont to say: "Struve -- now with the extreme right C-D Party, how shameful for a former Marxist!" But we have gotten free from the grip of rote memorised words, from the ready stereotypes, we attempt to deal radically with the new questions.

Struve is neither right nor left. He wants essentially, i.e. at root, *radically* to reconsider political matters, he wants to construct his politics upon more principled foundations, than glancing round at his right and left neighbours. He can be mistaken, he can make tactical blunders, but his radicalism is completely beyond doubt. He is the only one not banal, not unprincipled, not with merely a rote memory understanding of the word radicalism: this is a radical, who looks at the root of things, who best is conscious of the ends of the societal aspect and most harmonises these ends with the means of struggle. Struve criticises certain aspects of the revolution, since he sees in them a non-correlation between ends (freedom) and means (by violence). And least of all can the word radicalism be applied to those segments of our intelligentsia, who have but a poor understanding of the ends and hence get them confused with completely non-corresponding means. A true radicalism never is combined with mindlessness stuck in a rut, just as true revolutionism cannot find its sanction in the criteria of the gendarme-police. Struve more profoundly than the Social Democrats detests the autocracy and despotism and his "moderateness" can be defined by the strength of this loathing.

I have attempted to restore a sense of justice and to do right by P. B. Struve, the leader and ideologue of the C-D Party. But can the C-D Party be such a great, "all the people" party? Will Struve accomplish within it his potential for the people's politics; is there in it that historical breadth, is it capable of regenerating the nation? It grieves me, but I am compelled to answer in the negative. The C-D Party wants to be a party of the people, but the C-D's do not go to the people and do not make an approach to it, and therefore in its present condition it will not become a democratic party. The beautiful political dreams of Struve tend to crumble into dust under the stress of the irrational in Russian life. In what specifically is this failing? The programme of the C-D Party is very radical and fully democratic, and this is almost a Social Democratic programme at the minimum. Not in the programme is the defect. The tactics of the party are still not worked out, the party has still done little, but the absence of force in these tactics and the inclination towards cultural forms of struggle will not have situated the party to render itself democratic and of the people. I think, that this defect is psychological and deep-rooted.

The composition of the C-D Party and its spirit are such, that the members of this party, beyond the rarest exceptions, cannot get close to the heart of the people and have no wish to do so. One need not be a proponent of economic materialism, in order to see all the "bourgeoisness" of the C-D psychology. This -- is a trait of people, having a taste for peaceful parliamentary activity, but not capable for the creative work of national rebirth, by being bereft of fascination, of enthusiasm, of wide historical scope. Among the enormous majority of C-D's there is no perception of an "all the people's" politics, of which Struve dreams, their democratism is purely theoretical and not always sincere, their psychological premises are such, that they cannot speak in gatherings of the people amongst the peasants and workers, so as to attract the hearts of the masses of the people. Their words would be dry and lifeless, as to whether their programme be democratic, and they would be unconvincing, in lacking the expressive glance, and resounding voice, nor is their appearance suchlike. With the C-D's there is no belief, which they could offer to the people, no worldview, igniting the masses, there is no one who would want to suffer and die for this party, and it will not be of the people, it will disintegrate, and part of it will form a party openly bourgeois.

Yes, the position of P. B. Struve is very tragic. He finds himself suffocating in the atmosphere of the prejudices and stagnant beliefs of our "radical" intelligentsia, he cannot bear its narrowness, its constrainedness, he sees its alienation from the people, from the heart of Russia, its incapacity for large scale "all the people's" politics, and he goes... to the liberal lands and professors, which have not the prejudices of a traditional radicalism, though they have a fair amount of prejudices academic or of gentry-rule, likewise indeed little attractive, and likewise bereft of pathos, whilst suffering a political drabness. The absence of lunacy with almost all the C-D's is not an indication, that a great sense of reason is alive within it. In the C-D Party there is no sort of an organic aspect, of closeness to the soil, of roots in the people, and the unity of its democratic programme remains but of word. Evidently, an "all the people's" great politics needs to do otherwise, ought not to tie in with social groups, which would drag it down, as with heavy weights.

Struve is neither some "rightist", nor "bourgeois", undermining democracy, -- he is in much an utopian, despite his enormous political sense of reason. Struve -- is an idealist and tends to say: "I ought, and consequently, I must". This is fine, but only then will he fulfill his imperative, to accomplish his enormous historical task, when he finds a true antidote to the poison, vexing the soul of our intelligentsia, and poisoning the very wellsprings of the people's life. This poison I see first of all in the cultivation of politics, as an "abstract principle",[1] in the igniting of political passions as such, in admitting the path of politics and statecraft as the solely saving and most important thing, and in the severing off of politics from the integral life of the spirit. A great "all the people's" politics is possible only in this instance, if it be not only politics, not only salvation by "abstract" a political path, but instead be connected by mysterious threads with the full spiritual life of the people, with the religious centre of its life. But Struve himself and the C-D's are infected with this poison and they shove Russia further along the path of a soulless political struggle. And upon this path will blaze forth party passions to the extinguishing of religious and cultural life, on the example of Western Europe.

Struve is too caught up in the art of politics.

---

[1] A term of Vl. Solov'ev.

Social Democracy in contrast offers a religious pathos, which ignites the heart of the masses of the people, and attracts the youth. For the Social Democrats politics itself is a religion, a religious activity. What can the Constitutional Democrats oppose this with? With them there are no sort of ideas,[1] besides that indubitable, but bob-tailed idea, that the constitution, guaranteeing rights and freedom, is better than an autocratic-bureaucratic regime. Both the youth, and the working masses do not go in for the Const. Democrats, since they provide for them no spiritual nourishment, and desires and concerns to provide material nourishment they regard with suspicion.

Struve quite overstates the constructive role of Social Democracy within the Russian revolution, ascribing to it, that it makes for a revolutionary element of life, but he underestimates the real significance of the religious pathos of Social Democracy, against which he insufficiently opposes the empty and formal principles of liberalism, since no one is attracted to them. Russia has been consigned already by the caprice of fate into the grip of extremes, such as bear the black and the red colours, and here unneeded are pallid theories, moderate and unstirring, but rather new, and fiery ideas.

Suchlike ideas can only be ideas religious, no less radical, than those of the Social Democrats or the Black Hundredists. Until Struve comes to realise this, all the potentials lodged within him will come to but little. He is indeed the sceptic, and therefore he does not know the secret of gripping hearts, a secret, which the people of the red and the black colours know all too well.

Our Girondists are called forth by history to the rule of power, but they are afraid of power and are incapable of exerting it. The devils of reaction and revolution have got it all so tangled, have taken it so far, that every power of authority reeks with blood, and this stench is something that the idealistic professors and lands cannot stand. With the Constitutional Democrats there are two souls -- the one of statecraft, gravitating towards a rule of authority and the arranging of order, while the other soul -- is pervaded by intelligentsia morals, loathing all rule of power and all establishing of order, ever oppositional. Struve wants to reconcile

---

[1] I speak not about individual representatives, but rather about the party as a whole. Each regards it his duty to forget his own idea, in entering into the party.

the rule of power and freedom, the state and the person, and in the concrete terms of the given moment -- the monarchy and the people. He calls for a just rule of power and believes in it. Yet I fear, that a state order in Russia will be installed by an unjust rule of power, and the seal of the curse, hanging over statecraft, will not be removed from it.

Creative societal work is possible, and upon a path external to the state, and the creating of a new societal order is not a synonym for a new rule of power. Proudhon, unjustly forgotten, and cultured anarchists perchance, are closer to the truth, than the fashionable Marx and the liberals hostile towards him in statecraft. A people's party, close in much to the ideas of Struve, needs to be created, but it ought not to be a matter of classes, nor of politicising, it ought instead to be chiefly oriented towards the peasants and the workers, and on principle to stand against all forms of exploitation and rental profits together with a rejection of all forms of state oppression. The pathos of the "Declaration of Rights", about which Struve is so anxious for, can be revived within the people's movement, if the Social Democrat poison gets killed off by the religious antidote. But the Russian Gironde in its present outlook will not save Russia, since something greater and more important has to transpire for this salvation.

On the Paths of Politics

(1906 - 127)[1]

In his "Lectures on Godmanhood", Vl. Solov'ev began with the words: "I shall speak about the truths of positive religion -- about subjects very remote and foreign to the contemporary consciousness, to the interests of contemporary civilisation. The interests of contemporary civilisation are those, which were not yesterday and will not be tomorrow. Presumably one would prefer those, which are equally important at all times. However, I shall not happen to polemicise against those, who at the present time relate negatively towards the religious principle, I shall not happen to dispute with the modern antagonists of religion, -- because they are right. I say, that those rejecting religion at the present time are right, since the contemporary condition of religion itself evokes negation, since the religion in actuality is manifest otherwise, than what it ought to be. Religion, speaking in general and abstractly, is the connection of man and the world with an unconditional principle and the focal point of everything existing. It is evident, that if there be admitted the actuality of such an unconditional principle, then by it ought to be defined all the interests, all the content of human life and consciousness, upon it ought to depend and to it relate everything existing, in what man does, knows and produces. If one allow for the unconditional focal point, then all the points of the circle of life should have to be united with it by equal radiants. Only then will appear unity, wholeness and harmony in the life and consciousness of man, only then will all his deeds and sufferings in the great and the small aspects of life be transferred from aimless and meaningless appearances into reasoned, inwardly necessary events. It is quite without doubt, that such an all-encompassing, central significance should belong to the religious principle, and if in general it be admitted, and just the same it is without doubt, that in actuality for modern civilised mankind, even for those in its midst, who acknowledge the religious principle, that religion does not have this all-encompassing and central significance. Instead of

---

[1] O PUTYAKH POLITIKI. Article first published in St Peterburg weekly journal "Svoboda i kul'tura", 1906, № 2, p.106-121.

this, that it should be all in all, it is hidden away in a very small and a very remote corner of our inner world, it appears as but one of a multitude of various interests, dividing our attention".

These words are very interesting and important for us, the few, having raised the question about the relationship between religion and politics, and having been roused by their perplexing and misunderstood dream concerning a religious societal aspect. Soon, we would hope, there will ensue already a time, when this problem, "very remote and foreign to the contemporary consciousness, to the interests of contemporary civilisation", will be rendered quite great and important. They are aware, certainly, that "this, what is equally important at all times", is closer and more akin to the essence of humankind, than is that, what there "was not yesterday and will not be tomorrow". Then will be heard words, connecting "politics" and everything enormous, happening in Russia, with eternity, and then regarding its fate values will be established.

Still not so long ago there prevailed almost entirely the modern "intelligentsia" barbarians, the "positivist" savages, denying all religion and religiosity, rising up against religion with an almost religious fanaticism. But here along comes a new sort of people, more cultured, more refined. This transitory generation frees itself of the nihilistic manners and allows for religion amongst the number of other experiencings, and decides on it as a component part of culture. But religion for them remains penned up away into "a very small and very remote corner of our inward world, it appears as but one of a multitude of various interests, dividing our attention". They forbid the religious experiencings to emerge into the God-given light, they recommend rather to hide them away, hold them secret within oneself, lest they be embodied into something, to shun having a collective religious sense, a matter seen as though akin to sorcery and superstition, and rather instead thus to arrange the world and the conjoint life of people upon other, non-religious, positivist principles. I fear, that such an abstract, quite sterile and bloodless, and for it optional religiosity is what the editorship of the journal "Polarnaya zvezda" ("Polar Star") has come out for, insofar as one might judge concerning on this as regards the articles of P. B. Struve and S. L. Frank. This is terrible -- to reach such an abstract formalism, to which Struve has taken it, when he says, that -- "to be inwardly tolerant relates even to the religiosity of church",[1] though

---

[1] "Polarnaya zvezda", № 13, p. 130.

in the churchliness he tends to see falsehood and evil. Not only in the religious, but also in the cultural regard, that point of view proves itself sterile and uncreative, for which Voltaire is just as fine, as is the Catholic Church, and... it becomes a matter where all cats are grey. Voltaire is fine, fine also is the Catholic Church, aesthetically we delight in objects very contradictory, but a creator ought to be otherwise, than an empty form, to be endowed with qualitative content. If everyone thought and felt, as do Struve and Frank, they would have written a formal declaration of rights, and then there would not be either a Voltaire, or a Catholic Church, and no sort of embodiments and creative products, since formally Catholicism created the church, and Enlightenment rationalism created Voltaire. It is necessary to make the transition from abstract formalism, from "idealism" and "illusionism" to a realism in religion, to an organic fullness, to a content of future culture.

It is terrible and repulsive -- this fragmentation and ruination of the modern soul, this loss of individuality. Man in the fullness of his being has vanished, has melted away, disintegrated, and only pieces, bits, torn away and abstracted from the entirety of existence live a sort of independent, and essentially, phantasmic life. And the thirst for reunification, a return to the fullness and totality of existence, to the all-unity -- is religious a thirst, slaked within a vital mysticism. Vl. Solov'ev perceived this in his profound critique of "abstract principles", though he too sometimes fell into an assertion of "abstract principles", e.g. in morals and somewhat in statecraft.

That what we are speaking about, concerning the connection of politics with religion, concerning an eternal meaning within the temporal and the transitory, therefore *only tends to seem* sundered off from "life", whereas in life itself everything *actually has* gone to ruination, with one thing sundered off from the other. Whosoever actually lives by an "abstract" political life, reckoning politics as the only true basis of being, and sees in the political path his salvation, hence identifies this his "life" with a self-sufficing politics, while everything else remaining, all the infinite manifold of life -- is not admitted essentially "as life", gets termed an "abstraction", though it itself most of all be guilty of "abstraction". And thus the scholar sees true "life" in his science and often regards it as the solely-saving thing, be it Don Juan -- in his amourous adventures, or the artist -- in his art. The abstract, self-sufficing politics tends to reign in the contemporary world, just also as does an abstract and solely-saving morals, though they enslave us, employing the fragmentation of life and the ruination of soul. And all our essential being tends to rise up in revolt against the faith in this solely-saving politics, against the assertion of political passions and the political will to power, sundered off from the religious centre of life, and against the governmental arranging of the earth of bliss in it, as comprising a final measure and utmost value.

Political paths tend to be iniquitous, and it is impossible for a politics, torn away from the meaning of life, impossible to humanise it, impossible to kill in it the savage primordial and the savage yet to come. We cannot and we ought not to reconcile ourself with the sundered off aspect of modern politics from ultimate ideas, from religious passions, in contrast with that opportunism, which wants to arrange life independent of its meaning, both today and tomorrow distracted from the eternal. The fruits of these political paths, of this irreligiosity are already known, the human individuality is already being swallowed up upon these paths, the spirit being quenched and mankind led towards the abyss of desolation.

All the difficulty and abstractness of our position in an evaluation of the Russian revolution and in all the modern sort revolutions and in all our thirsting for a reunification of politics with religion is rooted in this, that we cannot look upon the historical process, as a process of the dying away of evil and the creativity of good, simply as an improvement, in which everything, to which we say "no", -- is in the past, and to which we say "yes", is in the future. For us the future is twofold, in it will come not only unprecedented good, but also unprecedented evil, within it there have to be separated apart for a final battle the opposing principles of world life. There is an evil not only primal and original, against which is conducted a liberation war, but also an evil ultimate, final, over which there is no outright winning, but merely a showing of progress. In this -- is the tragedy of world history and the impossibility of its purely human resolution. It is impossible thus to perfect and arrange this world by only the human, the rational paths, in order to have disappear in it the world evil (not the moral, but rather the religio-metaphysical evil), in order that it be forever strengthened, reformed to the point of perfection.

In revolution there conjoins a great truth, the sacred liberation of mankind from the primordial enslaving evil, in conjunction with two untruths: the untruth of the past and godless statecraft, with an autocracy, criminally denying the unconditional significance of the human person, and an untruth of the future, with a religion of an earthly ordering of mankind outside of God and against God, an all in-common depersonalisation, a new godless statecraft, already engendered within the positivist social democracy. The mystical sense of revolution consists in this, that within it two beasts have met face to face and at some mysterious point tend to coincide: the primordial beast, having imprinted its inhuman and godless nature upon coercive states, upon the monsters -- the Leviathans, upon earthly rulers, upon all the criminal transgressions, committed by the powerful and those holding authority, and the final end beast, engendered within the ideals of the human anthill, of an ultimate ordering, of a compulsory bliss and happiness, in exchange for which eternity and freedom are surrendered, into a religion of non-being, as proclaimed by positivism.

Against both these two images of the beast the eternal truth of revolution ought equally to struggle. By suchlike a truth is first of all manifest a proclaiming of freedoms, a revolt against every transforming of the person into an object, the declaration of the rights of man, which historically also has religious an origin, born within the religious societies of England. Here is the religious root of politics, which is there also in the Constitutional Democratic Party and other liberation parties, but there is not yet still a religious politics, not that integral unification, about which we dream. The human person possesses absolute a value, as a vessel, containing the infinitude Divine, and cannot be subordinated to such fictitious, godless and inhuman values, as the state, nationality, the utilitarian societal aspect, set in opposition to it as utmost, for such rather only possible is God and unity in God.

Russian statecraft, from which we now by bloody efforts are being torn away from, has to be surmounted, lest ultimately there be a perishing, and it has represented a most extreme, most monstrous, and within history an as yet unprecedented assertion of the "abstract" political principle. The autocracy has scoffingly conjoined itself with Orthodoxy, has received for appearances sake a religious sanctioning, and al our conservatives, now manifest as Black Hundredists and hooligans, have confessed their faith in the formula "Autocracy, Orthodoxy, Nationality", but we meet here with a most glaring example of the religious making a god of the state, its deification, the admitting of the state as the highest value. This absolute Caesarism is not of Christian an origin, it historically was inherited from pagan Rome through Byzantium, from primieval pagan Rus', and is religiously incompatible with the kingdom of Christ. Caesar is given the worship, proper to God, in which the state overshadows church, in a politics, godless and inhuman, and amidst this they have enslaved man, wrought in the image and likeness of God. Herein consists the fiction of statecraft and the nationalness bound up with it, severed off from the religious centre of existence, in an abstraction from all the human and divine values, it leads to an autonomous existence of the Leviathan-Beast, an existence illusory, deadening for true life. Only God can be set higher than man, only to Divine values can there be subordinated values human, and the state, nationality, lifestyle peculiarities, the old ways, which our conservatism worships, which it is endeared of moreso than it is by God and man, leads to a genuine cult of satanism. The Black Hundreds and our black governance has conducted already throughout all Russia its black mass.

The Russian violence-prone state is an organised criminality, an organised trampling upon laws Divine and human, and the dreadful beastly snout, which the present day reaction has unleashed, bespeaks clearly, what sort of religion is hid underneathe the autocracy, in having entered upon an historical pact with Orthodoxy. It would seem, that a religious man, loving God and affirming Christ as at the centre of everything, would have to say: to blazes with the nation, and the state, and all the set mode of life, all the illusory earthly values, if they be gotten at the price of trampling down the laws of God, if godless transgressions have to be committed in their name. But those confessing a religion of abstract statecraft have most of all been in love with the ordering of things upon the earth, the handling of its existence. The religion of statecraft, to which Russian conservatism has conjoined itself, always looks upon the human person, as merely a means, as a tool for the "higher" purposes of the state, the national, the lifestyle etc illusory sort of values. There seem no suchlike human sacrifices, before which the state as a religion would halt, where everything is permissible for the abstract politics of conservatism, where there are no limits to the outrages against man, committed in the name of Leviathan. The uniting of autocracy with Orthodoxy, of the state with the church, has not spiritualised nor made holy the state, on the contrary, it has deadened the sanctity of the church, has wreaked havoc with its soul. And the state has remained godless, shameless and beastly, serving neither God nor man, but rather instead a third aspect, as the source of evil in the world.

It is striking, that the selfsame godless and impersonal, the violence prone state principle, the selfsame false and "abstract" politics appears also at the opposite pole. The untruth of revolution -- consists in its viewing of every actual human generation as merely a means for future generations, and viewing the human person, as a means for the good of human society, for its new statecraft. Both reaction and revolution initially chop off politics away from the eternal values, they make it godless, and then they subordinate all values to politics, they transform politics into a false god. And thereof shows forth the snout of the selfsame beast. Both reaction and revolution alike discount all the content of life in accord with criteria political, in accord with usefulness for the ends of the state, be it the old or the new, and admit of nothing having value in itself. It is not right to ignite "abstract" political passions, be they Black Hundredist or Red Hundredist, since this is the path of beastly savagery, and not properly human. There is nothing beautiful in faces, distorted by political malice, and red faces, burning with human indignation. It is not right to admit of politics as the centre of life, where there is nothing to spiritualise the political flesh, and where all the wealth of existence becomes subordinated to it. It is not right, the path of political parties, severed off from the centre of life, from its meaning. It is not right, this thirst for political rule and domination, the intoxication with contemporary societal powers. To reduce politics, as such, to the extreme minimum, to the extirpation of politics, to its dissolution into culture and religion -- here is what ought to be our regulator, herein is our wish, herein the true liberation. *Liberation is a liberation from politics*. It is impossible to kill the beast of politics, the evil of the old statecraft, by way of "abstract" politics alone, by a new statecraft. It is necessary to oppose the statecraft, the violence, the rule of power, the "abstract" politics, with a different principle outside the state, a different non-coercive societal aspect, not a new political coercion, but rather of freedom along other paths. It is needful, not by another beast to tame and destroy the beast, but rather by an utmost might, casting down and transforming everything beastly. A profound and eternal truth was bespoken by L. Tolstoy concerning the state, concerning the beast of politics, concerning the godless recourse to violence. In this we shall have to learn from L. Tolstoy, and to acknowledge him moreso a Christian, than Dostoevsky, Vl. Solov'ev and the latest aspects of Merezhkovsky (who only most recently had stood the true path). But foreign and remote to us is the religious rationalism of L. Tolstoy and his attitude towards culture. The new religious societal views of Tolstoyanism cannot serve as a basis for building, cannot lead towards it, since the Tolstoyan truth is merely a matter of critique denying the creativity of religious mysticism. Of European thinkers, the relative but insufficiently noted truth is that of Proudhon, in his however idealistic anarchism, in his path to a societal edifice outside the state. We are not for a new sort "non-resistance to evil" and we do not deny the struggle, but rather for a different opposition, for different paths of struggle.

We admit, that there is the existence of a neutral human social medium, in which transpires a process of humanising, an emergence from the condition natural and savage, with an elementary liberation from primordial evil. This process can be endowed with a primal-principle sanctity and not include within itself as yet a trans-human principle on the religio-positive or religio-negative side. Thus, for example, in liberalism and socialism there is an human rightness, an elementary humanisation, an elementary liberation from beastly savage enslavement. The human image is revealed, the human person is raised up for the resolution of the meaning of history. But the liberal truth and the socialistic truth begotten of it is primarily negative and quite elemental. The purely liberal and the purely socialistic societal paths deal with an undoubtable evil, the evil of coercion and the exploitation of man, but they involve in them in the future not only good, but also a new evil. From the neutral human medium there ought to grow out, to polarly unfold from it the contrary religious principles, already trans-human, from which one can only say "yes" to. For example, in the positivist Social Democratic religion, from neutral human a medium (a rightful socialism, not regarding itself a religion) there is engendered a sort of trans-human principle, yet in its religious attitude it is for us hostile and contrary, in effect representing the kingdom of the prince of this world, of the Grand Inquisitor, of a new godless statecraft, that of the realm of philistinism.

The entire productive and economic process of mankind ought primarily to be relegated to a neutral human medium, it liberates man from the primal grip of nature, organises his food, creates the soil, upon which grows forth culture with its very contrary results. But this neutral social medium easily can be rendered a weapon of the devil, can transform human good into instead a trans-human evil. The eight-hour working day is an undoubtable human good in comparison with a 12 hour working day and it ought to be striven for, but from this human benefit can grow out flowers both white and black. We approve and support every liberation movement, the political and the economic, whilst humanly neutral, but we have to counteract its transition onto a trans-human path contrary for us, and a politics "abstract", torn off away from the religious centre of being, all too readily gets transformed from an indisputable human good into instead a trans-human lie. We approve of a neutral socialism, one that is not transformed into a religion, so as to defeat exploitation and arrange for food, but it has to be reunited with religious truth, in order to oppose the encroachment of a socialistic pseudo-religion. Unless we relate to a neutral social medium, with what things there be religiously-neutral, the humanly fine activities will not occur, and we now however ought to enter upon a new religious and not "abstract" a path. There ought to be formed not a religious political "party", which is something inwardly contradictory, but rather a religious societal movement, a religious culture.[1]

Every liberal, democratic, freedom-loving politician strives to resolve the opposition between the state and society, to relegate the state into society. A rightful state, they tend to say, is a state comprising the societal, the people, it is itself society, and not a power, situated external to society and oppressing it. We can and we ought to approve of the humanising process of the dissolution, the melding away of the state into society, but the godless and inhuman elements of statecraft, with the resorting to violence, power, the impersonal element, will not be defeated whether it be by a legislative state, neither by a socialistic state, nor even by an anarchistic state, nor by any sort of impersonal principle. I use the term "anarchistic state", because the anarchist-positivists, the materialists will never surmount the state, never exit the realm of violent force, never construct a free societal aspect, will never situate the person at the centre. The godless resorting to violence, the satanic love of power, the disregard of person is something we have to foresee also in the liberal and the socialistic state, and not only in autocracy. If in the past the state had some sort of good mission (requiring limitation), then this mission long ago has ceased, and the state no longer already serves as a culture, the times have ensued, when great state sort ideas cannot still prevail, and ideas external to and beyond the state have to govern and inspire. We do not believe in the rationalistic utopias of Tolstoy or of the anarchist-positivists, because

[1] With Merezhkovsky up to the present have been absent neutral concepts, that of an humanly rightful social medium, and therefore he has too abruptly divided everything into the kingdom of Christ and the kingdom of the Anti-Christ.

we do not think, that statecraft could now at present be abolished, since the recourse to violence and force are not now already banished from the world.[1] The savage propensity of recoursing to violence and force will continue to live on and appear in new forms. But there has to be chosen a path, upon which there is paralysed the element of statecraft, with its recourse to violence, savagery, the disregard for person, and upon which instead is formed an other and bright, a free power, there has to be found an antidote against the temptations of state positivism. And we can approve only of a "politics" that is culturo-anarchistic in its tendencies, anarchistic not in the sense of an affirmation of violence, but rather in the sense of the rejection of all recourse to violence, not an anarchy of chaos and worldly disintegration, but rather an anarchy comprised of free harmony and Divine unification. We are unable to participate in the realisation of the power of rule, since we do not admit of any sort of state power of rule as rightful, and since we do not believe in that actualised state condition, which would need to be sustained by force and upheld by law, since the person cannot be forgotten. To the old political and state passions there ought to be opposed not new indeed political and state passions, but rather new religio-societal and religio-cultural ideas. And upon this basis can be worked out a special sort of tactics, which can put forth for itself a series of stages, of steps, along which will proceed the new societal aspect outside the state, in an union of freedom and love. A societal aspect of freedom and love, not of the state and not of recourse to violence, this societal aspect of persons can only religiously be conceived of and religiously constructed, but in the rejection of the old forms of state oppression and economic exploitation we can join with the liberals and the socialists, can work with them, can stand upon the selfsame steps, whilst never melding in with whatever the "abstract" politics. In "politics" we have to be supportive of decentralisation and federation tendencies, all what weakens the power of the rule of authority, supportive of what renders the state into a rural zemstvo economy, into a self-administering community, everything what gives the balance of rights to the person over the state, all the societal formations outside the state.

---

[1] The necessity of the state is bound up with the depravity of mankind, and the liberation from it -- with the innate at-root regeneration of mankind.

It is incorrect to think, that only the striving for the rule of power, for state administration, is a creative political activity. Our "anarchism" is not disorganisation and destruction. By an evolutionary and reform path there can be constructed a societal aspect not of the state and non-coercive of the person, and there can die away in the hearts of people the love for power and the cult of the state. The most important matter -- is to deaden the state-loving, power-loving political passions and to fire up the hearts of people with a different love. "Abstract" politics never penetrates down to these roots, it remains always at the surface and will create only a phantasmic state existence. "Abstract" politics signifies per se a great rift between the individual and the universal, between the intimate and the collective, and attempts forever to consolidate this tormentive opposition.

Individualism says: the individual is the utmost value, but it ought not to possess any sort of relationship to the world, to history, to the societal aspect; whereas politics, in dealing with the individual, has to be abstracted away from what is most important and dear for each being. This individualism allows for religion, as an intimate experience of the individuum, but does not permit the transfer of this intimate experience over into the universum, to be embodied in history, to transform the societal aspect. The "individualists" tend to think, that this also is a genuine individualism, and they reproach us for a betrayal of individualism, in subjecting objectivity into the intimate, but herein is a dangerous misunderstanding, herein is a misuse of words. We, namely we -- are the individualists, since we desire, that with the world our individual principle should obtain, that our most intimate experiences should help turn round the world, we want all this seeming objectivity to bend to our values. For example, beauty is an intimate matter of worth and also an individual experience, and the so-called "individualists" as little as possible speak about it, as little as possible are they concerned over it, as little as possible manifest it and judge about it, wherein the non-beautiful, and the external to the beautiful, the "abstract" politics is out to save the world, and human society thus is jolted by history. Beauty, intimate and individual, has to save the world, to transform the societal aspect, say we on our side, and that without beauty there also cannot be a new and rightful societal awareness. Before the wonder of beauty worldly evil is humbled. This means, in what we say: individualism ought to be affirmed to the point of universalism, ought to be ruler of the universe, i.e. to be transformed into sobornost'-communality, to become embodied. And history on this is with us. It is filled with religious societal movements, with religious cultures, with individualism, having become communal, embodied, and not abstracted; it signifies great works of art, in which an intimate religiosity flows about into the world and it changes the course of history. Suchlike are all the organic, truly creative historical epochs. We thirst for an unprecedented new organic epoch, in which that, what now merely for a few is intimately of value, will become embodied within the world, will become a matter of communality, will take on flesh, and not abstraction; indeed examples of a similar sort have occurred both in Greek culture, and in the early Italian Renaissance, as well as in all the periods of a common mystical sensitivity. There is no sort of basis to see in the disintegration of modern times, in rationalistic abstractness, in the absence of an organic insensitivity -- any fullness of being, the eternal norm of life. It is necessary to get free from the hypnotic trance of the modern times, from the superstition of rationalism. The engendering and alacrity of a religious individualism is characteristic to our era, and with it has ensued the crisis of rationalism and anti-religious positivism, the protest against a reason-ordered and abstract culture, the terror of non-being, the restoration of the rights of a romantic dreaminess, but this is merely a transitory condition. The finalative transition to an organic and creative epoch, to that of a communality of religiosity, is possible not along the path of a restoration of the old historical form of religion, but rather by the path of the revealing of a new religious awareness, encompassing within it both all the old truth and together with this, creatively continuing the deed of the eternal, immeasurably full religion. The new universalism, the new religious communality will be begotten of individualism, and proceed on through the person and its freedom.

We do not want to fabricate a new religion, but rather to discern the solely eternal within a new religious creativity. Christianity alone cannot already save us, not because that it is false, but because [in its present state] it represents an incomplete truth, not encompassing all the fullness of our experience and our desires, and because that within it has been revealed, though very important and central, but partialised a truth. In Christianity, taken in its historical relativeness and limitation, there is not yet a positive societal truth, it does not as yet encompass all the richness of culture dear to us, such as there is in the God-Man, but not yet God-manhood. Historical Christianity, ascetic, sterile, -- is individualistic, it speaks only about a personal heavenly salvation, and it is impossible to find in it a truth earthy, a communality of salvation and transfiguration of the earth, of the flesh of the world. The religion of Christ has been a central point of world history, from which can be conceived all the meaning of history, but Christianity has remained split off from this meaning of world history, and for it as it were has been ignored everything that has happened of significance within history, all the creativity of culture, all the dreams about a societal transfiguration of the earth. The meaning of the religious crisis, which has become acute in modern mankind, though not many as yet realise it, consists in this, that it is impossible to find solace either upon the old, fleshless, non-societal and non-cultural sort of religion, or upon the new, the already grown stale, earthly irreligiosity. And therefore has come about the tendency to conjoin Christianity with whatever you please a political fanaticism blasphemously veiling over within it the cannibalistic reactionary instincts, -- because in Christianity, only in Christianity, there had not been revealed yet the truth about a religious societal aspect, about a religious earthly culture. And with the representatives of the historical church "hath fornicated the earthly kings" [Rev. 18; 9]. There has still not clearly come down upon societal mankind the Spirit the Comforter, promised us by Christ, the body of mankind has not as yet been rendered God-manly, with an holy societal aspect and an holy culture, encompassing the infinite plenitude of being. The Christian righteous have been saved by individual effort and they have prayed for the sins of the world, but a righteousness societal, cultural, world-historical we only await. And then it would defeat both the old godless statecraft and the new godless statecraft, then it would sanctify a great world culture, it would sanctify the earth.

Is it possible even to posit the question: has there been up to the present a true church in the historical embodiment, was not religion individual in its truth and thus sobornost'-communality -- not comprised instead within the circle of a free mysticism? The transgressions of the church against the earth, against an earthly truth, against culture and freedom are too terrible, too intolerable. With the old church it is impossible already to affirm new societal virtues, it is impossible to inspire a living spirit into it, to compel it to admit the good of a constitution and an 8 hour working day, this would be something mechanical, almost positivistic.[1] A new mysteried mysticism, long ago already having filtered

[1] In this regard I am in disagreement with S. N. Bulgakov.

up from the depths, ought to course out along the land, and a new love ought to ignite within the body of mankind. Revelations ought to continue, for sickly mankind anxiously awaits them.

We do not ascetically propose to turn away from the political liberation of mankind nor from the creativity of culture, now all amuck, no, all this ought to continue and has still its mission. But our consciousness obligates us to remember, that our task -- is to hasten the onset of an organic religious period, which will surmount the rationalistic abstraction, the disintegration, which will reunite in an utmost plenitude the fragmented parts of the human spirit. And we are only but precursors. There has to be brought to the quickest finish the "abstract" politics, there has to be conceived as the task of politics the abolition of politics, its dissolution into something higher, an as possible curtailment of its rule of power, its subordination to a supra-human good. This obligates to a new path, upon which can and ought to be supported also a purely political liberation, to be supported by this or some other party, but never to become conjoined with one path of politics, not become subordinated to it, but on the contrary, according to the measure of strength to subordinate it to oneself.

We can say, that the Constitutional Democratic Party at present in Russia -- is the least evil in the sphere of "abstract" politics, which ought to sustain it in a whole series of its rightful affairs. This is especially apparent at the present moment. In this party is least the cult of recourse to violence, it does not mutate from a real politics into a religion, though moreso in it is an human truth, than of that neutral social medium, about which I spoke above. But people, thirsting for a religious societal awareness, an organic reunification, the overcoming of "abstract" politics, just as with all "abstract" principles, cannot stand fully even with this party, for within it there is too much the feeling of a spiritual bourgeoisness. Let politics itself per se be as little as possible obligatory, but for this reason only, that it again become obligatory, as part of a religious totality.

Democracy and Philistinism

(1906 - 129)[1]

We have written much about the impending philistinism, about the "impending Hamism and boorishness", about the onset of forces, hostile to a noble and great culture, we have written -- and have come to alter the tone of certain of our words, but not our thoughts, not our outlooks. Some that are naive, and others malicious have termed us hostile to democracy, fearful of its coming victory, and have said: these representatives of the new religio-philosophic and religio-societal movement identify democracy with philistinism; they see in the people, in the toiling masses only a boorish Hamism[2], in them they proclaim aristocratic instincts and a bourgeois fear of losing their privileged cultural benefits. To a typical demagogic critic, exploiting the dark instincts of the masses, the hypnotic effect of the mob, any reply is of course useless, but misunderstandings have to be addressed, to show the true content of one's ideas.

We see in democracy an eternal truth, an acknowledging of the dignity of the human person, as regarding the considered value of his inner qualities, and consequently, the repudiation of everything, that hinders the person in the simple necessities, that forgets his nature, and prevents a man from rising to his full stature and manifesting his authentic visage. We are never in opposition to democracy on behalf of economic and political privileges, of social inequalities, nor do we seek protection from its negative sides through any social or state powers. Democracy ought to follow through on its pulling down of the coercive and inhuman social and state hierarchism, ought to provide a liberation from slavery to material objects. But in the name of what? We indeed say: in the name of a free and non-domineering hierarchism of human persons, organically subject to a

---

[1] DEMOKRATIYA I MESCHANSTVO. Article first published in gazette, "Moscow Weekly", 1906, № 11, p.332-335.

[2] *trans. note*: the term Hamism/Khamstvo idiomatically derives derisively from the Biblical personage of Ham, accursed son of Noah (Cf. Gen. 9: 20-27).

supra-human principle, in the name of values, higher than man, and determinative of the significance of man. The impending philistinism however says: in the name of the self-deification of man, of his self-satisfaction, in the name of human well-being, is to be admitted as higher and more valuable, than any supra-human benefits, than any values divine, the truly noble or cultural. But man, -- is a purposive-end, and not a means, and his person possesses absolute a significance. The man, having spurned all supra-human values, with no respect for holy churches, eternal books, great names, beautiful objects, esteeming neither beauty nor nobility, nor the wisdom and eternity manifest within living history, such a man, worshipping himself, considering "human" his ultimate sanctity, reflects but non-being, desolation and philistinism.

Philistinism is not democracy and it is not to be defined by social positions, no indeed, but democracy can be transformed into philistinism, if the object of religion becomes the self-deification of a future mankind, if its ultimate sanctity be only the "human", for by this the future man will get rendered into a nothingness, a nothing, bereft of his noble content. The proletariat is not philistinism, the proletariat -- is the working people, which ought to be liberated from oppression both economic and political, ought to manifest all the richness of the person, but the "idea" of the proletariat, which is so dearly beloved by the fourth estate, and also by the Social Democrat religion, in heart embracing the proletariat, is philistinism, the disdaining of noble values, those of sacred a culture, the betrayal of eternity in the name of self-worship.

Organically in the heart of the people, perhaps, there is less a philistinism, than in all the privileged classes, and it is not the people that we suspect of boorish sensibilities. The irreligious bourgeoise has wrought very desolate wastelands within human hearts, and has eroded the noblest feelings for the past -- for the eternal, whereas the democratic intelligentsia, an element so typical to a rationalistic century, so proud of its superficial revolutionism, has been infected by this poison of philistinism, this passion to build life, whilst having cast aside its meaning. They often nowadays think, that a boldness of negation and repudiation is a guarantee against philistinism, but they forget, that rooted in philistinism is *a lessening of values*, in a gradual transforming of the great into the small and then into nothing, and thereupon the world tragedy -- consists in but a philistine drama, a comedy and finally a complete farce. A truly liberating, anti-philistine revolt, a great revolution in spirit lies far deeper, and is immeasurably more radical. And from the modern "man-gods", from the self-worshipping man there wafts quite a stench of philistinism, and often around them is the feeling of a complete farce. The philistinism reeks of an irksome, banal "demonism". There is a stench of philistinism in the Social Democrat "demonism", dreaming of its detachment from eternity, from God, and thus to build a temporal replacement, that of a self-worshipping mankind, all indeed subject forever to death, with its liberation not indeed from slavery, but rather instead from nobility and reverence.

We are in a fight not against the people, nor against the working class, but rather against certain ideas and outlooks, which possibly also do not exist for real and ought even not to exist. We think, just like our opponents, that rightfully the socialist interests of the working people and its liberation have become inseparably caught up with philistinism in the sense that we have mentioned, and we seek to break this connection. The working people are indeed no less ancient, of no less aristocratic an origin, than the so-called "aristocracy", and they can, and they ought to follow out a noble, eternal, religious path. The malice against eternity, against things great, against what holds the earth in place, the reminders, that there is something higher, than human contentment, suchlike a malice is being imparted to the people by a various sort, themself of nowise lengthy an ancestry, but this is not at the roots of the people's life, and it is not needed for a triumph of the truth of democracy. We stand against the ignobility which, regretably, is manifest so often by the advocates and would-be builders of the future, which has become so characteristic of the impending religion of a positivist Social Democracy. It is comparable only with the ignoble fecklessness of our fading our enslavers and oppressors, the former governors and exploiters. A nobility of attitude always presupposes respect towards the human person and a reverence towards what is holy, beautiful, the supra-human aspects. Woe and misery, if people have been reduced down to this, that they are no longer able to be noble-minded, can no longer remember from whence their descent, having given up on their origin in eternity. Let those that caused this be accursed, but why indeed idealise this dreadful condition, why see in a fury against oppression the sole source of truth? The self-worship of man, of the human, the indeed self-loving thirst of each that is small to be so very great, to be higher than God, higher than truth and beauty; such maliciousness against what is higher cannot be noble, cannot be spiritually-aristocratic, for it is indeed the direct opposite to the chivalrant knight's serving in the honour of some "fair maiden". Why would they want to connect democracy with a religion of philistinism, of human self-contentment and human self-worship, rather than with a religion with a sense of chivalry, of reverence towards the supra-human beauty? Such anti-religious tendencies in our era -- all lead to a diminution in but the name of human well-being, with its arrangement of life. The past was filled with philistinism, with the philistine lifestyle tragedies, a sort of being we ought to be done with, but it is the philistinism of the future that even more frightens and grieves us, since we cherish the future all the moreso, in that it is a future we should want to create. Each sort of philistinism, both of the past and the future, is connected with an organising of the human mode of life, which tends to get loved more than the supra-human. We also desire democratic justice, we desire human liberation from the oppression over material matters, but we do not desire a philistine, ignoble, vile culture, of the sort that the proclaimers of a democratic religion want to shove on us, and we shall instead create, as we are able, different a culture. If it should be for the benefit of mankind, that for the "just" distribution of human benefits it be considered needful to abolish books, such as bear the imprint of eternity, along with the beautiful pictures, and the divine churches and memorials, if it be considered necessary to forget the great names and sacred graveyards, then we in turn would say: it will not indeed be to the benefit of mankind, and indeed it will not be a true mankind, since we cannot esteem it human, in having asserted oneself, -- as "only human" and thereby higher than the supra-human and Divine, wherefore also we do not desire suchlike philistine a sort of life, a philistine domain.

The deep antinomy between democracy and culture, between the human benefits and the supra-human benefits, seems tragic and implacable. And therefore they tend to regard us as enemies of democracy. And this gets projected on the positivist-empirical front, -- as evidently rational, that this is irresolvable an antinomy. But there is a religious way out from it, about which they tend to be too forgetful, and which indeed they do not want to see. The philistines think, that in the religious aspect there is not a single smidgeon of reality, that it is all a distraction, to amuse oneself with.

They do not believe in anything, that fails to pass muster in their autocratic judgement, their philistine sobriety. And thereby they win their judgemental-phantasmic victory over mystical a realism.

Only a religious democracy can surmount the philistinism, can save one from this poison. Only people such as are united in the name of the OneOnly Father can avoid the philistine aspect, and thus not worship their own tedious human existence. Only the religious life of the people, when in the people's heart there blazes a love for things supra-human, when the people with reverence enters into the church of immeasurable beauty and akin to chivalrant the knight serves its "Fairest Lady", only the life of the people, accomplishing the mysteried, can render democracy noble, can preserve it from smug self-contentment and the worshipping of the human only benefits, and abolish within it the malice against benefits supra-human. In the idea of God-manhood, as was proclaimed by Christ the God-Man, there is included both likewise the truth of democracy, -- in humanism, as well as also the truth of noble a culture, -- within the supra-human values, since within it both God and mankind are organically conjoined. On the path of God-manhood, a man grows not into a self-smug self-worshipping, philistine sort "superman", -- he instead uplifts himself towards God, the Divine aspect within grows, amidst a communing with the Divine and therefore one becomes more complete, noble, and immersed within the eternal. We dream of an organic, a creative religious era, when the life of the people reflects a living organism, in which all the parts are co-united harmoniously, aligned towards the supreme centre, radiating forth light. And in our dreams we should be of righteously just an era, instead of philistine a democracy. Only flourishing organic eras are free, allowing one to breathe fully; era however that are criticist and fragmented tend to writhe in the torments of philistine jealousy, and the rebellious person tends always still to be enslaved and broken.

Aesthetics is a great weapon in the struggle against the onrush of philistinism and as such it is full of religious presentiments. One, who reveres beauty, cannot still revere only himself, cannot worship only the human, since having tasted of the sweet, one does not prefer the bitter. To cultivate aesthetic experiences in oneself -- means to develope within oneself the beautiful, i.e. something higher than I myself, a supra-human principle, bringing one nigh closer to God. Morality can be rendered into a weapon of philistinism, self-infatuation can lead to a worshipping of man, but beauty never. Human malice, human self-love tends to wither in the human heart, when it bows to beauty, to beautiful objects, beautiful actions, beautiful works of art. Here is the mystical point, in which subjective experiences align with objective values. We well know, that democratic morals infuses into human hearts not only justice and righteous anger, but also meanness, malice and lack of civility; a true aesthetic however always leads to a noble humbleness before the MostHigh, before His miracles and brings one closer to the dream about love. How beautiful, how appealing the images of Mary, the ChristChild sitting upon Her knee and She hearkening to Him, and likewise of the sinner [Mary Magdalene] kissing the feet of Christ and lavishly anointing them with her tears and thereafter myrh [Lk. 7: 37-50].

Here is the mystical aesthetic, the saving peace.

The fate of democracy depends to a remarkable degree upon the aesthetic aspect in the life of the people, upon the cult of beauty amongst all the people, the respectful reverencing of beautiful things, upon the art and the embellishing of life amongst all the people. But the aesthetic life of the people, its regard for beauty cannot be and ought not to be merely "in the abstract". In the religious aesthetic aspect we are wont to see a great act of self-denial, of a voluntary refusal of that which for oneself is human, to instead honour God, amidst the higher assertion of the God-manly aspect of one's person, of an higher bliss in conjunction with God. That beauty will save the world, -- this is a religious truth [proclaimed by Dostoevsky], all hidden from philistinism. Woe to those democrats, who are afraid of beauty, who see in it an enemy of democratic truth. Typically also they are afraid of religion also, and they have had no liking for God, since they are focused on the human, the temporal and the relative, and the human has been rendered their ultimate passion. Yet they also tend to forget, that the God-Man co-unites love for man with love for God, and the love for people is derived from love for God. The Grand Inquisitor makes a mockery of the person, of freedom and love, tempting us with the temptations, spurned by Christ in the wilderness, with the temptation of a kingdom of this world, a kingdom of philistinism.

It is not against the great truth of democracy that we rebel, a truth revealed by Christ as a truth about the *person*, but rather against these temptations by the devil, the shovings onto paths of philistinism, paths of boorishness and non-being. None of us has written against the proletariat, in which we desire to see only human persons, but rather merely against the "idea of the proletariat", against the class mystique, a truly philistine non-personal idea; no one has opposed the values of the great culture of the people and its welfare, rather merely against a detachment and abandoning of this great culture. And we believe, that the great culture of all the people is possible only upon religious a basis, only religiously sacralised, and thence in it will be a true democracy rather than some mere philistine and impersonal sociability, and thence also it will become co-united with absolute values. Ahead we see two paths, the triumph of either one of two opposed principles, hostile each to the other: that of human self-worship and human self-smugness, amidst a love for the good things of this world, amidst universal and overall a depersonalisation, or -- a serving of the true God, an uniting of earth with heaven, of time with eternity, the affirmation of person in its absolute destiny. Only one of these religions is ours, only one alone of these paths do we ourself desire to go and assist others to go. Those, that have chosen the second path, will be neither understood nor loved, and will meet with hostility from people, such as want to tear away the world and mankind from that which is absolute and eternal.

Concerning the Will of the People

(1906 - #130)[1]

What is the will of the people? Where is one to seek its true expression and embodiment? Here is a question, which assumes at present an extraordinary acuteness. Having suffered, having been lacerated by a will foreign and strange, our people thirsts to live by its own will, through the self-accomplished expression of its will, by its self-accomplished embodiment in forms of a political existence. Here already for a long time has everywhere been heard, from the various ends of the land, the outraged will of the people letting loose with an outcry, resolute, constant: we demand the universal, equal, direct and secret suffrage right to vote, we demand a constituent assembly. This outcry signifies, that the people has aspired to an accomplished embodiment of its will, that it admits of only its own authority. Western Europe has worked out for this instance slogans and abstract formulas, by which we also express our needs. Woe to whoever admits even one part of a formula, in declaring a complete expression of the will of the people. And in the tumult of our days, in the furies of these days but few ponder over the problem, of what is the people, and in what is its will and power of authority.

We live in a very intense, a very responsible moment of our historical existence. The avid and searching glances of all the land had been fixed upon the Duma, and everyone felt, that this was the vessel, in which should be decanted a portion though of the people's will, that here finally it would be gathered, that here finally, would be heard the will of the people.

And yet amidst this from all sides they have chipped away at the Duma, from the left and from the right, they refused on principle that it should be a true representative of the will of the people. For both the one and the other of them they have no idea, in what consists the true will of the people, for some of them -- it is the Red Hundreds, and for others -- the Black Hundreds. The only content of will that they acknowledge as of the

---

[1] O NARODNOI VOLE. First published in weekly social-political newspaper "Moskovskii Ezhenedel'nik", 1906, № 20, p. 31-39.

people is what they wish for themselves, and this points already to a profound antinomy of the perception itself of the will of the people, to the possibility herein of a contradiction between form and content.

The left have said, that since the Duma is not a true popular representation, it therefore does not express the will of the people, because it is gathered not on the basis of an universal, equal, direct and secret suffrage of having a voice. By this is established a purely formal, an as yet bereft of content, indicator for the defining as to what the will of the people is, and in what is its true representation. Political democracy, in declaring formal signs for the expression of the will of the people within representative institutions, assents the truth purely in the negative. The four-part democratic formula of the suffrage right to vote is better than any limiting in the right to vote, with the predominance of any portion of the will of the people, whether of class or condition, with any coercive obstacles to the expression of the will of all the people in the selection of their representatives. But there is as yet nothing positive in political democracy, and it futilely attempts to set out a fortuitous, mechanical, arithmetic result for delimiting the will of the people. In political democracy the will of the people is the product of a quantitative combination, the adding up and deducing out of individual wills; in these quantitative combinations vanishes the qualitative aspect of the individual will and thus there does not obtain the qualitative aspect of the will of all the people. The parliamentary form is a characteristic product from a critical period of history, when everything becomes disjunctive and fragmented, when a people ceases to live an organic life and ceases to possess its own organic will. Our epoch is gravitating in its own abstract political existence towards a full and total rule by the people, -- this is an utmost, endpoint idea of societal radicalism. They tend to set off from the total will of the people (universal, equal etc voting right), and they arrive at a total ruling power of the people (a democratic republic). Let us analyse the concept of "people's-sovereignty" ["narodovlastie"] and there then will be exposed the falsity of the very path to people's-sovereignty, since neither an arbitrary human will nor a godless human rule of power ought to hold dominion over the earth.

And first of all I shall point to the ineradicable opposition between people's-sovereignty and the rights of the person. People's-sovereignty, as an utmost sovereign principle, cannot guarantee the person his inalienable, unconditional rights, since it puts the fate of the person into dependence upon the arbitrary, subjectively-mutable will of people. If the human will is made a god of and neither admits of nor loves anything higher than itself, then also there cannot be talk concerning any absolute values, such as might establish the unconditional significance of the person, nothing inalienable is demonstrated concerning it, and its rights are apprised according to expediency. Freedom of conscience possesses an absolute significance and not in the name of anything can it be taken away from a man, if it be bestown by a will supra-human, Divine and not dependent upon human caprice. Posit freedom of conscience as dependent upon human caprice, on the will of people, and its sanctity will be completely violated. J. J. Rousseau, from whom comes the teaching about a total and consistent people's-sovereignty, did not admit of freedom of conscience. The French Revolution, having attempted to establish a cult of the goddess of reason, tended to deny freedom of conscience at every step. Freedom of conscience has been violated by almost all revolutions, comparable in this to prior reactions, and its sanctity cannot be grasped by people with a pathos for people's-sovereignty, just as slaves under a single-power have not known it. The Social Democrats more than once have declared, that freedom of conscience, and freedom of the word, and every right based upon freedom will be taken from the person, if this be needful for the interests of the proletariat, if the proletariat should want this so.

The human person discovers his freedom and its rights obtain an absolute sanction, they are endowed with an inalienable worthiness, if there be repudiated making a god of the human will and there be respected the supra-human will, the will of God. The highest will has willed freedom for man, has established the absolute inalienability of his freedom of conscience and his other rights, and no human sort of will is empowered to take away this freedom, to infringe upon the Divine within man. When however the person and his freedom are made dependent upon the will of people, when sovereignty be naught else than human-power, then the person loses its absolute character, and its rights to freedom fall into becoming subject to capricious human passions. And thereby the subjective will of the proletariat, or of the tsar, or of some other human ruling-power can deprive the person of the freedom of conscience, and the right to life, and indeed of every right. There is nothing absolute, nothing precious, nothing untouchable in its inner significance, if the world be surrendered to a ruling-power which is subjective, capricious, mutable, before which there be nothing higher for the human will to bow. Pure people's-sovereignty is the making of the human will into a god, it surrenders the history of the world over into the grip of human desires, whatever they might be, it gives recognition to this human ruling-power within all its formal emptiness of content, it splits apart the will of the people (the form) from the righteous-truth of the people (the content). In this people's-sovereignty is a continuation of the matter of human self-power, begun with an acknowledging of the sovereignty of the state, -- a self-willed human invention, with making a god of the tsar, i.e. involving yet again human wills. The people's-sovereignty, -- as a total autocratic democracy is the selfsame bowing to an earthly governance, a state positivism, as is the deifying of an unlimited single-rule power, an absolute Caesarism, so hateful an autocracy for us. Both in an unlimited single-rule power and in an unlimited people's-sovereignty the will is only but human, arbitrary, capricious, and there is made a god of, in the first instance, -- the will of one, and in the second -- the will of all. Yet to Universal Reason needs to be limited, to be subordinated, not only the will of one or of several, but also the will of all people, since the human will, limited by nothing, subordinated to nothing, cannot arrive at freedom and world harmony. The fate of the world has to be subordinated to objective ideas, to a material, and not merely formal righteous-truth, issuing from a will supra-human, and not from subjective desires, empty of content in their self-sufficiency and self-smugness, issuing but from the human will, be it the will of one, the will of many or of all. Only in the universal, the Divine character of the will, such as governs the world, can there be the guarantee, that the significance of the person should be absolute, independent of anything temporal, that its rights be inalienable, that its freedom be posited higher than upon human usefulness and arbitrary human desires.

The idea of the rights of man, of the freedoms of man, is the expression of an universal, supra-human, reason-endowed will, and not by chance has the declaration of rights arisen in England upon religious a grounding. Liberalism in a pure, in an ideal form, contains within it an indubitable truth, but one yet still formal, bereft of real content and real footings, and therefore in its strivings to assert an absolute formalism, -- lawfulness, it leads to falseness, in which decays the spark of God's rightful-truth of governance.

The realm of formal governance, the realm of law, as utmost in the world, not only leaves everything hanging up in the air, dissociated from the living bosoms of the earth, but also in its "abstract" form it becomes transformed into something evil, inhuman and godless. The rule of law, possessed of a wellspring supra-human, proceeding upon the path of an abstract, formal "legality", in fatal a manner becomes subordinated to the state, in having a wellspring human, the changeable will of people, and the loud bustle of human interests which drown out the supreme voice, declaring the freedom of man. The formal truth of governance (objective an idea) only in union with the real truth of love can offer resistance to the unbridled power of the state, to the unlimited human will, declaring itself sovereign.

Social Democracy has introduced great improvements into the formula of people's-sovereignty, it has detailed and made concrete the concept of "the people". For Social Democracy the true people is the proletariat, and perfected people's-sovereignty is proletarian-sovereignty. But the full triumph of the proletariat abolishes classes, and the victorious proletariat is transformed into the sole mankind. The deifying of the proletariat, so characteristic for "the idea of the fourth estate", is the deifying of a future mankind yet to come, acknowledging the sovereignty of is human will and denying all supra-human values, denying the will of Universal Reason. Through the consummated people's-sovereignty -- proletarian-sovereignty, the fate of the world will be entrusted ultimately to the human will, to the human subjectivity, to human desires, from which by way of arithmetic combinations will be deduced the will of the sovereign people-mankind. Will there be a triumphing of freedom, will there be fortified the unconditional significance of the person, will there be the acknowledging of its inalienable rights? Will there be attained a perfected expression of *the will of the people*? In an unlimited, and subordinated to nothing higher, people's-sovereignty is extinguished both the person, and so also the people, and there is attained neither the rightful-truth of the person, nor the rightful-truth of Sobornost'-communality. Everything precious will be dependent upon the subjective desires of people and everything will have to be subordinated to their mechanical sum. And in this mechanical sum, -- a new Leviathan, is revealed neither the image of the person, nor the image of the people.

Social Democracy involves one contradiction, very dangerous for the developement of democracy and very instructive for us. It proclaims the principle of the will of the people, it reveres universal the equal etc suffrage right to vote, in people's-sovereignty it sees its political ideal, but not every, even though formally perfect, aspect of the will of the people does it tend to subordinate itself to. Social Democracy would boycott the most complete representation of the will of the people, if such were not to be endowed with the proletarian-socialist quality, if it did not make the object of its strivings the triumph of the "idea of the fourth estate". Thus bespeaks the Social Democratic thirst to surmount formalism, to transition over to the content of the will of the people, to its objects. But the frightful thing is in this, that the content of the Social Democratic religion shows itself to be a forever entrenched formalism -- the deifying of the will of a future mankind yet to come, loving nothing higher, and the objective "idea" of this religion -- is empty of content. Social Democrats have to be subordinate to the will of the people, since they know of nothing greater, nothing higher, than people's-sovereignty.

There mustneeds be surmounted the emptiness of content of the will of the people, the formalism of people's-sovereignty. It is time to admit, that the essence of the matter is not the will of the people, *but in rather the objects of this will, in the objectives, to which it is directed, in the ends of this will. Only a sobered will is striving to an end, directed to that, what is higher and greater than it, whereas a will, directed upon itself, locked up within its own human limitedness, asserting only itself -- is lacking in content and empty, and leads to non-being.* A mankind making a god of itself, worshipping its own human welfare, is a nothing, non-being. The human will only then becomes infinitely of content and full, if it has as its own objective end a worldwide All-Unity, the plenitude and harmony of universal life, when it catches sight of God in itself and over it and has the desire for Him. In the history of the world the human will came into being, when it was imbued with ideas and values, when it aspired to supra-human objectives, to a meaning worldwide, and otherwise came to non-being, when it made a god of itself, nowise aspiring to anything greater, than the human, nowise thirsting for All-Unity, having turned away from the One. And in the name of the person, of its content and freedom, it is necessary to disavow the self-involved deifying of the human will of the person, of a sovereign human power and instead devote oneself to the Divine-Power, in forever asserting the idea of the person itself, with the absolute grounding of the value of its freedom of conscience, its freedom of the word, its free self-determination.

But what indeed is the people? Avidly they seek to find the true representation of its will and they do not know, wherein is this reality, which they term the people. The people is neither a class, nor an estate.

The people is not and cannot be in an arithmetic combination of people's individual wills, in mechanical a combination. The people, as a reality, is a certain mystical organism, it is a communal-assemblage unity with a single object of the organic will, with a single love. The mystical organism of the people is difficult to find within the critical and fragmented epochs of history, and in them the organic will of the people, the organic love of the people gets replaced by an arithmetic, a mechanical quantity. The people's-sovereignty with all its representative institutions is also a substitute for the organic will of the people, wrought through a fatal necessity in an irreligious, critical epoch. The genuine will of the people, the will of the mystical organism always possesses a content, always has valuable objectives and only because it is a communal-assemblage, what it expresses is not the quantity of human wills, but rather a new supra-human quality of will, what it wanted is the All-Unity, a free worldwide harmony, that in it be given the triumph of subjective wishes with objective ideas, objective righteous-truth. In this sense the genuine will of the people is the will of God, is a will not arbitrarily-human, but rather supra-human and of reason. Before the will of the people ought to fall down every human power. Where however is to be sought the embodiment of this will of the people -- this will of God?

Its perfect and objective embodiment is possible only in religious Sobornost', in religious communality, in the uniting of people in the name of God, in the Church. Only in the Church, and not in the state, does the will of the people find itself an adequate expression and conjoin itself with the Divine-Power, whereby mankind comes to be of God-manhood. Concerning the Church, concerning true religious Sobornost'-communality we do not dare to speak self-assuredly and self-confidently, we yet know too little, we only seek and have presentiments. But we know already, that we have to choose this path. We know, that it is necessary to subjoin the human will to objective values and ideas, to conjoin subjective desires with worldwide righteous-truth, to delimit people's-sovereignty by rather the unconditional significance of the human person and its freedom. The human will has to become enkindled with love and reverence for sacred things, the centre of gravity has to shift from a will humanly-arbitrary, empty of content and self-sufficiency, to a will absolute, infinitely of content and universally liberative, and the formalism has to be overcome by realism. The declaration of the rights of man and citizen was already an expression not of the human will, but of the Divine, and therefore only therein do the rights of man obtain with absolute a significance. In this -- is the non-arbitrary truth of the teaching about natural truth. It is necessary to go further the path of explicating in the world the supra-human will, to strengthen and to sanctify these aspects of the world liberation movement.

In our -- alas -- quite tranquil State Duma, certainly, it would be impossible to seek for a perfect will of the people and not only because, that it was convened not on the basis of universal etc voting rights. It is not a true representation of the will of the people, since that it is not a Sobornost'-communality, the unity of the supra-human, since the people itself as it were is not seen. The people is not a combination of social groups, is not a sum of individuals, the people -- is an objective spirit, a supra-human organism, reflected also in Russian literature and in national creativity.

The people -- is an insoluble mystery and we thirst to be in communion with it. Yet only bits, only fragments of the will of the people, though also not communal, but merely gathered, and splintered, have spoken in our Duma, have bespoken within it the people's indignation against a government, tearing apart the people, constituting a people's tribunal over the old regime, and brought about a sense of the people's thirst for earthly freedom and righteous-truth. At the Duma via subterranean coursings wound its way the people's will -- the will of God, and in the weak voices of the people's representatives there began resonating the disunited parts of this will, though still mechanically consolidated not by love for a new good, but by hatred for an old evil. The Duma, as with any parliament, mirrored the will of the people during an era of fragmentation and disunity and therefore it was a least of evils, since for a greatest good there would have had to occur a turnabout of character religious, and not political.

The path of Russia is twofold, having apparent the struggle of two principles: human-power and Divine-power, man-worship or God-worship. We can only serve that path, upon which Russia, having become free of an human single-power, does not fall into a new slavery to an unlimited human-power, even though it be termed people's-sovereignty. A path upon which the mystical organism of the people, -- an unity supra-human, should determine our historical existence, and with objective ideas and values there should win out over the limitedness of all human passions, and empty desires. In categories purely political we by this deny the sovereignty of a state, such as is the expression of arbitrary human will, and we affirm sovereignty based upon law, and expressing supra-human will. Only in the person of the people, as a religious Sobornost'-communality, can be revealed a glint of the Divinity, and not in the mechanical aspect of a state, even though it be based upon people's-sovereignty or proletarian-power. We deny a merely *formal* politics, which but speaks about the *means* of life, in the name instead of a politics *material*, mystically-real, which addresses the *ends* of life, concerns itself with the *meaning* of life.

The truth of the liberation movement tends to set free the will of the person, denies oppressive dependence and the power of other, the alien human wills, and sunders the coercive and unjust connecting bonding of the atomised bits of the world. But let us not stumble down the path of some new whatever enslavement of the person by the human will, that of a new coercive and mechanical binding together. *The objective, universal right-truth has to issue forth through a mystical act of its free choice by the person,* and this act of freedom has to have its own political reflection. A liberative personal will should desire, should love worldwide an All-unity, Divine harmony, as its own absolute freedom and plenitude.

Reason and Healthy an Approach to Meaning

(A Postscript)

It is interesting a thing to look at the psychology of the critics of the modern religio-philosophic and religio-societal trends, the psychology of those enemies of mystical trends. And indeed it is impossible not to admit, that from all these critics, all apparently so varied, there has not been said essentially a single word, there has not been made a single effort to enter into the depths of the questions, so as to topple our basic principles and provide instead a basis for their own.

The critics in their sacredly and childishly naive a manner are convinced, that somewhere, some-when and someone once and for always has demonstratively proven (!), the absurdity and phantasy of every sort religion, mysticism, metaphysics etc etc, as once and for always solidly confirmed by healthy a positiveness. I beseech you, sir, in the interests of an objective truth situated outside us once having been recognised, by whom namely, when and where was all this demonstratively proven and toppled? What gives you the right to regard your own premises and your primary principles as undoubtable, not needing still further justification nor developement, while our premises, our primary principles are seen beforehand as folly and thus forever already overturned? Indeed we quite well know, that your sole solid position -- is this allegedly healthy sense of meaning and your singular demonstrative proof -- is in fanatical a faith in the autocraticness, the finalness and divineness of healthy a sense of meaning. And I invite you in the name of reason and its thousands-years traditions to scrutinise the alleged competency of healthy a meaning, towards a critical rejection of its excessive and absurd pretensions. You have jumbled it all together, sir, reason as the great objective reason with its healthy meaning, together with the smallish subjective judging, that human rascal, and therefore so snugly you are without any doubts, so scornful of everything inconceivable for you. Reason has its own sacred scripture, its own great books and great names. But where is the sacred scripture of the healthy meaning, where the great books, solidifying this assuredness, where are the geniuses of the healthy meaning? You always make it seem, that behind you stands a sacred scripture, that titans have carried you hence upon their shoulders, wherefore you reckon yourself free from having to provide any grounding and essential support. But behind you stands only one force -- the hypnosis of everydayness, a meaningless plethora of factiveness, the daily clutter, trite impressions, the healthiness of which has smoothed out what is nearby and close at hand, and has affected only what is seen, but remains blind to what is remote and deep.

Ye regard yourselves sceptics and therefore spurn all things holy, everything, that might bear you off to other worlds. But be then consistent sceptics right through to the end, sceptics consequential and honourable, and do not trust so blindly all the healthy-minded things, everything, that you impute to the empirical world. Unfamiliar to you is that ultimate and bold scepsis, that scepticism, which is a servant of reason and subjects equally to doubt everything earthly, as well as the heavenly, both matter as well as God, the reality of the sticks that have hit you upon the head, as well as the reality of the immortal soul. I can subject to doubt the reality of God and of immortality and even ought to engage these doubts, but I likewise have subjected to doubt the reality of the world, of that which is material, the reality of a world subject to necessity and laws, the reality of human well-being, the reality of human progress, in service to which you summon me. For the radicalism of my doubts, the this-sided world holds no sort of primacy over the other-sided world. You however absolutely believe in everything seemingly positive, on faith you arrange your life, and are absolutely doubtful of everything mystical and have even no doubts on this, but rather all the same believe, that such is all a phantasm and absurdity. Why, who has given you this right, on the texts of what sort of scriptures do you ground such a manner of faith and doubts? You can appeal only to healthy a meaning, but behind this healthy meaning lies concealed your mental-comprehending character, your desire to believe in everything positive, earthly, empirically rational, and your desire to repudiate everything mystical, heavenly, other-sidely. In this characteristic of your will there is nothing objective and nothing obligatory, and healthy meaning, your trite rationalness is merely a very subjective condition of your heart, nothing more.

I know, what you are prepared to say, that positive science has refuted religion, mysticism, metaphysics et al., has recognised them as superstition and an aspect of primitive times, that science has forever reinforced the triumph of the healthy meaning, that its rationality, its judgement -- bears witness to this. I would say that you are afraid not so much of God which causes you no fear, as rather that namely you are afraid of science and reasoning. Please indicate, how indeed has science repudiate the beliefs of religion, the experiences of mysticism, the knowledge of metaphysics? Is it astronomy, physics or chemistry, physiology or is it issuing from a still deficient sociology? Not a single one of the sciences, of the positive sciences, is involved with these questions and hence competent to decide, whether God exists, whether the soul is immortal, whether the miraculous and revelation be possible. Your spiel evidently involves not positive science, which indeed is not your monopoly and which in this matter should be left in peace, rather instead it is about positivist a philosophy and about your pseudo-religious faith. No sort of a science can prove, that in the world the miraculous is impossible, that Christ did not arise, that the nature of the Deity is not disclosed within the mystical experience, -- all this is simply outside the scope of science, and science has naught to say, whether it be something positive in this area, nor also anything negative. Positive science can tell us only: that which is according to the laws of nature, as revealed by physics, chemistry, physiology and other disciplines. Christ thus could not arise, but in this it concurs with religion, which likewise says, that Christ arose not in accord with the laws of nature, but rather that necessity was surmounted, with a victory over the law of perishability, that His Resurrection is a mysteried mystical act, which we share in within the religious life. What can the laws of physics and chemistry have to do, with that which outside of and beyond them, not begotten of physical and chemical forces? Science here is impotent and scientific physics and chemistry are nowise the worse off for this, since they establish the efficacy of law merely within certain dimensions and amidst the presence of defined conditions. I would even suggest, that the very concept of the miraculous can be philosophically established only then, when there is likewise established the concept of law, of its legitimacy, as revealed by science. Indeed for the primitive consciousness everything is alike miraculous, everything is begotten of mysterious forces and therefore in a strict sense there is no miracle. True religion can only follow out its own path of clarity and strictness independent from the developements of science and not only is it not afraid of this, but even needful, in the free philosophic process of reasoning.

Oh, I know, ye positivist gentlemen, your desired intent, that there should be nothing of the miraculous, that nothing should shake your earthly redoubt, should undermine your positive buttresses, and ye want to believe, that there can be nothing such, and sometimes ye believe naively, that everything, Lord willing, just has to happen. And so there is no miracle, since ye want no miracle, just only because.[1]

I have overheard, how ye pray secretly and clandestinely: Lord, render it thus, that Thou be not, render it, that the miraculous be not, that all should be according to law, else all would perish, all collapse, all our earthly calculations be brought to naught. The psychology of this paradoxical prayer is nigh intimate for positivist believers, for their subconscious sort of experience. Ye desire to believe in only one miracle, in the miracle of the laws of nature, in the confines of earthly a reasoning, with which ye connect your hopes to array the earth to your own benefit, and your heart is full of loathing and hatred towards any hindrances standing in your way. Your positivist philosophy of healthy reasoning and your positivist pseudo-religion never and nowhere will find a foundation, except as the lusting of your heart. Ye also want to believe, all the same just like us sinners; and on what side the objective reason is on, reason, and not merely healthy a meaning -- this is something we would still look into and dispute over, were it to change the modes of your criticism. It is time to admit, that in points of departure you have not any sort of advantage over us, and just the same you stand in need of providing a justification, a grounding and developing of your belief system, the same as us.

Ye ought not to proffer us impossible demands, indeed nowise corresponding to what ye proffer the representatives of all the other moreso "healthy minded" trends. If some perchance writer, for example a positivist, a Marxist or from the "Russian Riches" journalistic trend proves intellectual, talented, educated and sincere, then this is reckoned of itself sufficient and all praise him for these qualities, -- but a writer of mystical and religio-metaphysical a persuasion has to be at minimum a genius and a saint, otherwise they bestow him no significance nor do they even accord him the right to defend his ideas. If a writer of "positivist" a persuasion writes an article on some defined theme, then no one demands from him, that in this article he should provide a grounding and further develope all his basic principles, for they instead subject the article to slanted a criticism, on the mere say so and absurdity of such premises, as for

---

[1] In an era criticist, analytic, abstractly-rationalistic the miracles have ceased within history, whereas individual miracles, for the world typically unseen, have always been and continue to be.

example the purely empirical origin of all cognition or the admitting of human well-being and happiness as the final end in life, and no one disputes this nor objects. But if a writer of "mystical" a persuasion writes an article on some defined theme, then the article will not even merit a critique and everyone will complain about it, because that his initial premises in the article have not been spelled out and therefore it all just constitutes a matter of an absurd say so. If a writer of "positivist" a persuasion has penned a literary work, then it will merit a critique, as literary a work. But let a writer of "mystical" a persuasion pen some sort of literary work and everyone is set to pounce on him and issue demands, quite beyond the bounds of literature, and will shout, that its proper religion -- is literature, and they then will make use of this instance, to preen themself on their own moral astuteness. Hackneyed and hollow to you seem all our words: god, the absolute, eternity, love etc, but do you indeed know any words that are not hackneyed and hollow within your own useage? How fresh indeed are the words: the good of mankind, progress, "freedom, equality and brotherhood" or is it merely but some "social democratic jargon"? Yoi! All the words have become shabby, threadbare, and there is only one saving grace: to indeed love the eternal meaning, hidden beneathe the conditional signs, and thence this moreso stronger love will overcome such a loathing for trite sounding words.

Why such inconsistent demands, why such unfairness? There is indeed psychological a basis. For the prevalent "intelligentsia" masses the inherent condition of mindset is such, that every "mystical" a persuasion is considered from the onset *a priori* as assuredly silly, absurd, nonsense, whereas a "positivist" persuasion represents something truly self-evident for every healthy-minded man. To defend a known foolishness and absurdity can of course be permitted of a genius or a saint; the profundity and sincerity has to be especially scrutinised, the moral-examining portion has to be especially well posited relative to such people. It is presupposed, that the "positivist" possesses a natural right to existence, rooted in the known healthiness of his ideas. The "mystic" however has to prove his right to existence, has to win his way through unhuman an effort. To the "mystic" is simply denied a natural right and obligation to defend that which he regards as true, and he is viewed as particularly suspicious, his sincerity every second subject to doubt, which they do not do, relatively for example with a Marxist (likewise in his way a "mystic"); the "mystic" is as it were a pariah within contemporary society. Such a sort of unfairness in the realm of healthy a meaning, so touchy and narrow-minded the criticisms therein, and yet everything readily gets dealt with in that manner. Ye esteemed healthy-minded positivists, by all your mannerisms however ye yourself admit, that your ideas are mediocre and banal, that for them no higher capabilities are needed. And indeed in essence we are less pretentious than you, we do not think ourself gods, like unto the "positivists", making a god of men, we do not assemble together to create a god under the name of the coming happiness of mankind, of the perfecting of human society etc, nor do we look for a barren phantasy of a final rationalistic age as absolute a truth. We seek oneness with the eternally existent God, we desire a continuation of the thousands-years long deed of His revealing. In this realm of healthy meaning, strange is the manner in which progressives and radicals have united with reactionaries and conservatives, the government sort and the churchly, with this zoological view on equality, believing only in the healthiness of a coerced earthly arrangement, only in a trudgeon with which to painfully beat, and shamelessly via dead quasi-religious formulae whilst preserving its absolute non-belief in a mightiness mysteried and other-worldly. The typical type of our conservative, healthily subject to churchly authority, likewise is afraid of mysticism and hates it, just like the typical type radical, and both -- are slaves to the alleged healthy meaning.

I have said it already, said that you have hopelessly confused reasoning with the outcome of healthy a meaning and upon this you have erected your edifice of delimited a rationalism. Ye know not the history of human consciousness, ye have forgotten the history of philosophy and religion, mere insignificant decades have overshadowed for you centuries and millennia of human thought, the great efforts to grasp the meaning of the world-edifice. If ye indeed want to know, what reasoning actually is, in what comprises its titanic work and its fruits bequeathed to us, turn then to Plato and the Neo-Platonists, to Origen and to the Christian gnostics, to Spinoza and Leibniz, to Hegel and Schelling, and finally to Russian philosophy with Vl. Solov'ev at the head, whom none of you even knows of, and whom each of us ought to be proud.[1] Attempt to reverently fathom your way into the history of reasoning and the hypnotic effect of healthy

[1] Only an added mention also, that the recent remarkable book of N. Lossky, "On Intuitive Cognition" [1906], once again is emphatic, that Russian philosophy is original and full of creative tasks.

meaning will dissipate, there will ensue an end to bowing to the sway of judgement, and you will grasp the distinction between the greater, the supra-human reason, from that of the lesser, the human reasoning. The history of philosophy is not some fortuitous history of human errors and fictions, but rather instead is full of meaning, the gradual revealing of the absolute reason, similar to how the history of religion has been a revealing at various stages the same in mystical proclivities; these lines thread together and coalesce within the idea of the Logos, within a religious gnosis. The teaching about the Trinitarian aspect of the Deity is regarded by rationalists, by those heroes of healthy a meaning, as an absurdity and folly, but this truth was a revelation via reasoning among the great philosophers, engendered already within Greek philosophy, cultivated amongst profound mystics, and has found itself expression in Hegel, Schelling, Vl. Solov'ev, whereas for the Euclidian mind, the lesser human reasoning, too many truths seem incomprehensible and therefore absurd, and perchance is not within this limitedness of rationalism set at the root of all the misunderstood contention against God![1] For what preconceived notion do they think, that it is necessary to believe J. S. Mill or Spenser moreso, than Hegel or Schelling? Who is it that has proven, that reason has spoken via the mouths of the former, and folly by the latter? Why is the reasoning of Vl. Solov'ev less authoritative, than the reasoning of Mikhailovsky, and in Chicherin indeed is there less so a reasoning, than with Bel'tov? And do not allude to Kant, whom certain of you esteem, -- that old man was contemptuous of your healthy a meaning, and the idea of reason for him was something supra-human, beyond the human. The grip of non-reasoning traditional feelings and beliefs compels you to devote a preference to Mill or Bel'tov, to fawn over Avenarius, and a childish lack of knowledge inspires your esteem for a quasi-reasoning positivist spirit. Indeed the positivists and materialists do not admit of reasoning, they deny its grandeur and might, and even the rigour of logic, of which they are so proud, cannot be defended by them. They boastfully talk of their "experience" as their sole redoubt, but their experience also is limitedly-conditional, an experience too rationalised, similar to how their reasoning is too empiricised. Mystics from all times have drawn upon the insights from experience, but this experience was profound and deep, living,

[1] Ivan Karamazov's own Euclidian mind, -- reflects the healthy meaning outcome, set in opposition to God, to the World Reason.

primal, attuned to the very core of being, and not contrived and rationalised. On the side of mystical a philosophy stands both a primacy of reason and a primacy of experience. And within this there is no opposition between reason and experience, since reason is not an "abstract" principle, is not a cut-away portion, is not intellectualism and rationalism, but is rather a central, illuminative point of an integrally entire organism; reasoning is delimited and yet inseparably from what in psychology is termed the will and senses. All the psychological theories, deriving the emotional life from feelings, both the intellectualistic and the voluntaristic, alike remain at the surface level, since they do not penetrate down deeply to that primal source, in which organically coalesce elements sensory, volitional and intellectual, wherein reigns the greater reason. The primal basis and essence of the soul cannot be characterised, as "abstractly" the felt, the sensory, the volitional or cognitive. Even the most significant psychological trend -- that of voluntarism, assumes an abstractly volitional principle, with the will at the primal basis inseparable from reason. The metaphysics of voluntarism is connected with the pessimistic irrationalism of Schopenhauer. Truth however is not in rationalism nor in irrationalism, but situated rather in supra-rationalism. The supra-rational reason and the world will within it are not blind, but instead perceivable and expedient. Reason -- is not the human intellect, but rather supra-human an organism, and the reasoning cognition is a self-cognitive aspect of the Deity, amidst which we also participate in an intuitively-mystical cognitive act. Possible therefore only is a metaphysical and religious knowledge, whereby the reason within us is not merely individual and only human, rather that the ideas of reason are divine and supra-human, that within the reason subject and object align, that the cognitive reason is identical with the cognitive reason of the world, that the Logos shatters the limitedness of human reason. Thinking it a victory, positivism and criticistism advance the argument, that for man as relative an existent being, it is not given to have cognition of the absolute, but reason does indeed have cognition of the absolute, because it is of the absolute. Reason as manifest in man does not conform to the absolute being of rational categories such as are valid only for the relative being of the logical laws of identity, opposition etc, since it is intimately connected instead with Reason, as revealed in the world. There can be logical laws, which hold a tight grip upon us -- this is merely a defect of being, a defect of being itself, a result as it were of the sin-fall. The non-reason aspect of the empirical world is a sickness within being and to this blotch, veiling the face of the world, science in full is really aware. But it is not in the illness (the manifest matter) that comprises the essence of the face, and besides the pathology (science) there is still the physiology (metaphysics and religion), which is cognitive of the healthy body of the world. We posit reason in opposition to judgement, and in opposition to empiricism -- we posit experience in its mystical fullness.

Religion for us does not rest upon external an authority, nor upon a forced factual actuality. Religion -- is the free revelation of reason within me. The supra-rational truths of religion are truths of the reason, which can be philosophically given a basis and defended.[1] Religion -- is a product of mystical experience, as a thought process by reason, and this is a mysticism, in which the Logos has shown forth. They tend to say: the Gospel -- is an historical book, Christ -- is an historical fact. Yet I never mystically would sense nor mentally would ponder, who Christ was or what He is for me, if inwardly, within the reasoning there had not been revealed the truth about filiation, the sonship to God, about the Trinitarian aspect of the Deity, about the redemption, if these truths of the reasoning had not come into unity with my mystical experiencings. I could never comprehend a blind submission to the authority of writings nor of tradition, to an external authority, factually connected as such. I can make sense of the words of Christ and accede to them, when reason reveals their meaning and my free metaphysical experience compels me to sense all their depth. Otherwise, both Christ and the Gospel would remain for me an historical fact, just like any other. The bowing to an external authority of whatever the sort by the historical church,[2] and a traditional dogmatism, denying

---

[1] Suchlike was the view of John Scotus Erigena, very bold for the IX Century, blinded by authority. The gnosis of Origen is something infinitely close for me, and there seem kindred souls for me such figures as the Eastern theologian-philosophers, St. Dionysios the Areopagite and St. Maximos the Confessor.

[2] A bowing as such to the authority of the Church is inwardly contradictory, since the essence of the Church is in the mystical of the Holy Spirit within mankind, in Its free gifts, with the help of which mankind freely follows its way towards the supreme goal. I might best of all characterise my understanding of the Church with the words: a sort of mystical protestantism.

the free vitality and new prophetic insights is a betrayal of the supreme dignity of the Eternal Reason. There is not and cannot be any other authority in the world, besides the authority of the free Reason within me. But the truths of reason will become abstracted and deadened, if they are not united with a living concrete embodiment of the world meaning within history.

The worshipping, however, of healthy a meaning outcome as something external, connected with facticity, is a form of slavery and idolatry. The philosophic grounding and defense of religion and mysticism -- is an important task for our era, and in the defending of this we have to be not apologists, but rather investigators and seekers. My essays as a philosophic publicist, the attempts to examine aspects of the temporal *sub specie aeternitatis* -- represent a strong effort in a philosophic defense of religio-cultural and religio-societal ideas. They might mock us, that in such heated and difficult times we are occupied with eternity, and show interest in God, but this is the most strange and impermissible of all the objections. They say, there is no eternity and there is no God, and such perchance might be conceivable and would constitute essential an object. But grant for one second the reality of God -- and you are bound to admit, that all the time constantly you ought to be thinking about Him and seeking out the paths to an uniting with Him, and especially at moments of turbulence, of earthquakes and conflagrations. Long live reason and an end to the healthy meaning concept, the realm of darkness, the realm of paucity, of judgemental folly!

Bobaki, Kharkov gubernia.

5 June 1906

CPSIA information can be obtained
at www.ICGtesting.com
Printed in the USA
BVHW041521080421
604416BV00021B/1172

9 780999 197936